Nitobe Inazô

Japan's Bridge Across the Pacific

Nitobe Inazô and his wife, Mary, dressed up to go to the Imperial Palace on New Year's Day, 1916, their twenty-fifth wedding anniversary.

Nitobe Inazô

Japan's Bridge Across the Pacific

EDITED BY
John F. Howes

Routledge
Taylor & Francis Group
NEW YORK AND LONDON

First published 1995 by Westview Press, Inc.

Published 2021 by Routledge
605 Third Avenue, New York, NY 10017
2 Park Square, Milton Park, Abingdon, Oxon OX14 4RN

Routledge is an imprint of the Taylor & Francis Group, an informa business

Copyright © 1995 by Taylor & Francis

All rights reserved. No part of this book may be reprinted or reproduced or utilised in any form or by any electronic, mechanical, or other means, now known or hereafter invented, including photocopying and recording, or in any information storage or retrieval system, without permission in writing from the publishers.

Notice:
Product or corporate names may be trademarks or registered trademarks, and are used only for identification and explanation without intent to infringe.

A CIP catalog record for this book is available from the Library of Congress.
ISBN 0-8133-8924-0

ISBN 13: 978-0-3670-1735-4 (hbk)
ISBN 13: 978-0-3671-6722-6 (pbk)

DOI: 10.4324/9780429047213

*To
the memories of
Matsumoto Shigeharu
Takagi Yasaka
Yanaihara Tadao
who implemented
Nitobe's vision*

Contents

Foreword, Mark W. Fruin — ix
Preface — xi
Acknowledgments — xiii
About the Contributors — xv
Editorial Conventions — xvii

PART ONE
Introduction

1 Who Was Nitobe? *John F. Howes and George Oshiro* — 3

PART TWO
Maturation

2 Roots, *John F. Howes* — 27
3 Graduate Student and Quaker, *Furuya Jun* — 55

PART THREE
Cultural Identity

4 Japan Watchers 1903–1931, *A. Hamish Ion* — 79
5 *Bushido*: Its Admirers and Critics, *Cyril H. Powles* — 107
6 Philippine Bushido, *Grant K. Goodman* — 119
7 Toward Remaking Manliness, *Donald Roden* — 133

PART FOUR
Japan in the World

8 Colonial Theories and Practices in Prewar Japan, *Miwa Kimitada* — 159
9 The Geneva Spirit, *Thomas W. Burkman* — 177

PART FIVE
Evaluation

10 Journalism: The Last Bridge, *Satô Masahiro* — 217
11 Mediation Between Cultures, *Yuzo Ota* — 237

12 The End: 1929–1933, *George Oshiro* 253
13 Darkened Lanterns in a Distant Garden,
      Richard Eldridge Copley 279
14 Conclusion, *John F. Howes* 303

About the Book and Editor 317
Index 319

Foreword

The chapters in this volume were prepared for and presented at the Nitobe-Ohira Memorial Conference held at the University of British Columbia, May 23–25, 1984. The conference was named in part to honor Prime Minister Masayoshi Ôhira (1910–1980), whose last public appearances abroad took place in Vancouver. He died suddenly and unexpectedly a few days later in Japan. The Japanese government through the Japan Foundation had given generously to the promotion of Japan Studies in Canada during the tenures of Prime Ministers Tanaka Kakuei, Nakasone Yasuhira, and Ôhira himself. Some of the monies from this Ôhira Commemorative Program provided generous funding for the conference.

The conference consisted of fourteen panels with over 160 participants. Topics, all of which dealt with Japan, varied as widely as theater, linguistics, literature, trade, investment, politics, and modern history—as represented in this volume. Activities took place in the Asian Centre adjacent to the Nitobe Memorial Garden.

In the years since the conference, the activities of the institute have continued to develop. In 1992, the Institute of Asian Research was expanded to include five regional centers for research on Japan, China, Korea, Southeast, and South Asia, and in 1993 the Canada Asia Pacific Research Initiative (CAPRI), a public policy research program was launched. In 1996, the Institute will move to a new 30,000-square-foot building of its own adjacent to the present Asian Center and Nitobe Memorial Gardens. In the meantime, faculty concerned with Japan and the emerging Asia-Pacific Century continue to be hired with five new faculty positions in the Institute of Asian Research.

These activities represent an historical continuum which would have pleased both Nitobe Inazô (1862–1933) and Ôhira. Ôhira was known for his particular interest in international relations. One of the most persistent rumors in Tokyo about how Nitobe's face was chosen to adorn the new ¥5000 note attributes the decision to Ôhira. Nitobe, who died a few miles from Vancouver in nearby Victoria, would also have been pleased. At the time of his death, he was probably the most famous Japanese outside Japan. Those responsible for the foundation of Asian Studies in the University of British Columbia, both before and immediately after World War II, included a number of his close friends. They sponsored the building of the

Nitobe Memorial Garden in his honor. The details that undergird the relationship between Nitobe and North America, commemorated in the Garden, unfold in the pages that follow.

Mark W. Fruin
Director, Institute of Asian Research
University of British Columbia

Preface

In the world of the Quakers, which Nitobe Inazô joined as a young man, the alternate to the use of force to solve disputes is what the Quakers call "friendly persuasion." By that they reflect a quiet confidence in the basic rationality of individuals whose better nature will respond to quiet and well-meaning logic presented in the understanding that all people are children of God.

Nitobe Inazô resorted to quiet verbal persuasion aided by his impressive ability at language, humor, knowledge and broad human understanding. In the following pages, we read of only one instance where he used force of any kind. At this time his Japanese rickshaw puller abused an innocent Korean on the street in Seoul when Korea was under Japanese control before World War II. Nitobe tells us that he thereupon gave the rickshaw man a "good thrashing," because he "did not know that a patriot loves his country so well that he would not countenance any act which might reflect on the good name of his own people" (see p. 231). It would appear that in this instance Nitobe felt that the rickshaw man could not be approached through quiet rhetoric or that his action toward the Korean put him beyond the pale of reasoned discussion.

Rather than with bombast or warlike rhetoric of any kind, those who knew Nitobe associated him with the ability to listen closely to what others said and the regular retreat to common ground when matters moved to a point where violence might result. These qualities served him well in a career devoted to the development of harmony between individuals and nations, but they made him no match for the Japanese Army intent on control of the portions of Asia adjacent to Japan. Their moves in this direction developed into World War II in the Pacific.

In his life we learn of how a talented and dedicated individual who tried to serve his God and nation through quietly reasoned words died when events beyond any single individual's control threatened much of his life's work. Yet in the closing years of the twentieth century, many of the causes for which Nitobe fought have become an accepted part of human relations. In many ways, he serves as a model for all those who regularly deal with people of other cultures.

John F. Howes

Acknowledgments

As Professor Fruin has mentioned in his foreword, the essays in this volume were prepared for the Nitobe-Ohira Conference held at the University of British Columbia in Vancouver. The conference was held with the most generous support of the Japan Foundation. Publication of this volume has been made possible through the additional support of a sizable grant from Obirin University in Tokyo.

Three of the essays in this study have been published previously and are reprinted here with permission of the original publishers: Furuya Jun's article was originally published as "Nitobe Inazô in Baltimore," in *Kokusaigaku ronshû 1986* (Tokyo: Jôchi Daigaku Kokusai Kankei Kenkyûjo 1985), pp. 43–71; Grant Goodman's article was originally published as "Nitobe's *Bushido:* The Samurai Ethic in a Philippine Setting," in Emerita S. Quita, ed., *Festschrift in Honor of Dr. Marcelina Faronda, Jr.* (Manila: De La Salle University Press, 1987); George Oshiro's article was originally published in Japanese as Chapter Eight, *Bannen, 1927–1933* in his *Nitobe Inazô: kokusai shugi no kaitakusha* (Tokyo: Chûô Daigaku Shuppanbu, 1992), pp. 199–245.

Numerous individuals assisted in the preparation of the text. They included Karl Broedhecker and Susan MacDermid, who skillfully edited the entire manuscript in 1989–1990. Members of the department of computer services and communication at the University of British Columbia helped over a long period of time. Special thanks are due to Frank Flynn and Christopher Law. Professor Boyd Davis of the University of North Carolina, Charlotte, helpfully read the entire manuscript with the critical eye of an experienced editor, while Sandra Koritzin provided particular assistance in the final stages of production. Mark Hatfield and Charisse Kiino also read over the whole final text and helped correct irregularities in formatting. The editors of Westview Press have also done everything to make the production accurate and quick.

Although thanks go out to each of these individuals, they bear no responsibility for the remaining errors, which accrue solely to the editor.

J. F. H.

About the Contributors

Each of the authors has spent decades studying, teaching and publishing about Asia. More specifically:

Thomas W. Burkman taught at Old Dominion University when he prepared his chapter but now directs the Asian Studies Program at The State University of New York at Buffalo where he also teaches Japanese history. Burkman's research specializes in the history of Japan and the League of Nations. The College of Arts and Letters of Old Dominion University and the Northeast Asia Council of the Association for Asian Studies helped fund his research.

Richard Eldridge Copley teaches geography at the University of British Columbia, Vancouver, Canada. A student of cultural landscapes in the Sinitic world, Copley is currently preparing a book on the location of sacred places in traditional East Asia. It will include more of the theory that he employs in his discussion of the Nitobe Memorial Garden.

Furuya Jun teaches American political and diplomatic history at Hokkaido University in Sapporo. When he prepared this chapter, Furuya was a Nitobe Fellow at The Johns Hopkins University in Baltimore.

Grant K. Goodman taught history at the University of Kansas when his chapter was prepared. He is now professor emeritus. Goodman's extensive publications on Philippine-Japanese relations during the American colonial period include *Davao: a Case Study in Japanese-Philippine Relations; Four Aspects of Philippine-Japanese Relations, 1930–1940; From Bataan to Tokyo, diary of a Filipino Student in Wartime Japan, 1943–1944.*

John F. Howes taught at the University of British Columbia when his chapters were written. He now teaches Japan studies at Obirin University in Tokyo. He has published numerous articles on Nitobe and Uchimura Kanzô. Research for Howes' work was supported by grants from the Japan Foundation as well as the University of British Columbia and Obirin University.

A. Hamish Ion teaches history at Royal Military College of Canada (Collège militaire royal du Canada), Kingston, Ontario, Canada. Ion has published two volumes on the history of Commonwealth Protestant missionaries in Japan and its empire.

Miwa Kimitada teaches international relations at Sophia University, Tokyo. He is former director of its Institute of International Relations and now directs its Institute of American and Canadian Studies. He also serves as president of the Japanese Assocation for Canadian Studies. Author of numerous books and articles, Miwa's recent publications include "Perry's Fourth Letter and Nitobe Inazo."

George Oshiro teaches history at Obirin University, Tokyo. He wrote his essay as an advanced graduate student in the University of British Columbia. Oshiro's subsequent Japanese-language biography of Nitobe is the most comprehensive to date.

Yuzo Ota teaches history at McGill University, Montreal. He has published numerous Japanese-language biographical studies of important individuals in modern Japanese history. They include a book on Nitobe. Ota acknowledges the assistance of the Japan Foundation for a leave grant to develop his thoughts on Nitobe.

Cyril H. Powles taught Asian history at the University of Trinity College, University of Toronto, when he wrote his chapter. He is now professor emeritus. Powles has published books on the history of Commonwealth missionaries in Japan and contemporary theology.

Donald Roden teaches history at Rutgers University, New Brunswick, New Jersey. Roden is the author of *Schooldays in Imperial Japan*, which includes a chapter devoted to Nitobe's tenure as headmaster at the First Higher School.

Satô Masahiro taught philosophy at Osaka City University when he wrote this chapter. He is now professor emeritus and teaches philosophy at *Kansai Gaidai* University. Satô served as an editor of the *Complete Works of Nitobe Inazô* and has published widely on Nitobe and Uchimura Kanzô as well as the history of German philosophy.

Editorial Conventions

Abbreviations for works frequently cited in the text:
FHLNP refers to Friends Historical Library, Nitobe Papers. The Friends Historical Library is located in Swarthmore College, Swarthmore, Pennsylvania.

NHTS refers to Takagi Yasaka and Maeda Tamon eds., *Nitobe hakushi tsuioku shû* (Tokyo: Ko Nitobe hakushi kinen jigyô jikkô iin, 1936).

NIK refers to Tokyo joshi daigaku Nitobe Inazô kenkyû kai ed., *Nitobe Inazô Kenkyû* (Tokyo: Shunjûsha, 1969). This should not be confused with the annual of the same name issued beginning in 1991 by the Nitobe Inazô kai, 2–10 Uchimura, Moriokashi, 020.

NIZ refers to the *Nitobe Inazô Zenshû* (Tokyo: Kyôbunkan, 1983–1987), 23 volumes, the most recent and comprehensive collection of works by Nitobe. Volumes 12 through 16 were later published separately as the *English Language Words of Inazo Nitobe*, see following. Volumes 17 through 22 include the same material translated into Japanese. Volumes 1 through 16 were first issued by the same publisher in 1969–1970. A supplementary 24th volume contains the material previously published in *NHTS*.

NYT refers to the *New York Times*.

UKZ refers to the *Uchimura Kanzô Zenshû* (Tokyo: Iwanami, 1981–1984), 40 volumes, the most comprehensive collection of works by Uchimura. Most of the works cited in this volume are also available in any of several multi volume reprints of Uchimura's works. In 1984–1985 the same publisher added two volumes, *Uchimura Kanzô eibun ronsetsu hon'yaku hen*, *jô* (tr. Dôke Hiroichirô), and *ge* (tr. Kamei Shunsuke), which present Japanese-language translations of Uchimura's many short English-language essays.

Works refers to the *English Language Works of Inazo Nitobe* (Tokyo: Tokyo University Press, 1972), 5 volumes.

Citations to multivolumed works indicate the volume number followed by a colon and page number.

Names in the text are given in normal order for the country concerned. Japanese names appear with the family name first followed by the given name. Exceptions are the few Japanese whose names written in the English order are well known to those outside Japan. Names of authors of essays are listed in whichever order the individual author desires. Names of authors in footnote references are given in the normal order for footnotes in the language of the text.

ONE
Introduction

1

Who Was Nitobe?

John F. Howes and George Oshiro

This book deals with the enigmatic Nitobe Inazô (1862–1933), a man who during his lifetime regularly made headlines throughout the world but was forgotten after Japan's disastrous defeat in 1945. Yet with the disappearance of the man from the public consciousness many of the causes for which he worked have become an accepted part of Japanese society. One of the first Japanese to learn English, he achieved a fluency only now being approached as Japan makes the mastery of English a major element in its educational planning. The first Japanese to attempt in one volume to interpret his people's culture to those outside Japan, his *Bushido: the Soul of Japan* became a best seller and spawned a host of similar works; their intellectual descendants continue to make frequent appearances. The first Japanese to achieve a responsible position as an international civil servant when he became the Under-Secretary General of the League of Nations, Nitobe founded what would become UNESCO. His unexpected death in Canada five thousand miles from home was world news; two days later 750 people in Vancouver attended a memorial service for this most international of Japanese individuals.

Nitobe's career, which spanned four decades and several continents, makes in itself fascinating reading but also illuminates broader ideas and topics. The operations of important twentieth-century institutions, such as the League of Nations or the Institute of Pacific Relations, both of which Nitobe served brilliantly, are two examples. The wide range of Nitobe's activities both within Japan and abroad makes his biography an ideal prism through which to view how pressing issues in prewar Japan impinged upon Japanese leaders.

Nitobe's historical importance extends to other areas. As a noted educator, he played a crucial role in the development of higher education for both men and women. He made an important contribution to both the theory and practice of Japanese colonial policy. And his articles on popular morality helped shape the ideals and aspirations of young people for decades.

One would expect that the name of such a man would be memorialized in numerous institutions and studies, but this is not the case. Sixty years later almost no one remembers Nitobe. A student will seek in vain reference to him in standard sources. As a result, an introduction to a series of essays on his life and works must begin with an introduction to the man. Interlinked with an outline of his life in these pages we will refer to the relation of the essays which follow to the stages of his career.

One first asks why so little attention has been paid Nitobe since his death? Like all negative questions asked of the past, there can be no convincing answer, but in this case it is worth a try, since to discover why so little interpretation has been attempted bears directly upon the study of Nitobe's career itself.

Almost all the essays in this collection help one understand the tension that surrounds Nitobe's memory, but three deserve special mention at the outset. The final essay demonstrates how a Japanese landscape garden designer worked into his plan for a garden to commemorate Nitobe's life numerous references to Nitobe's tragic end. The garden seems to tell us that the designer, a contemporary of Nitobe, sensed a greater than normal pathos in the final days of the man he commemorated.

The other two essays take opposing stands on the question of Nitobe's contribution to history. Satô's "Journalism: The Last Bridge" introduces newly discovered articles which Nitobe wrote during the final days of his life which demonstrate greater opposition to government policy during the early 1930s than those which have been available earlier. These works strengthen the image of Nitobe as a man of peace dedicated to diplomacy. Ota's "Mediation Between Cultures" takes an opposing position. His careful assessment of Nitobe's works which introduced Japan to the West concludes that Nitobe has been greatly overrated. His fuller treatment in a separate volume has marshalled evidence quite contrary to what Satô introduces with regard to Nitobe's words and acts in the early 1930s. Here Ota contends that Nitobe did not necessarily favor diplomatic solutions which ran contrary to what the Japanese army was doing on the Asiatic mainland. If one accepts Ota's thesis, Nitobe's reputation as a man of peace suffers.

Taken together, these three articles hint at something not otherwise directly stated. This is that when postwar Japanese have looked at Nitobe's total career they have differed greatly on the extent to which he in fact served the ends of peacefully inclined Japanese. How one interprets Nitobe in this regard has been of more than incidental interest to most thinking men of his generation, for the decisions of his career paralleled those which others of his own age and their children made in response to immediate developments up to 1945. One is tempted to say that study of Nitobe has been a taboo topic since 1945 precisely because he, like other thoughtful

Japanese, did not unequivocally oppose the road to war from 1931 until his death in 1933.

A look at the career of a close friend provides a contrast. Uchimura Kanzô had studied along with Nitobe for most of their education from elementary school through university. They remained close friends and colleagues. Uchimura became a professional Christian evangelist and scholar of the Bible after he publicly opposed government policies which led to the Russo-Japanese War of 1904–05. He had earlier made history as the most famous Japanese who opposed the government's attempt to foster unquestioning nationalism. After his declaration of pacifism, Uchimura did not engage in public debate over government policy but instead retired to nourish the faith of those whom he had converted to Christianity. They in their turn developed into a significant proportion of the few Japanese who opposed the road to World War II. Uchimura himself died in bed in 1930, revered for the steadfast consistency with which he opposed government excesses. After the end of World War II, he became a cultural hero as the embodiment of the loyal citizen who opposed his government's follies.

Uchimura's death in 1930 a year earlier meant that he did not need to decide how to react to the Japanese takeover of Manchuria in 1931. But it was during the succeeding two years, 1932–33, that Nitobe found himself forced to choose between his internationalism and his support of the Japanese invasion of China. It is Nitobe's writings and actions in this period that most sully his reputation.

The problem of reaction to Nitobe comes from the similar experience of others in his generation who shared his aims and his experience. They faced the same dilemmas, and they, like Nitobe, did not clearly oppose the acts of their government. All Japanese in the late nineteenth century and early twentieth century found themselves trying to catch up with what they considered the advanced nations of the world. Nitobe represented the best that an individual Japanese could do to live as a respected member of a leading nation in international society. The bewildering array of activities during his lifetime all rest on his achievements in this regard. He consciously developed himself to serve as a role model for the modern and well-educated Japanese and accepted many posts, convinced that he could assist his countrymen who wanted to make themselves into international men. Those who followed him as a group disliked the acts of the army leaders whose expansionism earned Japan the increasing antipathy of the Western powers. They wanted Japan to be respected and mistrusted their countrymen whose invasion of China squandered hard-won international respect. At the same time, as loyal Japanese these well-educated individuals shared the fear that the Western powers might unite against Japan to block what seemed its rightful contribution to Asian development.

The essays in this work show how this conundrum affected Nitobe. As the dust settled after 1945, most educated Japanese preferred to think of themselves in the mold of heroic opposition provided by Uchimura rather than the accommodation to government policy that Nitobe seemed to typify. It was psychologically more nurturing to remember that their number had included Uchimura with his unquestioning obedience to his pacifist Christian conscience than to recall Nitobe who, like themselves, had vacillated when faced with the challenge to his conscience that the Japanese army presented.

In 1994, remembrances of the fiftieth anniversary of the cessation of hostilities in 1945 were being planned. Only at this point did many Japanese begin to think about who was responsible for the war and its atrocities. Early in 1994 the Minister of Justice publicly declared that the Rape of Nanking was nothing more than a fabrication of Chinese publicists. He thereby sided with those among the Japanese who prefer not to deal with uncomfortable reality. Immediate public outcry forced the minister to resign. Subsequently the younger brother of the Shôwa Emperor reaffirmed his opinions first set down in writing as part of his military service in Nanking. They strongly castigated the army for its actions and, by inference, the luckless former justice minister. A few months later the city of Hiroshima opened a new branch of its famous war museum. Exhibits in this new building detail the extent to which the citizens of Hiroshima contributed to the war effort and suggest how they were as a result much more than unsuspecting and innocent victims in August 1945. It appears that the trend exemplified by Hiroshima will continue so that Japanese will look at the effects of World War II much as citizens of other countries do. If this in fact happens, one can expect that the Japanese will learn, among other things, how to appreciate the suffering of the aged Nitobe.

The facts to which we have briefly alluded, taken together, form one of the main currents in modern Japanese history. Not they, but the reactions of an individual who identified with them and whose reputation was badly damaged by them form the subject of this volume.

To begin the study of Nitobe, one notes that he was a man of letters. The most recent version of his complete works consists of twenty-four volumes of about six hundred pages each, in their very bulk a testimony to Nitobe's energy. The works may be divided into four categories. The first consists of essays on agricultural development, and in particular the development of agronomy and of agricultural policy in the Japanese colonies before World War II. This was Nitobe's own specialty for which he studied in both Japan and Germany. A second group of writings includes works on the masterpieces of English literature, a field in which Nitobe acquired expertise as an inspired amateur. He interpreted these classics as part of a third section of his works which comprise a large part of the total. These expound popular philosophy and ethics, and are written for adolescents and young adults who seek a personal philosophy for their own lives. A final group of books, written in English, introduce Japan, its history and people, to English speakers. All express an optimism and desire for individual perfection that invite readers to follow in Nitobe's footsteps.

The beginning student of Nitobe also learns that he was an educator. Almost all studies of Nitobe until very recently have come from the pens of his students who knew him and wrote recollections. These recollections assume knowledge of the circumstances in which Nitobe worked with his students. The essays in this volume set the information about Nitobe in perspective for readers who neither know him nor the world in which he worked.

The first section, "Maturation," locates Nitobe's forebears in modern Japanese history and describes the intellectual development that prepared him for a career in agricultural development.

The following section, "Cultural Identity," deals with his emphasis on character development and what he saw as distinct to the Japanese view of it. This he called "Bushido," a word which became part of the international understanding of Japan largely because of his most famous book.

The next section, "Japan in the World," deals with Nitobe's dedication to Japan's international position, both as an enlightened colonial power and as one of the advanced nations. In this dedication, one discovers the origins of Nitobe's ambivalent legacy, which depicts him as an internationalist dedicated to world peace who at the same time shared many assumptions of the Japanese army's plan to control East Asia.

The final section, "Evaluation," describes Nitobe's last days and introduces what we have mentioned above as the conflicting assessments of his actions during the early 1930s.

In the following pages, we introduce these four divisions in order.

Maturation

The boy Inazô started life in Morioka, about five hundred kilometers north of Tokyo. Since 1983 it has been linked to Tokyo by a high-speed passenger railroad, but the trip took over ten days when Inazô was carried there in a palanquin at the age of nine.

A mini-park that occupies part of the area formerly given over to the Nitobe home stands about a hundred meters to the east of the Nakatsu River. Adult males in the Nitobe family served as advisors to the daimyo and could easily enter his castle which stood on the other side of the river.

What we know about the young Inazô's life comes for the most part from his autobiography, *Reminiscences of Childhood*, composed a few years before his death. It reflects the delightful life which family position and loving relatives could make available to a talented and sensitive boy. The articles by Howes, Roden, and Satô each make use of this information. When Nitobe was born in 1862, the American Commodore Matthew Perry had ended Japan's isolation some eight years earlier, and the resultant tides of change flooded into every corner of the country. Even in the far northeastern section of Honshu, it profoundly affected Inazô's childhood.

The Edo regime, which had ruled Japan for over 250 years, was toppled when Inazô was five. Changes initiated by the new Meiji government soon swept aside feudal institutions and replaced them with models based upon new ideas of Western egalitarianism. Individuals of Nitobe's generation, by this accident of history, grew up in a world which promised exciting new possibilities as well as new perils. No longer could individuals limit their allegiance to their local areas; they must now think of themselves as Japanese as opposed to the peoples of many countries who began to appear among them. The opening up of Japan destroyed the insular Edo world and presented the people of Meiji with new challenges and opportunities to exercise their talents. During this period of rapid and fundamental change, ambitious youths like Inazô dreamed about future greatness unfettered by concern over the past.

In his *Reminiscences,* Nitobe tells us that at age nine he went with his brother to study in Tokyo. His father had died, and his father's brother had moved to Tokyo where, childless, he welcomed his two nephews. There Inazô continued the study of English in which he had already received rudimentary instruction. He also met a number of other boys whose families, like his, felt that their sons should have the advantage of the superior education available in the capital. Nitobe tells us how they met a number of personality types among their foreign instructors. Some knew almost nothing, like the teacher of mathematics who airily responded to a student question about fractions with, "Fractions! I don't understand them at all."[1] Others immediately impressed their young students with their sincerity and ability. The one who would become the most famous among Inazô's fellow students, Uchimura Kanzô, describes in his own autobiography an innocent outing to watch a Western missionary preach. The boys went to "a certain place in foreigners' quarter, where we can hear pretty women sing, and a tall big man with long beard shout and howl upon an elevated place, flinging his arms and twisting his body in all fantastic manners, to all which admittance is entirely free."[2]

None of them realized it, but the young schoolboys had come together in Tokyo at the beginning of a Japanese enthusiasm for everything Western which would characterize society for the next decade and a half. The Japanese whose government had denied its people contact with Westerners for over two centuries identified the source of the strength represented by superior Western armaments with the lifestyle of individual Westerners. Those claiming the most imagination and foresight wanted to speak, dress and eat like these exotic newcomers. The families of Uchimura, Nitobe and the other boys agreed with this viewpoint.

Since they excelled in English, both Nitobe and Uchimura were selected to study in the new Sapporo Agricultural College, which the government had established to train officials who would help develop Hokkaido. They travelled to the port city nearest Sapporo by a coastal steamer. Nitobe's *Reminiscences* ends as the steamer which carries the new students heads north along the coast of Honshu to the east of his old hometown, Morioka. Howes in his essay shows how the events, places and individuals of Nitobe's childhood became important to him once again after his retirement.

When the students eased their sore limbs off the horses which had taken them overland about 150 kilometers from the port of Otaru to Sapporo, they found themselves in a community modeled in most details on a small college town in the United States. A clock intoned the hours from a tower atop the main building of the college. Dormitories provided western-style rooms complete with Franklin stoves for heat. The school uniforms made the boys look like cadets at an American military school, and the food with its lavish use of bread, venison and sugar reflected contemporary American tastes. Most of the faculty members were American, and their lectures in English accustomed the students to its use as a practical tool. Inazô entered this society at the age of fifteen. By the time he and his classmates were graduated in 1881, they corresponded with each other in English, because, as another one of them said, "we felt that only with English could we express our innermost emotions and thoughts."[3]

In several particulars, the boys had achieved what those who had established the school had wanted. They hoped to develop a college similar to the Land Grant institutions in the United States which had been established after the War Between the States to train engineers with commissions in the military reserves. Graduates of the new Japanese school would be able to assist the development of virgin lands and could quickly be called up for military duty. The Japanese saw in Hokkaido an area very like the American frontier and suspected Russian designs on it. The new graduates, required to spend some years in Hokkaido in return for their free education, would help the government achieve its aims.

Though in general happy with what the school achieved, the authorities felt less enthusiasm for a final element which characterized the young graduates. Most of them, and all of the academic leaders, had become Christians. The American whose name is most associated with this development is William S. Clark, a professor of chemistry who had received the best technical training his own land and Germany could afford; he had also served in the northern forces in the War Between the States, ending with the rank of colonel, and had taught in Amherst College before he went on to help found what later became the University of Massachusetts.

Clark went to Japan in 1876 to preside over a new college in Sapporo modeled upon what he had set up in Massachusetts. After obtaining the reluctant consent of the Japanese authorities, he based his instruction in ethics, a key element in any Japanese curriculum, on the Bible instead of on the Confucian classics which informed Japanese ethical instruction. Although he had returned to the United States before Nitobe and Uchimura arrived in Sapporo, the best students among those who had studied under Clark quickly set about to convert Nitobe, Uchimura and a number of other leaders among the freshmen. Alone and otherwise friendless, newcomers capitulated. They were baptized by a young American Methodist missionary, Merriman C. Harris, who had taken an arduous trip overland from Hakodate to meet them. Harris would go on to become one of the most outstanding missionary churchmen of his generation, and the young converts, who went on to be known collectively as the "Sapporo Band" of Christians, founded a vigorous branch of Protestantism which continues today in Japan, long after their deaths.

Nitobe's letters from this period impress us with his competitive ambition and ability. His friend Uchimura's biography tells us that Inazô also suffered a period of depression after the unexpected death of his mother. Reading avidly in the school library, Nitobe found solace in the great works of English literature, helping thereby to polish his own English further and provide himself with a strong personal philosophy based on the literary culture of the British Isles. His later conversion to Quakerism gave him a kind of Christian faith which did not seem at odds with his Japanese background and enabled him to move easily in the company of educated individuals both within Japan and the West.

Nitobe was graduated with a specialty in agricultural development, while Uchimura had become a fisheries scientist. Though they had both had training greatly in demand in Hokkaido and had agreed to serve some years there, ambition drove them to Tokyo. Nitobe enrolled in Tokyo University; he later recalls that one of his professors asked him why he wanted to major in economics and English literature and that he replied that he hoped to become a "bridge across the Pacific." Though the tenor of the story inclines one to consider it apocryphal, the intent expressed in these words matches quite clearly what Nitobe in fact went on to do.

The first step was to further his study abroad. He quickly concluded that the instruction by Japanese in the new university did not match what he had received in Sapporo from his American teachers and determined to go to the United States for further study. The wife of the Reverend Harris who had baptized him introduced him to Allegheny College in Pennsylvania. Nitobe enrolled there in the fall of 1884 but quickly succumbed to the suggestion of a good friend and fellow graduate from the Sapporo Agricultural College that he continue on at the graduate school of the new Johns Hopkins University in Baltimore.

Furuya's "Graduate Student and Quaker" tells us how, at Johns Hopkins, Nitobe associated with some of the best teachers and students in America. The school had an exciting new approach to education, one which combined normal classroom study with independent research topics. Nitobe, at first by far the junior man both in terms of linguistic ability and other accomplishments, could not compete. After he had been in Baltimore three years, the same friend who had urged him to come to Baltimore, now an official at the Sapporo Agricultural College, appointed Nitobe to a teaching post there, to take effect after further study in Germany.

The government stipend which accompanied the European study eased Nitobe's need for funds while he gained necessary additional training. Before he left Baltimore, he took two other steps which would greatly affect his future. He joined the Baltimore meeting of the Friends, and he made the acquaintance of the woman he would later marry. She was Mary Passmore Elkinton, the daughter of one of the foremost Philadelphia Quakers and an active leader among their women.

During the years 1887–1889 in Germany, Nitobe followed the normal custom of German students with study at a number of universities. He also guided visiting Japanese on their tours of Europe and through visits to craftsmen's shops gained experience in a number of traditional skills. He finished his doctorate at Halle University in the field of agricultural economics in 1890. His thesis on Japanese patterns of land use was published as *Über den Japanischen Grundbesetz, dessen Verteilung und landwirtschafliche Verwertung. Eine hisorische and statistiche Studie*, a first publication, doubly impressive since it was written in Nitobe's second foreign language. Another book, *The Intercourse Between the United States and Japan: An historical sketch*,[4] was published shortly after Nitobe had returned to the United States from Germany.

In 1891, the same year he published *Intercourse*, Nitobe and Mary married. Mary became an executive housewife, subordinating her own very real abilities to her husband's career. She realized that she would learn Japanese only with great difficulty and decided instead to provide a suitable domestic environment for her husband. It emphasized the non-Japanese parts of his personality and experience.

These years abroad, between ages twenty-two and twenty-nine, left an indelible mark upon Nitobe. The fundamental views of man, society and God, which he would espouse throughout his long career, took shape. He acquired the impeccable manners and bearing of a cultivated gentleman able to manipulate with ease the conventionalities of educated Westerners. These personal qualities would serve him well as he mingled with world leaders later on; at this point, he returned from the United States to work in the Sapporo Agricultural College a far different being from the hesitant and insecure one who left Tokyo for the United States in 1884.

Cultural Identity

Back in Sapporo, Nitobe set about what would become the single element of his career to which he would devote the largest part of his energy: instruction of young adults. He helped administer and taught at institutions of higher learning, founded night schools to supplement the education of those who had to stop school to work, and published frequent magazine articles for young people which supplemented the national educational curriculum.

He launched his teaching career in 1891 at the Sapporo Agricultural College. Beginning in 1903 he lectured on political economy, first at Kyoto University, and then at the University of Tokyo. Between 1906 and 1911 he served concurrently as the principal of the Number One Higher School, also known affectionately by the abbreviation of its Japanese name, "Ichikô." It was the preparatory school for the University of Tokyo. When Nitobe left Ichikô in 1913, he became professor and the chair of Colonial Policy at the University of Tokyo. In 1918, he became the first president of the New Tokyo Women's Christian College while he continued at Tokyo University until he took up an appointment in the League of Nations in 1920.

To the bewildering array of institutions outlined here must be added Nitobe's continuing involvement in other sorts of education. He helped administer two private schools in Sapporo; while teaching in Tokyo, he helped edit a magazine for young students, and constantly counselled young people who sought guidance about future plans. One senses throughout his career the personality of a relentless instructor. Even while serving as an Under-Secretary of the League of Nations, he felt that non-Japanese knew so little about Japan that he must always teach them.

This career of instruction began officially with Nitobe's return to the Sapporo Agricultural College. Here he and Mary settled down to represent North America in the rude Hokkaido forest. Nitobe's main work was to instruct in economics, but he quickly volunteered classes on English literature and the Bible. He also supervised the dormitory. This constant activity seemed to reflect an almost conscious need to prove himself after the many years when he had soaked up knowledge rather than used it on behalf of society.

Mary found the adjustment to backwoods Japan difficult, so the two of them returned to Philadelphia for the summer the year after they had arrived in Sapporo. Back in Japan, they lost their only child, Thomas, a few days after his birth. Their inability to have further children led them later on to adopt two relatives of Inazô who married each other and continued the family name. The exceptionally warm relationships that developed between Nitobe and his best students seems to have compensated in part for his own lack of children.

All this activity resulted in physical and emotional exhaustion. In 1897, the doctor told Inazô that he must leave Sapporo to recuperate for an extended period. He and Mary rested for a while in a mountain hot springs resort and then went to Monterey, California, where the invigorating climate and distance from his many obligations brought back Nitobe's strength much more quickly than physicians had anticipated.

Within three years he had recovered and produced what would become his most famous work, *Bushido*. He tells us in the introduction that it resulted from a chance inquiry by a professor whom Nitobe had met in Europe. This gentleman asked how the Japanese taught ethics lacking Christianity. Nitobe as a result turned his mind to how the Japanese did handle this part of their education. His calm acceptance of the professor's point reflects Nitobe's basic conviction that Christianity posed the ultimate solution to ethical problems, but his own background had taught him that Japan must have had good solutions of its own before it knew Christianity. He discussed the progress of each chapter with Mary and then dictated his prose to a friend of hers who took shorthand.

Bushido achieved an international reputation for Nitobe while still in his early forties. Published first in 1900, the book was fortuitously reissued by a major publisher in 1905 and appeared in bookstores just after the decisive Japanese naval victory over a huge Russian Fleet. To William E. Griffis, one of the foremost American experts on Japan, the main selling point of the book was that it was "written by a Japanese," an "insider." Griffis found that Nitobe had explained the moral fortitude of these "yellow men" who had taken on and defeated Russia in what the world perceived as a David-and-Goliath conflict. The book became a best seller as part of this interest in the Russo-Japanese War. Book reviewers called it a magnificent achievement. Nathaniel Hawthorne's nephew, Julian, extolled its virtues in a review:

> Inazo Nitobe has edited an essay, a little more than a hundred pages long, which must be studied as well as read: and since it is as fascinating as it is important, that is no hardship. This English which the professor writes is so singularly pure, easy and effective that no one would imagine it to be the work of a foreigner—and of a foreigner so very foreign as a Japanese. But that is little: The author seems to be the master of all the knowledge proper to a learned man of the West, as well as of that Oriental lore of which Westerners know not much.... It is foolish to pretend to review an essay of this depth and scope in a paragraph. The professor shows not only learning, but in-

sight, judgement, magnanimity: his arguments are cogently reasoned: he touches his subject with satire here and there: he is always patriotic, but never bigoted or narrow. He gives us a better knowledge of the spirit of his nation than any foreign observers.... You may read the book through in a couple of hours, but you may return to it profitably for years.[5]

Bushido has enjoyed the greatest longevity in a tradition of books which start from a single premise: that the Japanese are so different that one can more exactly deal with them by pointing out their uniqueness rather than assuming universal human similarities. Nitobe addressed a world of readers outside Japan who, particularly after the Japanese victory over Russia, wanted to know what made these otherwise so strange people so capable. After Nitobe's success with this work, non-Japanese readers have with remarkable consistency sought handy explanations about how the Japanese differ from themselves. This search for the one-volume quick fix on Japanese culture continues almost a century after Nitobe's work first appeared. It is not surprising, therefore, to learn that once he had established a worldwide reputation with *Bushido*, Nitobe found that it followed him around as his career progressed.

By the time he finished *Bushido*, Nitobe's health had improved so that he could consider further employment. After some consideration he accepted a job which would enable him to implement his theories about agricultural development in the new Japanese colony of Taiwan, which Japan had received as part of the settlement after the Sino-Japanese War of 1894–95. There, in 1901, Nitobe entered upon a phase of his career which is best discussed in the following section for, though while in Taiwan he demonstrated great concern for the education of the Taiwanese, he spent most of his time in the improvement of their economy.

In 1903, he left full-time employment in the colonial government of Taiwan to return to the mainland and teach at Kyoto University. Then, in 1906, Nitobe accepted the position of headmaster of the Ichikô. He concurrently received an appointment to Tokyo University which developed in 1909 into a chair position of Colonial Studies. Nitobe continued in it until he left for the League of Nations in 1920.

Though Nitobe served both the Number One Higher School and Tokyo University, the former position gained him the most recognition. In the new Japanese education system after World War II, the two institutions became one. Even when Nitobe served there, students who managed to enter the First Higher School could usually depend on further study in Tokyo University. Since that in turn formed the apex of the Japanese pyramid of higher education, the best talented and motivated young Japanese men routinely hoped to enter the First Higher School. There they, as teenagers, lived in dormitories which they themselves administered with the crude sort of self-government which Roden describes in his "Toward Remaking Manliness."

The mature students in the University courses could benefit from Nitobe's professional interest in colonial administration, but their younger and less formed colleagues required more general leadership. To become the kind of Western-oriented gentlemen that Nitobe thought Japan required, they must be taught the many related skills of modern international life.

The character formation of these young men became Nitobe's chief concern as the principal of Ichikô. Opinions vary on how well he succeeded. Many students disliked his homilies, while others found in them great inspiration. Nitobe referred those with a specific interest in Christianity to his friend Uchimura Kanzô, now an independent teacher of the Bible who lived near the Ichikô campus.

While thus involved both in instruction and educational administration, Nitobe also joined the magazine *Jitsugyô no Nihon*, perhaps best translated as "Japanese Enterprise." Through the pages of this biweekly which enjoyed a large audience of aspiring young people, Nitobe shared his preoccupation with morality and the need for an individual to develop a rich inner life. The popularity of his regular columns for over ten years boosted the circulation of the magazine which then republished the Nitobe articles in books of essays. Each dealt with the need for inner development as a precondition to success and contribution to one's fellow human beings.

Nitobe's final educational endeavor was his presidency, which began in 1918, of the new Tokyo Women's Christian College, affectionately known as "Tokyo Joshi Dai." His resignation from the headship of Ichikô in 1913 had left him free to devote his administrative energies to the education of women. Students under him at Tokyo Women's Christian College recall with fondness his avuncular attitude to their development and his readiness to listen to their questions and comments.

Taken together, this work as an educator, beginning with Sapporo and extending to Tokyo, forms the major thread that ties together Nitobe's activities. The institutions he helped shape each became leaders in their fields, but what has come through in the testimony of former students is Nitobe's interest in the inner personal development of each of them. This counsel on the importance of quality in one's inner life stood in stark contrast to the compulsive drive for personal gain that characterized the philosophy of many other leaders in his generation.

Authors of chapters in the section "Cultural Identity" deal with a number of the elements in Nitobe's career which grow out of his concern for education. They recognize that Nitobe's writings in English, and particularly his *Bushido*, involved him in a discussion that went far beyond his normal academic activities within Japan.

Ion's "Japan Watchers: 1903–1931" looks at Nitobe as an interpreter of Japan to the West in comparison with others who did the same thing. Japan had been opened just as the nineteenth-century developments in transportation had rendered world travel for the first time predictable and comfortable. Almost from the time that the first foreigners could reside in Japan in 1859, globe trotters stopped off to form their own conclusions regarding a land about which almost nothing had been written for two centuries. Travel books which detailed visitors' experiences emphasized Japan's differences. As a community of foreigners regularly resident in Japan developed, a number of its members interpreted Japan more broadly and with more insight. Foremost among them was Basil Hall Chamberlain whose *Things Japanese* appeared a decade before Nitobe wrote his *Bushido*. When the Nitobes returned to Tokyo, their combination of Japanese and American points of view plus the fame that *Bushido* had conferred upon Inazô made them an important part of the dialogue about Japanese character. Interpretations by expatriate Westerners had to take into account what Nitobe said. Ion points out that later Japanese aggression in Asia rendered Nitobe's words less persuasive.

Powles' "*Bushido*: Its Admirers and Critics" analyzes the reactions to Nitobe's interpretation of Bushido. It shows how Nitobe's work, in addition to meeting with general agreement, evoked vigorous dissent from the time of its first publication. Critics found its generalization too sweeping and its evaluation of the Japanese tradition too complimentary. Goodman's "Philippine Bushido" introduces us to what Nitobe would have considered a most unusual interpretation of his ideas. Philippine leaders, faced in the late 1930s with the need to develop a strong nation to succeed American colonial rule, thought they found in Nitobe's formulation of the strength of the Japanese spirit something which might point the way to a similar core philosophy for the Philippines.

Roden's careful analysis of the divergent elements in Nitobe's psychic makeup links the apparent contradictions of his leadership to what happened in other nations when an hereditary elite lost its position in favor of those trained as specialists in a new educational system. Although some students under Nitobe could not understand his apparent lack of what they considered masculine virtues, his approach made sense to others who themselves appreciated the need for Japanese formed in the mold of contemporary Western gentlemen.

Each of these authors contributes to our understanding of how Nitobe's attempt to define the essential elements of what it was to be Japanese influenced those who came into contact with them. There was no clear message, for each reader interpreted the words in terms of his or her own experience, experience which differed as greatly, for instance, as that between European leaders and Philippine officials.

Japan in the World

The other general area covered by Nitobe's writings and activities is the relation between Japan and other nations. Because of Nitobe's training, his profession of colonial administration and his view of himself as a "bridge," he enjoyed a great reputation as a diplomat. Part of that reputation resulted from his vaunted ability to explain Japan to Westerners. It also rested on the results of his plans for the colonies which Japan acquired during Nitobe's lifetime.

The first colonies were the island of Taiwan, Korea, and the southern half of Sakhalin (called by the Japanese "Karafuto") which lies to the north of Hokkaido, along with assorted islands in the western Pacific. Japan received Taiwan from China after the end of the First Sino-Japanese War in 1895. The Treaty of Portsmouth which ended the Russo-Japanese War in 1905 granted Japan the southern half of Sakhalin and Russian rights in Manchuria. Japan's hegemony over Korea gradually increased beginning with the First Sino-Japanese War until it integrated Korea into the Japanese empire in 1910. Nitobe, first as an official in the development of Taiwan and then as a professor of colonial administration, helped develop and implement policy for these areas.

The outbreak of World War I in 1914 gave those who wanted to enlarge Japan's empire the chance for greater activity on the Asiatic mainland. Japan had become an ally of Great Britain in 1902; the terms of the Anglo-Japanese Alliance imposed upon the Japanese the responsibility to help their ally when hostilities broke out between Germany and its allies on one side and Great Britain with its allies on the other side. When hostilities broke out, the Japanese responded with alacrity but limited their assistance to possession of nearby German territories.

They quickly took over the island of Yap in the Southwest Pacific. It had strategic importance as the point where undersea telegraph cables came to the surface; possession of Yap included the ability to monitor or disrupt those communications, by far the fastest at a time when the next closest means was mail carried by passenger liners. At the same time, the Japanese took over the city of Qingdao on the east coast of Shandong where the Germans had established their major East Asian base.

The Revolution in Russia led to further involvement. Czarist Russia had fought on the side of Germany. After the overthrow of the Czarist forces, the new revolutionary government withdrew the Soviet Union from the war in 1917. As a result, a number of Czech prisoners of war whom the Czarist forces had captured desired to return to Western Europe. They had been forced by the Germans to fight for Germany and now wanted revenge. The Allies in Western Europe badly needed the help. The only way to get the eager volunteers to where they were needed in Western Europe was to send them by rail to Vladivostok and then by ship to France. The

Revolutionary forces had not yet consolidated control over the Trans-Siberian Railroad, and an expeditionary force of troops from eight Allied nations entered Siberia by rail from Vladivostok to keep the trains running. The forces of all the nations but Japan quickly returned home after the war ended in 1918. Japanese troops remained in control of the railroad as far as Lake Baikal, about halfway to Moscow from the Pacific Coast. They did not leave until 1922. While active in East Asia, the Japanese limited their assistance in Europe to the delayed dispatch of two destroyers. Japan's inattention to the major theater of war along with the seizure of territory for itself aroused British suspicions; British leaders eased out of their alliance with the Japanese and established a multilateral arrangement with other powers to guarantee China against interference from Japan.

This shift in British policy would have fateful consequences for Nitobe. Before it, the Japanese who agreed with Nitobe had every reason to believe that Japan could develop into a first-rate colonial power in the best tradition of the British. After the change, they could only feel great concern as Westerners, and in particular the British and Americans, increasingly opposed Japanese policies.

If one keeps in mind this watershed in its relations with Europe and America brought about by Japan's actions in World War I, it is possible to see how Nitobe's point of view and training would lead to two quite different results. The discussion begins with the recognition that Nitobe was, first and foremost, a civil servant and a scholar who helped formulate Japan's colonial policy. This aspect of Nitobe's career, in reality his main vocation, has received only slight attention from biographers. Only after the Ministry of Finance announced that in 1984 the 5000-yen note would carry Nitobe's picture did the subject become the focus of attention. Iinuma Jirô, Professor Emeritus of Kyoto University and a specialist on prewar Korean agriculture, questioned the decision to put Nitobe's portrait on the bill. Iinuma attacked Nitobe as an imperialist because of his professional connection with the colonial ventures in Taiwan, Korea and Manchuria, all areas acquired by military expansion.

When Nitobe fashioned specific policies for Japanese colonies, no one, certainly not he, could foresee how the colonies would later be mishandled. He concentrated on the improvement of colonial economies in the belief that improved living standards would benefit the Chinese and Koreans as well as the colonial overlords. Nitobe's plan to increase agricultural production during his short tenure in Taiwan demonstrated how one could implement this theory.

When the Japanese took over Taiwan after the Sino-Japanese War, they had set about with great energy to provide the infrastructure of transportation, communication and education that would enable the Taiwanese to improve their standard of living by methods similar to those the Japanese themselves had used in early Meiji. These methods had not, by the end of the nineteenth century, produced an economy in Taiwan which could pay for them. It continued to drain finances rather than to enrich the homeland as colonial theory had led the Japanese to expect. The great increase in the production of sugar which resulted from Nitobe's plans obviated the need for imports and put the economy of Taiwan solidly in the black.

Although his success with the Taiwan economy demonstrated the utility of Nitobe's training in agronomy, he himself had other objectives in Taiwan. He felt that the Japanese colonial administrators should adopt a fatherly attitude toward their charges and help bring them into the warm embrace of Japanese civilization. Miwa's "Colonial Theories and Practices in Prewar Japan" shows that in this regard Nitobe continued a long tradition of Japanese and Chinese attitudes toward their neighbors. For Nitobe, who had modeled himself on the Christian gentlemen in the English tradition, this paternalism would have seemed to approximate the European attitude of the White man's burden. Roden's "Toward Remaking Manliness" shows us how Nitobe defined that tradition in his attempts to instill it in bright young Japanese students.

The nation whose colonial policies most nearly seemed to approach this ideal was Great Britain. Though many other factors influenced relations between Japan and Great Britain, Nitobe's own professional experience in colonial administration and his admiration of the British gentleman would have inclined him to a benign view of British foreign relations. The British desire to distance themselves from their East Asian ally after World War I could not help but give Nitobe pause.

Although the long-term effects of the shift were profound, the short-term effects in Nitobe's life gave him hope that Japan would continue to find acceptance among Europeans and Americans. In 1919 he was quite unexpectedly named to the post of Under-Secretary General of the new League of Nations. Burkman's "Geneva Spirit" demonstrates how Nitobe at the League became the embodiment of Japanese international cooperation. From 1920 to his retirement in 1926, Nitobe remained one of the League's most effective publicists. Sir Eric Drummond, the Secretary General, was an efficient administrator but an ineffectual speaker. "Frightened of speech making" himself, Drummond often asked Nitobe to publicize and solicit support for the League in various countries because, the Secretary General is said to have explained, that Nitobe was the best speaker the League had.[6] He could bring listeners to his point of view as well as entertain them with well chosen, often humorous, anecdotes based on his own experience.

Within Geneva, Nitobe became well known for his personable human relations. F. L. Whelen, who worked for many years at the League, wrote:

In the League's early days, at a Christmas party, [with] many members of the Secretariat present, the guests were asked to write down in order of 1,2,3 three names...they regarded as the most popular people in Geneva. My recollection is that all put Inazo Nitobe, no. 1.[7]

Nitobe's younger colleagues in the Secretariat reverently called him "Dr. Nitobe," and the rest spoke kindly of him. Professor James Shotwell of Columbia University, who came to know Nitobe in these years, called him "one of the finest gentlemen of any nationality I have ever met."[8]

William Faunce, President of Brown University, had struck up a friendship with Nitobe when he lectured at Brown in 1911. Faunce wrote to his wife Sadie from Geneva after meeting Nitobe again in 1922 that he was "an urbane, witty cosmopolitan, tenderhearted Christian who will have a front-seat in Heaven."[9]

When in 1926 Nitobe retired from the League of Nations in his sixty-fifth year, he returned to Japan a hero who spoke of retirement but continued active, taking on increasing loads until he died. He had been appointed, in 1925, to the Imperial Academy, and, when he returned from the League, the Wakatsuki government appointed him to the House of Peers, the upper house of the legislature. He also took on numerous other lecturing and writing assignments, most visibly as a columnist beginning in 1929 for the English-language version of the *Osaka Mainichi*.

Evaluation

Nitobe's new profession as a journalist in an English-language newspaper gave him the podium from which to espouse his own homely philosophy and with the passage of time try to sway readers to agreement with Japanese policies.

Satô's "Journalism: The Last Bridge" examines some of Nitobe's controversial articles in reaction to crucial contemporary events like the Stock Market Crash of 1929, the London Naval Disarmament Conference, the Manchurian Incident, and Japan's departure from the League of Nations in 1933. Historians have come to recognize that these events initiated a departure from the internationalism of the 1920s and the pursuit, through the 1930s, of an independent and autonomous Japanese Asian policy which culminated in the disastrous Pacific War. Though these articles seem to a North American reader seventy years later inoffensive enough, they concerned editors of Nitobe's *Complete Works* sufficiently after his death so that they did not include the articles in the *Complete Works*.

In 1929, the same year that he started to write for the *English Osaka Mainichi*, Nitobe also became the chairman of the Japan branch of the Institute of Pacific Relations (IPR). The Institute had been founded in 1925 by businessmen, for the most part Christian, and missionary statesmen interested in the preservation of peace in the Pacific. Governments as such could not join, and officers could not hold important government posts. Branches in the various nations around the Pacific were united by a secretariat in New York. Although its publications nowhere said so, the organization in fact concentrated on problems posed by the increasing Japanese presence in the area because the chief possible threat to peace in the Pacific was the Japanese army.

Nitobe succeeded to the chairmanship of the Japan branch when the previous incumbent became finance minister in July 1929. The new chairman immediately engrossed himself in plans for an October international conference of the IPR to be held in Kyoto. In a world which depended on surface transport, international conferences were still a rarity. The Japanese felt flattered that they had been asked to host the second international conference of the IPR, and Nitobe worked hard to assure its success, as Burkman's "The Geneva Spirit" and Oshiro's "The End: 1929–1933" demonstrate. Nitobe continued to head the Japan branch of the IPR until his death in 1933. In this position, he led Japanese delegates to the IPR's succeeding two international conferences: Shanghai in 1931 and Banff, Canada in 1933. Death claimed him shortly after his dramatic inability to sway international opinion in Japan's favor at Banff.

As these paragraphs show, the conditions under which Nitobe tried to function as a bridge changed greatly during his four decades of professional service. When he started, he rode the ascending wave of Japanese internationalism so well that in the course of his career he came to symbolize it. During the last four years of his life, it became increasingly difficult to bridge the chasm within Japan between the internationalists like Nitobe and the expansionists of the Japanese army.

Nitobe's urbane and witty championship of Japanese internationalism at the Kyoto Conference signalled the approaching end of his career as an internationalist, though no one in the halls of the Miyako Hotel could then foresee the extent of his eventual defeat. It became clear a few days before the Shanghai IPR conference in October 1931. By that time the Japanese army seizure of Manchuria had initiated a pattern of increasing involvement in China that led to Pearl Harbor and abject defeat. In his final years, Nitobe could do no more than oppose with ineffective words the increasing army domination of foreign affairs.

The first onslaught of deteriorating health forced him to rely on the assistance of two nurses *en route* to the Shanghai conference. There he faced representatives of the host country China enraged by the Japanese army's actions. From then on, as Nitobe gradually weakened in mind and body, he could do no more than importune representatives of the Western nations to give the Japanese time to work through their problems, even though the actions of the Japanese army nullified all he had sought to achieve. In the process he tarnished his reputation so that few would remember his name and so that those who do remember him disagree on his legacy. In their chapters, Howes, Oshiro, and Satô each deal with elements of the problem, while Ota has written an entire separate book on the subject.

The major difficulty resulted from the pride in their nation and its accomplishments common to every Japanese mingled with the fear that the army's actions engendered in those who opposed it. At each step of the way there was no point at which any significant group of people said, "This is too much." As the military brought increasing areas under Japanese control, even the most thoughtful Japanese could feel with conscience that this action might help those whose land was being taken over as the Japanese had improved general conditions in Taiwan. Japanese technology, according to such logic, could help the Manchurians produce enough foodstuffs to better themselves and export the remainder to Japan. Nitobe with his accomplishments in Taiwan could himself be seen to personify the benign effects of Japanese colonial benevolence.

This pervasive popular faith in the rectitude of government policies provided fertile ground for actions, however otherwise reprehensible, by those who claimed to act in the Emperor's name. Youthful military officers, convinced that martial rule could better address pressing economic problems than the lackluster elected officials, started to kill civilian politicians in distressing displays of violence. In a society with effective institutions that insured due process, the actions of the military officers might have been contained, but the Japanese Constitution placed almost no constraints on the military, and in a showdown, they controlled brute power.

As a result, those who in 1929 agreed with Nitobe on the need for greater Japanese commitment to international cooperation found themselves three years later increasingly on the defensive. Nitobe started to show the strain by a series of erratic acts quite at variance with his earlier career, as Howes and Oshiro show.

Satô examines articles that Nitobe wrote during these years which the censors passed for publication at the time but which were considered too critical of the government for republication after Nitobe's death. Satô finds that Nitobe championed peaceable solutions to international problems in the face of crucial contemporary events between 1929 and 1933. These events seem in hindsight to have initiated a departure from the internationalism of the 1920s and the pursuit, through the 1930s, of an independent and autonomous Japanese Asian policy which culminated in the disastrous Pacific War.

Those who find fault with Nitobe point out that he did not go far enough in his criticism. Oshiro shows that when Nitobe did speak frankly against the excesses of the army, angry self-proclaimed patriots threatened bodily injury and exacted a humiliating apology. In the light of this evidence,

Nitobe's general silence on the issue of army activity seems more understandable. Close friends who as officials shared his internationalism were being shot by enraged ultrarightists. Nitobe would have understood that to continue open criticism might well cost him his life, while to continue what must have seemed even to him at best ineffectual protests would ensure that one voice of caution remained among those with high positions in Japan. Nitobe's caution meant that at least he lived to express circumspect criticism of contemporary foreign policy.

Yet it would appear that Nitobe's lack of more vigorous dissent in the years right before his death led his countrymen to forget after 1945 his very real accomplishments, a point to which we return in the conclusion. Nitobe himself recognized that people's memories were short. He had confided at one point to his secretary at the League that he hoped to be remembered "by at least one person with affection and gratitude" twenty years after his death.[10] Copley's "Darkened Lanterns in a Distant Garden" indicates how one individual, a landscape garden designer, remembered Nitobe's accomplishments sufficiently a quarter of a century after Nitobe had passed on to create a quiet and serene Japanese garden that included many references to Nitobe's career. It shows that, however great the disagreements in the latter years of the twentieth century about Nitobe's place in the world, a sensitive artist who lived through the same events felt moved to commemorate Nitobe in a form that will live on indefinitely.

Notes

1. Miyabe Kingo Hakushi kinen shuppan kankôkai, ed., *Miyabe Kingo* (Tokyo,1953), p. 29.

2. *How I Became a Christian: out of my diary*, UKZ 3:13

3. Introduction to Yamamoto Taijirô, *Miyabe hakase ate no shokan ni yoru Uchimura Kanzô* (Tokyo, Tôkai shobô, 1952) p.1.

4. (Baltimore: Johns Hopkins Press, 1891).

5. As quoted in Kimura Ki, trans. Philip Yampolsky, *Japanese Literature, Manners and Customs in the Meiji-Taishô Era* (Tokyo: Ôbunsha,1957), pp. 59–61.

6. Drummond quoted in Kitasawa, *The Life of Dr. Nitobe*, p. 66; for details on Eric Drummond, see George Slocombe, *Mirror to Geneva: Its Growth, Grandeur and Decay* (1938; reprint ed., Freeport, New York: Books for Libraries Press, 1970), pp. 82–83.

7. F. L. Whelen, Letter to Passmore Elkinton, January 5, 1940, in Friends Historical Library, Nitobe Papers.

8. James Shotwell, *The Autobiography of James Shotwell* (New York: Bobbs and Merrill, 1960), p. 133.

9. Letter to Sadie Faunce, August 23, 1922, in Faunce Papers, Brown University Library.

10. K. I. Stafford, "Dr. Nitobe" in *NHTS*, p. 460.

TWO

Maturation

2

Roots

John F. Howes

When Nitobe died in Victoria, British Columbia, he left behind him a number of unpublished manuscripts. They included six essays in English on the events of his first years. These essays had been prepared for a proposed American magazine that "never materialized."[1] Inazô's widow, Mary Elkinton Nitobe, readied the manuscripts for publication during the year after her husband's death. In an epilogue dated on Inazô's birthday in 1934, she added material about the Nitobe family. It expanded a number of points that Inazô had noted in passing. They deal with his progenitors for the three immediately preceding generations.

Mary ended her comments with these words:

> My husband sometimes pained me by saying '*I have not been loyal to my ancestors in suffering more.*' With all due reverence, I feel they were combining to slay him; these three immediate progenitors—the savant, the pioneer and the diplomat who had each and all contributed to the make-up of his gifts and character. To their legacies of personality, it is true, was added endeavor— from youth, until the '*three score years and ten*' happily allotted men were passed. (pp. 560–61)

Mary, the daughter of a prosperous Philadelphia Quaker businessman, did not regularly use metaphors of violence. This one came to her mind as she finished her additions to her late husband's recollections. That the thought occurred to her at this point gives it added significance. The gentlemen in question had all died by the time her husband was nine years old. In this case, then, what was it about them that led his widow in her bereavement to cast such aspersions on their memories? She had been at Inazô's side almost constantly for over four decades. Her statement therefore should be accorded due weight in any attempt to link the internationalist Nitobe Inazô to the forces which molded the individual Inazô's innermost being. He was so urbane and witty in his command of the traditions of modern Japan and the Western world that it is possible to overlook his specific rural roots. They were far removed from his adult world. His *Reminiscences of Childhood* aimed to introduce Western readers to these specifics in a systematic way. Passing references to the same material appear in a number of his other writings. Mary's mention of the three immediate forebears directly before her sudden reference to their posthumous effects on her husband suggests that we should look carefully at their achievements.

Here I deal with three elements: the facts of Inazô's childhood, the work of his forebears, and the renewed relationship to his childhood home that marked his final years.

Childhood

Inazô started life in the attractive castle town of Morioka, then a small city of 40,000. It nestled into the hills of an interior valley in northern Honshu and served as the capital of Nambu-han. This was the name for the semi-independent area of northeastern Honshu up to the Tsugaru Straits. Our best single source for how life here affected the young Inazô is the adult recollections of Nitobe. They are supplemented by letters from his mother. These were written while Inazô studied in Tokyo and Sapporo from 1871 to 1881. They urged the lad to study out of respect for his forebears. During these same years, the members in the generation which immediately preceded Inazô demonstrated just how important the question of succession was to them. As a mature man, Nitobe became world famous. He then looked back on the events of his youth to explain the great disparity between his childhood environment and the international stage whose boards he trod daily. A discussion of his upbringing and how he subsequently viewed it precedes our later analysis of exactly what his family members had done and how these accomplishments attracted him back to his native place.

Inazô was born on September 1, 1862. His father Jûjirô was the eldest son. His mother Seki was talented and strong, stronger than a man, according to family tradition. Seki required strength to bring up a family of seven children in a home where her husband's work took him away for long periods and where he died when the youngest child was five. Along with all this, Seki learned sericulture well enough to instruct local women in its arts.[2]

The spacious compound in which the Nitobe family lived when Inazô was born has since been broken up into several lots. One of these has become a small park with a statue of the mature Nitobe. He sits immaculately dressed in a Western suit. He leans forward with his right elbow supported on the arm of the chair; the fingers of his right hand cradle his chin. The statue is a reproduction of one which marks his grave in suburban Tokyo. It depicts the attitude of careful attention to others' opinions which characterized Nitobe in conversation. We see here the man who wrote the *Reminiscences*. The child Inazô never sat in a chair and seems, as an active boy, to have sat in any fashion as little as possible. A few steps away from the home, the Nakatsu River flowed gracefully through the residential area which nestled under the castle walls. The neighborhood housed samurai officials whose business took them frequently within the castle.

Inazô's father, Jûjirô, died in 1867 when the boy was five; Inazô's grandfather, Tsutô, still active, seems to have overseen the upbringing of his grandson. Tsutô died in 1871. Seki was left with three boys and four girls. Her eldest son had died in infancy. The remaining sons were Shichirô, at that time twenty-eight, Michirô, eleven, and Inazô, nine. At least in part according to the prior decision of the grandfather Tsutô,[3] Inazô and Michirô left almost immediately to study in Tokyo. There the two boys lived with their father's younger brother, Tokitoshi. He had been adopted into a closely related family, the Ôtas, who had not produced an heir. He himself, in his thirties, had no children. Inazô became his adopted son. When Inazô left Morioka, therefore, he left both the scenes of his childhood and the Nitobe family. He would remain Ôta Inazô for twenty years. Then the same concern for family tradition would prompt the Nitobe family elders to return him to their fold.

In Tokyo, Inazô studied hard enough to proceed easily up the elite ladder of success to Japanese leadership. As he advanced in school, he formed fast friendships with Satô Shôsuke, Miyabe Kingo and Uchimura Kanzô. The four boys, already proficient in the English language, gained admittance to the new Sapporo Agricultural College. There most of the instruction was in English. Satô left to join the first class at this new school in 1876. The other three followed a year later. The story of these four and the others in the school forms an exhilarating chapter in the history of early Western-style Japanese education. The later careers of the others deserve separate mention.

At this time the childhood of Inazô had ended. Nitobe completed his *Reminiscences* with a description of how he and two of his friends went north by ship to Sapporo. They passed along the coast of Japan about sixty miles to the east of Morioka and separated from it by a mountain range.

The *Reminiscences* was written while Nitobe was one of the Under-Secretaries of the League of Nations in Geneva. At this time he was in his early sixties and one of the League's top officials. He was also the only non-European among them. As such, he felt a strong duty to represent all of Japanese culture and to show that the Japanese were a cultivated and civilized people. He had discovered that Europeans had endless questions about upbringing in Japan. And he himself seems to have found his mind returning to the scenes of his own childhood as those of an old man do.

As he reflected on these events of years past, his memory does not seem to have played many tricks on him, nor does his version of his own past seem to plead a special point of view. The *Reminiscences* lacks any obvious bias, but it manifests characteristics of Nitobe's thought which bear mention. They show us a Nitobe almost overly modest about his family background. They also picture a child who craved affection and stood in awe before unseen forces.

Looking back to his youth in Morioka, Nitobe concluded that his *Reminiscences* constituted "human documents relating to the life of a plain and average individual who has passed through the most eventful period of Japanese history" (p. 496). He went on to say that the family, "thanks to grandfather's financial abilities, lived in comparative opulence." They enjoyed in Morioka "a rather high position both in rank and in worldly possessions,...the more respectable of the middle class" (p. 501).

In these words Nitobe reflected his own apparent perplexity with the use of the word "middle class." Acquainted with the huge expanses of lawn and spacious homes in the mainline suburbs to the west of Philadelphia, he knew that their owners considered themselves "middle class." Certainly the Nitobes had enjoyed no such extravagant exterior or interior space. Judging by what seemed to Nitobe international standards, he could not accord his family a higher social rank.

To a citizen of Morioka he would have seemed unduly self-effacing. The Japanese among whom Inazô grew up considered apparent evidence of wealth both poor taste and an offense to public morality. They knew that the Nitobe position in Morioka was anything but modest. Rank in this bureaucratic society came first through official position. Wealth was a far lesser consideration. Yet the Nitobes had both. Grandfather Tsutô's "financial abilities" had provided them with extensive capital which they were investing in an ambitious land development. Tsutô during the years which immediately preceded his death had represented Nambu in the negotiations which determined its fate after the War of the Restoration. Inazô's father, as a "sort of minister-resident," represented Nambu in Edo (p. 500). Years after the Restoration, according to Mary Nitobe, people in what had been Nambu said "If Jûjirô Nitobe had lived, the fate of Nambu would not have been so hard" (p. 560). The little boy in such a family was not seen by adults around him as in any way "middle class." Inazô and Michirô rode five hundred kilometers to Tokyo in a palanquin. Its bearers knew that they were dealing with children whose family wielded great power. Both the adults in the family and the society around them recognized that the Nitobes stood at the center of regional authority.

Though the family had considerable influence and confidence in its use, Nitobe remembers that Inazô felt a perhaps excessive need for security. After he describes his first contact with English-language works, he continues, "Being...of an emotional nature, the stories related in reading books full of religious ideas, made a strong impression on my plastic mind. I was craving for sympathy.... There often came over my soul an immense sense of loneliness, and I was ready to clutch at a straw that would afford the least promise of succor" (p. 543). Here in one short passage, Nitobe combines two elements common to human experience but not usually mentioned in descriptions of childhood.

They are, first, the need for assurances and understanding from an authority figure and, second, the sense that beyond human assistance one must depend on unseen but nonetheless real forces. Human beings require affection from other human beings. When such affection has reached its limits, human beings must depend on religious convictions. The first English-language works Inazô studied came from strongly Protestant North America and brimmed over with contemporary piety.

Inazô's reference to religion requires further comment, but only after some mention of his "craving for sympathy." There is good reason to agree with his analysis that he needed much more than he received. As the youngest of seven children, he seems to have enjoyed probably more than his share of maternal attention, but Seki cannot have had much time for him. He tells us of the considerable pains to which the family went, first to make his initiation into samurai status at the age five both enjoyable and meaningful, and then to get him a proper uniform as a drummer. On the first occasion he received the dagger of a samurai; "the lacquered sheath—sprayed with gold—bore the family crest; but the steel!—what should I cut first?" (p. 508) He did not find out. The dagger was whisked away and replaced with party food. Shortly after the Restoration, the gun rather than the sword seemed to hold the future for a warrior. Friends urged Seki to get instruction for the Nitobe boys in Western-style military drill. Inazô, too young for guns, was persuaded of the important role performed by the drummer boy. "It was argued...that in Western tactics the drummer always marched at the head of the army and practically led it. This explanation entirely "satisfied my vanity" (p. 509). In this home, Inazô's father had already died, so the final decisions on training the children rested with Inazô's mother, Seki. The references in the *Reminiscences* to the home over which she presided all reflect the happy memories usually associated with childhood and a loving mother.

The home of Inazô's Tokyo adoptive father, Ôta Tokitoshi, lacked such warmth. Tokitoshi's first "beautiful young wife" (p. 529) had died. A suspicious and apparently vindictive woman took her place. She was later divorced. There was no one to continue the succor that had made the Morioka home a place of such contentment for Inazô.

Although Seki seems to have showered affection on Inazô, she kept in mind his preparation for entry into a man's world as a samurai. Inazô's happiest recorded memories of her home dealt, after all, with how to introduce the sword and rifle into the life of a young boy. Mary tells us that after the funeral of Inazô's father, Jûjirô, when the boy was five, Inazô slunk into a corner of the room while he cried. "He was bidden to come out—'to remember that a samurai should not shed tears.' 'I know it,' was the response, 'but I cannot help it. I am ashamed—so I came into the corner to hide them'" (p. 487). Here already, it seems, Inazô knew what a samurai should do and opted to hide when he had to vent his grief in tears.

The need for a source of psychic support beyond human means seems to have turned Inazô's mind at an early age to religion. His next elder brother, Michirô, suffered from a constitution so weak that he eventually had to return to Morioka. This frail body disturbed Inazô so that he attempted penance as a means to cure his brother. He gave up certain foods and vowed that he would bathe in cold water every morning at six, beginning in late fall. "The question of conscience," he goes on to say, "had always bothered me—not that mine was particularly sensitive, but perhaps because I knew I had paid less heed than I should to its alarming voice" (p. 533). In circumstances of this sort, the religiosity of the English-language primers seems to have given Inazô a certain solace. And when an unexpected gift came his way, he used the money to purchase an English-language Bible. It was his part of a present from the Emperor to his family. Inazô "felt exalted by the past of my family and by the greatness of my future responsibility" (p. 549).

Here then Nitobe directly links the boy Inazô's developing interest in religion with his consciousness of his place in the Nitobe family and their role in history. Inazô seems to have felt that he required the strength that religion could provide as he considered his own future. The chapter in which these remarks occur is entitled "Choice of a Calling." Uchimura Kanzô's autobiography describes how Inazô continued to be withdrawn and moody in the Sapporo Agricultural College.[4]

A strong source of solace and goad to future accomplishment came Inazô's way in the form of letters from his mother. Thirteen of them remain. They date from 1876, five years after Inazô left Morioka for Tokyo, until 1880, three months before Seki's death.[5] We can presume that there must have been more sent to the lad in Tokyo that he did not preserve, but as he matured, Inazô saved them.

And later, Nitobe had these mementoes of his mother mounted into a beautiful scroll. Each year on the anniversary of Seki's death, Nitobe retired into a room by himself, read the letters and reflected in silence on his mother's contributions to him. Mary Nitobe said, "I learned early to respect my husband's desire for a quiet apartness on this hallowed anniversary, and to recognize the fact that there is an innermost recess of the stoutest heart, that *no* one can or should penetrate" (p. 487). Mary's sensitive restraint demonstrates both her respect for her husband and his filial piety.

In 1880, after Inazô had finished his third year in college, he started on a leisurely trip back to Morioka. He savored the prospect of reunion after nine years of separation from his mother and the rest of the family. When he made his way into the familiar compound, he discovered that his mother's funeral had taken place the day before.[6] His mother's health had gradually deteriorated, and it seems that she concerned herself more for his body than her own,[7] perhaps had even restrained members of the family who wanted to inform Inazô, because such tidings would disturb his study. His adult recollections rested simply on his contact with his mother to the age of nine and her thirteen letters.

There is thus small wonder that he preserved them. And what did they say? At first they contained regular requests for letters to her. Later she included a message for Shichirô, Inazô's eldest brother, who was also in Tokyo. This would indicate that Inazô answered her letters, whereas Shichirô did not. Finally, when Inazô got to Sapporo and started minute and illustrated descriptions of his life there, she marvelled at all he did and cautioned him not to ruin his health with too much study. And she apologized for not writing him more.

Nitobe summarizes the sense of two among the letters in his *Reminiscences*. The first one was sent very shortly after Seki had dispatched two yen to him. It was Inazô's share of the Imperial gift made to the family when the Emperor stayed at a second home of grandfather Tsutô in a place called Sambongi in the far northern reaches of Nambu-han. The Emperor had given the money to commemorate the work of agricultural development, principally by Tsutô and Inazô's father, Jûjirô. They had developed new rice land in this remote area. Nothing could have honored any Meiji Japanese family more than such a gift. Inazô quotes Seki, "Your grandfather was a famous man and so was your father. If you do not attain to greatness, people will laugh at you and say that you were only your mother's child and not your father's. If you disgrace yourself, you will drag me down, too. Strive for renown" (p. 545).[8] The next year Inazô's adoptive father and both elder brothers joined the army to help put down the Satsuma Rebellion. Inazô, in contrast, went north to the new Sapporo Agricultural College.

> Poor Mother! She wrote to each of us a brave letter of comfort. "You left me when you were eight," she wrote me, "and you have grown in body and mind.... There has been falling snow on my head of late, but if you flourish and attain to greatness I shall not mind how much whiter it may become. Ten years are nothing. You must not be so weak as to yearn for home. Remember you have an important work to do, and to do it you must be strong-minded.

When I, who am only a feeble old woman, can bear separation, certainly you can and must, with a cheerful heart" (pp. 553–54).

The patient student who compares the original of these texts with the Nitobe paraphrase will recognize significant differences. This is true in particular of the lines which follow the ellipsis in the second quotation: "There has been..." They do not occur in this letter and appear[9] to be a simple addendum. This is not to say that Nitobe imagined things, for these words certainly reflect the spirit of the original letters taken as a whole. Most important, it does not matter to history so much what Seki said as what Nitobe remembered her as saying.

There is one more passage which should be mentioned. In the spring of 1878, a few months after he had arrived in Sapporo, Inazô asked his mother for travel money to visit the family. She referred the request to Inazô's adoptive father. He refused with the reason that Inazô had so recently arrived in Sapporo.[10]

If he had gone home in 1878, Inazô might have been party to deliberations which demonstrated the care that the Nitobe family took with questions of family continuity. In that year, they established a *bunke*, or branch family, in Sambongi, the settlement established near the paddy land that Tsutô and Jûjirô had developed. The family now had considerable interests there which could not conveniently be managed from Morioka. The Sambongi branch of the family would be able to perform this function. Inazô's immediate elder brother, Michirô, became head of the new branch. The eldest brother, Shichirô, remained as head of the Morioka family. In 1884, four months before Inazô left Tokyo for the United States, Michirô died without issue. In an attempt to provide continuity, the family first sent Michirô's wife back to her parents. This was customary in the case of young widows without children. Then they adopted into the *bunke* Waka, the youngest daughter of Tsutô. She had been born in Tsutô's seventy-second year. Tsutô, as was the custom at the time for those whose job forced them to spend long periods away from home, had a concubine in Sambongi. The Sambongi family tradition holds that she was the daughter of the personal secretary to the last daimyo of Nambu and therefore of samurai stock. Waka, two years Inazô's junior and his half aunt, became by this act his adopted niece. The family then adopted a bright young man, Ryôsuke, from an entirely different family as Waka's husband.[11] Biographers who deal with individuals of status in a status-conscious society know that concubines disturb family lines. The introduction of a concubine into the Nitobe line opened the way for later controversy. The information in the preceding paragraph is based on the understanding of the Sambongi branch of the family.

The Morioka family tradition, increasingly supported by evidence, holds that Waka was not adopted as Michirô's successor and that the records were falsified to indicate that she was.[12] The details in the preceding paragraph are presented here because they fit in with the facts as seen in Towada-shi, the current name for Sambongi, and because its citizens considered them fact for at least three quarters of a century. These perceptions formed an important basis for what would happen in Towada-shi as Nitobe aged.

The concern for family continuity would influence Inazô's later life. When the eldest son of Jûjirô and Inazô's remaining brother Shichirô died in 1889, there was no male left to continue the Morioka line of the Nitobes. As a result, Inazô was returned to the Nitobe family. From the point of view of his own self image, Nitobe Inazô who had become in 1871 Ôta Inazô became in 1889 once again Nitobe Inazô. A son of Ryôsuke and Waka took Inazô's place as an Ôta in Tokyo.

Nitobe's own recollections of his childhood, plus what other information we have, demonstrate that he came from a family that took itself very seriously. Inazô grew up feeling a strong need for "sympathy" because of concerns which he tried to solve in religious terms. During most of his youth Inazô seems to have felt that it was his mother who did the most to give him the emotional security that only affection can provide. Satô Masahiro in a sensitive analysis of the letters links Nitobe's appreciation for his mother's words to his own later considerable work on behalf of women.[13]

While accepting this evaluation, it is also possible to derive some quite different conclusions from the letters and other materials. In a large number of cases, Seki's expressions of affection are directly linked to and conditioned on Inazô's success through study. Such a conclusion seems possible from the passages Nitobe quoted; "If you disgrace yourself, you will drag me down too, strive for renown" (p. 437). Or again, in another letter, not quoted in *Reminiscences*, "You must at all times and without reservation devote yourself only to study. There are many other things I want to say, but I simply cry out with this *[oi oi môshiagesôrô]*. Please, please, if only you bear up diligently, that will be the greatest kindness to your family *[nani yori no kôkô.]*."[14]

One would feel that these letters place a heavy burden indeed upon a fifteen-year-old who as an adult remembers he craved affection. The words of support from his mother he later so cherished were always linked with need for academic achievement. It would be easy for a homesick lad to assume that these expressions of affection were conditional, that his mother loved him to the extent that he got good grades.

And what of the family for whom all this was to be done? They could uproot a boy from his mother at one whim, ask him to engraft another set of family loyalties, and then take him back. In some cultures a person so treated would feel considerable antagonism.

As far as we know, neither the child Inazô nor the adult Nitobe ever indicated displeasure over these developments. His cultural conditioning was such that he would not have said it, and if he had said it, those that heard him would not have understood. Yet the fact remains: Removed as he grew up, both in time and space from close contact with members of his own family, he could easily have idealized them out of all proportion if he did not first reject their claims on him.

He might have rejected them if his own objective research into his roots had persuaded him that his mother's views were the roseate recollections of a widow. He turned to study his forebears, he tells us, shortly after the Imperial visit and gift in 1876 (p. 549). The more he studied them, the more remarkable he would have found their legacy. They put a heavy burden on him to achieve. A brief glimpse at them precedes our discussion of how these elements worked on Inazô during his final years.

Giants in Their Time

There is general agreement among the sources that the three forebears Mary mentioned, Koretami, Tsutô and Jûjirô, were all men of distinction. The three patriarchs are each mentioned both by Nitobe and Mary in the *Reminiscences*, and each has left behind copious writings which are preserved in Towada-shi.[15] The summaries given by the two authors of the *Reminiscences* are accurate, particularly when one considers the distance in space and cultural background which separated the authors from the records with which they worked.

Koretami (1769–1845) taught military arts in a small castle which guarded the southern approaches to Morioka. It had been constructed to ward off the very real danger of an attack from the much more powerful Date family in Sendai. Two hundred peaceful years later, Date no longer threatened, but Russian explorers off the coast of Hokkaido did. The Nambu leaders proposed to demolish the castle and divert the defense funds to the north. Samurai in the castle under Koretami appear to have threatened revolt over the decision.[16] He petitioned that the decision be reconsidered. For his temerity he was divested of half his income and sent at age fifty-one to a distant and forlorn community. It faced Mutsu Bay from the south side of the hook-like peninsula at the northern end of Honshu.

This amounted to exile. The winters were severe. In the winter of 1983–84, admittedly worse than most, the village made the news when it reported 1.5 meters of new snow in one day.[17] After six years, Koretami was pardoned and returned with his family to his home. Some time before his death, he cleaned up the family records. The genealogy, which had been badly eaten into by worms *(mushi)*, was recopied on heavy paper. Koretami also started an accompanying less formal list of individuals with their vital statistics and accomplishments. In the introductions to both the genealogy and comments, he urged his successors to continue his tradition of record keeping as an act of filial piety.[18]

The genealogy traced the family back to the fifth son of the Emperor Kammu. Kammu's name lives in history as one of the most vigorous among the Japanese Emperors. He was responsible for the removal of the capital to Kyoto in the final years of the eighth century and the dispatch of Kûkai to China. A biographer acquainted with Japanese genealogies might well doubt this claim, but for a young lad to find himself situated some forty generations removed from such an illustrious beginning would give any youth of Inazô's generation a strong sense of identity and responsibility.

Koretami's son Tsutô (1793–1871) accomplished the most of the three outstanding progenitors of Inazô. Tsutô's outstanding career started when Koretami was exiled. At that time, Tsutô was given the choice, according to tradition, to accompany his father or live in Morioka closely supervised.[19] He chose the former alternative. At the same time, in order to supplement what had become with his father's exile quite straightened circumstances, Tsutô went into business. Samurai were not supposed to sully themselves with business, so this act in itself reflected considerable independence. Tsutô traded in lumber, shipping logs to the Kanto. After four years, he left his parents to move to Edo. Here he started on a decade of successful entrepreneurship. He became fast friends with many businessmen and studied various aspects of the economy.

As part of this, he lumbered the area around Lake Towada for the first time. Natives thought the *kamisama*, the guardian gods of the lake, would take revenge if it was used for transport. Tsutô overcame their fears and floated logs on it. The logs were then sent down to the sea by river. A disastrous fire in Edo in 1828 produced a lively market for lumber which brought Tsutô great profit. Five years later, he traveled for nine months from Edo to Shimonoseki. His autobiography for this period indicates that he used the time to study how others did their jobs.[20] He also observed the disasters caused by rice shortages and tried to alleviate some of their worst effects. At the same time, he benefitted from his own investment in the rice market. At the end of 1837, he sold out his business and returned to serve the administration of Nambu.[21]

Nambu now had at its service a man of extraordinary experience. In his forties, he had behind him almost fifteen years of business success, much of it in the capital. He had traveled widely and observed conditions all over Honshu. His lifetime career in the government utilized this background until his death. He devoted himself to fiscal management, increased production and diplomatic negotiations.

Nambu, like so many of the other local governments, found itself in great difficulty with what would in the late twentieth century be called cash-flow problems. In 1858, Tsutô was in Edo. The daimyo planned to start home, and the date of departure had been announced, but the money to pay his considerable travel expenses had not arrived. Tsutô and another official tried to borrow money. They approached various firms with no success. The daimyo left on schedule without funds but awaited them at the first station outside Edo. Just then a ship arrived from Nambu. Its goods were sold and the income earmarked for the daimyo's expenses. Just as the messenger bearing the money caught up to the daimyo, another envoy arrived from Morioka with the funds that had originally been requested.[22] If the daimyo's credit had been good, the loan could have been easily arranged.

For one with Tsutô's experience, it was natural to consider an increase in income to prevent such embarrassment. To this end, he enlarged the tax base through numerous land-improvement schemes. In 1852, he started twenty-four such projects. They opened land with an anticipated production of 641 *koku*, enough rice to feed about the same number of people for a year. He also started surveys for the very ambitious program at Sambongi. In 1854, Nambu forced all samurai with incomes above a certain minimum to return some of them as loans. Its officers also initiated the "ten-year samurai" system.[23] Under this system, samurai were bound to reclaim within ten years sufficient land to provide their own stipend. If they did not, they would lose their status.[24] Specific incentives of this sort helped persuade numerous samurai to invest in the Sambongi project.[25]

The major development work took five years. It brought water from a river which drains Lake Towada to irrigate what otherwise was a barren upland plateau. This was about sixteen kilometers square. The work required over five kilometers of tunnels to bring the water along the side of a mountain plus fills for canals between the tunnels. Once the water had been brought to the plain, a system of sluices had to be built to distribute it. The land had earlier supported a few settlers who scratched out a living raising horses. Now communities had to be provided for many more people. Tsutô moved to Sambongi to supervise the entire project. He is now as a result revered as the *kamisama* who founded the city.

By the time the work was finished, Tsutô was sixty-six. His son Jûjirô (1820–67) had become deeply involved in the development. At the age of eighteen Jûjirô had gone to Edo to study. Shortly thereafter, he became a favorite of the daimyo and accompanied him on many trips. At the age of thirty-three he became a *kanjô bugyô*. This term referred to an officer with considerable responsibility for financial development. It usually went to men with more experience.

Tsutô followed the career of his capable son with great interest, noting each time Jûjirô received a new appointment. After the visits of Commodore Perry, Nambu started to erect cannon emplacements on the coast. Jûjirô divided his interest while the work was in progress at Sambongi between the erection of such emplacements and the construction of the irrigation projects. In 1860, he laid out the town of Sambongi with wide streets and a checkerboard pattern. He modeled it on Kyoto. The following year, he built a home in Sambongi. He also ran surveys for a canal that would have linked Mutsu Bay with the Pacific and thus cut days off the time required by ships for the trip from Edo to Aomori. In 1862, he moved to Edo to represent Nambu, and remained there until 1867. In this year, he sold some Nambu silk, produced in part at his suggestion, to the French. It was his plan to use some of the profits to help defray costs in Sambongi. This act incurred the wrath of the daimyo; Jûjirô returned to Morioka a prisoner. Although cleared of the charges, he refused to leave the house and died of a heart attack late in that year.[26] His accusers seem to have assumed that he planned to establish a separate government under his control. That his integrity could not endure this suspicion led Mary Nitobe to conclude that the cause of death was a *"broken heart."*[27]

Little more is known about Jûjirô. His numerous writings exist only in manuscript form and have not been available to scholars. In February 1984, a group of specialists on old texts started to transcribe them into modern language for publication. They will thus become available so that scholars can judge Jûjirô's abilities on the basis of his writings. Until that time, a number of diagrams and charts in the Nitobe Memorial Museum (*Kinenkan*) in Towada-shi attests to his abilities as a draftsman. One short published work dated 1860 also outlines his proposal for further development of the successful Sambongi scheme.[28] It was his attempt to seek funds to implement this new venture that caused his disgrace. The suggestions as a result merit attention.

In them Jûjirô proposes the further development of an area some twenty-two kilometers by forty kilometers, an increase of the completed work by about three-and-one-half times. His text exudes the air of a confident developer who requires only capital. The argument runs as follows. Sambongi is just at the median latitude between the south and north of Japan. The weather is temperate with well differentiated seasons. It is a "fecund land, the best in the world for the fertility of its soil and the enrichment of its inhabitants."[29] It abounds in useful products. During the first year of production after the completion of the irrigation project, the area is already producing 200 koku of rice and 100 koku of dry-field products. This could increase to tens of thousands of koku. Specific suggestions for development include a horse market along with the encouragement of pottery production, silk production, Irish potatoes, fishing nets, tea and carrots.

Jûjirô then considers the human engineering the project requires. This includes the subsidy of girls with unwanted pregnancies so that they and their progeny can help; the importation of prisoners and the indigent as laborers; and even the establishment of brothels. The document is signed by Tsutô, Jûjirô and by the seventeen-year old eldest son of Jûjirô and eldest brother of Inazô, Shichirô.[30]

Although the family tradition as passed along by Mary considers Jûjirô to have been most distinguished as a diplomat,[31] the work we have just examined portrays him as a practical doer-of-things. He had a vision of man shaping his environment to the advantage of his society that would become popular in Japan in about two decades. And it seems to have been if anything the lack of skills in prudent persuasion that led to the eventual suspicions of him and his subsequent downfall.

Tsutô is considered by most people as a doer-of-things, but the record also reveals consummate diplomatic ability. He presented his point of view in a way that made it look as if he was simply transmitting the views of others. This enabled him to relax as he engaged in important and complicated discussions.

His skills were demonstrated in his representation of Nambu in the discussions which brought about the surrender of the Nambu forces to those of the Restoration. They took place in the fall of 1869. At the time, Britain and France had representatives in Hakodate and were helping the Bakufu forces there. The Restoration army had come up along the Japan Sea coast. Sambongi lay close to its approach from Aomori. Tsutô, now seventy-six, alternated between Morioka and Sambongi.

During the summer, the elders of Nambu had met for long hours to discuss whether they would side with the Imperial or the Tokugawa forces. They had decided on the Tokugawa for reasons of the daimyo's family: The wife of the daimyo had come from Mito which was related to the Tokugawas. This left Tsutô, who had favored the cause of the Restoration forces, "very concerned."[32]

Some days later, he left Morioka to confer with the leaders of Tsugaru in Hirosaki, through which the Imperial forces were approaching.[33] The Tsugaru leaders warned him that the Imperial forces were expected any minute and might kill him. He responded that he was seventy-six and did not fear death. He then proceeded to show the Tsugaru leaders that they had backed the Imperial Forces because of marriage ties between their daimyo and an Imperial prince. Both groups had thus based their allegiance on family considerations which bore little relation to the problems Japan faced. What mattered was concern for the defense of all Japan against the foreigners.[34]

A month and a half later, the two forces clashed near the coast of Mutsu Bay to the east of Aomori. The Nambu forces won, and Nambu leaders decided to use their success to ease themselves out of the war. Tsutô's ideas were already known in Tsugaru and therefore probably to the leader of the Imperial forces. Tsutô represented Nambu in the discussions.

The commanding general of the Imperial forces, Tamura Kanzaemon, gradually warmed to Tsutô's arguments which resembled those he had used with the Tsugaru officials, though Tamura remained adamant on one point. He wanted the head of the Nambu commanding officer. Tsutô had succeeded in his aim to deflect anger from the daimyo of Nambu. He replied to the request of Tamura with the statement that his demand must be relayed to Morioka for an answer. That would take time. If Tamura wanted faster action, he could take Tsutô's head. After this argument had been put forth a number of times, Tamura emphasized that Tsutô's head would not do. Well, in that case, came the reply, there was nothing to do but wait. Troops from both sides went home when Tsutô signed a guarantee that the head would come within a week.[35]

Tamura's assent gave the Nambu forces some time to consider their strategy. They discussed the possibility of another head, since Tamura had not met the man whose sacrifice he required. When the head did not come by the date promised, Tsutô negotiated a postponement.[36] To all of the Nambu representatives it seemed a very cruel demand. In the end they had to accede.

By that time Tsutô had been sent on to other things. A year later he was in Tokyo to negotiate supplies of rice to ward off starvation after a local crop failure. In the following year, 1871, he died after an illness of two months. He was buried in a stand of trees he had planted atop a slight eminence in Sambongi.[37]

Inazô had been seven and in Morioka as Tsutô negotiated the end of the hostilities. Inazô's father's plan for the development of the Sambongi area had been put forth two years before Inazô's birth. Jûjirô had later been in Edo for all but a few months of Inazô's life but had died in Morioka. Inazô knew and loved him. Nitobe goes on to say how Inazô had "felt deeply humiliated" over the defeat in 1869.[38] He also tells us how the man who would become his adoptive father had been ordered as a close friend of the victim to sever the head that Tamura Kanzaemon required after the Nambu general's seppuku. Inazô's uncle had refused because the request seemed so heartless.[39] Although neither topic may have been dinner-table conversation, the young Inazô learned quite young what an important role his family members had played in this opening chapter of "the most eventful period in Japanese history."[40] And he must have learned that his very unusual given name, first as Inanosuke and then, after age nine, Inazô—"to make rice"—linked the date of his birth to the first rice harvest from the reclaimed land in Sambongi.

Half a century later, he appears to have given the matter systematic thought for the first time. When his term with the League of Nations ended, he began to pay much more attention to his home in northern Honshu.

Last Rites

Inazô had retired from the League at sixty-five. On a visit to Sambongi a newspaper reporter interviewed him. The resulting article quoted Nitobe to the effect that he wanted a life where he could avoid constant callers and enjoy afternoon naps.[41] He was far enough along on the process that leads to retirement to appreciate some of its amenities. But he would never, in fact, harvest the fruits of his many labors. His own drive to accomplish, his sense of duty to assist worthwhile efforts, and his recognition of his own unique capabilities kept him at the center of developments. When he died the members of a delegation from Sambongi insisted that his ashes be interred there. Their request surprised Nitobe's Tokyo friends. The story that leads to this development revolves about Nitobe's activities in his last year, his visits to Sambongi, and the events of his funeral in Tokyo.

Uchikawa Eijirô has uncovered a whole new segment of Nitobe's career which links his final years to Morioka. This is Nitobe's chairmanship of the Iwate Prefectural branch of the national agricultural cooperative association. In the spring of 1928 Nitobe had addressed their national meeting in Tokyo. His topic was "The Spirit of Cooperatives" (Sangyô kumiai no seishin ni tsuite), and reports indicate that he held his large audience spellbound. He talked in part about the influence on his own development of the German agricultural reformer Friedrich Wilhelm von Raichffeisen.[42]

During the late 1920s, agricultural conditions in the Tôhoku demanded attention. Frequent crop failures, usurious interest rates and plummeting agricultural commodity prices reduced many farmers to desperation. A few months after Nitobe spoke in Tokyo, the army held war games in the area around Morioka. The Emperor attended. To celebrate the end of the games, the government announced a program to encourage agricultural cooperatives. This flurry of official interest implicitly recognized that many of the hotheads in the army came from these farms now in such distress. The sons of these farmers, as army officers, demanded decisive solutions to economic problems.

Local cooperative officials realized how, in these circumstances, the participation of Nitobe would strengthen their movement. They plotted a careful approach to him and then savored unanticipated success when he acceded. He took up his duties at the annual meeting in May 1931. In his opening remarks, he mentioned the work of his forebears. He also said that he planned to act as more than a nominal head. Ever conscious of his time, he added that he would gladly give the Iwate Agricultural Cooperative ten days a year to do anything they needed.[43]

Two years earlier, Nitobe had taken on other specific responsibilities which put insistent demands upon his time. The first of these was to contribute a regular column for *The English Osaka Mainichi*. As Satô Masahiro shows elsewhere in this volume,[44] this required considerable effort.

Second, Nitobe had become chairman of the Japan branch of the Institute of Pacific Relations(IPR). Nitobe took on this duty when the previous incumbent accepted a cabinet post and so, under IPR rules, became ineligible to lead a delegation. Nitobe had, almost immediately, to host the 1929 conference in Kyoto. This included responsibility for Japan's contributions to the conference proceedings. Nitobe continued to head the Japan IPR until his death. The two later conferences, in 1931 at Shanghai, and 1933 at Banff, became, with the ever-worsening international situation, major crises in Japanese international relations. The Emperor asked Nitobe, as the representative of moderate forces, to ameliorate relations between Japan and the West. This became increasingly difficult as Japanese military advances into China incurred the wrath of other powers.

Nitobe sandwiched his responsibilities to the cooperative movement between these other duties. Perhaps his most important contribution to it was his work on behalf of medical cooperatives. Through this, he deepened his acquaintance with the highly respected Protestant pastor and social reformer, Kagawa Toyohiko. Both men realized that fear of high medical expenses formed a considerable threat to the well being of the poor. Kagawa, like Nitobe, had also worked hard to improve understanding across the Pacific. Both men suffered as they saw their attempts at bridge building fail. Perhaps that is why Kagawa wrote a very moving eulogy when Nitobe died.[45]

For Japanese like Kagawa and Nitobe, the passage of time from 1931 to 1933 brought ever-increasing tension. Nitobe suffered an unexpected and painful attack of *shinkeitsû*, variously translated in this volume as "lumbago" or "neuralgia." It forced him to use crutches and lean on two nurses as he boarded ship en route to Shanghai in 1931. In Shanghai he found himself under attack because of the recent Japanese takeover of Manchuria.

Seven months later in February 1932, a remark which Nitobe thought he had made in confidence was widely quoted and criticized. In it he had compared the danger that militarism posed to Japan to that of communism. Ultra-rightists attacked him immediately. Uchikawa's sensitive treatment of this lecture in Matsuyama and its aftermath provides fascinating insight into the way that individual human ambitions and national concerns combined to make this series of events a nightmare for Nitobe (pp.

137–63). The members of his family also suffered. For some time afterward, police guarded the gates to his Tokyo residence because of threats on his life.

Relations with the United States in particular continued to deteriorate. Nitobe had vowed never to visit the United States again after the Exclusion Act of 1924, but he considered the circumstances grave enough to warrant an exception at this time. He and Mary left in April 1932, two months after the visit to Matsuyama. In the states, Nitobe lectured widely and met with many important people, but he could not stem the widespread suspicion of Japan's actions in Manchuria and Shanghai. On the way back, Mary developed heart trouble. She remained behind in a Pasadena hospital with a faithful family retainer attending to her needs. Inazô and Mary were not to be reunited until September 1, 1933. By then Mary had recovered sufficiently to move to Oak Bay Beach Hotel in Victoria where Inazô met her. This was after the Banff Conference of the IPR and six weeks before Inazô's death.

Inazô had returned alone to Japan five months earlier. Two days after he disembarked, Japan left the League of Nations. For one reputed to have been the League's most eloquent spokesman, this must have come as a terrible shock. Uchikawa says, "After Japan withdrew from the League of Nations, Inazô's statements [and actions] became very contradictory."[46] Little wonder, with the pressures that crowded in on him, the increasing frailty of age, and the absence of his wife's support.

Two months later, in May, he traveled north to Morioka. He spoke there and then observed damage caused by a huge tidal wave that had hit the coast about fifty miles to the east. In Morioka, he left a written statement in English and Japanese. The English version said:

> To live is to work for others;
> to die is to do nothing. Self-renunciation is
> the beginning of life. Inazô Nitobe[47]

This became his final message to the people of his birthplace. On May 18, he left Morioka for Sambongi. It appears to have been Inazô's ninth or tenth visit to the area that Tsutô and Jûjirô had developed. His first trip had been in 1908 when he addressed the local agricultural cooperative. In 1915 he had represented the family when Tsutô was given a posthumous Imperial decoration. Family records, newspaper articles, and group photographs attest to four more visits between 1927 and 1931. They reflect a continuing interest in Sambongi that increased with the passage of time; the story of Sambongi further illuminates the interconnections.

In 1924, Inazô and two relatives in Sambongi ordered the construction of a fireproof building to hold family archives and artifacts.[48] The two relatives were Ôta Tsunetoshi and Nitobe Kun who were blood brothers. To describe their relation to Inazô demonstrates the web of ties and affections that had resulted from family attempts to insure its survival. Tsunetoshi and Kun were two of the sons of Waka and Ryôsuke. These in turn were the two who, according to the Sambongi tradition, had been adopted into the Nitobe family to continue the Sambongi branch established by Inazô's immediately elder brother, Michirô. One son of Waka and Ryôsuke, Tsunetoshi, had been adopted into the Ôta family in 1907. Waka's and Ryôsuke's next son, Kun, had stayed in Sambongi to head that branch of the family.

Ôta Tsunetoshi had thus taken Inazô's place as the son of Ôta Tokitoshi. Tokitoshi had earlier, among other things, refused to sever the head of his leader at the time of the Restoration. He had remained childless for eighteen years after the death of Inazô's eldest brother, Shichirô, had led to Inazô's return from the Ôta family to the Nitobes. At that time the child who would become the adoptive son, Ôta Tsunetoshi, had been three years old. One suspects that Tokitoshi had observed his development carefully. Tsunetoshi joined the Ôta family when he went to Tokyo for further education. He later become a naval officer and had risen to the rank of lieutenant commander before the early retirement which resulted from Japan's accession to the Naval Arms Limitation Treaties of 1921–1922.

Tsunetoshi then returned to Sambongi where he built an impressive Western-style house. It sat across the street from the grave of his ancestor Tsutô. Tsutô was a grandfather if one counted through the mother, Waka, a great grandfather if one counted with the adopted lineage through Ryôsuke and Michirô. Tsunetoshi was also Inazô's great nephew by adoption. Both of them knew through their own experience the methods the family employed to ensure continuity.

The two shared a special affection. After the uproar caused by Nitobe's statement in Matsuyama, Tsunetoshi accompanied Inazô on a number of occasions as a self-appointed bodyguard. His photograph pictures him as tall, well built and thick necked—the type who would make a persuasive bodyguard. Tsunetoshi also, alone among the Morioka and Sambongi relatives, would have had, because of his naval experience, some acquaintance with Western ways. His house symbolized this difference.

It was with these two grandnephews, Tsunetoshi and Kun, that Inazô joined to preserve family records and artifacts. Their prescience preserved many items from destruction in the disastrous fire of 1941. It wiped out the house that the Meiji Emperor had visited and Kun had later inhabited as the head of the family. The materials saved in the storehouse are now displayed in the Nitobe Memorial Museum in Towada-shi. The records are outstanding, as Uno Shûhei[49] and Mori Nobu, specialist on old documents (komonjô) at the Iwate Prefectural Library, attest.[50] Nitobe tells us he enjoyed his first acquaintance with these documents at age fourteen.[51] He may have read further in them during visits to Sambongi. If he did, he discovered for himself what an extraordinary collection they are. And they, he would have realized in 1933, reflected Tsutô's and Jûjirô's dedication to the cause of others—exactly what he had indicated as life's main aim when he wrote out his holograph in Morioka a few days earlier.

Beside Tsutô's grave lies another one with Jûjirô's name. Jûjirô was in fact buried in Morioka. This grave represents what is known in Sambongi as *bunkotsu*. The term, "division of the bones," calls up unpleasant associations of dissection. In fact, the process is a much more benign means by which society can provide more than one locus for the material remains of an individual it wants to remember.

In the first place, bodies are cremated. This means that ashes can be put in two urns rather than one. Or if interment has already taken place, hairs from combs or fingernail clippings or even earth from the first grave can be moved to a second location. Jûjirô's grave in Towada-shi contains in fact only a bit of earth from the grave in Morioka.[52] He thus rests beside his father at the sight of their great triumph on behalf of their fellow human beings. When Inazô visited the grave site on his trip in 1933, it contained only his grandfather's remains. A photograph taken in front of Tsutô's grave shows Inazô wan and stooped.

A baker in Towada, Matoba Kiyoshi, ninety-three in the spring of 1984, remembered at that time a number of visits by Inazô. On one occasion, Matoba tells us, he carried his infirm grandmother to pay her respects to Mary Nitobe. Mary shook her hand, and the old lady demanded that she be taken back every day for the rest of the Nitobe visit to receive more handshakes. Matoba also remembers that in 1933 he and Ôta Tsunetoshi accompanied Inazô on a walk to Tsutô's grave. At a point at the side of Tsutô's grave, Inazô marked with his cane the place where he wanted to be buried if "after my forthcoming trip to America, I do not return alive."[53] Others in Towada heard the same story from Ôta Tsunetoshi. One of them remembers how Tsunetoshi said that during this same visit Inazô pointed out a place where he would like to build a retirement home when he returned from his forthcoming journey.[54]

Two weeks before he left for Canada, Inazô traveled briefly to Shimoda. It was the day before the anniversary of his mother's death. He and two friends visited the sights associated with the sojourn of Townsend Harris, the first consul to Japan from the United States. A Japanese woman who served Harris at that time is memorialized at Shimoda for the self-sacrifice which cost her life in the interest of better relations between Japan and the United States. While viewing the various sights of Shimoda, Inazô suddenly ordered a small roadside statue (*jizô*), of a sort usually associated with children; he further specified that the death date of his mother be carved into the stone.[55]

It is convenient in Japanese terms to think of this as a simple act of filial piety along with Inazô's many others. If one does so, he has difficulty with the metaphor. In what way was Seki a sacrifice on behalf of Japanese-American relations? She was not; it was not she but her son Inazô who was the sacrifice. As the Japanese government had ordered the girl who served Townsend Harris to what became her doom, so the same government now ordered Inazô on a similar mission. Seki became part of the sacrifice because Inazô would fail; he had not succeeded in the high demands she had placed on him.

This is one of the irrational acts to which Uchikawa alludes. In terms of Inazô's psychodynamics it does not seem irrational. He had hardly any choice. He wanted to succeed for Seki, and in the moment of his greatest test he appeared about to fail. Other men might have cried out for understanding or sympathy. Even at this point, Inazô sublimated his own pain to what he considered his mother's interests.

On August 2, 1933, Inazô left for Vancouver. After he rejoined Mary on September 1, they had eleven days together before Inazô entered hospital. Five weeks after that he died.

Inazô's death was world news. People everywhere knew about it the next day. Yet it took a month for Mary to return home by ship with the urn which contained Inazô's ashes. During this period, those concerned with the obsequies had time to make detailed plans. Mary Duguid, a niece of Mary Nitobe, and Yoshio Nitobe, Inazô's son, have left us a description of the events which started with Mary's return on November 16, and ended four days later after the ceremonies.[56] The description is in a family letter which runs to four thousand words. Within a few days of the news of the death, it says, Inazô's various protégés had formed twenty-three committees to handle arrangements. The word here translated as "protégés" is "*deshi*" in the original. Deshi are students of a highly respected individual. In return for what they have learned from him, they owe him limitless gratitude. This includes assistance with funeral arrangements. In Inazô's case, the committees totaled more than one hundred persons with assigned tasks.

A committee of six met the ashes at the boat. They then supervised the formalities at the dock where over a thousand persons had come for the same purpose. The following day, in addition to many individual callers, an Imperial messenger brought condolences. And on the eighteenth itself, there was a home family service in the morning. It was followed by a general funeral at one P.M. and by individuals who came to express their last respects between two and three. Duguid estimates that some three thousand people came during this time.

After the funeral, the ashes were brought home, since "Aunt Mary wanted to take time to decide upon the grave."[57] While Mary thought about what to do with them, the ashes were being guarded downstairs by "Lieut. Commander Tsune Ôta." This is the Ôta Tsunetoshi in whose presence Inazô is said to have requested burial in Sambongi. To Mary Duguid and Yoshio, Tsunetoshi appeared "large and stout and with a ruddy face...in his naval uniform wearing his decorations."[58]

The letter does not tell us why Mary Nitobe "wanted to take time to decide upon the grave." The recollections of those who were in Sambongi at the time give us at least part of the answer. Akanuma Heitarô recalls that the members of the Young Mens' Association had heard of Inazô's desires. Ôta Tsunetoshi had told them. They therefore petitioned Tokyo "three or four times"[59] to bury Inazô in Sambongi but were told that Mary would not hear of it. Finally, Ôta, who had acted as their middleman, persuaded them to agree to a form of bunkotsu burial in Sambongi.

Katô Takeko, Inazô's granddaughter, has told Uchikawa how she remembers Mary Nitobe cradling the box which contained the urn as she looked out at the September moon.[60] Nitobe Kotoko (also called Koto), Takeko's mother and Mary's daughter, remembers how strongly Mary first opposed the idea of bunkotsu. She also remembers how later Mary wondered how the ashes could be divided. The Vancouver urn had been manufactured so that, once closed, it could not be opened again without ruining it.[61] Mary's desire to learn how to open the urn seems to say that she was considering bunkotsu. What went in the small receptacle to Sambongi are some hairs from a hair brush and some fingernail clippings.[62]

Mary and Inazô lie together in the Tama cemetery in suburban Tokyo. Inazô also sleeps with his father and grandfather in Sambongi.

Conclusion

As we consider the facts which faced Mary in November 1933, it is not hard to understand how she came to feel that Inazô's forebears combined to "slay him." She alone, she remembered him as saying, understood him.[63] And in the events of the funeral, she was to understand what a burden that in fact placed on her.

As with all couples who marry across a wide cultural gap, she and Inazô had been forced to make greater accommodations than most people, and they had succeeded. Their daughter, Koto, remembered in her nineties only one occasion when they seem to have argued.[64] On that occasion, Koto recalls that Mary rushed into her room where Koto was working, slammed into a chair and began to write furiously until Inazô came and called her out. Mary seems to have spent a great deal of time in her room writing letters to distant correspondents. One wonders whether these letters may not have served as her psychic safety valve when pressures built up too high.

Whatever problems there may have been did not interfere with the smooth operation of the household. The Nitobes appeared to all observers to have set up an ideal home. Its members and their belongings typified Japan as a respected member of the international community. The Nitobe home became a model for Japanese who aspired to a life that bridged the apparent great gap between Japan and the West. Life within it followed Western conventions.

Koto describes her first few hours in the Nitobe home when they adopted her as a high-school girl. Both her parents had died. Inazô was a great uncle but only some twenty-five years her senior. He took her into the dining room. "In this house we eat Western food from morning to night. We will teach you table manners.... We have many foreign guests. Since there are times when you too will eat with them, you will embarrass us if you do not learn Western table manners."[65]

The many deshi who came to the house seem to have felt that they found in Inazô's home the ideal surroundings. Koto mentions a number of these students, including Takagi Yasaka and Tsurumi Yûsuke. These two were at the Nitobe home so much as students that Koto "wondered when they studied."[66] Twenty years later, men like these maturing professionals formed the committees that helped Mary after Inazô's death. Takagi flew from New York to Vancouver as soon as he heard the news. It was a grueling trip in 1933. He arrived in time to stand in at the autopsy and to accompany Inazô's body to the crematory.[67] In Japan, Tsurumi "in silk hat 'directed traffic'"[68] as the crowds came to pay their respects.

These deshi assisted the family greatly in its time of need. They knew how to live like Westerners and willingly used their skills on behalf of their master's family. In Tokyo, they could act for the family almost better than anyone else. Outside Tokyo they were not as helpful. Their success in the transformation of themselves from Japanese into international men seems to have made them less able to appreciate ordinary Japanese. They must have felt perplexed over the pushy provincials who came, it seemed, from nowhere, to demand that the remains of their mentor—one of the world's great leaders—be removed far to the north. To the deshi with their Tokyo-centric view of life, it must have seemed that no one would provide proper care for a grave so removed from them and their world.

At least partly as a result, the decision of where to inter Inazô devolved upon Mary, with her own special understanding of her husband. She had visited Sambongi and knew Tsutô's grave, so she could picture the possibility of burial there under the trees, but she finally decided on Tokyo, thus according with the deshis' understanding of Inazô.

She also told Kotoko that she wanted Inazô near her so that she could visit his grave daily and place flowers on it.[69] And after she overcame her original revulsion at the idea of bunkotsu, she did not object when wisps of hair were taken from a hairbrush and, along with fingernail clippings, buried in Sambongi.

Over the following months she studied his forebears and introduced them with respect in her portion of the *Reminiscences*. Even though in the end she had to conclude that Inazô's perception of them made them seem to threaten him, she recognized in them a commendable humanity which had existed far from the center of nineteenth century world power. Thus in an act of devotion she extended Inazô's bridge back to the farms of the Tôhoku. This was something the deshi could not do. Her actions seemed to reflect a sensitivity for traditional Japan greater than their own.

In sum, what of the combination to "slay" Inazô? One is tempted to read Mary's verb "combine" as "conspire"—as if somewhere there was evil intent. That does not seem to be her meaning. Rather, she refers to the multiplicity of demands that he felt they placed on him. In the end, the resultant pressures from his past and from the ever worsening international developments became too great. At least on occasion, he wanted to return to the quiet shade of the Eden that his grandfather and father had brought into being. Mary enabled him to find the repose he desired. At the same time, she recognized how the demands for perfection of Tsutô, Jûjirô and Seki had hounded Inazô. Mary seems to have been correct in her singular perception of the burden that these expectations put upon her husband. The story has further ramifications which deserve brief mention here.

In the first place, Inazô seems to have stated on various occasions a desire for burial in a number of places. Kobayashi Masatsune, the grandson of Inazô's elder sister, remembers hearing Inazô say that he wanted to be buried in Tama cemetery.[70] And Katô Takeko, Inazô's granddaughter, remembers hearing Inazô say that he would like to have his ashes scattered on the ocean.[71]

These recollections by loving members of the family would indicate that, like many aging men, Nitobe had a romantic streak in him. He expressed it by stating a preference for burial in a number of places which appealed to him. It would appear that Mary did not have a clear recollection of where he wanted to lie. Those who had the most specific recollection of Inazô's desires were in Sambongi. They revered Inazô with the awe of small-town individuals for the local boy who has made good. And to them there was no doubt. They had heard him say he wanted to sleep with his grandfather.

Their attitude, and the attitude of people in Towada-shi sixty years later toward the Nitobe family, brings up the theoretical question which inheres in the story of Inazô's choice of a burial place. Inazô had become the symbol of the new international Japanese. This was a man who could walk easily throughout the world. Though such men were very few in Japan at the time, he was not alone. Others with fluency in English, including his close friend Uchimura Kanzô, felt cut off from their fellow Japanese. At least in his final years, Nitobe differed from these individuals. He recognized his local roots and tried to bridge the chasm that separated them from the modern international world, and he affiliated himself with the attitudes toward family taken for granted there.

They included an imperative that the physical remains of one's predecessors receive proper care. This was part of the concern for the ancestors which had given Inazô difficulty when he tried to describe his mother's religious views in the *Reminiscences* (p. 529). Whether the attitude toward ancestors was "worship" in the Christian sense of the term, or "commemoration" requires careful consideration of definitions. The cultural fact that they represent cannot be denied. In traditional Japan, no act has a greater claim on the religious part of one's personality than respect for one's forebears as demonstrated in care for their graves. When the people of Sambongi heard Inazô request burial among them, they knew they were taking on this responsibility. Their petition reflected as a result a moral imperative. He had to be buried there because they had to attend to his grave. Mary's solution enabled them to fulfill their psychic and spiritual need.

The people of Sambongi represent all those who value old and respected local customs in a world where individuals are gradually losing all sense of cultural differences. Inazô and Uchimura Kanzô did not expect traditions to die out so quickly when they became Christians in 1877. This process of deracination, losing one's roots, is a natural concomitant of the unity toward which so many forces work in the modern world. Individuals who respect their ancestors and their local roots may feel the strains imposed by modernization in a deep personal sense. Inazô probably did not understand when he expressed a quondam desire for burial in Sambongi how deeply it reverberated in the psychic depths of those who heard him. His return to them had taken place after a lifetime in which he represented modern Japan's concerns in the rest of the world, so it could not help surprise those that knew him only as an international man.

Notes

1. *Reminiscences Of Childhood*, in *NIZ* 15: 485 (hereafter *Reminiscences*). Unless otherwise noted, all references to the end of the section, "Childhood," (p. 36) are to this work.

2. Nitobe Kenji interview, March 27, 1984.

3. Satô Masahiro, "Nitobe Inazô to sono haha," in *Kindai Fûdo* (Higashi Osaka Kinki Daigaku shuppan kyoku), p. 9. (hereafter *Haha*).

4. *How I Became a Christian; Out Of My Diary* (Tokyo: Keieisha, 1896). (hereafter *How I*). Reprinted many times, most recently in *UKZ* 3. See pp. 23, 35–36, 47. Uchimura here refers to Nitobe as "Paul," the Christian name Inazô had chosen.

5. Kaide Sumiko, ed., "Ôta (Nitobe) Inazô shokan," in *NIK* (Tokyo: Shunjûsha, 1969). p. 393, 435–43. (This extremely important article is referred to hereafter as *Letters*).

6. *Nitobe Hakase bunshû*, p. 18, as quoted in *Haha*, p. 15.

7. Uchimura, *How I*; *UKZ* 36: 7. See also in this volume Roden, p. 135–37.

8. See also letter #5 (August 22, 1876), *Letters*, p. 437.

9. Letter #10 (August 14, 1877), *Letters*, p. 440.

10. Letter #11 (May 14, 1878), *Letters*, p. 441.

11. This material on the Sanbongi branch of the family is based on the family records preserved in Towada-shi (hereafter *Records*). Nitobe Kenji told me about the family tradition with regard to the identity of the woman listed as a "concubine" of Tsutô; April 28, 1984.

12. Katô Takeko interviews and correspondence, May–August 1984.

13. *Haha*, pp. 16–20. See also in this volume, Roden pp. 134–38.

14. Letter #7 (February 24, 1877), *Letters*, p. 438.

15. This analysis owes much to Nitobe Kenji, *Nitobe Tsutô to Sambongihara Towada-shi kaitaku no shiori* (Towada-shi: Taisô kenshôkai, 1983). Though flawed in a number of respects, this is the best avaiable source (hereafter *Shiori*).

16. Mary E. Nitobe, epilogue to *Reminiscences*, p. 556.

17. Aomori Television newscast, January 1984.

18. "Nitbe-shi keifu," *Records*, pp. 3–4.

19. Mary E. Nitobe, *ibid.*, p. 557.

20. *Sambongi kaitakushi* 1 (Towada-shi: Sambongi kaitakushi fukkoku kankôkai, 1980): 28–33 (hereafter *Kaitakushi*).

21. *Kaitakushi* 1: 43.

22. *Kaitakushi* 1: 109.

23. *Kaitakushi* 1: 98.

24. Kawai Yûtarô, *Sambongi kaihatsu shôshi* (Sambongimachi: Nitobe ô kenshô kai, 1936), p. 8. (hereafter *Kaihatsushi*).

25. *Kaitakushi* 1: 98.

26. *Shiori*, pp. 63–64.

27. *Reminiscences*, p. 560.

28. "Sambongidaira kaigyô no ki," in *Shiori*, pp. 84–93.

29. *Shiori*, p. 86.

30. *Shiori*, p. 84.

31. *Reminiscences*, p. 560.

32. *Kaihatsushi* 1: 173.

33. *Kaihatsushi*, 1: 176.

34. *Kaihatsushi*, 1: 178.

35. *Kaihatsushi*, 1: 192–96.

36. *Kaihatsushi*, 1: 204.

37. *Shiori*, p. 61. For more information on Tsutô, see John F. Howes, "Nitobe Inazô's Grandfather Tsutô," in *Transactions of the Asiatic Society of Japan*, 3rd Series, Vol. 20, 1985, pp. 47–88.

38. *Reminiscences*, p. 516.
39. *Reminiscences*, p. 517.
40. *Reminiscences*, p. 496.
41. *Tôô Nippô*, October 8, 1927; as quoted in Uchikawa Eijirô, *Bannen no Inazô* (Morioka: Iwate Nippôsha, 1983), p. 24. (Hereafter *"Bannen."*) This significant and highly original work provides entirely new information. Uchikawa, chief editorial writer for the *Iwate Nippô*, uses newspaper files written between 1881 and 1883 to shed light on many obscure elements in Nitobe's own works. Uchikawa's painstaking archival research also provides the most trustworthy study of Nitobe's last years. English quotations cited in the text are by Michael Newton who translated Uchikawa's book into English. The translation is entitled *Nitobe Inazô, The Twilight Years* (Tokyo: Kyôbunkan, 1985) (hereafter "Newton.") Page citations after *"Bannen"* refer to the Japanese original, while those after "Newton" refer to the English translation). Newton, p. 18.
42. *Bannen*, pp. 31–33; Newton, pp. 23–25.
43. *Bannen*, pp. 85–86; Newton, pp. 65–66.
44. pp. 217–36.
45. "Eien no seinen," in Maeda Tamon and Takagi Yasaka, eds., *Nitobe Hakase tsuioku shû* (Tokyo: Ko Nitobe hakase kinen jigyô iin, 1936), pp. 561–66.
46. *Bannen*, p. 203; Newton, p. 146.
47. *Bannen*, p. 207; Newton, p. 149.
48. This material on Towada-shi is based on an interview with Nitobe Kenji May 10, 1984.
49. "Nitobe no keifu," in *NIK*, p. 376.
50. Interview, March 1984.
51. *Reminiscences*, p. 549.
52. Uchikawa Eijirô, *Yobunroku Nitobe Inazô...*, (Morioka: Iwate Nippôsha, 1985), p. 24. Pages 4–24 correct a number of misapprehensions about Nitobe's career. These include several which result from the "tug of war"(p. 15) between contemporary Morioka and Towada-shi to appropriate the memory of Nitobe. The Morioka position resembles that of the Tokyo branch of the family.
53. Matoba Kiyoshi interview, June 15, 1984.
54. Akanuma Heitarô in *Nitobe Inazô Hakase no omoide* (Towada-shi: Towada-shi kaitaku hyaku nijûgonen oyobi Nitobe Inazô hakase botsugo gojû shûnen kinen jigyô jikkô iin kai, 1983), pp. 46–47, 52 (this collection of reminiscences is referred to hereafter with the name of the individual quoted plus *"Omoide"*).
55. Irisawa Tatsuyoshi, "Nitobe Inazô to Okichi jizô," *Tokyo Asahi Shimbun*, December 10, 1933; as quoted in *Bannen*, pp. 218–19; Newton, p. 154–5. Also, *Haha*, pp. 6–7.
56. Mary E. Duguid and Yoshio Nitobe, "On Funeral of Dr. Nitobe," November 19, 1933, in *NIK* pp. 503–9 (hereafter *Funeral*).
57. *Funeral*, p. 504.
58. *Funeral*, p. 506.
59. Akinuma Heitarô in *Omoide*, p. 47.
60. *Bannen*, p. 240; Newton, p. 169.
61. Nitobe Koto interview, May 19, 1984.

62. Katô Takeko interview, March 2, 1984. See also Nitobe Kenji in *Omoide*, p. 48.
63. *Reminiscences*, p. 485.
64. Akaishi Seietsu, "Musume kara mita Nitobe Inazô fusai," in *Bungei hiroba* 30 (September 9, 1982): 8–9 (hereafter "Musume").
65. Musume, p. 5.
66. Musume, p. 10.
67. "Takagi Yasaka shi yori no shoshinsha." Takagi sent this letter from the Oak Bay Beach Hotel on October 21, 1933. Katô Takeko kindly gave me a photocopy.
68. *Funeral*, p. 503.
69. Nitobe Koto, interview, May 19, 1984.
70. Interview, June 10, 1984.
71. Interview, June 10, 1984.

3

Graduate Student and Quaker

Furuya Jun

One day in October 1884, Ôta Inazô, later better known as Nitobe Inazô, arrived in Baltimore to study at the city's new, but already famous, academic institute, The Johns Hopkins University.[1] At this university a Japanese friend of Ôta, Satô Shôsuke, had already been studying for a year.

Satô Shôsuke was also born in Nambu, but six years before Inazô. Partly because they came from the same area and partly because Ôta and Satô's fathers were very close friends, the two boys attended the same schools in Tokyo. Ôta's adoptive father regarded Satô Shôsuke as an exemplary student, and so entrusted Inazô to Satô's guardianship. For a time the two boys shared the same boarding house. From then on, whether in Sapporo or in Baltimore, Ôta almost always followed Satô's lead.[2] Now Ôta settled in at Satô's apartment and on October 17 went to the university with his friend to fill out an application form. On the form he listed as his purpose for going to Johns Hopkins, "To complete my education and to qualify myself for teaching on my return to Japan."[3]

Ôta lived in Baltimore as a graduate student for three academic years. Then, in May 1887, he moved to Germany, where he continued his graduate study and received a doctorate from the University of Halle. Six years of studying abroad qualified him to teach upon his return to Japan. At the age of thirty, he thus began his career as a prominent scholar, teacher, author, social activist, and diplomat. His later reputation as a leader in the promotion of friendship between America and Japan rested in large part on his extended youthful sojourn in the United States. His death in 1933 prevented him from participation in the final rupture between the two countries he loved the most.

Here we focus on Nitobe's first encounter with America as a graduate student at The Johns Hopkins University between 1884 and 1887. This period, little known in comparison with his later years, requires fresh scrutiny, for almost all previous studies of Nitobe in Baltimore have relied on his own accounts. Among his writings two memoirs are regarded as basic sources: A series of talks on his life in Baltimore, and a collection of retrospective fragments on life and study abroad.[4] In them, Nitobe seems particularly reluctant to recount unpleasant aspects of his life in foreign countries and characteristically dismisses them with accounts of his courageous actions against them.

This is not to say that Nitobe consciously covered up parts of his experience abroad. Born into a high-ranking samurai family, he early learned the virtue of stoic self-discipline. He acted on the conviction that one should retain personal integrity and persevere in the face of any adversity. While in America, Ôta occasionally experienced serious physical, mental, and financial hardships. His memoirs mention them briefly, but he obviously overcame them only after long and lonely effort. Nitobe seems to have felt that if one survived hardships without complaint, one need not later confess their severity. This ethic, deeply ingrained in the psyches of former samurai and therefore in many Meiji leaders, may have contributed to his reticence.

A second reason for the mature Nitobe's reluctance to dwell on past hardships relates to his personality. As Nitobe swiftly established his career on his return home, he considered teaching his chief vocation. His students and biographers found in his lectures and speeches particular inspiration and encouragement. One can assume that Nitobe hoped to teach the youthful members of his audiences, "something useful."[5] Since he mainly hoped to encourage foreign study, he had no reason to discourage it with details of his own depressing experiences.

In Nitobe's own recollections, the Ôta Inazô of Baltimore seems courageous, or if naive, sometimes to the point of stupidity, forward-looking, and full of promise. Most biographers uncritically accept this self-image. They view his youth in the light of his later success and neglect hard facts at odds with this success. Those that turn up are simply ignored or passed on without critical interpretation, so that customary portrayals of the young Nitobe differ considerably from what the record shows.

A clearer picture of Ôta Inazô results from the use of new sources. In addition to his own famous memoirs, this chapter relies on the scholarly and religious articles and the letters he composed in Baltimore. They present Ôta's reactions to American society at the time. Secondly, through the letters and diaries of his contemporaries, records from the Seminary at The Johns Hopkins University, minutes of religious meetings he attended, and other sources, we discover how Ôta impressed others. The resultant more complex and balanced portrait better resembles historical reality.

For an able and ambitious young man in Meiji Japan, study abroad promised future influence and status. The government encouraged talented students to go abroad as part of its modernization program. Those who brought back knowledge of Western institutions and technology were welcomed into the oligarchy. When, as Nitobe tells us:

I came to Tokyo for the first time [at the age of 9 in 1871], to go abroad was in itself a great feat.... Anyone who had gone abroad once, even for a short time, became famous and respected for that reason alone. As boys, we regarded a trip abroad and eventual appointment as Councillor of State to be our greatest aim in life.[6]

Ôta's trip resembled that of any normally ambitious young man.

In contrast to this typical act was the atypical reason behind his choice of the United States. Discounting for the moment the famous, but perhaps apocryphal, episode concerning his early determination to become "a bridge across the Pacific," Ôta's attachment to America developed gradually throughout his long education. It first appeared in his predilection for the English language, in which he became so proficient that when he left the Sapporo Agricultural College, he regularly wrote in English to his closest classmates.[7]

The second reason he chose America was religious. Educated by Americans who taught not only secular subjects but also their faith, Ôta became interested in Christianity in his early teens.[8] When he arrived at the frontier town of Sapporo in 1877, his immediate involvement in a group of active Christian students led to his baptism by the Methodist missionary, M. C. Harris.[9]

Ôta later wrote occasional letters to the Harrises and visited their home in Tokyo. The relationship with the Harris family, which would last in Japan and in the United States until Mrs. Harris's death, helped Ôta decide to cross the Pacific in 1884. It was Mrs. Harris who, in reply to his letter, suggested study at her alma mater, Allegheny College, in Meadville, Pennsylvania, and recommended him to its President, Rev. David H. Wheeler.[10] Ôta, disillusioned with the lectures at Tokyo University responded at once to her proposal. A few months later, Ôta wrote: "I shall leave Tokio for America. I go off unprovided with ample funds. I run a risk; it may be too bold. But thinking that life is at best but a bold attempt at adventure, I decide to go."[11]

Thus, on September 1, 1884, Ôta Inazô, equipped with considerable ability in English and Christian belief, left Yokohama for America. Much has been written about his sea voyage to San Francisco and his transcontinental trip by rail to Meadville. He found himself, typically for a first-time Japanese visitor to America, awed by the vastness of the continent, puzzled by the variety of its people, racked by the tremendous cultural gap between America and Japan, and plagued by dreadful anxiety. He bewailed the depravity of Japanese immigrants in San Francisco.[12] As he shepherded a young compatriot onto the transcontinental train, tried to behave himself in a more distinguished manner than the segregated Chinese immigrants, and argued religion with American fellow passengers, Ôta struggled to survive his initial cultural shock by presenting himself as a member of the elite from a new and rising country.[13] It does not seem so far-fetched to associate this struggling young man with his struggling nation. By Westernizing itself as quickly as possible in the 1880s, by identifying its cultural uniqueness and fortifying its nationalism, Japan hoped to survive in the imperialistic world. Like his nation, Ôta strengthened his sense of Japaneseness through his own struggles for survival in a new world.

On September 30, Ôta arrived in Meadville in northwestern Pennsylvania, but he stayed only half a month. This stopover was not insignificant, because it showed him small-town America, an important phase of American civilization inaccessible to those in big eastern cities like Baltimore. A few days after he arrived in Meadville, Ôta writes in a letter to his friend:

> It is calm.... All about the place maples are abundant. This place is a quiet town of some ten thousand souls. It is a beautiful site.... [Mrs. Harris's] family is all very kind and all students here are also kind hearted happy fellows. In the evening paper of the day when we came, there was put a news of our coming, and this was read by all folks, and therefore people know that we (strange young lads to them!) are Japanese...and not [Chinese].... So that, if I ask a way in a street one will say, "Ah, you're a stranger, ha, ha. How do you like your College?" [S]urrounded by religious folks, the very physical conditions being religious, I hope to shuffle off the doubts.[14]

Meadville seemed a serene, self-contained, autonomous, and homogeneous community inhabited by religious people who knew each other. What we now know as the tradition of pre-industrial America still appeared viable.[15]

Allegheny College, where Ôta studied German, History of Philosophy, and the "Art of Discourse" for two weeks, also belonged to this tradition. Allegheny College had been established by the Presbyterian church in 1815 and taken over in 1833 by the Methodist Church. A half century after its founding, it retained a traditional orientation. Ôta writes with satisfaction that he "attended a Student Prayer Meeting." The college stuck to the old traditions in its organization and curriculum as well as its spiritual life. It had both a preparatory and collegiate department, but the latter included only a "classical course" and not a "scientific course." Ôta's recollection that President Wheeler frequently recommended the mastery of Latin and Greek reflects the characteristic philosophy in the college.[16]

In an age of industrialization and urbanization, both Meadville and Allegheny College lagged behind the times. Ôta, with his idealistic view of Christianity, relished the serenity, religiosity, and the hospitality of Meadville, but he also aspired to great things and knew just what kind of knowledge his modernizing nation needed. One wonders what he would have learned and what he would have become if he had stayed in Meadville and studied in Allegheny College for three years. But he did not stay; when he received a letter from Satô which urged Ôta to leave the "outmoded" college and come to study with him at The Johns Hopkins University, Ôta agreed and left Meadville.[17]

He found Baltimore a bustling, large port city. Several railroads connected it with other big cities on the Atlantic coast as well as with western Maryland and Pennsylvania. From the railway stations, a network of horsecar lines extended to various parts of the city. Wide and paved downtown streets were lined by brick buildings of four or five stories. As Ôta later recalled, it was "the big city whose prosperous streets and facilities of civilization astonished the stranger."[18]

When Ôta arrived in Baltimore, The Johns Hopkins University stood at the corner of Howard and Ross Streets, northwest of the downtown and about a mile from the harbor. Several blocks east of the university were the Washington Monument and the university's sister institution, Peabody Institute. Quiet homes surrounded the university. All of the faculty and students lived nearby in a closely knit scholarly community. Satô and Ôta formed part of this community by living in a boarding house at 54 McCulloh Street, where the young J. Franklin Jameson, an Associate of Johns Hopkins, lived as well.[19] Woodrow Wilson, who had entered Johns Hopkins one year before Ôta, lived also in this "neighborhood of dignified old brick houses with blinds." In a letter to his fiancée, Wilson wrote of the intellectual community he cherished:

> I am...surrounded by what I may, I think, call 'picked specimens' of the University men, fellows of various characters, of course, but of equal enthusiasm in intellectual pursuits, sensible, well-informed, jolly, and unaffected....
> I shall try to describe my companions here...in some future letter...for they are all well worth knowing, and each one seems to have a strong individuality which will make a descriptive introduction of him comparatively easy.[20]

According to historians of higher education in America, The Johns Hopkins University "represented the most important innovation in graduate instruction launched during the whole period between the Civil War and the First World War."[21] The university's founder, Johns Hopkins, intended to give the institution a distinctive purpose: To further "the increase of knowledge and the great facility of its practical application." The Board of Trustees, appointed by Hopkins and Daniel Gilman, the first president, designed the institution according to this statement of purpose. The university thus from its inception differed greatly from more traditional colleges. It emphasized productive research rather than traditional liberal arts. Professors were selected from "men now standing in the front rank in their own fields," and were given "students far enough advanced to keep them stimulated." In order to gather such students, the university offered fellowships to college graduates. University life made little allowance for anything which was thought to hamper the pursuit of knowledge. Hence it was wholly non-sectarian and non-partisan. Even fellowship among students, which had a long and acclaimed history in American higher education, was slighted here, along with the four-year class system. As one magazine article pointed out: "The principle at the new university will be that attainments rather than time shall be the condition of promotion. It will regard individuals rather than classes." This truly was "a school consecrated to study."[22]

No sooner had Ôta arrived in Baltimore than he was involved in the life of this unusual institution. His student deposit had already been paid to the university, and his name had been registered as a graduate student in the Department of History and Political Science. Moreover, Professor Herbert Baxter Adams, the director of the department, had agreed to give some secretarial work to Ôta, who needed money.[23] All these arrangements had been made while Ôta was still in Meadville and had not yet decided to go to Baltimore. It was probably Satô, Ôta's mentor since they had studied English in Tokyo, who made them. Thanks to the help from his friend, Ôta could start graduate work immediately, though as a graduate student at this highly advanced institution, he seemed very unprepared, with little to offer which would "keep the professors stimulated." On his application form, an item asking him "to state in what subjects you are prepared to be examined," was left completely blank.[24] Ôta, who had intended to study at the traditional Allegheny College until only a few weeks before, grasped the scope and purpose of this new university only with difficulty.

On his first day at Hopkins, Ôta must have recognized his lack of preparation. On the evening of October 17, Ôta attended one meeting of what historian Arthur Link has called perhaps the most famous seminar in the history of higher education in the United States.[25] That evening Woodrow Wilson, a promising student in his second year, spoke first to read the evening's principal paper, "The House of Representatives, Revenue and Supply." Wilson's argument seems to have been complex; even the secretary of the evening, an American native, complained: "It is to be regretted that no abstract has been furnished for insertion in the minutes." Then Herbert Baxter Adams made some remarks on civil service reform and presented a card from James Bryce to the seminar. A book by a former member of the seminar, Albert Shaw, was reviewed by Davis R. Dewey, and finally, Jameson reviewed a study on the local parliaments in France and brought in the schedule for the year's reviews of periodicals.[26] This was how the seminar was conducted, and it is not difficult to imagine how dazzling and overwhelming the ill-prepared new foreign student found the evening.

The seminar, which had started with the university and developed in the 1880s by the careful and energetic directorship of Herbert Baxter Adams, was one of the outstanding features of the young institution. By the time

Ôta arrived, it was regarded as a center for the study of the incipient field of social sciences in America. Two associates, Richard T. Ely and J. Franklin Jameson, would by the turn of the century become illustrious leaders in, respectively, economics and American history. Here they helped Adams as they did their own research. The thirty graduate students in the seminar for the academic year 1884–1885 were also expected to have their own research topics.[27]

As a research and educational organization, the Seminary, as the seminar was called, tried to attain three sets of seemingly incompatible purposes. First, it required each participant to obtain at the same time both a bird's eye view of social sciences and his own speciality. By covering a wide variety of discussion topics, the seminar provided all the participants with a general perspective of the intellectual world. At the same time, it expected each participant to have his own topic, pursue original investigation and become a first-rate specialist in his field. In other words, through his familiarity with his individual subject each member could contribute to the general increase of knowledge. Second, the seminar tried to integrate nationalism and cosmopolitanism in the study of history and politics. Adams often suggested to the seminar that "history should be studied from the standpoint of nationality," and that "the student in history should put a chief stress on the history of his own country."[28] Consequently, studies on American institutions and economics occupied the most honored place in the seminar. Comparative and international viewpoints were also encouraged to provide a better understanding of national history. Thus "international law, politics, administration, economics and social science, history (European, ecclesiastical, classical, oriental), each [had] their proper place."[29] Finally, the seminar sought to combine knowledge of the past and present. Although archival study of American state and national institutions formed the core of the seminar's research,[30] various contemporary problems were also covered. As encapsuled in the famous slogan of the department, "History is past Politics and Politics is present History," the two disciplines were considered "as inseparable branches of the same science."[31] To the members of the seminar, a group of people who were or would be national leaders, no subject which dealt with society could seem irrelevant.

The various topics discussed in the seminar reflected these diverse purposes.[32] Among the titles of papers were "History of Witchcraft in Connecticut," "The State Constitutions of the Revolutionary Period," "The Land-Laws of the United States," "Progress of Cooperation in England," "Railroad Tariff in Germany," "The Government and Civil Service in China," "City Government in Baltimore," "The Progress of Civil Service Reform in the United States," and "The Negro in Mississippi Politics."[33] These subjects were discussed not only among regular members of the seminar, but also by occasional scholars, professionals, and governmental officials invited from outside the university. To include those visitors, the Seminary was regularly held after working hours, between 8 and 10 P.M. Friday evening. It was, as Adams proudly said, a scientific laboratory, where diverse participants analyzed various information from the points of view of individual specialists.[34]

Although Adams was "not a noteworthy scholar in his own right," he was no doubt a superb educator and leader.[35] To the graduate students in the seminar, he was not merely a "genial" professor.[36] He helped them find research topics, write reports for the seminar, and publish works—in effect pioneering modern graduate education in America by introducing a system invented and developed in German universities half a century earlier.[37] Adams's thoughtful instruction provided graduate students with a focal point for their academic life and a basis for mutual competition.

Although Ôta took several other lecture courses on history and political economy and had to do some odd jobs for Adams and the Newspaper Bureau of the department,[38] he concentrated his efforts on the seminar. He must have spent most of his time at Hopkins in the Bluntschli Library, the seminar's meeting room, which was also well-equipped for research by graduate students.[39] According to his memoirs he worked very hard here, so hard that in his second year he injured his health.[40]

Despite his labors, Ôta did not speak up in the seminar. On January 30, 1885, about four months after Ôta had arrived at Hopkins, Jameson wrote in his diary: "Ôta [as the secretary] came up with some questions about his report of my paper last Friday night. Got some talk with him. He and Satô oughtn't to have been so shy of wasting my time this year; but I haven't been generous in respect to urging them to come up and see me."[41] Here again Ôta's behavior was typical for a Japanese student abroad. Although he enjoyed a high reputation as an English conversationalist later in life, he apparently could not overcome his shyness or ask questions freely in the classes at Hopkins. Consequently his name seldom appears in the minutes of the seminar. During his first year he served as secretary pro-tempore twice, but otherwise Ôta reviewed only one magazine and one article.[42] In the second year, he participated even less. A one-page note taken by him at the first meeting in the year remains the sole record of his presence at the seminar.[43]

Difficulty in English probably limited his participation, but it was not language alone. Though a good student in Sapporo and Tokyo, he was now no more than a puzzled novice amongst highly capable and competitive young professionals. Unlike higher education in Meiji Japan which taught students to imitate established Western ideas, education at Johns Hopkins, particularly in the Seminary, centered around the discovery of new knowledge. Ôta's inability to participate began with this difference in educational philosophy. Because he lacked a speciality, the only means through which one could fully participate in the seminar, Ôta spent three years at Hopkins in the endless search for a scholarly identity.

In this regard Satô contrasted greatly. First, he came to Hopkins much better prepared than Ôta. Satô had stayed at a large farm near New York City where he had studied agricultural business and economics for a year before coming to Baltimore. Moreover, he enrolled at Hopkins after careful preparation. Half a year prior to his enrollment, he wrote a letter to President Gilman in which he informed the President of his academic interests and requested an application form and information about the university. Satô continued this correspondence with Gilman and Adams until September.[44] When he came to the university, he was no longer a stranger. Secondly, Satô acquired a respected status and his own research subject at an earlier stage of his university life. Half a year after coming to Hopkins, Satô had the good fortune to receive an appointment by the Japanese government "as special commissioner for the study of the land laws of the United States." This gave him more than just a salary from his government. When the *Baltimore Sun* reported this appointment, Adams and Ely recommended Satô as a "Fellow by Courtesy," and President Gilman approved the recommendation.[45] Moreover, he now had a research topic of his own. Therefore, when Ôta joined him, Satô had already started work on the history of land questions in the United States and had begun to gain recognition as a specialist on this topic which fit well into the seminar's emphasis on institutional history. Thus Satô found a secure place in the seminar early in his second year. Although Jameson thought that Satô was also too shy in the class, Satô had already impressed him on their first acquaintance as "a pleasant and intelligent fellow...likely to prove a good student" for the department.[46] As Jameson expected, Satô soon began to take an active part in the seminar. His participation proved much more consistent and substantial than Ôta's. Satô structured his seminar activities around his special research on land problems. He selected materials pertaining to his speciality for magazine and book reviews. His papers submitted to the seminar dealt not only with archival records but also current views on land reform. Thus he completed a very good dissertation and received a doctoral degree by the end of his stay at Hopkins. When Satô left the seminar, Adams paid a special tribute to "the value of Mr. Satô's work."[47]

There is little doubt that Satô became a role model for Ôta. Had it not been for this kindly older friend, Ôta would have enjoyed Baltimore much less. Although later both Satô and Ôta looked back upon their warm mutual cooperation at the time, Ôta owed more to Satô than vice versa. Satô's success in the seminar must have made Ôta proud of his compatriot, but

Satô's presence as an example may not have entirely benefitted Ôta. It probably made Ôta feel eager to achieve his own success and caused him to recognize his relative immaturity. From a vacation site in Pennsylvania in the summer of 1886, Ôta indicated to Adams a degree of jealousy: "I am not studying hard at all.... I cannot...work half as much as I would like to.... P.S. Sato (I mean Dr. Sato!) will come to Phila. tomorrow."[48] Then a few months after Satô went home with honors, Ôta clipped many favourable reviews of Satô's published thesis for the Newspaper Bureau. One of them, similar to others, says:

> It is remarkable as a clear straightforward, systematic review of a somewhat complicated subject. It betrays hardly a trace of foreign origins either in matter or in style. Americans may well be grateful to this Japanese scholar for giving them so good a review of an important chapter of their own policy and laws.[49]

It is intriguing to speculate how Ôta felt when he read such reviews, perhaps the best that a Japanese scholar could hope to get. Now Satô left and Ôta stayed, impressed at how Satô had become "a bridge across the Pacific."

Ôta could not match Satô as a scholar and remained an industrious but unproductive student for his first two years. He did too much besides study. In particular, he spent much time on his religious life, of which more later. Further, he lacked funds. Although his foster father had given Ôta money before he left Japan, it did not suffice for a full year.[50] As a result he had to work to support himself, and his study suffered accordingly.

Second, his manic-depressive tendencies hindered his work. Although he suffered repeated bouts of nervous depression in the United States, the one of the spring and summer in 1886 was the most severe. Even before he had finished classes, he left Baltimore to recuperate in Pennsylvania. Lack of money along with Satô's success in contrast to his own delay probably worsened the condition.[51]

Finally, unlike Satô, Ôta lacked a close connection with his nation. Perhaps for this reason he could not decide on a research topic. Meiji youth who wanted to succeed abroad needed strong relations with their nation which included encouragement and direction from home. Satô was given such motivation by the Japanese government while Ôta was not. It is interesting to note that once in Germany Ôta worked under government auspices similar to those Satô had enjoyed in America and seemed more motivated and productive than earlier.

For these reasons Ôta's life in Baltimore reached its nadir in the summer of 1886; by the end of the summer, things had begun to improve. Adams encouraged him with frequent letters, with an editorial job for the newly founded American Historical Association, and above all, with advice on a research topic.[52] Ôta was also by this time the most experienced among a small group of Japanese students at Hopkins,[53] and so became their natural leader. He also faced the need to reorient his life, to which we turn after consideration of his religious activities. Ôta had begun to associate with American Christians, particularly Quakers. In this religious life he proved more active, eloquent, and influential than in his studies.

Since his baptism in Sapporo, Ôta had almost invariably shared with his classmates a missionary zeal to Christianize Japan. Ôta and his friends believed rather naively in a congruity between the two "J"s, Jesus and Japan, and his long stay abroad strengthened this belief. In letters to Christian friends he often wrote of their "nucleus of a National Christian organization" in Sapporo.[54] In the Bluntschli Library he wrote: "You see that all my thoughts are invariably associated with Sapporo. It is, indeed, my earnest desire and sincere prayer that I may one day be able to do something for my God and for my country in Sapporo."[55] God, Japan, and Sapporo constitute a recurrent triad in his letters. At that time Ôta lacked any official position in Japan. It would seem that only his dream of future evangelization there and his memories of past friendships in Sapporo supplied him with an identity as a Japanese. His passionate activities among American Christians may have been motivated by this need to seem to himself Japanese.

But why was Ôta drawn to Quakerism, particularly Orthodox Quakerism? About this question, too, he has left us an often quoted anecdote. He tells us how he fortuitously discovered a Friends' meeting house on the way from school and was favorably impressed with the Quakers' way of religion from his first attendance at a meeting on the following Sunday.[56] This otherwise unverifiable anecdote may be true, for the meeting house of Baltimore's Orthodox Quakers was then located just one block north of the university.[57] Nevertheless, it also seems plausible that Nitobe overdramatized his encounter with Orthodox Quakerism in order to impress his readers with its favorable characteristics. And the singling out of this anecdote as the reason for his subscription to Quakerism may have led him to neglect other equally important causes which helped him gradually strengthen his Quaker beliefs.

First of all, one must consider the Orthodox Quakers' influence on The Johns Hopkins University. Although the founder had conceived an institution dedicated solely to science and the original board of trustees had kept it non-sectarian, Quakerism was still by far the most visible and influential religious force at the university. Johns Hopkins himself was, after all, a Quaker, and half of the trustees of the university shared his faith. When Ôta came to Baltimore, two elders of the city's Monthly Meeting of Friends, Francis T. King and James Carey, were the most influential trustees of the university.⁵⁸ Through their occasional attendance at the Adams seminar and their writings in the university publications, the influence of these Quakers must have been evident to the members of the university.⁵⁹ Perhaps partly because of this influence, Adams once spoke on "The Quaker Settlement at Ellicott's Mills" in the seminar.⁶⁰

Ôta cannot have escaped this influence but may not have recognized its importance. He believed in his own version of Christianity with such passion that he constantly criticized the university for its lack of deep and obvious religious sentiment. A Bible class, sponsored by the Quaker meeting and conducted by J. Rendel Harris, a Hopkins professor of New Testament Greek and Paleography, probably helped to slake his thirst for religion.⁶¹

These various influences may have gradually attracted Ôta to Orthodox Quakerism. About a year after his arrival in Baltimore, he wrote to his friend: "I am attending a Quakers' Meeting every Sunday. I like very much their simplicity and earnestness."⁶² By this time, he had already established a close tie with the Philadelphia Quaker meeting.

In the 1880s, the Philadelphia Quakers included a very influential group of women. They, in their enthusiasm for reform, began to challenge the male dominance which otherwise characterized Quakerism. Most members of the men's meetings opposed the idea of a foreign missionary because of their quietist opposition to outward religious activities and individualist objection to a paid professional ministry. To these male Quakers, it was more important to maintain their traditional inward faith than to convert others. In spite of this male opposition, the reform-minded women organized the Women's Foreign Mission Association of Friends of Philadelphia under the influence of the vigorous evangelical Quakerism of the Western states. Their energetic association started to send missionaries to various countries including India, Syria, Mexico, and Japan.⁶³

In order to prepare themselves, members of the association gathered information from foreign students about countries to which they would send missionaries. Ôta and other Japanese received frequent invitations to the meeting houses or private homes of influential Quakers in Philadelphia. The most noted of those meetings met regularly on Saturday at the house of Wistar Morris, a famous Japanophile Quaker. As Uchimura Kanzô, one of Ôta's closest friends in Sapporo and a regular at those meetings, recollected later, there were few Japanese who came to Philadelphia without enjoying the Morris's benevolence.⁶⁴ Ôta also visited the Morris' home regularly.

In the years around 1885 when the women's association sent their first missionaries to Japan, Ôta and Uchimura provided the bulk of their information. In the annual meeting of the association held on January 23, 1885, Uchimura spoke of Japanese religiosity and urged the Quakers to bring their least ostentatious Christianity to Japan.[65] In June of the same year Ôta wrote to the corresponding secretary how Japan needed able, educated, and sympathetic Christian missionaries, and why he hoped Friends would "fill a vacancy in the mission field" in Japan.[66] Both Ôta and Uchimura addressed a special meeting of the association on June 20 of that year. Their testimony helped the association fix policy for its new mission.[67]

The more the women's association interested itself in Japan, the more fervent became Ôta's missionary zeal. As he informed the women about religion in Japan, he gradually included Quakerism in his scheme for the Christianization of Japan: The greatest merit of Quakerism lay in its simple "non-sacramental mode of worship."[68] It was "the nearest approach to an ideal church, and therefore the most rational, or better to say, the most spiritual way of divine service." Though he praised it so highly, he also recognized that Quakerism did not appeal to the popular desire for ritual. He consequently warned Quakers against an immediate approach to the members of the Japanese lower class. They immersed themselves in Buddhism whose rituals resembled those of Roman Catholicism. Instead he urged the missionaries to direct their work to a different stratum of the society. He thought that, though a great majority of Japanese were Buddhist, there were other individuals who disliked ritual and longed for spiritual fulfillment. He recommended that the Friends work among them, because they comprised "the most influential part of the population by whom public opinion [was] guided and the future of the nation [was] moulded." Japanese Quakers would as a result form an elite who would enlighten the masses and found a true Japanese Christianity. As he made these recommendations, Ôta also prepared himself as an evangelist of social and religious ideas.

By the summer of 1886, Ôta had contributed more to the Society of Friends in Philadelphia than to the Adams seminar. While he said nothing in the seminar, he made lively speeches on Japan to sizable Quaker audiences. Although he could not find any definite research topic for his graduate work, he wrote eloquent letters to *The Friends' Review* on Japanese culture and history, its religions and women's education, and even the crisis of American religiosity.[69] In contrast to the rigid academic framework of Hopkins, here he could speak and write freely. American people of whose religious orientation he approved and who had a sincere interest in his home country attentively listened to his every word. He could talk about his home with passion and sentiment. While speaking, memories and dreams of Japan would surface. Here he could speak to the hearts of other Japanese students who shared similar anxieties and ambitions. These students even included a few of his Christian friends from Sapporo. At Philadelphia Ôta had found in the desert of his American life an oasis which recalled the verdure of Japan.

And so for Ôta, Philadelphia and its surroundings could heal the depression which assailed him the summer of 1886. Among the Pennsylvania Quakers, he at last began to inch toward a research topic. In a letter to Adams of June 22, he states: "The thesis, I find very interesting and instructive. I am glad that you have suggested the subject. Some reliable accounts of the coming of Com. Perry have been sent me from home: also my father (adoptive) has sent me several [manuscripts] on the subject."[70] The topic concerned the course of diplomatic relations between the United States and Japan. Adams may have suggested the topic because he himself had been interested in it since his encounter with Niijima Jô at Amherst College.[71] But Ôta himself had an interest in the topic, for five months before he wrote this letter, he had addressed the Friends' Institute in Philadelphia on the same subject.[72] By describing his country to Americans, Ôta had perhaps recognized the need to treat Japan's international position with some objectivity. Adams, an astute educator, could have suggested the topic when he perceived Ôta's passion for the cause of Japan.

Thus Ôta finally acquired a specialization in the seminar. His choice fit well within some of the rules, for in it Ôta had "put a chief stress on the history of his own country," in a way that lay between history and politics.[73] As the fall semester of 1886–1887 started, he seems to have begun his research.[74] Though the topic lay within normal guidelines, Ôta charged it with more missionary spirit than one would expect in scholarly research. As a nationalist, Ôta felt a particular concern over two sorts of news from Japan. One was the snail-paced progress toward revision of the humiliatingly unequal treaties with the Western powers. The other was the damage occurring to Japanese culture because of precipitate Westernization. It was Japanese policy at the time to seek treaty revision by impressing Westerners with Japanese success in Westernization. Reports about these issues must have kept Ôta informed about the major domestic and foreign problems the Japanese faced. How could he confine his deep indignation over these apparent crises within a purely scholastic work? Again he found an outlet for his sentiment in the Quaker meetings. A friend of Ôta's who shared his religious activity, later recalled:

[B]efore leaving America for Germany, Nitobe started an energetic propaganda campaign for treaty revision. Although the question is now [1936] forgotten, in those years it was Japan's most exasperating problem in foreign relations. Even though we said that Japan was an independent country, the independence was incomplete [because of the existence of unequal treaties].... Nitobe, therefore, made numerous speeches advocating revisions for almost three months. As he spoke, tears sometimes interfered with his words. Quakers so sympathized that many meeting houses asked him to present his appeal to them. In reply to these requests he made about thirty speeches.[75]

Meanwhile, as if trying to make up for his previous silence, Ôta hastily read portions of his papers three different times in the Adams seminar during his last half year at Hopkins. Judging from the minutes of the seminar, these reports did not differ remarkably from his speeches to the Quaker meetings. He made his first report of an hour at the seminar of November 19, 1886. In it he poured out his knowledge of Japanese history, starting from the country's "first intercourse with Corea in 157 B.C.," referring to Marco Polo and Francis Xavier, touching on the "extirpation of the Christians in 1637," and ending with the Russians' unsuccessful attempts to open Japan since the seventeenth century. The speech apparently evoked less reaction from the seminar members than it had from Quakers. Adams noted that "it was the reports of Marco Polo of the fabulous wealth in Japan that induced Columbus to set out on his voyage." Then he asked that Ôta share any recent news about Satô with members of the seminar.[76]

Ôta's second report defined a narrower topic. He talked only about the diplomatic relations between the United States and Japan which led to Perry's expedition. In spite of his care, this report also failed to impress the seminar, probably because, as the minutes revealed, it consisted of little more than a list of events. The record makes no reference to questions or discussion occasioned by the report.[77] Ôta's last presentation took place on April 22, 1887. Under the title of "American Influence on Japan," he again packed his paper with too many details, including references to American pioneers of commerce in Japan, the work and influence of Townsend Harris, the growth of Yokohama, the currency question in Japan from 1854 to 1869, and the influences of American Missionaries from 1859 to 1881. He clearly could not construct an inspiring scholarly argument on so many important topics in an hour. Again there was no record of discussion, and neither Adams, Jameson, nor Ely seems to have praised the presentation, Ôta's last in his three-year stay at Hopkins.[78]

His papers to the seminar formed in fact nothing more than a thesis outline. In Germany he would continue work on this thesis along with his major study of agrarian economy. All in all, it seems clear that Ôta did not succeed as a graduate student in Baltimore. At Hopkins, he probably felt more frustrated than satisfied, and he could curb his frustration only through his deepening association with Quakerism in Baltimore and in Philadelphia. On October 26, 1886, Ôta applied for membership to the Baltimore Monthly Meeting of Friends. He wrote:

> Dear friends
> Being convinced of the doctrines and precepts of Christ, as presented and testified to by the Society of Friends and believing in the efficiency of an organization for furthering the Same, I hereby request to be admitted into your society as a member.[79]

Then in the December meeting, after the committee appointed to examine Ôta reported about "a very satisfactory interview with him," the Baltimore Monthly Meeting granted Ôta membership,[80] an association he maintained for the rest of his life.

In early March of 1887, Ôta was appointed Assistant Professor at Sapporo Agricultural College and ordered to study agricultural economy in Germany. Again Satô, who had become a professor at the Sapporo college on his return to Japan, sponsored Ôta.[81] This appointment must have given Ôta a clear perspective on his life. Now he could continue his longstanding interest in agricultural economy, which The Johns Hopkins University had unfortunately not nourished.[82] By his assumption of official status, he now joined his own destiny with that of Japan. He appears to have felt even more responsibility and loyalty to Japan, and he became almost pathetically emphatic about treaty revision.

Passionate as he was about his nation's fate, he did not at all despair. On May 9, just before he left Baltimore, he requested a certificate of membership from the Society of Friends. He appeared jovial:

> Having recently recd an appointment from the home government, with the title of assistant Professor in the Imperial College of Agriculture Japan Sapporo, to proceed to Germany then to prosecute studies for three years in Agrarian Economics, I expect to leave this country on the 28th inst & I wish to be provided with a certificate of membership of Baltimore Monthly Meeting—I therefore ask the meeting to furnish me with one. In closing, I wish to express my sincere thanks for the kindness shown me by the members of the meeting during my stay here, the memory of which I will always carry with me with pleasure.[83]

The meeting then duly decided to issue a lengthy letter identifying Ôta as "an esteemed member" of the meeting, "a student of Johns Hopkins University for the past three years," and now assistant professor of a Japanese college going to Germany.[84] An identification more accurately describing him at this point is almost inconceivable. With this letter in his possession, Ôta Inazô left Baltimore.

In Philadelphia on the way to New York, he made his last speech at the regular Monthly Meeting of the Women's Foreign Missionary Association on May 27. In this "deeply touching and interesting" speech, he reiterated the need for American Quakers to aid Japan and the possibilities for Quakerism there. But by far the most interesting remark was his confession about patriotism and Friends' anti-war testimony. He said that in his mind "this question of war remained unsettled for two years after he became convinced on the other points of Friends' doctrines." To him, a young elite official in an increasingly belligerent nation, the question must now have perplexed him even more. He simply concluded that finally he had become convinced of the views of Friends on this important subject.[85]

Notes

1. He informed his professor at Johns Hopkins, Herbert Baxter Adams, of the name change in a letter from Germany; see Ôta (Nitobe) to Herbert B. Adams, September 21, 1889, Herbert Baxter Adams Collection, Milton S. Eisenhower Library, Johns Hopkins University (hereafter "Adams Collection"). In this paper, I principally use Ôta, which was his only name in Baltimore.

2. Torii Kiyoharu, ed., *Nitobe Inazô no tegami* (Sapporo: Hokkaidô Daigaku tosho kankôkai, 1976), pp. 76–78; and Matsukuma Toshiko, *Nitobe Inazô* (Tokyo: Misuzu shobô, 1969), p. 14.

3. Nitobe File, Application Documents, Office of the Registrar, Ferdinand Hamburger Jr. Archives, Johns Hopkins University (hereafter "Nitobe File").

4. "Ryûgaku dan," *Keirin* 16 (June 1895): 57–63; *Gakugeikai zasshi* 19 (April 1896): 59–61; 20 (June 1896): 60–63; 21 (November 1896): 75–82; and *Kigan no ashi* (Tokyo: Kôdôkan, 1907). "Ryûgaku dan" consists of lectures to students at Sapporo Agricultural College, transcribed by one of them and published in the student magazine. *Kigan no ashi* contains in addition transcriptions of informal talks to his family and close friends at the Nitobe home and published several years later; it is reprinted in *NIZ* 6: 5–177, which I used.

5. *Kigan no ashi*, p. 19.

6. *Ibid.*

7. Torii Kiyoharu, "Postscript," to Torii, ed., *Nitobe Inazô no tegami*, p. 190.

8. Matsukuma Toshiko, *Nitobe Inazô*, pp. 23–25.

9. *Ibid.*, pp. 36–52. For his skepticism, see *Ibid.*, pp. 77–83; and his letters to Miyabe Kingo, March 29, 1884, November 13, 1885, *Nitobe Inazô no tegami*, pp. 22, 69. See also "Who Was Nitobe?" this volume, pp. 9–10.

10. Torii's annotation to a letter from Ôta to Miyabe, *Nitobe Inazô no tegami*, pp. 60–61.

11. *Ibid.*, pp. 42–43.

12. As the number of Japanese in America (420 in 1884) indicates, large-scale Japanese immigration had not yet started, but the Japanese minister in San Francisco had already noted poverty, prostitution and gambling among the few Japanese there. See Kaikoku hyakunen kinenbunka jigyô dan, ed., *Nichi bei bunka kôshôshi* 5 (Tokyo: Yôyôsha, 1955), *Ijû*, ed., Nagai Matsuzô, pp. 42, 50.

13. These travel episodes appear originally in Nitobe's letters and memoirs and are cited uncritically by most of his biographies. See Ôta to Miyabe, 5 October 1884, *Nitobe Inazô no tegami*, pp. 57–58; "Ryûgaku dan", *Keirin* 16: 62–63; *Gakugeikai zasshi* 19: 59–61; *Kigan no ashi*, pp. 26–30. What seems the most interesting episode concerns Ôta's view of Chinese immigrants. His writings reflect little sympathy for their plight as fellow Asians. It is probable that Nitobe's view of China after the Sino-Japanese War of 1894–1895 is reflected in both "Ryûgaku dan" and *Kigan no ashi*, both of which he wrote after the war. In them, he viewed China as a bad example for Japan. Although there is little to go on, the influence of his years in America on Nitobe's view of China seems worth further study.

14. Nitobe to Miyabe, October 5, 1884, *Nitobe Inazô no tegami*, pp. 57–59. For Nitobe's impression of Meadville, especially for his favorable comment on its religious atmosphere, see also "Ryûgaku dan," *Gakugei zasshi* 20: 62.

15. The population of Meadville was 8,860 in 1880 and 9,520 in 1890, a 7.3 per cent increase in the decade. In the latter year, foreign-born inhabitants numbered 1,005, and there were just 194 blacks, 4 Chinese, and 1 Japanese. See *Eleventh Census of the United States, 1890, Report on Population, Part I* (Washington, D. C.: Governmental Printing Office, 1893), pp. 294, 386, 477. In contrast, Baltimore in 1890 had a population of 434,439, a 30.73 per cent increase from the number in 1880, and had 69,003 foreign born, 67,104 blacks, 178 Chinese, 4 Japanese, and 10 American Indians. *Ibid.*, pp. 371–374, 460.

16. James Pyle Wichersham, *A History of Education in Pennsylvania, Private and Public, Elementary and Higher: From the Time The Swedes Settled on the Delaware to the Present Day* (Lancaster, PA: Inquirer Publishing Company, 1886), pp. 403–5; U.S. Bureau of Education, *Report of the Commissioner of Education for The Year 1884–1885* (Washington D.C.: Government Printing Office, 1886); Ôta to Miyabe, October 5, 1884, *Nitobe Inazô no tegami*, pp. 58–59; "Ryûgaku dan," *Gakugei zasshi* 20: 61–62.

17. *Ibid.*, pp. 62–63; Satô Shôsuke, "Kyûyû Nitobe Hakushi o omou," *Nitobe Hakushi tsuioku shû*, eds. Maeda Tamon and Takagi Yasaka (Tokyo: Ko Nitobe hakushi kinen jigyô jikkô iin, 1936), pp. 6–7.

18. "Ryûgaku dan," *Gakugeikai zasshi* 20: 62.

19. Satô had lived across the hall from Jameson since September 1883, and Ôta shared Satô's room. Soon after Ôta arrived, Jameson "called dutifully...on Sato and Ota." After that, Ôta visited Jameson occasionally in order to ask questions about the Seminary. Elizabeth Donnan and Leo F. Stock, eds., *An Historian's World: Selections from the Correspondence of John Franklin Jameson* (Philadelphia: The American Philosophical Society, 1956), p. 34; John Franklin Jameson, Diary, October 20, 1884, January 30, 1885; Jameson Papers, Box 3, Diaries, Manuscript Division, Library of Congress. At that time most students and faculty members lived within half a mile of the university.

20. Ray Stannard Baker, *Woodrow Wilson, Life and Letters: Youth, 1856–1890* (Garden City, New York: Doubleday, Page & Co., 1927), p. 176; Woodrow Wilson to Ellen Axson, January 16, 1884, in Arthur S. Link et al., eds, *The Papers of Woodrow Wilson 1881–1884* (Princeton: Princeton University Press, 1967), p. 658.

21. John S. Brubacher and Willis Rudy, *Higher Education in Transition: A History of American Colleges and Universities, 1636–1976* (New York: Harper & Row, Publishers, 1976), p. 178.

22. *Ibid.*, pp. 178–182; John C. French, *A History of the University Founded by Johns Hopkins* (Baltimore: Johns Hopkins Press, 1946), pp. 3–4, 22–25, 39–41; *Harper's New Monthly Magazine* 54 (February 1877): 463–64. Reflecting the university's emphasis on scientific research, the majority of students enrolled between 1876 and 1885 (590 out of 923) were in graduate school. James Carey Thomas, "A Brief Review of the Ten Years' Work of the University," *Johns Hopkins University Circulars* 5 (June 1886): 109.

23. While Ôta wrote to Miyabe on October 5, about the life in Meadville, his student deposit had been paid on October 3, and his name had been recorded as absent in the minutes of a seminar of The Johns Hopkins University held also on

October 3. See note 16; Cash Book, September 1881–December 1885, Ferdinand Hamburger Jr. Archives, The Johns Hopkins University, p. 396; "Minutes of the Seminary of History and Politics," October 3, 1884, Ferdinand Hamburger Jr. Archives, The Johns Hopkins University (hereafter "Minutes of the Seminary").

24. Application form, Nitobe File. To the same questionnaire, for example, Woodrow Wilson stated his interest in "the Constitutional machinery of the English Government." See "Wilson's Application for Admission to The Johns Hopkins University," September 18, 1883, in *The Papers of Woodrow Wilson 1881–1884*, 4: 430.

25. Arthur S. Link, *Woodrow Wilson: a Brief Biography* (New York: World, 1963), p. 22.

26. Minutes of the Seminary, October 17, 1884, pp. 108–9.

27. As to the history and general characteristics of the seminar, see Herbert B. Adams, *The Study of History in American Colleges and Universities* (Bureau of Education, Circular of Information, no. 2, 1887) (Washington: Government Printing Office, 1887), pp. 171–179. For a vivid description of the seminar at the time, see Baker, *Wilson*, pp. 176–79.

28. Minutes of the Seminary, November 21, 1884, pp. 120–21.

29. Adams, *The Study of History in American Colleges and Universities*, p. 177.

30. This was what was known as "institutional history." It flourished in late nineteenth century America. Convinced of a continuity between the communities of the old Germanic village and of colonial New England, many historians started to study colonial and local records. About the seminar's emphasis on institutional history, Wilson complained:

> When I got within range of these professors here, however, I found that they wanted to set everybody under their authority, to working on what they called 'institutional history,' to digging, that is, into the dusty records of old settlements and colonial cities, to rehabilitating in authentic form the stories, now almost mythical, of the struggles, the ups and the downs, of the first colonists here, there and everywhere on this then interesting continent.

Ray Stannard Baker, *Wilson*, p. 174.

31. Minutes of the Seminary, 6 March 1885, February 12, 1886, pp. 154, 209.

32. Here again Wilson was critical: "Adams skipped too lightly...over too many subjects." Baker, *Wilson*, p. 178.

33. *Johns Hopkins University Circulars* 4 (December 1884, March, May, July, 1885): 28, 66, 82, 122.

34. Adams, *The Study of History in American Colleges and Universities*, p. 175.

35. John Higham, *History: Professional Scholarship in America* (Baltimore: Johns Hopkins University Press, 1983), p. 11; Baker, *Wilson*, p. 178.

36. Raymond J. Cunningham, "History of the Department. The Genial Mr. Adams: 1850–1901," *The History Department Newsletter* 1, The Johns Hopkins University, (Winter 1984): 3–4.

37. Brubacher and Rudy, *Higher Education in Transition*, pp. 174–78, 187.

38. The Newspaper Bureau was one of the department's important features. Some graduate students worked for the bureau by selecting and clipping newspaper articles which became source material on current affairs for the seminar. Adams, *The Study of History in American Colleges and Universities*, pp. 184–86. Nitobe de-

scribes the bureau and his work for it in his memoir. "Ryûgaku dan," *Gakugeikai zasshi* 20: 63.

39. Every graduate student had his own place and his own drawer around a long seminar table in the library. Adams, *The Study of History in American Colleges and Universities*, p. 177.

40. Nitobe Inazô, "Gakusei jidai no Uiruson," *Chûô kôron* (March 1917), pp. 86–87; "Ryûgaku dan,"*Gakugeikai zasshi* 20: 63.

41. Jameson, Diary, January 30, 1885, Jameson Papers.

42. He served as the secretary on January 23, and April 17, 1885, reviewed *Antiquarian Magazine* on February 6, 1885 and read "a review of the different races of men" on April 24, 1885. Minutes of the Seminary, pp. 137–40, 142, 160–62, 162a.

43. *Ibid.*, October 15, 1885, p. 171.

44. For his letters to Gilman of March 15, June 14 and 27, 1883, see Satô Shôsuke File, Application Documents, Office of the Registrar, Ferdinand Hamburger Jr. Archives, The Johns Hopkins University. Satô's letters to Adams of June 11, 25, 30, and September 14, 1883, are found in the Adams Collection.

45. A clipping from the *Baltimore Sun* of February 11, 1884 was attached to the letter from Adams and Ely to Gilman, October 30, 1884, Adams Collection.

46. Elizabeth Donnan and Leo F. Stock, eds., *An Historian's World: Selections from the Correspondence of John Franklin Jameson*, (Philadelphia: American Philosophical Society, 1956), p. 34.

47. Satô Shôsuke, *History of the Land Question in the United States* (The Johns Hopkins University Studies in Historical and Political Science, Fourth Series, nos. 7–9) (Baltimore: The Johns Hopkins University, 1886); Minutes of the Seminary, May 13, 1885, p. 248.

48. Ôta to Adams, June 22, 1886, Adams Collection.

49. A clipping from *The Morning Oregonians*, August 29, 1886, Newspaper clippings, Box 37, Adams Collection. In this collection, there are several other clippings of favorable reviews from various periodicals. The titles of the periodicals and dates of the reviews were written on the clippings in Ôta's handwriting.

50. Matsukuma, *Nitobe Inazô*, pp. 124–28, 143; Ôta to Miyabe, August 4, 1884, *Nitobe Inazô no tegami*, pp. 42–43.

51. In his several letters to Adams written from Pennsylvania between April and July, Ôta frequently regrets his inability to study due to illness and financial hardship. Ôta to Adams, April 23, May 21, June 22, July 29, 1886, Adams Collection. In "Ryûgaku dan," Nitobe mentions the crisis very briefly and reduces its cause to his financial difficulties. See *Gakugeikai zasshi*, 20: 63.

52. See the letters from Ôta to Adams mentioned in the previous footnote.

53. In the year 1884–1885, Satô and Ôta were the only Japanese at Hopkins. In the following year Motora Yûjirô, a graduate of Dôshisha, joined them in their new residence. Motora was affiliated with the philosophy department as a graduate student and obtained a fellowship from the psychology department one year later. In the year 1886–7, Watase Shôzaburô, another graduate from Sapporo Agricultural College, enrolled as a graduate student in Biology, and two other Japanese came as undergraduates "not yet fully matriculated." The last two students were obviously unhappy in the university. When one of them failed and had to go home, he wrote a letter to Adams full of criticism against the other Japanese. *Johns Hopkins*

University Circulars 5 (November 1885): 33; 6 (November 1886): 2–7; Nagase Hosuke to Adams, n.d. [1888], Box 34, Adams Collection.
54. Ôta to Miyabe, August 7, 1887, *Nitobe Inazô no tegami*, p. 90.
55. Ôta to Miyabe, November 13, 1885, *Ibid.*, p. 66.
56. "Ryûgaku dan,"*Gakugeikai zasshi* 21: 79," in *Kigan no ashi*, p. 138.
57. The house was at the corner of Eutaw and Monument Street.
58. French, *A History of the University*, pp. 10–26; Anna Braithwaite Thomas, comp., *The Story of Baltimore Yearly Meeting from 1672–1938* (Baltimore: The Weant Press, Inc., [1938]), pp. 86–88. In contrast to large numbers of Quakers on the board, relatively few of the faculty members were Quakers. A Quaker magazine reported in January 1886, that three members of their society occupied responsible positions at Hopkins. *The Friends' Review*, January 16, 1886, p. 375.
59. For example, in the seminar of 1885, Francis T. King "by request made some remarks on importance of slavery question in [the] history of Society of Friends." Minutes of the Seminary, p. 170. Also see James Carey Thomas's "A Brief Review of the Ten Years' Work of the University," written for *Johns Hopkins University Circulars* 5 (June 1886).
60. Minutes of the Seminary, December 5, 1884, p. 122.
61. Thomas, comp., *The Story of Baltimore Yearly Meeting*, pp. 111–12. As a pious Quaker, Professor Harris seemed to share Ôta's criticism of the university's secularism. In 1885, Harris joined a controversy over experiments on "warm–blooded animals" conducted by a Hopkins physiologist. He so criticized vivisection and President Gilman's official support of it that he left the university. See French, *A History of the University*, p. 430.
62. Ôta to Miyabe, November 13, 1885, *Nitobe Inazô no tegami*, p. 69.
63. Philip S. Benjamin, *The Philadelphia Quakers in the Industrial Age, 1865–1920* (Philadelphia: Temple University Press, 1976), pp. 6–7, 151–52; Elbert Russell, *The History of Quakerism* (New York: The Macmillan Company,1942), p. 435. For general details see, for example, "Women's Foreign Missionary Association of Friends of Philadelphia," *The Friends' Review*, February 7, 1885, p. 427; and for Japan see "An Appeal for Japan," *Ibid.*, March 14, 1885.
64. Uchimura also came to the United States in the fall of 1884. He was introduced to Morris by Mrs. M. C. Harris and visited the Morris family often while working for a mental home in Pennsylvania. Torii's annotation to Ôta's letter to Miyabe of November 13, 1885, *Nitobe Inazô no tegami*, p. 83; Koizumi Ichirô, "Nitobe Hakushi to Kueikaa shugi" in *NIK*, p. 48. Uchimura Kanzô, "Uisutaa Morisu shi nikansuru yo no kaikô," *UKZ* 1: 196–98.
65. *The Friends' Review* [Hereafter "Review"], February 7, 1885, pp. 422–23, 427.
66. Ôta to Margaret W. Haines, June 10, 1885, Review, pp. 29–30.
67. Margaret W. Haines, "Friends' Missionary to Japan," Review, December 12, 1885, pp. 294–95; Women's Foreign Mission Association of Friends of Philadelphia, "Annual Report," Review, February 20, 1886, p. 456.
68. Ôta Inazo, "Friends' Mission in Japan," Review, January 30, 1886, pp. 413–14. All quotations in this paragraph come from this article.
69. *Ibid.*; "Women's Foreign Mission Association of Friends of Philadelphia," Review, Feburuary 20, 1886, p. 456; Ôta Inazô, "Religious Impressions of America," Review, November 18, pp. 241–43; "Baltimore Yearly Meeting," Review, p. 250; Ôta Inazô, "American Influence in Japan," Review, April 14, 1887, pp. 578–81.

70. Ôta to Adams, June 22, 1886, Adams Collection.

71. Herbert Baxter Adams, "Joseph Neesima, The Japanese," "Joseph Neesima on the Japanese Revolution," (unpublished typescript) Box 13, file no. 5, Adams Collection. This file contains much of Adams's typescripts on Japan written in the 1890s. They demonstrate a considerable interest in Japanese history.

72. "Japan and the Japanese," *The Friends' Review*, February 13, 1886, pp. 437–38.

73. See pp. 61.

74. See Ôta to William E. Griffis, November 9, 1886, cited in *NIK*, pp. 451–52.

75. Saeki Riichirô, "Yonjûgo nen kan kawaranu yûjô," in *Nitobe Hakushi tsuiokushû*, pp. 35–36.

76. Minutes of the Seminary, November 19, 1886, pp. 277–80.

77. *Ibid.*, January 28, 1887, pp. 314–16.

78. *Ibid.*, April 22, 1887, pp. 359–60.

79. Minutes of Baltimore Monthly Meeting of Friends for the Eastern and Western District held October 28, 1886, Minutebook of Baltimore Monthly Meeting of Friends from July 10, 1884 to January 8, 1891 (microfilmed), The Religious Society of Friends, Homewood, Baltimore (hereafter "Minutes of Baltimore Quaker Meeting"), pp. 128–29.

80. *Ibid.*, p. 130; List of Members of Baltimore Monthly Meeting of Friends, Membership, 1882–1906, (M789), Papers of Baltimore Monthly Meetings of Friends, Orthodox (microfilmed), Hall of Records, Annapolis, Maryland, pp. 54–55.

81. Matsukuma, *Nitobe Inazô*, pp. 155–56; Satô, "*Kyûyû Nitobe Hakushi o omou*," p. 8.

82. Nitobe, "Gakusei jidai no Uiruson," p. 86.

83. Minutes of Baltimore Monthly Meeting, May 19, 1887, pp. 174–75.

84. *Ibid.*, pp. 175–76.

85. "Inazô Ôta," *The Friends' Review*, July 21, 1887, p. 806.

THREE

Cultural Identity

4

Japan Watchers: 1903–1931

A. Hamish Ion

> [T]he sudden revulsion of feeling has come when those who, not a generation ago, were thought of as pretty, interesting, artistic, little dolls or children, fantastic and whimsical, unsettled in purpose and loose in morals, dishonest in business, and cruel if you scratched through the skin, "great in little things and little in great things," have come out on the broad stage of the world.
>
> —Bishop William Awdry of South Tokyo,
> "The Character of the Japanese People," *London Times*, October 2, 1905.

During the years from 1905 to 1931, Western images of Japan and the Japanese underwent several dramatic changes almost as radical as those of the preceding half-century. The cultic attitude, whose undiluted praise characterized Western public opinion in the decade following Japan's defeat of Russia, grew until the World War I and then shifted to an increasingly negative perception which culminated with the invasion of Manchuria in 1931. As one of the leading propagandists for things Japanese, the ubiquitous Nitobe Inazô played an influential role in the creation of a positive image of Japan in the West prior to 1914, but in subsequent years he failed to convince many Westerners of the continued need to cultivate "a sympathetic understanding between peoples trained at opposite poles of tradition."[1] His inability should not surprise us, for Western images of Japan depended on the perception of Japan's significance to the West. By 1931 this significance differed profoundly from that in the years immediately following the Treaty of Portsmouth. As a self-appointed "cultural bridge" between Japan and the West, Nitobe's rise and fall depended in large part on Western perceptions of the Japanese rather than Japanese perceptions of themselves. Nitobe rose to fame on the crest of a craze for Japan in the West. His influence abroad after the World War I also foundered on the ebb-tide of Western interest in *his* Japan. Western authors on contemporary Japan no longer agreed with him. The support of those like the Edwardian G. W. Knox had given way by the late 1920s to the critical views of A. Morgan Young, and the breach had been opened for the vitriol of Taid O'Conroy and the phosphoric fury of Amleto Vespa which followed hard on Nitobe's *Japan: Some Phases of her Problems and Development*.[2] Nitobe may have possessed a charming avuncular personality, a quaint written English style and an excellent command of spoken English, but these in themselves do not necessarily make a successful cultural bridge. An essential ingredient to his success or failure was the broad context in which his ideas at first flourished and eventually withered.

This chapter provides such a context. It studies the Western intellectual community in Japan to help explain why Nitobe exerted such great influence before 1914 and so little after 1919. The rise and fall of Nitobe as a popular spokesman for Japan was paralleled by the reverse fall and rise in influence of the Western intellectuals in Japan. These two phenomena are closely related.

Here we concentrate on the opinions of some of the more notable British and Canadian residents in Japan with specific reference to political and social changes, military affairs and literary endeavour. The views of British and Canadian residents are of particular interest because between 1905 and 1931 Britain was not only the most important foreign power in East Asia but also closely allied to Japan.[3] Further, the majority of Western pioneers in Japanese studies during the late nineteenth century happened to be British, and Britons continued to lead the field after 1905. Our intention here is to give an impression of the concerns and changes within the Western intellectual community in order to define the intellectual community within which Nitobe worked.

Nitobe and Western residents in Japan were not the only interpreters of Japan to the West during the twenty-five years after 1905. Indeed, it might be suggested that the West suffered from a surfeit of experts on Japan, both Japanese and domestic. As early as 1904, one observer cynically noted that English works on almost every aspect of Japanese life "abound."[4] In 1924, M.D. Kennedy suggested that the number of publications about Japan would be three or four times greater than the four hundred pages of book titles listed by von Wenckstern in the 1890s.[5] The burgeoning literature on Japan was impressive. It went from simple Christian tales like Herbert Moore's still charming *In Peace and War*[6] to H. H. Coates' scholarly treatment of Hônen.[7] The activity of these Westerners in Japan takes on considerable importance because of their special position as interpreters of Japan for audiences at home. British residents in Japan held the middle ground between Japanese experts such as Nitobe and peripatetic Britons like the Webbs or Bertrand Russell. While Britons in Japan lacked the intuitive knowledge possessed by the Japanese, they usually did possess the decided advantage over the visiting traveller—long acquaintance with the Japanese and their culture. They also held the advantage over the Japanese with his intuitive knowledge of what the West did not and would not know of Japan, and so what would seem unique. Of all Westerners, it was the one who lived in Japan who could confirm or contradict those views which the Japanese wished to impress upon Western audiences about their island empire. The Western resident or academic who specialized in Japan at home competed for similar Western audiences with Nitobe and other Japanese spokesmen. The eventual eclipse of Nitobe as a "cultural bridge" lay not in his Japaneseness nor in the extent of his knowledge about Japan but in the more astute sensitivity of Western authors to the changing concerns of Western audiences.

Pioneers

The views of these expatriates reflected changing British public opinion about Japan. As has been argued elsewhere, the cult of Japan had a particularly profound impact on British public opinion between 1894 and 1914.[8] The reason for this cult during those twenty years lay in the belief that Bushido played a prominent role in the industrial and military successes of the Japanese and that the samurai society afforded lessons through which the British might solve their internal problems.[9] After World War I, a different image of Japan emerged. In this image, Japan appeared, not as a model in the continuing debate over how to arrest the decline of Britain, but more simply as an Asian imperialist power which posed a potential threat to British interests east of Suez. This new perception of Japan is clearly illustrated in the recommendations concerning Royal Navy deployment in the Pacific made by Lord Jellicoe in 1919.[10] Such an interpretation of Japan as a threat had roots which stretched back to the fears of the Yellow Peril in the 19th century. British public opinion about Japan was formed by the linkages made between Japanese actions and the British.

During World War I, the Japanese made very clear their designs on China. This brought them into conflict with both British and American imperialism and the incipient Peoples' Movement in China. What had become important about Japan for the British after 1919 was the second half of the Japanese political slogan, "constitutionalism at home, imperialism abroad," which was in vogue after 1905.[11] It was Japan's actions in China and to a lesser extent in Korea, not the positive achievements of Japanese domestic change, which altered British attitudes toward Japan. By 1931 China had become more important than Japan to the British. This, again, reflected a reversion to a nineteenth-century view of East Asia before the First Sino-Japanese War of 1894–95. Political change within Japan seemed important to the West only insofar as it might ameliorate Japan's overseas policies.

As British public opinion toward Japan changed, so did Western tastes as to whose opinions about Japan the public would accept. In the years immediately following the end of the Russo-Japanese War, Western audiences generally accepted the views of articulate Japanese spokesmen. A university degree from a prestigious Western institution ensured that one's opinions would be received as gospel. If the expert happened also to be a peer so much the better; Japan in 1905 did not lack noblemen with Western degrees. Included among them were such men as Kikuchi Dairoku (Baron, Wrangler in Mathematics from Cambridge), Kaneko Kentarô (Viscount, Harvard) and Suematsu Kenchô (Baron, later Viscount, Cambridge). Although they lacked noble titles, others such as Fujisawa Rikitarô (Strasburg) and Nitobe Inazô (Johns Hopkins) held prestigious professorial positions in Japan. Nitobe was doubly acceptable because he was also a Christian.

After World War I, Westerners were more discerning and could strongly criticize Japanese propagandists such as Fujisawa Rikitarô who attempted to construe apparent democratic changes in Japanese government as something that they were patently not.[12] There still remained a place for the Japanese expert such as German-trained Anasaki Masaharu, but as a specialist on Japanese Buddhism rather than a general propagandist for broad Japanese cultural values. As general interpreters of Japan, the opinions of A. Morgan Young and other foreigners in Japan were, by 1920, gaining greater acceptance because they were not Japanese propagandists. To some extent, this shift reflected the trend away from interest in Japanese ideas toward Japan in the context of international power rivalries. It also represented a return to the earlier nineteenth-century pattern in which foreigners had largely transmitted knowledge about Japan to the West. In fact, the decade after 1905 represented an anomaly, because for this short period Westerners placed great emphasis upon what the Japanese thought of themselves and their culture.

This anomaly requires explanation. An important cause for the emergence of Japanese spokesmen in this decade was the departure by 1905 of the great figures associated with the pioneer era of Western scholarship on Japan. Some of them had become disenchanted with Japan. The most famous British pioneer of things Japanese, Basil Hall Chamberlain, summed up his feelings to a fellow specialist on Japan, Sir Ernest Satow, in March, 1906:

> Here I am on my way home perhaps for the last time. I find it takes a great deal of courage to start off on one's travels nowadays. But I very specially want to see my old aunt, who is now 91 and quite alone; and I want to hear music and see a little of other art, pictures, statues, cathedrals—and to rub off colonial rust and re-adjust the point of view before it is too late. Brinkley [the editor of the *Japan Mail*] and a few others in Japan are ever-present warnings of what may—what almost must—happen to such as remain stuck forever in

one rut. Even the London rut is grotesquer, viewed from the outside. How much more so the Tokyo or Yokohama rut![13]

This utterance of remorse and desolation suggests that after some thirty years in Japan, Chamberlain had concluded that Japanese ideas did not compare with those of Europe. Satow's reply to Chamberlain is unknown, but *A Diplomat in Japan* published in 1922 was the only book which Satow wrote about Japan after he returned home.[14] In itself this book, which was concerned with a Japan that had long since disappeared, revealed Satow's lack of interest in contemporary events. Perhaps Satow, like Chamberlain, had concluded that Japanese attitudes resembled those of the colonies.

While both Satow and Chamberlain lived to an advanced age, two other major figures, William Aston and Frank Brinkley (who remained to the end in the Tokyo rut) both died only a few years after 1905. Among the younger members of the first generation of Western scholars, Sir Harold Parlett, who became a professor at London University when he retired from the diplomatic corps after World War I, wrote no major work on Japan. J. H. Gubbins, who also retired from the consular service to become a professor, wrote for publications but with more interest in history than contemporary affairs.[15] The departure of the first generation of Western scholars from Japan created this vacuum from 1905 until 1918. During this time Japanese experts provided authoritative opinions about Japan until the emergence of a second generation of Western scholars in the 1920s.

Anglican Missionaries

During the hiatus before the appearance of the second generation of British experts, men such as Hugh Byas, A. Morgan Young, Sir Charles Eliot and M. D. Kennedy, many of those Britishers who retained interest in Japanese trends were definitely of "second" quality. Some of these agreed with Chamberlain's curmudgeonly attitude toward changes in Japan. A major concern for them after the Treaty of Portsmouth was concern over the undue adulation of Japan. Foremost among such critics were the Anglican missionaries in Japan.

William Awdry, premier among them, wrote this about the Japanese national character in a letter to the *Times* in October 1905:

> It is true to say that the Japanese in Rome does as Rome does. He fits into his surroundings, is always gracious and desirous to please, has few angles. Among jockeys he will live and talk as a jockey, among gentlemen as a gentleman. In a clerical family in England he will go to church and behave in all ways as a religious man. In the ballroom he will be agreeable but not forward: and he catches quickly the tone of the society in which he is. If the Oxford undergraduate from Japan has gone to France or Germany by way of

utilizing his vacation you will know which it was on his return by his manners as well as by his tones. This is not hypocrisy, except as all adaptability, conscious or unconscious, is hypocrisy. It is a great gift and also a great snare both to himself and to those who interpret him as they would interpret an Englishman.[16]

In seeing the Japanese abroad as mirrors of Westerners, Awdry did not intend any unkindness. He wished instead to indicate to Britons that one should not place too easy faith in the seeming attributes of the Japanese. In a letter to the *Times* two-and-a-half-years later and shortly before his death, he stated that events had already borne out his earlier observations.[17] Such remarks did not go uncontested by the Japanese.

In November 1905, after Awdry's first letter, Baron Suematsu, then serving as a senior Japanese diplomatic spokesman in London, criticized Bishop Awdry's hostility.[18] Suematsu mistakenly supposed that Awdry's comments resulted from the burning of some churches in the Hibiya riots.[19] In fact, Awdry's comments rested on a more broad-minded consideration of Anglo-Japanese relations. He feared that subsequent disillusion might invite unfavourable consequences for the "efficiency and continuity of the Anglo-Japanese Alliance."[20] He believed that the Alliance promised to become the "best guarantee for the peace and progress of the world"[21] in East Asia.

Suematsu was not the only Japanese expert with whom Anglican clerics crossed swords. In 1910, Cecil Boutflower, Awdry's successor as Bishop of South Tokyo, vented his annoyance with Kikuchi Dairoku, then President of Kyoto Imperial University, whom many Britons regarded as an authority on Japanese education. Boutflower wrote that:

> When Baron Kikuchi, the great authority, lectures in England and America, he solemnly says that *the* all important thing, to explain their perfect (educational) system, is to get a correct translation of the Imperial Rescript! This abject humbug (for really it's nothing else) is a thing Japan can play at for ever, especially where the Emperor is concerned, and one daren't smile about it before one's most intimate Japanese friends.[22]

Boutflower further warned that British people, who might be impressed by Kikuchi's Cambridge degree, should not expect him to mention any flaws in the Japanese educational system. The Bishop noted, "don't expect Baron Kikuchi to tell you *that* sort of thing! You may rely that any sort of official information about Japan, from history onwards, is carefully 'cooked' if necessary for the world's eye."[23] Boutflower felt that Kikuchi and his ilk spread deliberate falsehoods about Japan's educational system and history so as to impress foreigners with Japan's uniqueness.

In their concern to reduce the excessive veneration accorded Japanese after 1905, it was only natural that Anglican missionaries should have little regard for Nitobe Inazô. The danger to the missionary was that British admiration for Bushido might reduce support for his religious efforts. A number of Anglicans in England received Bushido in surprisingly favourable terms. The Anglican missionaries responded in 1906 through John Imai, a Japanese clergyman of marked ability, to play down the importance of Bushido. He stressed that there was still a need to purify, renew and perfect what existed in Japan.[24] Saeki Yoshi, another Japanese Anglican who taught at Waseda University, agreed that, notwithstanding Bushido, Japan still needed Christianity.[25]

Among those with reservations about traditional Japanese ethics, possibly the most trenchant attack upon the cult of Bushido came from Basil Hall Chamberlain in his *The Invention of a New Religion*, published in London by the Rationalist Press Association in 1912. In this, Chamberlain identified the Bushido cult as a part of the "fabric of ideas" being promulgated by the ruling elite in Japan to bolster its own influence, and he categorized it as part of the reaction after 1888 against foreign influences.[26] He argued that the emergence of Bushido as a code of rules was part of "Mikado worship and Japan worship," an indication of the rejection of Western ideas and a reflection of an emerging Japanese imperialism. While Chamberlain's attack on Bushido must be considered in part a rationalist criticism of a secular religion, it does further illustrate the depth of his alienation from contemporary Japanese developments. Similarly, it shows that the Japanese rejection of Western ideas deeply concerned Westerners who knew Japan.

Some British in Japan perceived that the Japanese government and their propagandists strove to project uniquely Japanese religious and cultural values which they expected the West to accept as equal to the values of Western civilization. As Chamberlain argued, traditional Japanese ideas had been "sifted, altered, freshly compounded and turned to new uses."[27] Lionel Cholmondeley, the honorary Chaplain at the British Embassy in Tokyo, wrote to his friend Sir Ernest Satow in December 1909, that there was "a growing determination in high places to emphasize Emperor worship to extremes."[28] Cholmondeley would undoubtedly have agreed with Chamberlain that this projection of uniquely Japanese values—of which Bushido and Emperor worship were only a part—endangered not only Christianity but also Anglo-Japanese relations and especially the Anglo-Japanese Alliance.

Cholmondeley merely stated a widely accepted British view when he told Satow that he felt the Anglo-Japanese Alliance should be continued because it was the "safest way to keep the Japanese out of mischief."[29] In spite of this support of close diplomatic ties between Britain and Japan, Cholmondeley highly criticized general Japanese views of politics. He noted that:

The Japanese people, as far as politics are concerned, are profoundly incapable of thinking; they leave the thinking to their statesmen. They are content with the one axiom that their country can not possibly be in the wrong; for the rest they allow themselves to be swayed in whatever direction the government for the time chooses to sway them, e.g. the whole country must either be pro-English or anti-English; and herein is one of the great differences between our two countries—the child people and the people who rebel against being treated like children.[30]

This patronizing view of Japanese public opinion reflects the convictions that united Japanese on issues of foreign policy. It was difficult for Britons, especially those who had lived for a long time in Japan, to accept the Japanese as equals. And it was most important for them that "the Island Empire, and the Navy, and the police and the Parliamentary Monarchy, topped by the Alliance, make old England count first here."[31] Their desire that Britain would always "count first" and their genuine support for the Anglo-Japanese Alliance tempered their criticism of Japanese attitudes.

While this patronizing attitude of the British in Japan reflected class background and should not be mistaken for racism, British concerns were real. They worried that the excessive English admiration at home for Japan might eventually lead to a similarly excessive reaction against Japan that could damage the Anglo-Japanese Alliance. Rightly or wrongly, many considered Bushido a part of a conscious attempt to create "a fabric of ideas" that would lead to the rejection of Western influences, one of their overriding fears. Nitobe did not share this concern, nor did many audiences in the West after the Russo-Japanese War. The attitudes of Britons in Japan rested upon their convictions about the issues essential to Western attitudes about Japan.

Military Observers

As a result of the Alliance, Britain, other than Japan, was the chief beneficiary from Japan's victory over Russia in East Asia. The signing of the Anglo-Japanese Alliance in 1902 and the Russo-Japanese War created a wide British interest in the Japanese military. It was definitely in Britain's strategic interest to maintain good relations with Japan, especially as the growing threat of Germany caused Britain in the decade after 1905 to reduce its naval strength in the Far East. Like their civilian counterparts, British officers serving in Japan between 1905 and 1914 found themselves trying to temper popular British enthusiasm for the fighting qualities of the Japanese. They concentrated instead on practical military conclusions that the British military could draw from Japanese experiences.

In 1903, the British Army began to send British officers to Japan to work with Japanese regiments and study its military system. In the eleven years to 1914, some fifty or sixty of these "language officers" served in Japan for periods of one to four years.[32] During the Russo-Japanese War, over twenty British Army officers accompanied the Japanese forces in Manchuria, and four British naval officers served at various times on board Japanese ships. The majority of these officers went out directly from Britain or India, though one went from Canada.[33]

Since British troops in the South African War had performed so poorly, the British looked to the Japanese for inspiration: "efficiency in war" or "efficiency for war" as "God's test of a nation's soul."[34] There was little concern that Japanese military efficiency might lead to a Yellow Peril. Sir Ian Hamilton, an influential and rising British officer, noted that "the Japanese army, battalion for battalion, surpasses any European army, excepting only the British army at its best (not at its second best, which is the state in which it usually finds itself)."[35] Hamilton obviously shared the view that this excellence arose from the quality of sacrifice of the self for the state which stemmed from the spirit of Bushido and so found himself in agreement with Nitobe:

> The most improved guns and cannon do not shoot of their own accord; the most modern educational system does not make a coward a hero. No! What won the battles of the Yalu, in Corea and Manchuria, were the ghosts of our fathers, guiding our hands and beating in our hearts. They are not dead, those ghosts, the spirits of our ancestors. To those who have eyes to see, they are clearly visible. Scratch a Japanese of the most advanced ideas, and he will show a samurai.[36]

Sir Ian Hamilton and Charles A'Court Repington, the *Times* military correspondent whose writings did much to engender the cult of Japan in the aftermath of the war, did not need to scratch very hard to be convinced. For Repinton, Bushido provided that "deep and abiding moral principle of action which supports and sustains the frailty of human nature," something that "inculcates high ideals, encourages emulation in noble deeds, and inspires both moderation in victory and constancy in defeat" necessary to preeminence in the arts of war.[37] Moderation in victory, which was seen in Japan's decision not to demand an indemnity from Russia at the Treaty of Portsmouth, was viewed by Alfred Stead, one of the most influential advocates of Japan in Britain, to stem from the nature of the Japanese; the fact that "the idea of war for money and territory was abhorrent to the Japanese mind; all the ideas of Bushido, the instincts of the samurai rose up against it in horror."[38] Events in Korea would soon challenge this conclusion.

Indeed, after the first flush of euphoria about the war, the "language officers" who continued on in Japan began to speculate on the wellspring of the fighting qualities of the Japanese. The most outstanding British officer who served in Japan prior to World War I was Captain Everard F. Calthrop R. F. A., a language officer from 1903 to 1908, and the first and only British officer to pass through the Japanese Staff College. According to Major-General F. S. G. Piggott, himself a language officer at this time, Calthrop quickly gained a knowledge of Japanese language which "has been rarely equalled and never surpassed."[39] Piggott further wrote of Calthrop:

> Amongst his countrymen, Japan had no firmer friend, and few had penetrated so deeply below the hard-frozen and unyielding surface of Japanese social life. His principal aim was to remove misunderstandings between the two races, and to bridge the gulf that lies between East and West. No other officer amassed more knowledge of, or had more sympathy with, the Japanese.[40]

Calthrop was a most unusual Army officer. His friend Field Marshal Lord Wavell, himself one of the greatest of British soldier scholars, always wondered why Calthrop had chosen the Army as a career, for despite his ability as a soldier he appeared to be more interested in art and ideas than soldiering.[41] Perhaps his artistic temperament attracted him to the Japanese.

Despite his empathy for Japan, Calthrop's enquiring mind led him to see that its military success resulted from more than the spirit of the Japanese troops. He saw its roots in the broad East Asian philosophy of war in which *esprit d'armée* was only a part. In his pioneering English translation of the Chinese military theorist Sun Tzu's *Art of War*,[42] Calthrop in fact refuted the idea that Japan's success resulted from uniquely Japanese attributes by revealing that the East Asian philosophy of war came from a Chinese source. In this he approached his Anglican missionary friends who saw Bushido as an offshoot from Chinese thought. Calthrop had scratched beyond the samurai to find Wu and Sun. They taught him that spirit in battle is important but so also are the principles of war.

Calthrop's debunking did not stop here. In 1907, he translated an article on modern trends in strategy and tactics by Lt. Colonel Yoda Shokei. In it Yoda noted that "military questions must be looked at from two points of view: the material aspect, constantly changing with the development of mechanical science; and secondly, the moral aspect, which remains constant."[43] Concerning the latter, Yoda went on to state:

> [A] high moral (or spiritual) standard, or, in other words, the possession of loyalty and patriotism, is of absolute importance in war. Further, the qualities of endurance, thoroughness, quickness, and courage must be cultivated, and especially, in view of the difficulties and stress of the modern battle, a spirit of attack is of the first necessity. The endeavour of peace training should be to cultivate this quality to a high degree.[44]

Yoda makes no mention of a special Japanese mystique, but emphasizes the need for military training. The key to the quotation is the term "spirit of attack." It reveals the influence of French military thought. Yoda understood that the war had been fought according to contemporary European standards. He did not attribute victory to any Japanese characteristic, for to do so was obviously to misinterpret the lessons of the war.

Calthrop succeeded only partially. The idea of a special Japanese mystique had some adherents among language officers. In 1907, Major J. A. C. Somerville, a language officer from 1905 to 1907, continued to maintain that the Japanese Army "has arrived at a pitch of excellence which it is never likely to exceed for the reason that the ancient, fighting, feudal spirit still flourishes as yet practically untouched by the refinements and luxuries of our civilization; and to it is united a highly specialized knowledge of the science of modern war."[45] While Somerville in his stress on "knowledge of the science of modern war" refers to Japanese indebtedness to Von Moltke and the Prussian Army, he clearly felt that "the pitch of excellence" resulted from Japanese characteristics. Calthrop, following Yoda, would have stressed French influence.

Nor was Calthrop alone. The idea that Japanese success in the Russo-Japanese War resulted from traditional ideas was vigorously condemned by Brevet Major Sir Alexander Bannerman, a language officer from 1903 to 1905, in a lecture given at the Royal United Services Institute in 1910. Bannerman believed that "Bushido has on the modern Japanese spirit much the same influence that the principles of the Sermon on the Mount have at the present time in England."[46] A kindred spirit and fellow language officer in the audience, Captain C. A. L. Yate, agreed and in doing so revealed a contempt for Nitobe:

> The lecturer referred to Bushido, about which there has been an enormous amount of nonsense written. Who was the writer of the English book entitled "Bushido"? He was a Japanese Professor educated in America, and—I speak subject to correction—I think he is a Christian. In any case, he must certainly have been out of touch with the military and naval circles which formed the repository of the knightly traditions, such as they were. I have read "Bushido" from cover to cover. There is much that is beautiful in it, but there are certain things in it that would not appeal to people brought up in the English style. In any case, I feel convinced that the ancient feudal classes knew and cared little about a great deal that is written in it. The samurai had one great virtue—devotion to their masters; but they also had big vices. They were not always warriors; history tells us that in Japan, too, there were long periods of peace, and during those periods the samurai degenerated and became lazy, bullying parasites.[47]

Both Bannerman and Yate mentioned the failure of the samurai in the rebellion of 1877 which proved, according to Bannerman, that "under more modern conditions a farmer made as good a soldier as any hereditary warrior."[48]

To Bannerman, the Japanese army had beaten Russia because of its system of military conscription. He did not believe that the Japanese soldier was a "demi-god," for he felt the Japanese, like other soldiers, had their breaking point and had no special desire to die in battle. The reason for the Japanese citizen army's success was the mass educational system of the Japanese with its "little elementary schools" which taught loyalty, self-sacrifice, discipline, courage, and self-respect.[49] The seeds of victory were sown in the discipline of the Japanese people through their educational system. It allowed the Japanese in time of crisis to submerge their personal opinions and wholeheartedly attack the enemy. As one of the most distinguished of British soldiers, Lt. General Sir H. C. O. Plumer, sadly noted as he took up Bannerman's point, "we take little or no pains to teach them [British children] to be loyal, to be patriotic, and to feel—each boy and each girl—that when they come into the world as British citizens they owe something during the whole of their lives to their country."[50] Plumer was very much involved in the Boy Scout Movement ("the modern Bushido" as another referred to it)[51] which he saw as an attempt to teach the values of good citizenship and service to young people. Plumer regretted that the British educational system did not give these values first place, as in Japan.

Whereas in the immediate aftermath of the Russo-Japanese War, Hamilton and others had stressed the importance of traditional Japanese values, opinion considerably changed by Bannerman's time. By 1910, it was not traditional Japanese values that were considered important but Japan's modern mass-educational system and its implications for the modern Japanese army. There was nothing uniquely Japanese about this in purely military terms. The Japanese model remained important, not because it was uniquely Japanese but because its citizen army influenced by French ideas predicted success for the French Army against the Germans. At the same time, the success of the Japanese Army provided ammunition for those who wished to introduce conscription in Great Britain.

The pragmatic attitude of British language officers to the Japanese military related to the ongoing concerns of the British Army. Prosaic though their minds might have been in comparison to those of civilians, both Japanese and British, who conceived Japan's military achievements in terms of traditional martial spirit, the language officers' knowledge of the practical world of arms and men led them away from this to the more familiar ground of how known military theory explained victory. The attractiveness of the Japanese Army as a model disappeared with the events of World War I. By 1918, the Japanese Army was considered to be out of date in terms of its tactical formations and its lack of modern weaponry.[52] World War I caused the civilian residents, too, to see more clearly the negative aspects of Japanese militarism.

Canadian Optimism

Although Japan entered World War I as an ally of Britain because of the Anglo-Japanese Alliance, British residents soon started to complain that many Japanese admired Germany. Lionel Cholmondeley wrote in 1915:

> These childishly vain Japanese may some day be brought to a bitter repenting of their folly. Military arrogance runs high, and they would like to make Japan as formidable a war power as Germany. Very well, the militarists will bid for, as they are doing today, ascendancy in the country. Conscience will be thrown over for ambition. Taxation will increase and those naturally peace loving and contented people, under their hard task masters, will lose their charms of kindliness and courtesy and become a curse to themselves and others.[53]

In spite of the hyperbole, there was an element of accurate long-term prophecy in this analysis. The British in Japan feared "the unvarnished admiration of German powers which goes on openly behind the secure screen of a language whose press none of the other civilised countries can read."[54] They feared as well that widespread Japanese admiration for Germany might lessen Japanese support of the Allies for the Great War then being fought in Europe. The Foreign Office shared this concern[55] and sent its own propagandist to Japan to counter this trend. Missionary commentaries reflected cynicism about Japan's behaviour. For some years after the end of the war, British missionaries thought Japan had let Britain down.

A more positive attitude toward political developments within Japan also appealed to some observers. In 1914, C. P. Holmes, a Canadian Methodist missionary, noted:

> [A] new democracy of thought is growing up. The man in the street is beginning to think, and we know that it takes a thinking man to make a Christian. A year-and-a-half ago Count Okuma said that the present Emperor's reign would be remarkable for one thing and that would be the growth of democracy.[56]

By no means was this the view of everybody; Bishop Boutflower discounted the possibility of democracy. In November 1917, he wrote:

> Even from the official point of view all the present tosh that is being talked about 'democracy' may be good business *vis a vis* America, but it certainly won't help things over here, where the whole fabric of the Constitution, reflected down to the demeanour of the police and railway officials, rests on the extremest 'divine' theory of the Monarchy. The *Demos* of Japan consists, like our own, of some 'fifty million people mostly fools,' but they are wise enough to know (though Count Okuma and others blow a bit about demo-

cratic institutions) that on the whole they have been well guided and governed; and the spectacle of Russia's experiment (and China's next door), both hailed with acclamation in the West, are not likely to encourage premature plungings for Democracy in Japan.[57]

These sentiments vividly illustrate the deep scepticism with which many upper-class Englishmen regarded democracy and felt further disillusioned with Japan. Canadian views on Japan at the time reflected Canadian attitudes toward race.

In early 1918, C. J. L. Bates pictured Japan's future in Asia as extremely bright.[58] He felt that for the next twenty-five years Japan would lead East Asia, and that the West had nothing to fear from this. Bates believed that there was no basis for the idea of the "Yellow Peril," which he considered had been manufactured in Germany with no basis in reality.[59] He believed that the basic tenet of Japanese foreign policy was to prevent any Western power from establishing itself in force on the "Far Eastern coast of Asia." He saw that the Anglo-Japanese Alliance and the Lansing-Ishii agreements both unequivocally affirmed the territorial integrity of China and both recognized Japan's special position in East Asia.[60] Further, Bates considered that Japan had no intention to colonize China; rather its China policy, even the "badly worded" Twenty-One Demands of 1915, had as its real intention the prevention of Western domination of China.[61] Though his opinion now appears thoroughly naive, Bates wished to remove any apprehension of a Japanese threat to the Western powers and China in the post-war world. He clearly wanted to mollify Canadian concern about Japan.

Bates' missionary colleague, J. W. Saunby, was even more explicit. He noted that the people on the west coast of Canada would have to prepare themselves for "the mingling of races because the East was becoming a mighty competitor in manufactured goods" and that trade relations were annually becoming more extensive.[62] In view of the problems of Oriental immigration which affected both Canada and the United States, it is not surprising that race relations were always an important element among Canadian Methodists who knew Japan. The British, on the other hand, generally felt little concern over race. They knew no racial tension in Britain itself, but Britain stood at the head of an Empire which was largely composed of colored races. To question Britain's leadership of its Empire on racial grounds might seriously undermine its overall position. Conversely, it was definitely in the interest of Canadians to project a sympathetic view of the Japanese because of the racial tensions in Canada.

During the negotiations at the Versailles Conference, the Britons and Canadians differed on Japan's racial equality resolution. Dan Norman, a Canadian Methodist missionary living in Nagano, expressed sympathy for Japanese racial aspirations. He said that Japan needed all the sympathy and help that could be mustered while it was "in the throes of social and political ferment and evolution" which made it foolish to show a "spirit of disdain or resentment."[63] Boutflower inevitably differed. He felt gratitude that "Japan was making the painful discovery that in the opinion of the world Japan did not count for much because of her lack of ideas."[64]

The different national interests of Britain and Canada appeared clearly in the divergent opinions of Britons and Canadians in Japan. The attitudes of members of both groups toward Japan had to be either "yea" or "nay" because the "extraordinary national sensitiveness of Japan" made it difficult for them to hold a middle ground. The innate conservatism and political proclivities of the British made it hard for them to see the Japanese in other than paternalistic terms. British frustration with Japan during the war stemmed in part from the sense of isolation and impotence of Britons in Japan while Britain struggled in far-off Europe for its very existence. They also realized that World War I probably marked the beginning of a new era in world history which would be less certain than the old. Canadians, more susceptible to Wilsonian idealism, viewed the future with greater optimism and hope. Less suspicious than the British, they more easily accepted the Japanese at face value. While this might have led to positive opinions of Japan, as extreme in their way as the negativism of the British, the ultimate Canadian intent concurred with the need for a broad range of views concerning Japan. Whereas prior to 1914 foreign residents wanted to counteract uncritical admiration of Japan, Canadians by the end of World War I had recognized the importance of approval for Japan to counterbalance the prevailing negative Western perceptions. In that sense, Canadians now felt more sympathy with Nitobe's view of the need to cultivate understanding between peoples trained at opposite poles of tradition. Despite the inclination toward sympathy, the events of the post-war years made this predisposition difficult to sustain.

Opposing Evaluations of Japan's Domestic and Colonial Policies

Westerners in Japan after 1919 reflected in their ideas both disillusion with the past and hope for the future. In the first instance, there was a pervading nostalgia. In the second, there was an awareness that the disappearance of the Anglo-Japanese Alliance brought on a new need to stress informal bonds of friendship. This was necessary to counter the fulminations of those who were patently anti-Japanese. The task of Westerners in Japan was complicated by the two Japans which had emerged after 1919: metropolitan Japan in the throes of political evolution and Imperial Japan caught in the grip of protest against Japanese colonial rule. A consistency in the views of Westerners allowed them to sympathize with changes in metropolitan Japan while at the same time they criticized Japanese colonial policies in Korea. Events in metropolitan Japan defined attitudes toward the island empire, but it is wrong to assume that Westerners saw metropolitan Japan in isolation from the actions of Imperial Japan. The foci for the two opposing views of Japan were, in metropolitan regions, democracy, and, in colonial Japan, the treatment of Korea.

As for life in metropolitan Japan, some among the older Western residents found it far less pleasant than before World War I. W. F. France, an Anglican missionary, expressed a familiar British disdain for the times when in 1921 he unfavorably compared post-war Japan with the stable world at the end of the Meiji era. France lamented the disintegration of past standards and ideals that could be summed up in the word "democracy."[65] He felt that this term was used to justify the rapid disappearance of courtesy and good manners which had helped make life in Japan so pleasant. Others disagreed with him.

One constant thread in Major-General Piggott's memoirs written in 1950 was that the affability and courtesy of the Japanese toward foreigners, at least on a person-to-person basis, always remained.[66] A. W. Medley, a teacher at the Tokyo School of Foreign Languages, who knew both the good and bad points of the Japanese found himself "occasionally, *against my better judgement*, adopting an attitude more pro-Japanese than I really intended."[67] It was difficult to dislike the Japanese when Katô Takaaki could inadvertently refer to England as "*waga Eikoku*," ("our England") during a debate in the Diet[68] or when Japanese crowds welcomed the arrival of *HMS Renown* with its royal passenger, the Prince of Wales, as "no other country had welcomed them."[69]

Pomp and ceremony, so dear to the hearts of those from the sceptered isle, took on an added meaning at the time of the abrogation of the Anglo-Japanese Alliance. In the enthusiasm for Prince Edward's visit was seen hope that good relations between the two island peoples would continue unabated. Many Britons genuinely respected leading Japanese statesmen. Itô Hirobumi, Terauchi Masatake, and Yamagata Aritomo were all regarded with some affection as were such military heroes as Admiral Tôgo and Field Marshal Kawamura. Yet most of these, beginning with Itô in 1909, died during this period, and the warm feelings toward these aged men can also be interpreted in terms of nostalgia for past friendship with Britain. While Prince Arthur might hand the Japanese Emperor a British Field Marshal's baton or a visiting Crown Prince could pin the Order of the Rising Sun Class on the chest of the Governor of Ceylon, such symbolic gestures could only paper over the changes in the Anglo-Japanese relationship. Even so, such visible manifestations of friendship undoubtedly helped to engender goodwill, if only to the extent that they allowed Medley and others to be pro-Japanese "against their better judgement."

In keeping with their idealistic hopes for the post-war world, Canadians sympathized with the direction of political and social change in Japan. In 1922, Loretta L. Shaw, a Canadian Anglican missionary, noted that while "Japan seldom invents," the country did quickly adapt new ideas for its own needs and "Western democratic ideals are influencing the national life increasingly."[70] Shaw obviously felt that the growth of democracy would result in the growth of Christianity. Yet it is also clear that she and other Canadians saw that the development of general prosperity would lead to an improvement in the lot of the average Japanese. Again, altruistic concern for the Japanese led C. J. L. Bates to oppose the new restrictions upon Japanese immigration to Canada.[71] Despite this general agreement with Japanese developments among Canadians, it was also clear to them that metropolitan Japan had problems.

By the mid-1920s, Japanese militarism seemed too strong. In 1924, a missionary warned that even though the Japanese Government contemplated reducing the Japanese Army by four divisions, military training for all boys over fourteen continued in Japanese schools.[72]

Others at this stage did not see any danger in militarism. Captain Kennedy, a language officer and later journalist, was one of these. He contended that the "best brains" were found in the army or navy and the best of those in the General Staff: "The Foreign Office generally sends out men with less brains and less money than the General Staff and therefore, when it comes to the final point, almost invariably loses."[73] Coupled with this, he admired the strong Japanese tradition of the soldier-statesmen, Saitô Makoto and Katô Tomosaburô. Kennedy later contended that while Yamagata had been alive, he had ensured that the Army obeyed the Meiji Emperor's injunction to the armed forces to "neither be led astray by prevailing opinions nor meddle with politics."[74]

Although the death of Yamagata in 1922 allowed for the emergence of rival factions within the General Staff, it was by no means clear until the late 1920s that the former prohibition against political meddling no longer held. While the Meiji Constitution did provide the military ample opportunity to interfere in politics (by contrast the ingrained ideas of Sun Tzu warned against the civilian politician meddling in military affairs), the proponents of anti-militarism tended to overlook how well Japan had been served in the past by its soldier-statesmen.

In strictly military terms, Sir Charles Eliot, the British Ambassador, considered that the Japanese were a weak rather than a strong power.[75] The major reason for this was the Japanese lack of modern military equipment. Even though the British in the late 1920s began to develop their strategic base at Singapore and the absence of a first-class facility in Eastern waters in itself was sound justification given British imperial commitments, until the mid-1930s the Japanese were more a hypothetical enemy in the minds of Admiralty planners than a real threat. Although a British Aviation Mission had started to train Japanese naval pilots, the Master of Semphill, Kennedy wondered in the 1920s whether the Japanese, unlike the British and French, possessed the natural qualities necessary to make good pilots.[76] He showed prescience when he argued that Japanese cities were particularly vulnerable to long-range air raids which he believed would characterize any major future war.[77] He considered that the inadequacy of Japanese anti-aircraft defences in the 1920s imperiled Japan's chances in a future war, since morale on the home front would collapse even if the Army and Navy remained intact. In modern war, Kennedy contended, martial spirit alone did not suffice, for a modern army simply courted disaster unless it possessed the new machines. He gave the example of General Nogi's attempt to capture Port Arthur through numbers of troops rather than wait for the arrival of his heavy artillery to illustrate the very high casualties which would result from inadequate equipment.[78] As Japan did not possess many modern weapons, the Japanese did not in reality pose a threat to the major powers.

Japan did not pose a consequential military threat, but its attitude toward things military did cause concern. The goose-step of the Japanese infantryman, the organization of the General Staff and the position of the military under the Meiji Constitution drew attention to the German influence on the Japanese Army. Many Western observers equated militarism in Japan with Prussianism. Westerners opposed to militarism, including many in Japan, saw continuing German military influence in the Japanese army. Some further believed that Japanese militarism was incompatible with democracy because German militarism had been so undemocratic. This concern with Germany failed to take into consideration both the influence of French military thought in Japan and the compatibility of a strong military in both France and Great Britain with their forms of democracy. Although there was disagreement over the potential danger of militarism in Japan, the actions of the Japanese Army overseas provided a plentiful supply of ammunition for those who saw it as a danger.

The actions of the Japanese in Korea, for instance, did much to destroy missionary goodwill toward Japan. Canadian Presbyterian missionaries in the peninsula harshly criticized Japan, particularly after the suppression of the March 1st Movement in 1919. Canadians in Korea regarded the Japanese colonial administration as a "German machine" independent of the Japanese civilian government.[79] For Canadian missionaries who considered themselves the champions of democracy fighting the evils of militarism, the struggle for justice in Korea became a humanitarian crusade. It was more important to them than any consideration of anti-Japanese publicity on missionary work in Korea. Canadians went out of their way to publicize the atrocities committed by the Japanese military against Koreans.[80] While the anti-Japanese sentiments of Frank Schofield or Robert Grierson in Korea stemmed from the same Wilsonian idealism which made C. J. L. Bates pro-Japanese, the negativism of Canadian missionaries in Korea toward the Japanese compromised the attempt of Westerners in metropolitan Japan to foster sympathy for Japan's developments at home.

Just as the crisis over the Japanese suppression of the independence movement in Korea had died down, Canadians found themselves in a new controversy. This time, a Japanese punitive expedition had invaded the Kantô (Chientao) region of Manchuria in October 1920. They said they went to repay the murder of Japanese consular and civilian personnel by those whom they considered Chinese brigands. Canadian missionaries who worked among the Koreans in the Kantô quickly publicized atrocities against Korean Christians. The Japanese Army responded with a public accusation that Canadian Presbyterian missionaries were fomenting anti-Japanese feelings.[81] This resulted in a diplomatic incident between Britain, representing the Canadians, and Japan.

Just at the time, the British were debating whether they should renew the Anglo-Japanese Alliance. The actions of the Japanese army embarrassed both the British and the Japanese. Yet D. M. MacRae, a veteran missionary in Korea, probably summed up the views of his fellow Canadian missionaries when he argued that Britain had, through the Anglo-Japanese Alliance, forfeited her good name in order to satisfy the "prussianism" of Japan.[82] Long after the events of 1920, MacRae's colleague, Robert Grierson, wrote of Japan's defeat in the Pacific War "no wonder that Divine Providence reproved Japan for cruelty and injustice. Hurrah for Korea."[83] While this statement illustrates the depth of missionary sympathy for Koreans, the importance of Korea was that it provided real grounds for continuous criticism of the Japanese. As a result, the task of the apologist for Japan was made that much more difficult. He must both justify Japanese actions and counter the prevailing Western attitude that Koreans were the equals of the Japanese rather than inferior to them. Indeed, to missionary backers in Canada and the United States, Korea was a more important mission field than Japan. This put those who argued for sympathetic understanding of Japan at a disadvantage.

While foreigners in Japan disagreed over the political and social changes taking place during the 1920s, it is evident that many Westerners now saw Japan in a more sophisticated way. The paternalism of the British prior to 1914 had given way to an acceptance of Japanese as equals. Foreigners in metropolitan Japan were more predisposed than before World War I toward the Japanese. What weakened their case were Japan's actions in Korea. Nitobe might argue for a sympathetic understanding of Japan, but the onus to bring this about lay with Japan itself. As far as Western writings about Japan in the post-World War I period, the most prominent feature of much of the literary work is distance—cultural, psychological, and often geographic, between author and subject.

Escapism

Few would disagree that the finest piece of literature written by an English resident during this period was the poet Edmund Blunden's autobiographical prose essay *Undertones of War*[84] which was written in the early 1920s. While this anti-war book is not about Japan, it was written in Tokyo where Blunden was surrounded by an alien society. These surroundings provided the psychological distance necessary to produce such a work. Another example of distance is Arthur Waley's translation of the classic *Tale of Genji*, which introduced English readers to a new world.[85] Waley never set foot in Japan. He compared traditional Japanese culture's rich literature favourably with European literary masterpieces. While Heian Japan was a far cry from the fringes of Bloomsbury where Waley lived and the Noh drama of the Muromachi period hardly less from Yeats' Dublin, lesser luminaries in Japan also showed a marked propensity to look far into the past.

The considerable energy devoted to the investigation of traditional religions, particularly Buddhism, demonstrates this interest. In part, the study of Buddhism stemmed from a competitive missionary interest in other religions as revealed in the rather lackluster work of R. C. Armstrong.[86] In a more affirmative sense, concern with Buddhism also arose from the burgeoning interest in comparative religions as in the pioneer work of Arthur Lloyd or Sir Charles Eliot.[87] They focused on the traditional values of Buddhism, rather than on its contemporary role in Japanese society. The significant biography of Hônen written by H. H. Coates also reflected this antiquarian interest.[88] The scant works of Mark Napier Trolope, the greatest British scholar of Korea, on Korean Buddhism reflect a similar preoccupation with the past.[89] To some extent, especially in the case of the British, this classical concern demonstrated the preoccupations of the Oxbridge dons transferred to an Oriental setting. To others, like J. S. Gale with his superlative *History of the Korean People*, concern with the past had obvious, though perhaps subconscious, political overtones.[90]

While it can be said that the interest in tradition was perfectly legitimate and a manifestation of growing foreign knowledge of Japan, it can equally be held that the concentration on the past reflected an unease with the present. Westerners could more easily evoke an impression of Japan's past glory than deal with the contemporary situation where imagination had little play. Contemporary developments also worried them. Backward glances at Japanese tradition, which underlined the attributes of considerable merit within Japanese culture, also emphasized a comforting "lack of ideas" emerging from modern Japan. Although their knowledge of Japan was often superior to those who had lived there in the late nineteenth century, the Western residents of the 1920s still demonstrated a greater affinity with the past than the present. Indeed, it was only the critic Robert Young, deeply interested in the work of Uchimura Kanzô, who had a real interest in current intellectual thought for its own sake.[91] Despite numerous studies of the Japanese past which made the work of a generalist like Nitobe increasingly peripheral, the cultural gulf between Westerners and Japanese still remained.

A prime reason for this gap was the life-style of many of the Westerners in Japan. Its most striking aspect in the first decades of the twentieth century was the extraordinary lengths to which Westerners went to protect their own cultural identity against the surrounding alien society. The Western-style houses, the clubs and the summer resorts all testify to this concern. Westerners separated themselves from all but a selected few Japanese. The missionary or the businessman cloistered in the foreign community on James-yama in Kobe strove to control his environment by purposely distancing himself from the unknown. In this respect, to study the golden past of Japanese Buddhism did not challenge the Westerner's own cultural views. Samuel Heaslett, a British Anglican bishop, sarcastically berated his fellow missionaries in 1921 with the words: "If a missionary did not have a gospel to preach he filled his time by studying Buddhism."[92] Such study could indeed be seen as escapist.

Yet "escapism" could have significant value for an understanding of Japan. The writings of Walter Weston, the British Anglican, seemed deliberately escapist, for they dealt with his love of mountaineering.[93] Weston, who was one of the pioneers of Japanese mountain climbing as a leisure sport, in fact both opened a new side of Japan to the West and carried on a literary genre that had its antecedents in the late-nineteenth century descriptive accounts of Isabella Bird Bishop, Canon Tristam and A. H. Savage Landor. Yet Weston, like his contemporaries studying religions, was trying to impress upon his readers that Japan did possess facets which were of relevance to the wider world community. These were as permanent as the Japan Alps or Zen Buddhism and would remain constant regardless of the rise and fall of democracy or militarism.

While some looked for permanent features, others concerned themselves with that which was disappearing. Lionel Cholmondeley's history of the English community in the Bonin Islands is a clear example of this.[94] The ongoing debate between John Batchelor and Neil Munro over things Ainu offered another illustration.[95] Sir Josiah Conder, the architect, delighted in ephemeral beauty as is shown by his writings on Japanese floral art and landscape gardening.[96] Bernard Leach used his hands to imitate the fragile beauty of the traditional potter's art and in so doing helped to popularize it abroad.

Yet another strand of thought criticized foreign thinking about Japan. The irascible monk, Herbert Kelly, berated fellow Westerners in Japan with his complaints that everybody in the group knew all the others and that all their ideas were American which he considered "very intellectually conventional."[97] Kelly criticized everybody except Uchimura Kanzô and himself. Even if one agrees with Kelly that the members of the Asiatic Society of Japan emphasized the past at the expense of the present, by the 1920s Westerners with experience in Japan had re-established themselves as the leading interpreters of Japan to Western audiences. In 1930 Arnold Toynbee, as part of a report on the Kyoto Conference of the Institute of Pacific Relations, criticized the Japanese delegation in a vein reminiscent of Awdry and Cholmondeley. "They behaved," as Toynbee wrote, "as if they were in public school, where every boy knows his exact place and relationship to every other boy, and is self-conscious if a junior, when a prefect is present."[98] In simple terms, the Japanese were not their own best apologists.

Conclusion

How, then, does an account of the intellectual community in Japan expand our knowledge of the way in which Nitobe was accepted in the West? In investigating the period from 1903 to 1931, it has been shown that there was a brief time between 1903 and 1914 when the Japanese were their own best apologists. Nitobe emerged as a leading spokesman in part because his meteoric rise coincided with the departure from Japan of the respected Western pioneer scholars on Japan. As a result, the Japanese graduates of Oxbridge had the opportunity to fill a need for information about Japan. As far as the British were concerned, Nitobe himself was at a cultural disadvantage, for he was American educated. This entailed all that Herbert Kelly implied in a different context. It is hardly surprising, then, that Chamberlain and other Britons should be among Nitobe's most virulent critics. It is probably more correct to see Nitobe as a cultural mediator, not between East and West, but between Japan and the United States.

In looking at Nitobe and the other Japanese spokesmen, Tsurumi Shunsuke says that "English-speaking Japanese are unreliable," a proposition to which Yuzo Ota alludes.[99] Tsurumi's concern does not in this case appear to reflect a major question. More important than the veracity of the speaker is the relevance of his ideas to the foreign audience. In order for Nitobe's ideas to be accepted, there had to be a clear linkage between them and the concerns of his audience. Happily for Nitobe, his ideas were seen to be relevant to the ongoing British debate over national efficiency, if not also military efficiency. The fact that Nitobe's understanding of Bushido may well have been flawed, or that foreigners misinterpreted his intentions in writing the book, is clearly academic compared to the linkages which the foreign audience decided to make between it and their own particular needs. For the British, the samurai were seen to represent spirit, vigour and loyalty—they were the ancient Boy Scouts. Whether Bushido was true or not really did not matter. For in Bushido, the British saw only what they wanted to see.

The impact of the publication of *Bushido* was instantaneous, but it resulted in fleeting interest rather than a lasting effect. The case of British language officers illustrates this. To the British Army, what was important about the Japanese Army's success in the Russo-Japanese War was what it revealed by analogy about the French Army and also to a lesser extent about their own military organization. Bannerman and other language officers came to see that Japan's educational system, its conscript army and European military thought were more important to Japan's victories in Manchuria than Bushido. While the very high casualties suffered in storming Port Arthur might show the spirit of Bushido, they also, as Kennedy later pointed out, resulted from General Nogi's basic tactical error. Nitobe's work obviously stimulated interest in East Asian military philosophy, but the key to this thought was found by Calthrop, not in Japan but in the China of Sun Tzu. In reality, Nitobe offered nothing of substance to the military officer which could not be gleaned from Jomini or Foch.

Nitobe, as a Christian, might have been surprised by the reaction of the British Anglicans to his version of Bushido. Again, they saw in it only what they wanted or did not want. The very popularity of *Bushido* in England posed a perceived threat to the continued financial support of their mission work. Beyond this, they saw Nitobe's book as part of an attempt to create a new religion in Japan based on Emperor worship. It goes without saying that Nitobe did not view his work in that light. He was not attempting to compromise Christianity. The reaction of the British Anglicans does illustrate the truism that an author cannot predict how his readers may interpret his ideas. That depends on the linkages which they choose to make. One difference between Nitobe and some of the other Japanese spokesmen lies in his work's redeeming quality of sincerity. This makes the criticism of him all the more poignant.

The tragedy of Nitobe as a cultural mediator after World War I was that regardless of the sympathy which his ideas on mutual understanding between civilizations might invoke in principle, they said little to British readers. In a generalized way, Japan had ceased to exist. This does not mean that links between Britain and Japan disappeared, but it was the traditions of a remote Japan as seen in Heian literature or Buddhism that attracted Britons, not modern Japan. As a generalist seeking to explain modern Japan, Nitobe represented an older, pre-war type of cultural bridge in a world demanding more specific and specialized knowledge. More sensitive perhaps to shifts away from interest in contemporary Japan in the West, Westerners in Japan were able to provide much of this specialized knowledge for British audiences. That, after World War I, British or Canadian interpreters of Japan should supercede their Japanese counterparts should not surprise us, for cultural mediation is also a matter of distance.

Notes

1. Quotation from a review of Nitobe's *Japanese Traits and Foreign Influences* in *Journal of The Royal Institute of International Affairs* 7 (1928): 58.

2. See G. W. Knox, *Imperial Japan* (London: G. Newnes Ltd., 1905); A. Morgan Young, *Japan Under Taisho Tenno* (London: G. Allen and Unwin Ltd., 1928); Taid O'Conroy, *The Menace of Japan* (London: Paternoster Library, 1936); Amleto Vespa, *Secret Agents of Japan: A Handbook to Japanese Imperialism* (London: Victor Gollancz, 1938).

3. A great many monographs have been written on Anglo-Japanese relations during this period. A good survey of these relations in the broader context of British interests in East Asia is Peter Lowe, *Britain in the Far East: A Survey from 1819 to the Present* (London: Longman, 1981). In terms of diplomatic affairs, Ian Nish's work remains unsurpassed. Ian H. Nish, *The Anglo-Japanese Alliance: The Diplomacy of Two Island Empires* (London: Athlone Press, 1966), and *Alliance in Decline: Anglo-Japanese Relations, 1908–1923* (London: Athlone Press, 1972). An interesting account from a contemporary observer is Captain Malcolm D. Kennedy, *The Estrangement of Great Britain and Japan 1917–35* (Manchester: Manchester University Press, 1969).

4. T. W. H. Crosland, *The Truth About Japan* (London: G. Richards, 1904), p. 9.

5. Captain M. D. Kennedy, *The Military Side of Japanese Life* (Westport, 1924; Greenwood Press Reprint, 1973), p. vii.

6. Herbert Moore, In *Peace and War in Japan: A Tale* (Westminster: The Society for the Propagation of the Gospel in Foreign Parts, 1915).

7. Harper H. Coates and Ryûtarô Ishizuka, *Honen, the Buddhist Saint: His Life and Teaching* (Kyoto: Chionin, 1925).

8. Colin Holmes and A. H. Ion, "Bushido and the Samurai: Images in British Public Opinion, 1894–1914," *Modern Asian Studies* 14, no. 2, (April 1980): 309–29.

9. Holmes and Ion, "Bushido," p. 328.

10. Barry D. Hunt, "The Road to Washington: Canada and Empire Naval Defence, 1918–1921" in James A. Boutilier, ed., *The RCN in Retrospect 1910–1968* (Vancouver: University of British Columbia Press, 1982), pp. 44–61, pp. 50–53.

11. Matsuo Takayoshi, *Taishô demokurashii* (Tokyo: Iwanami shoten, 1974), pp. 37–38.

12. See review of Fujisawa Rikitarô, *The Recent Aims and Political Development of Japan* (Oxford: Oxford University Press, 1923) in *Journal of the Royal Institute of International Affairs* 1–2, 1922–1923 (September 1923): 204–05.

13. Quoted in Hagihara Nobutoshi, "Some Impressions of Sir Ernest Satow," unpublished typescript in the possession of A. H. Ion.

14. Sir Ernest Satow, *A Diplomat in Japan* (London: Seeley, Service & Co., 1921).

15. J. H. Gubbins, *The Making of Modern Japan: An Account of the Progress of Japan from Pre-Feudal Days to Constitutional Government and the Position of a Great Power, With Chapters of Religion, the Complex Family System, Education, etc.* (London: Seeley, Service & Co., 1922).

16. *The Times*, October 2, 1905.

17. *The Times*, May 18, 1908.

18. *The Times*, November 18, 1905.

19. Awdry, in a different article, dismissed the attacks on the Christian Churches as the work of "roughs" which should not be taken as a sign of anti-Christian feeling. See *South Tokyo Diocesan Magazine* 9, no. 28, (December 1905): 68–69.

20. *The Times*, October 2, 1905.

21. *Ibid.*

22. *Cecil Boutflower Papers*, cycle letter #11(April 10, 1910), in the United Society for the Propagation of the Gospel Archives, London, England.

23. *Ibid.*

24. John Imai, *Bushido: In the Past and in the Present* (Tokyo: 1906).

25. P. Y. Saeki, "The Sources of Bushido," *South Tokyo Diocesan Magazine* 12, no. 35, (March 1908): 5–12. Japanese Anglicans would have undoubtedly agreed with Uchimura Kanzô who in 1920 remarked that "Bushido is the finest product of Japan. But Bushido by itself cannot save Japan. Christianity grafted upon Bushido will be the finest product of the world. It will save not only Japan, but the whole world." See "Bushido and Christianity," *UKZ* 22: 161. Although British Anglicans might have chosen to ignore it, Nitobe himself clearly saw the highest type of *bushi* to possess Christian-like qualities. This is clearly seen in his 1906 article "Ascent of Bushido" in *NIZ* 12: 282–85.

26. Holmes and Ion, p. 327.

27. *Ibid.*, p. 327.

28. L. B. Cholmondeley to E. M. Satow, December 1909, *Satow Papers*, P.R.O. 30/33/12/4 2679 in Public Record Office, London, England.

29. L. B. Cholmondeley to E. M. Satow, July 7, 1910, *Satow Papers*, P.R.O. 30/33/12/5 2683.

30. *Ibid.*

31. *Cecil Boutflower Papers*, cycleletter, #12 (June 6, 1910).

32. Kennedy, *The Military Side of Japanese Life*, p. 3.

33. See Captain John J. Armstrong, "A Gunner in Manchuria: Canada Observes the Russo-Japanese War," *Canadian Defence Quarterly* 12, no.4, (Spring 1983): 37–44.

34. Holmes and Ion, p. 319. See H. F. Wyatt, *God's Test By War* (London: 1912), pp. 9, 14.

35. Sir Ian Hamilton, *A Staff Officer's Scrapbook: The War in the Far East 1904–1905.* (London: John Murray, 1905), p. 238.

36. Nitobe Inazô, *Bushido: The Soul of Japan* (Rutland, Vermont: Charles E. Tuttle Co., 1980), pp. 188–89.

37. Homes and Ion, p. 318.

38. *Ibid.*, p. 320.

39. Major-General F. S. G. Piggott, *Broken Thread* (Aldershot: Gale and Polden Ltd., 1950), p. 25.

40. *Ibid.*, p. 90.

41. John Connell, *Wavell: Scholar and Soldier*, 1 (London: Collins, 1964), p. 522, also pp. 63, 76–77.
42. E. F. Calthrop, *The Book of War* (London: John Murray, 1908).
43. Lt. Colonel Yoda, "Modern Tendencies in Strategy and Tactics as Shown in Campaigns in the Far East," translated from the *Kaikosha kiji* 352 (December 1906), by Captain E. F. Calthrop, R.F.A., *Journal of the Royal United Services Institute* 51 (July–December 1907): 854–71, 870.
44. *Ibid.*, pp. 870–71.
45. Quoted in Towle, "British Estimates of Japanese Military Power," p. 128.
46. Brevet Major Sir Alexander Bannerman, Bart., R. E., "The Creation of the Japanese National Spirit," *Journal of the Royal United Services Institute*, 54 (January–June 1910): 697–710, with comments 710–719, 697–698.
47. Bannerman, "The Creation of the Japanese National Spirit," Yate's comment, p. 714.
48. *Ibid.*, p. 708.
49. *Ibid.*, p. 704.
50. *Ibid.*, comment of Lt. General Sir H. C. O. Plumer, p. 718.
51. *Ibid.*, comment of Colonel J. A. Rosseter, p. 713.
52 Kennedy, *The Military Side of Japanese Life*, p. 32. Kennedy was a language officer 1917–20.
53. L. B. Cholmondeley to F. Cholmondeley, October 10, 1915, copy of letter in *Cholmondeley Diaries 1915* in *Nihon seikôkai kyômin*, Tokyo.
54. *Cecil Boutflower Papers*, cycle-letter #36 (November 15, 1917).
55. See Peter Lowe, *Britain in the Far East*, p. 110.
56. C. P. Holmes, "Address to Hamilton Conference," June 19, 1914, H13F1 Box 1 in United Church of Canada Archives, Toronto, hereafter cited as *UCCA*.
57. *Cecil Boutflower Papers*, cycle-letter # 36 (November 15, 1917).
58. C. J. L. Bates, "Japan's Place in the Orient," 11-page typescript dated February 1918, H13 G4 Box File 112 (UCCA).
59. *Ibid.*
60. *Ibid.*
61. *Ibid.*
62. J. W. Saunby, "The Question of Japanese Immigration," *Christian Guardian*, April 24, 1918.
63. D. Norman, "Political Change in Japan Influenced by Christian Teaching," *Missionary Bulletin* 15, no.4, (October–December 1919): 579.
64. *Cecil Boutflower Papers*, cycle-letter #42 (May 13, 1919).
65. W. F. France, June 1921, S.P.G. Series E 1921.
66. Piggott, *Broken Thread*, passim. This courtesy even extended to critics of the Japanese, as was illustrated in the generous tributes in the Japanese press to Robert Young of the *Japan Chronicle* after he died in 1923. Kennedy, *The Military Side of Japanese Life*, p. 329.
67. Quoted in Piggott, *Broken Thread*, p. 159.
68. *Ibid.*, p. 159.
69. *C.M.S. Japan Quarterly* (June 1922), p. 6.
70. Lorretta L. Shaw, *Japan in Transition* (London: Church Missionary Society, 1922), pp. 8–9.

71. See *Canada File 1925, Japan Government*, in Foreign Ministry Archives, Tokyo.
72. C. M. S. *Japan Quarterly* (December 1924), p. 1.
73. Kennedy, *The Military Side of Japanese Life*, p. 321.
74. Kennedy, *Estrangement of Great Britain and Japan*, p. 64.
75. Quoted in Dennis Smith, "The Royal Navy and Japan: In the Aftermath of the Washington Conference, 1922-26," in Gordon Daniels, ed., *Proceedings of the British Association for Japanese Studies* 3, no. 1, (Sheffield: Sheffield University Press, 1978): 69-86, p. 76.
76. Kennedy, *The Military Side of Japanese Life*, p. 325.
77. *Ibid.*, p. 328.
78. *Ibid.*, p. 333.
79. See R. P. MacKay to N. W. Powell, April 9, 1919. PCC GA 41 Box 4 File April 1919 (UCCA).
80. See my "British and Canadian Missionaries' Attitudes to Japanese Colonialism in Korea, 1910-1925," in Peter Lowe, ed., *Proceedings of the British Association for Japanese Studies* 1, no.1, (Sheffield: Sheffield University Press, 1976): 60-77.
81. *The Times*, December 7, 1920.
82. D. M. MacRae to A. G. Armstrong, December 24, 1920. PCC GA 41 B6K Box 5, File December 1920 (UCCA). MacRae, one of Canada's most distinguished missionaries, is the subject of Helen Fraser MacRae, *A Tiger on Dragon Mountain* (Charlottetown, P.E.I.: A. James Haslam, Q.C., 1993).
83. Robert Grierson, "Episodes on a Long, Long Trail," unpublished autobiographical typescript in the possession of Dr. Horace Underwood, Seoul, Korea, p. 66.
84. Edmund Blunden, *Undertones of War* (1928; reprint ed., Harmondsworth: Penguin Books, 1982).
85. Arthur Waley, *The Tale of Genji* (London: G. Allen & Unwin, 1925-1933).
86. See, for instance, R. C. Armstrong, *An Introduction to Japanese Buddhist Sects* (Toronto: Oxford University Press, 1950).
87. Arthur Lloyd, *The Wheat Among the Tares: Studies of Buddhism in Japan*. A collection of essays and lectures, giving an unsystematic position of certain missionary problems of the Far East, with a plea for more systematic research (London: 1968 edition). Also important is Lloyd's *The Creed of Half Japan* (London: Smith, Elder, & Co., 1911); and Sir Charles Eliot, *Japanese Buddhism* (London: Edward Arnold and Co., 1935).
88. Harper H. Coates and Ryûtarô Ishizuka, *Hônen, the Buddhist Saint: His Life and Teaching* (Kyoto: Chionin, 1925).
89. For M. N. Trollope see: "Obituary: The Right Reverend Mark Napier Trollope D. D. Bishop in Korea," *Transactions of the Korea Branch of the Royal Asiatic Society* 20 (1931).
90. See Richard Rutt, *James Scarth Gale and his History of the Korean People* (Seoul: Talwon, 1972).
91. See Kakegawa Tomiko, "Japan Keronikeru to Robaato Yangu 1," (The Japan Chronicle and Robert Young), *UKZ Geppô* 32: 6-9.
92. Quoted in A. C. Hutchinson, *Autobiography*, typescript in the possession of Canon A. D. Hutchinson, Bristol.

93. Walter Weston, *Mountaineering in the Japan Alps* (London: J. Murray, 1913); *The Playground of the Far East* (London: J. Murray, 1918); *A Wayfarer in Unfamiliar Japan* (London: Methuen & Co. Ltd., 1925).

94. Lionel Bernes Cholmondeley, *The History of the Bonin Islands from the Year 1827 to the Year 1876, and of Nathaniel Savoy, one of the Original Settlers, to which is added a short supplement dealing with the islands after their occupation by the Japanese* (London: Constable, 1915.)

95. John Batchelor, *Ainu Life and Lore: Echoes of a Departing Race* (Tokyo: Kyobunkwan,1930). For Neil Munro, see *Who's Who in Japan 1914*.

96. See *Who's Who in Japan 1914*, Prof. Josiah Conder, "Landscape Gardening in Japan" and "The Floral Art of Japan."

97. Alan William Jones, "Herbert Hamilton Kelly, S.S.M. 1860–1950: A Study in Failure (a contribution to the search for a credible Catholicism)," Ph.D. thesis, Nottingham University, 1971, pp. 212–13.

98. A. J. Toynbee, "The Third Biennial Conference of the Institute of Pacific Relations, Kyoto, October 31st to November 8th, 1929," *Journal of the Royal Institute of International Affairs* 9, no.2, (March 1930): 189–201, 191.

99. See Ota, p. 238, 250 of this volume.

5

Bushido: Its Admirers and Critics

Cyril H. Powles

The distance which separated Nitobe from his critics revolved largely around Nitobe's early and controversial work *Bushido*. This work deserves special attention, for it became one of the most widely read books about Japan and exerted an influence far greater than its author could have imagined as he set out to write it. It dealt with the relations between Japan's warlike proclivities and the ethical training of Japanese individuals. Through Nitobe's interpretation, Bushido achieved the status of a unitary explanation for Japan's success at modernization. Some foreigners even hoped to appropriate its secrets to the solution of their own domestic concerns. *Bushido, the Soul of Japan: An Exposition of Japanese Thought*, was a runaway best-seller in the early twentieth century. The original English text went into at least twenty-five editions and reprints. A succession of Japanese translations and others in at least ten languages soon followed. After the defeat in 1945, few readers found the subject of interest, but twenty years later, a right-wing author republished it in a new translation to recall Japanese youth to the old values.[1] Reprint editions continue to make it easily available to readers in the original. In this way, *Bushido* has enjoyed both early popularity and a long life.

At the same time, it poses for the late-twentieth-century historian a number of puzzling paradoxes and problems. Written by a convert to Quaker pacifism, it appears to go out of its way to glorify martial virtues. The Ministry of Education so admired it in the 1930s that it made a reading of *Bushido* a part of its notorious moral training program.[2]

Since we know it was used to inculcate martial virtues, it should not surprise us to learn that *Bushido*'s argument seems to approve the nationalistic Meiji-Taishô emperor system. Nitobe's words reflect little tension between Japanese nationalism and the cosmopolitan humanism for which he later became famous. Finally, how does the chapter on the "Training and Position of Women"—one of the longest in the book—which appears to approve the subordination of women, harmonize with the author's own personal choice of an independent American wife?

These and other contradictions provide clues to help us understand the complexities of Nitobe's character and thought, as well as of the context out of which they arose. How far, for instance, did Woodrow Wilson's democratic internationalism, for which Nitobe became known, represent the core of his thought, and how far did his background and career as a member of Japan's bureaucratic elite govern his ideas? Does *Bushido* reflect only the romantic enthusiasm of a young intellectual, eager to explain his country to contemporaries abroad, or does it reveal something hard and irreducible in its writer's nature which remained with him, alongside the cosmopolitanism, to the end of his life?

In order to explore such questions, this chapter considers the context out of which *Bushido* grew, its content, what others have said about it, and its significance for the questions we have raised.

Like the majority of Meiji converts to Christianity, Nitobe came from a domain whose leaders sided with the old Edo regime in the War of the Restoration (1867–69).[3] Unlike most early converts, who remained outsiders to the new government leaders, Nitobe served as a loyal public servant for most of his life. The quiet eclecticism of his faith reveals some striking contrasts to that of his lifelong friend, Uchimura Kanzô, whose stormy career reflected the ambivalence and conflict more characteristic of converts to Protestantism at that time.[4]

To anyone reading the pages of *Bushido* at the end of the twentieth century, Nitobe's apparent ability to hold a cosmopolitan humanism at the personal level together with obedience to a ruthless colonial government appears at best like inconsistency. Little of the fiery criticism of imperialism reflected in the writings of the early Uchimura or other pacifist contemporaries like Abe Isoo, Kôtoku Shùsui, or Kinoshita Naoe appears in its pages.[5]

And yet, the publication of *Bushido* coincides with the first climax of criticism against the authoritarian structure of the emperor-centered modern state.[6] The Constitution of 1889, closely followed in 1890 by the Imperial Rescript on Education, marked the consolidation of a bureaucratically controlled society whose transcendental focus in a "sacred and inviolable" emperor allowed for irresponsible government.[7] The transmogrified Confucian–Shinto ideology enshrined in the two documents reflected the intention of Japan's ex-samurai leaders to maintain their peculiar understanding of the nation's spirit (*wakon, yamato damashii*) as a thought structure able to hold the people together while potentially subversive foreign techniques (*yôzai*) were being imported. That the spirit might prove to be incompatible with the techniques, or that techniques might bring in with them a different spirit, troubled the rulers only to the extent that they carefully combined indoctrination with repression to ensure the survival of the ancient mythology. In the process, the mythology itself changed its nature. Shinto, in its earliest form, had arisen as a local cult whose scope was limited to one discrete community. As Harada Toshiaki has described it, "Not only did they not allow people from other villages to participate in their life, they also made light of the worship of other Gods thinking it to be sinful....Each village regarded its own Matsuri as the most unique one."[8]

Traditionally, even with the imperial cult, it had been a case of *primus inter pares*, where Amaterasu, the clan goddess *(ujigami)* of the imperial household, reigned as chief among the eight thousand myriad Gods or spirits *(kami)*. But now, in the modern scheme, a "new religion" was invented. As B. H. Chamberlain pointed out at the time, and many scholars since World War II have noted, the imported idea of a universal religion was applied to the Meiji emperor cult.[9] As a result, State Shinto became the messianic faith of a new-born imperialism which burst upon the international scene with the victory over China in 1895. It is true that the early party movement of the late nineteenth century and a nascent socialism among others attempted to propose alternate visions of Japan's future, but the government largely succeeded in co-opting or repressing them all. The failure of the movement against war with Russia (1903–1904) and the ruthless suppression of the socialists in 1911 mark the almost total triumph of the official ideology.[10] Until Japan's defeat in 1945, it remained the virtually undisputed expression of the spirit, or soul, of Japan.

Little of the turmoil which surrounded the subject at the time appears on the pages of *Bushido*. In the course of his exposition, Nitobe quotes from, or refers to, over a hundred different American, Chinese, European and Japanese authorities, ancient and modern, in itself a considerable tour de force. Yet nowhere do names like Tokutomi Sohô, Nakae Chômin, or Miyake Setsurei, to name only three of Nitobe's contemporaries who expressed widely differing ideas in the argument about the Japanese spirit, appear. Although modern Western political thinkers—Marx, Nietzsche, Veblen— are named, it is largely classical figures—Confucius, Wan Yang Ming, or Yamaga Sokô—who represent the Eastern tradition. Roughly, what emerges is an objective, albeit romantic and rather aristocratic, account of the feudal origins and characteristics of Bushido, replete with analogies from, and comparisons with, the Western tradition. Along the way and briefly at the end, Nitobe interjects some almost unconnected reflections on the Japanese heritage from a kind of liberal Christian and Western standpoint.

To scan the content a little more thoroughly, Nitobe writes in his introduction to the original edition (dated December 1899) that he first decided to write *Bushido* in order to answer the questions of foreigners close to him, "why such and such ideas and customs prevail in Japan" (vi).[11] At least ten years earlier the Belgian jurist, de Laveleye, whom Nitobe had met while studying in Europe, had questioned him about religious instruction in the schools of Japan. In his attempts "to give satisfactory replies...I found that without understanding Feudalism and Bushido, the moral ideas of present Japan are a sealed volume." These ideas "consist mainly of what I was taught and told in my youthful days, when Feudalism was still in force" (vi). As the formal end of feudal society had taken place a scant thirty years before, it was important to realize how basic a part its attitudes and customs still played in the formation of the Japanese character.

Finally, lest Christian friends should question his attitude to the faith, he takes care to point out that the ideas he is about to expound represent a kind of preparation for evangelism in Japan: "I believe that God hath made a testament which may be called 'old' with every people and nation—Gentile or Jew, Christian or Heathen" (vii–viii). In effect, Bushido represents for Japan a kind of natural morality, capable of evolution toward something higher, but at the same time of unique value in its own right.

A detailed exposition then follows, divided into seventeen short chapters. As stated in the Introduction, Bushido is to be treated as an ethical code, parallel to chivalry in the West. Because of their distinct origins, however, the two cannot be compared exhaustively. "My attempt is rather to relate, *firstly*, the origin...; *secondly*, its character and teaching; *thirdly*, its influence among the masses; and, *fourthly*, the continuity and permanence of its influence." What then follows resembles an urbane and sophisticated exposition of what used to be known as "manners and morals of the Japanese," rather than of Bushido as such.[12] A discussion of the religious and ethical contributions of Shinto, Buddhism, and Confucianism (Chapter 2) leads on to descriptions of particular characteristics like *giri* (justice, duty) (3), courage (4), *nasake* (benevolence) (5), and *reigi* (politeness) (6). Throughout, the author emphasizes the peaceful, artistic and literary side of the warrior's training, interpreting in detail the significance of etiquette and the tea ceremony as methods for inculcating self control and regard for others. The chapters on truthfulness (*bushi no ichigon*), honor (*memmoku* vs. *haji*) and loyalty which follow, make one wonder whether Ruth Benedict's identification of terms like these as basic to Japanese character may not be traced back to this venerable work.[13]

For Nitobe, though, "the sense of shame seems...to be the earliest indication of the moral consciousness of our race" (67). This remark allows the reader to glimpse the author's method, traces of which reappear in later passages. For example, in the chapter on suicide and redress (*seppuku, katakiuchi*) (12), he treats these bloody customs as quasi-legal institutions to mete out rough justice before the reign of law made both unnecessary (117). What he seems to say in both passages is that the ethical practices of Japan represent old, intuitive ways to deal with human relations which provided the nation with a firm foundation on which to build a newer, more humane, structure of morality.

For Nitobe, such a newer, better morality would not come exclusively from the West. In recurring passages he contrasts the "individualism of the West" unfavorably with the familial, communal, solidarity of the East (79, 91, 136). Qualities like loyalty (9), self-control (11), and self-surrender (136), all characteristic of samurai training, go to build up this solidarity. And such qualities can lead on to an even higher ideal of service to God and neighbor when the opportunity to follow Christ presents itself. Thus, in agreement with his friend Uchimura, Nitobe sees the Japanese Christian as the fruit of a grafting process in which a new branch is united with an old root grounded in Japanese culture.[14]

This old root can never be neglected because it provides the foundation on which any new structure must be built. To change metaphors yet again, the root or foundation represents (Japan's soul) *Yamato damaishii* (16: 157–61), the reason why that country was able to retain its own spiritual autonomy and to modernize without dependence on foreign ideologies. It is in this soul or spirit that Bushido lives on despite the disappearance of the feudal society that once embodied it (169–70). "It is dead as a system; but it is alive as a virtue: Like its symbolic flower (*sakura*), after it is blown to the four winds, it will still bless mankind with the perfume with which it will enrich life" (176–77).

Nowhere does this concentration on the root nature of Japanese culture appear so clearly as in the chapter entitled, "Training and Position of Woman" (14). A long section, it is one of the few passages in which the struggle in its author's mind between Japanese-feudal-corporate and Western-"Christian"-individual is allowed to surface. According to Nitobe, the Bushido view of woman itself contains a paradox: "Bushido being a teaching primarily intended for the masculine sex, the virtues it prized in woman were naturally far from being distinctly feminine" (128). Thus the Amazon, wielding her *naginata*, a long staff with a sword tip, and schooled in all the samurai virtues of fortitude and self control, represents one side. But a warrior society also required the submissive housewife (*shufu*), willing to take her place on the ladder of the feudal hierarchy, surrendering herself to her husband as he in turn surrenders himself to his lord (135). In contrast to the Western, "Christian" view, which "requires of each and every living soul direct response to its Creator" (136), this hierarchical plan demands that the Amazon never replace—only reinforce—the qualities and duties of the housewife.

So persuasive is Nitobe's picture of the Japanese woman that this passage has been used again and again as an authoritative portrayal of the "traditional" feminine estate.[15] Yet in spite of the sympathetic objectivity with which he approaches his subject, one wonders how it all fits in with the Nitobe who, when he had himself taken a wife, turned to one who clearly stood outside the hierarchical society. Indeed, the contrast could hardly be sharper. The Quaker society from which Mary Elkinton came had itself grown out of a challenge to an earlier hierarchical society. By joining the Society of Friends, as he did even before his marriage, Nitobe was placed outside the pale of the culture whose values he appears so sympathetically to be describing.

This brief summary has allowed us to glimpse the ideal aspect of Bushido: to sense what made it attractive to Western readers in its day. The English style is idiomatic, albeit flowery as was the style at the end of the nineteenth century, with a few of the slips to which a non-native writer might be prone. The use and variety of foreign sources is meant to dazzle, though many of the Victorian authorities quoted now mean little to the reader. Until Nitobe's generation, as Hamish Ion has shown in chapter four, America and Europe had depended on eyewitness accounts from outside, by foreign observers who rarely escaped treating Japanese culture as in some way exotic. With Nitobe's generation, writers, termed by Yuzo Ota "Masters of English," had emerged. They could interpret their own culture from within.[16] Like his contemporary Okakura Tenshin, Nitobe sketched a picture that fitted neatly into the image of an aesthetic Orient to complement the utilitarian drabness of an industrializing West. How the popularity of *Bushido* was perceived in its day—and its weaknesses also noted—forms the theme of our next section.

Reactions

Bushido gained rapid acceptance as an authoritative description of the Japanese character and remained for many years the yardstick against which others were measured. In the preface to the tenth, revised, edition of 1905 Nitobe notes that:

> Since its first publication in Philadelphia, more than 6 years ago, this little book...has passed through twenty-five editions, the present thus being its tenth appearance in the English language.
>
> In the meantime, *Bushido* has been translated into Mahratti, ...German, ...Bohemian, ...Polish, ...into Norwegian and into French. [Chinese, Russian and Hungarian versions are under way, as well as Japanese. Finally,] exceedingly flattering is the news that has reached me from official sources, that President Roosevelt has done it the undeserved honor by reading it and distributing several dozens of copies among his friends.[17]

Bushido enjoyed a high reputation among liberal missionaries in Japan. This was particularly true of Americans with whom Nitobe most frequently associated. For instance, W. E. Griffis, author of an earlier best seller, *The*

Mikado's Empire, along with biographies of Niijima Jô and Guido Verbeck, wrote an introduction to the American edition of 1905 in which he praised the work in fulsome tones:

> Nitobe has limned with masterly art and reproduced the colouring of the picture which a thousand years of Japanese literature reflects so gloriously.
> This little book on Bushido is more than a weighty message to the Anglo-Saxon nations. It is a notable contribution to the solution of this century's problem—the reconciliation and unity of the East and the West.[18]

Nearly thirty years later, another missionary work, *Religious Values in Japanese Culture*, by T. T. Brumbaugh, was still quoting *Bushido* as an authority: "It was Dr. Nitobe who first ventured to enunciate these virtues for the Western world.... [T]here is much in *Bushido* which deserves to be forever recapitulated in the hearts and lives of her youth if Japan is to merit and to maintain her place in 'the Rising Sun' of the world's advancement."[19] Nor was it only missionaries from the U.S. who seemed to approve. *Bushido* turns up in the footnotes of Anesaki Masaharu's famous *History of Japanese Religion* and in a now forgotten work by a colleague at the University of Tokyo, Arthur Lloyd.[20]

Finally, although the reaction against militarism which followed World War II discredited *Bushido*'s martial teachings, the book continued to be read as a guide to traditional manners and customs. One colleague has confessed that he was attracted to Japanese studies through reading *Bushido*, while even more recently comments have appeared in studies which deal with subjects as diverse as pacifism and feminism.[21]

Yet not all readers gave the work unqualified praise. In his standard guide, *Things Japanese*, Basil Hall Chamberlain included it in a list of "Books on Japan," with the following, rather sour, comment: "The work...that has made the most noise of late years is a little volume by Nitobe entitled *Bushido, the Soul of Japan*, which sets forth in popular style the system of practical ethics that guided the conduct of the Samurai of old."[22]

A Canadian missionary, J. C. Robinson, gave it the same kind of left-handed compliment: "During the past few years attention has been called to a teaching called *Bushido* which means literally, 'The Warrior's Way.'...Dr. Nitobe's little book, '*Bushido, the Soul of Japan*,' describes this 'Warrior's Way' in a very interesting though flattering manner."[23] Motivation for the criticisms differed. The missionary, Robinson, preferred a treatment of the subject by a fellow Anglican, Imai Toshimichi, which clearly judged Bushido in more negative terms.[24] Chamberlain, on the other hand, saw Nitobe's romantic portrait as one more element of what he called the New Religion of the Meiji Emperor Cult. His remarks on the subject are worth quoting at some length, not merely because they have been forgotten, but because they reflect a position which aroused some controversy at the time. "As for Bushido," he wrote in 1912:

> so modern a thing is it that neither Kaempfer, Siebold, Satow, nor Rein—all men knowing their Japan by heart—ever once allude to it in their voluminous writings. The cause of their silence is not far to seek: Bushido was unknown until a decade or two ago!
> *The very word appears in no dictionary, native or foreign, before the year 1900.* Chivalrous individuals of course existed in Japan, as in all countries at every period; but Bushido, as an institution or a code of rules, has never existed. The accounts given of it have been fabricated out of whole cloth, chiefly for foreign consumption.[25]

Was Chamberlain right? It would be interesting to trace the history of the term—which certainly appears to have been in its meaning, if not the actual word, part of the ideological armament of the young restorationists who grouped around Yoshida Shôin—but we have neither the space nor the time to do that here. Yuzo Ota has called my attention to an anonymous review of *Bushido* in the English literary journal, *The Athenaeum*, for August 19, 1905. The attitude of the writer reflects Chamberlain's opinion so accurately that it is tempting to conclude that they are one and the same person. Here is the relevant passage:

> The discovery is quite recent. Neither Sir Ernest Satow nor Dr. Aston even mentions the word Bushido; Prof. Chamberlain, in his *Things Japanese* (1898), does not refer to it; the word is not contained in the admirable dictionary prepared by Capt. Brinkley...nor is it to be found in the principal native dictionary, the *Kotoba no Izumi (Source of Language)*."[26]

This opinion provoked a strong refutation from Baron Suyematsu (Kenchô), who quoted from the twelfth-century *Hôgen monogatari*, where the term "Bushi-no-michi (i.e., *Bushido*)" is used.[27] But the reviewer would not be persuaded: "What I wrote about *bushido* is strictly accurate. The word is a new coinage, otherwise as a word it would be in the dictionaries. Baron Suyematsu gives no instance of its older use.... I altogether disbelieve in *bushido*, as described by Prof. Nitobe, being a virtue of old Japan."[28]

Whether right or wrong, Chamberlain certainly convinced other Japanophiles in his day about the correctness of his stand. In another popular work, *Everyday Japan*, the English missionary, educator and student of Buddhism, Arthur Lloyd, writes, "The name is quite new—I never heard it used until a few years ago—but the thing itself is as old as the hills in Japan.... I have found the spirit of *bushido* as strong amongst the young men preparing themselves for business life as amongst the cadets and officers of the Naval Academy."[29]

Characteristically, Lloyd takes a middle-of-the-road position on the technicalities of the argument. But his opinion is useful because it points to a question which, implicitly, worried both Robinson and Chamberlain. Did the romantic view of Bushido implied in Nitobe's exposition lend itself to the encouragement of aggressive nationalism, whether by commercial or militaristic expansion? When Robinson expressed preference for Imai's view of Bushido he probably meant, first and foremost, that Imai stressed the superiority of Christianity over Buddhism. Robinson had no use for Nitobe's liberal eclecticism.[30] But Imai's treatment—though less sophisticated than Nitobe's—has other merits. In the first place, he gives clearer evidence of familiarity with Japanese sources than Nitobe, whose virtuosity depends on wide reading among Western authors. About half of Imai's essay consists in an exposition of Yamaga Sokô's *Shidô*. In the second place, Imai describes the limitations of Bushido much more distinctly than Nitobe. It was developed within a feudal society, so it is now "out of date and New Japan cannot be its second cradle."[31] "The scope of loyalty was narrow," which unfitted it for a society in which a constitutional monarchy and democracy became the norm. Finally, its ethical standards would not stand up in a modern society whose values have been influenced by contact, "directly or indirectly with Christianity through our intercourse with the West."[32] Imai directly contradicts Nitobe's assertion that the Red Cross had succeeded in Japan by the training of the samurai in *nasake* when he states categorically:

> Let us not be misled for a moment into supposing that the Bushido spirit could ever have originated institutions like the Red Cross Society, or could have lifted into principles such ideas as humanity to prisoners, generosity to the conquered, refraining from loot, and respect for female virtue.[33]

Imai nowhere openly criticizes Nitobe's point of view; indeed he never even mentions Nitobe's name. On the whole, their common understanding of the tradition probably outweighed their disagreements. Both acknowledge the feudal origins of Bushido; both agree that only its spirit, in some way transformed by interaction with Christianity, can persist in the New Japan.[34] At that date it is likely that neither foresaw how militarists would use the idea. Perhaps Imai thought, on the whole, that he was supplementing Nitobe's effort by presenting the kind of explanation for British (Anglican) readers that Nitobe had designed for Americans.

This construction would help explain the more negative approach of the English-trained Imai. If Chamberlain and the anonymous *Athenaeum* reviewer represent a trend in the British approach, we might justifiably conclude that they were able, earlier than their counterparts in the United States, to see the dangers inherent in a mode of modernization whose ideology appealed excessively to irrational and nativistic elements in the national heritage. They included the samurai's worship of his sword, or his blind obedience to his overlord. Perhaps the British were reacting to similar elements in their own culture that they had just left behind. Or perhaps, more likely, Japanese imperialism was beginning to threaten their own imperial interests.

Reflections

So in the end we find ourselves forced to confront the contradiction between Nitobe's indigestible nationalism, or closedness, in Bushido, and his longing for a world of international goodwill, or openness. One modern student of his thought, Takeda Kiyoko, has argued that throughout his life Nitobe was quite conscious of the clash between the old and the new. But, unlike some of his contemporaries, who teetered wildly between radicalism and reaction, he chiefly attempted quietly to engraft onto the ancient root of Japan's culture a new growth from the Christian West. *Bushido* (the book), according to Takeda, represented an early experiment with this method. "Today in Japan," she writes:

> [Nitobe] says that Christianity's role is to inherit the spirit of Bushido which, with the end of feudalism,... is left an orphan, fated to fade away. This spirit Christianity will transform into something filled with new life. In effect, he attempts to graft Christianity onto Bushido, whose roots go back to Buddhism, Shinto and Confucianism. He tries to listen quietly to what Buddhism, Shinto, and Confucianism—and Bushido, which has combined their essence—have to say.[35]

If we follow Takeda's analysis, Nitobe's method can be seen to resemble that of the medieval European Catholics like Aquinas, who attempted to graft Christianity onto Teutonic culture. Or, closer to our own day, he anticipates the theologians of dialogue in India and Japan. As such he can be affirmed as a pioneer, ahead of his time. Japan's future, he would say, lies neither in adopting Western ideas undigested and whole, nor in recoiling from their foreignness into some dream-world of a romantic past. There must be a process of interaction, so that something new can be born; a Japan ready to take its place among the family of nations.

This great idealism of Nitobe contained within it one fatal flaw. No society can live by ideas alone. The intellectual cannot function apart from the world of economics and politics, the ever-changing context of historical process. Just as St. Thomas Aquinas' magnificent synthesis became the basis for the fascism of Franco's Spain, so Nitobe's attempt at cultural grafting lent itself to the ideological manipulation of Japanese militarists. So, in the end, Nitobe's loyalty to the state structure of Imperial Japan overcame his dream of a family of nations. We can celebrate that dream as prophecy of things to come. But its fulfillment must await a society in which exploitation and national self-aggrandizement, differences of wealth and poverty, have been overcome, and human beings can with confidence live in peace, without fear.

Notes

1. Nawa Kazuo, trans. and ed., *Bushido* (Tokyo: Rekishi bunkô, 1969), pp. 185–93. This edition carries a memoir by Nitobe's daughter, Koto, which stresses Nitobe's liberalism and conversion to Christianity.

2. Nobuya Bamba and John F. Howes ed., *Pacifism in Japan* (Vancouver: University of British Columbia Press, 1978), p. 7.

3. Sumiya Mikio's original hypothesis on the background of early Christian leaders in *Kindai Nihon no keisei to Kirisutokyô* (1950) was backed up by the empirical study of Kudô Eiichi, *Shodai Nihon purotesutanto no shakaisô* (1949). See also E. E. Best, *Christian Faith and Cultural Crisis, The Japanese Case* (Leiden: E. J. Brill, 1966), p. 95.

4. Takeda Kiyoko terms Uchimura a "confrontative type" (*taigetsugata*). "Kirisutokyô juyô no hôhô to sono kadai," in Takeda Kiyoko ed., *Shisôshi no hôhô to taishô* (Tokyo: Sôbunsha, 1961), p. 280.

5. For Abe, see *Chijô no risôkoku Suisu* (1905), *Gendai Nihon bungaku zenshû* 39; Kinoshita, *Shin Kigen* articles in Sumiya Mikio, *Nihon no shakai shisô* (Tokyo: Tokyo University Press, 1968), pp. 261–71; and Kôtoku, *Nijusseiki no kaibutsu teikokushugi* (1901).

6. For Uchimura, see Ozawa Saburô, *Uchimura Kanzô fukei jiken* (Tokyo: Shinkyô shuppansha, 1961), pp. 52–55. For others, see Kudô Eiichi, *Shakai undô to kirisutokyô* (Tokyo: Nihon YMCA, 1972), Chapter 1.

7. Maruyama Masao, *Gendai seiji no shisô to kôdô* 1 (Tokyo: Miraisha, 1959):123. See also the same author's *Thought and Behaviour in Japanese Politics* (London: Oxford University Press, 1963), pp. 5–8.

8. Harada, "The Development of Matsuri," *Philosophical Studies of Japan* 2 (Tokyo: Japan National Commission for UNESCO, 1961):100. English slightly altered.

9. B. H. Chamberlain, *The Invention of a New Religion* (London: Rationalist Press, 1912), pp. 1–2; and Murakami Shigeyoshi, *Tennô no saishi* (Tokyo: Iwanami shoten, 1977), pp. ii, 65.

10. Kôsaka Masaaki, *Japanese Thought in the Meiji Era* (Tokyo: Ôbunsha, 1958), p. 358.

11. Page and chapter numbers in brackets refer to the edition of 1920 published by Teibi, Tokyo, checked with other editions, mainly the composite edition in *NIZ* 12.

12. Compare the anonymously edited *Manners and Customs of the Japanese* (London, 1841) and many other works, such as Alcock's *Capital of the Tycoon*, 2 vols. (London, 1863).

13. Ruth Benedict, *The Chrysanthemum and the Sword* (Boston: Houghton Mifflin Co., 1946).

14. Epilogue of the German edition of *Representative Men of Japan*, in *UKZ* 3:295.

See also Takeda, *Shisôshi*, p. 292.

15. For a recent example, see Dorothy Robins-Mowry, *The Hidden Sun* (Boulder, Colorado: Westview Press, 1983), p. 21.

16. The phrase forms the title of Chapter 2, Ôta Yûzô, *Eigo to Nihonjin* (Tokyo: TBS-Britannica, 1981), p. 61.

17. Teibi edition, p. ix.

18. *NIZ* 12:17–9.

19. *Religious Values* (Tokyo: Kyobunkwan, 1934), pp. 65–66.

20. (London: Kegan Paul, 1930), p. 264; Arthur Lloyd, *Everyday Japan* (London: Cassell, 1912), p. 15.

21. Bamba and Howes, ed. *Pacifism* (see footnote 1); Robins-Mowry (see footnote 15).

22. 1905 ed., (reprinted by Tuttle Books, 1971), p. 72.

23. *The Island Empire of the East* (Toronto: MSCC, 1912), p. 39.

24. *Ibid.*, pp. 39–40.

25. Chamberlain, *The Invention of a New Religion*, p. 6.

26. *Athenaeum*, August 19, 1905, p. 229.

27. *Athenaeum*, September 2, 1905, pp. 302–3.

28. *Ibid.*, p. 303.

29. Lloyd, *Everyday Japan*, p. 15.

30. Robinson, *Island Empire*, p. 40.

31. Imai Toshimichi, *Bushido: In the Past and in the Present* (Tokyo: Kanazashi, 1906), p. 67.

32. *Ibid.*, p. 71.

33. *Ibid.*, p. 71.

34. For Nitobe, Teibi ed., p. 175; Imai, p. 72.

35. Takeda, "Kirisutokyô juyô," p. 292.

6

Philippine Bushido

Grant K. Goodman

On November 15, 1935, Manuel L. Quezon was inaugurated as President of the Commonwealth of the Philippines. Thus began what was to have been, under the Tydings-McDuffie Act passed by the United States Congress in 1934, a ten-year period leading to full Philippine independence. Although World War II with all of its tragic consequences for the Philippines intervened, on July 4, 1946, the American flag was indeed lowered over the Islands for the last time. Accordingly, the life span of the Commonwealth was fulfilled, and the freedom of the Philippines began.

During the period from November 15, 1935 until the Japanese invasion of January 1942, President Quezon dominated the political life of the Commonwealth. For those six years and nearly three months until his enforced departure for Australia and the United States where he died in 1944, examination of almost any aspect of the Commonwealth requires the closest attention to the multi-faceted and politically astute man in the presidential office at Malacanang. In what follows, an unusual and seemingly peripheral aspect of Quezon's presidential career will be investigated. The purposes of this chapter are: (1) to examine the sources and methods of the intended transposition of the samurai ethic from Japanese society into Philippine society and (2) to enhance an understanding of Quezon's presidency of the Commonwealth as well as of the character and thought of this central figure in modern Philippine history.

As far as I have been able to determine, President Quezon and Nitobe Inazô never met. Yet, as the comments which follow demonstrate, Nitobe's famous and influential volume *Bushido* stimulated and informed the President's intriguing attempt to engender a Philippine Bushido. As I have already demonstrated in previous writings, Quezon had admired Japan and its society for a long time.[1] Nevertheless, not unlike many others among the Filipino colonial elite, and despite the relative geographic proximity of Japan, he knew little of Japan. Among the limiting factors were the language barrier, the traditional Euro-American, i.e., non-Asian, orientation of Philippine intellectual life, the general lack of in-depth, direct, personal contact with Japan and, probably most significant, the seemingly purposeful effort of the American colonial authorities to encourage Filipino mistrust of Japan.

In the latter instance, almost since annexation, the Americans had, to their embarrassment and consternation, increasingly recognized that the Philippines were indefensible. Given that recognition and the growing concern that Japan was the only identifiable potential invader in the Pacific region, the American colonial government increasingly worried about possible Japanese subversion of the Filipinos. Therefore, the Americans were not at all averse to scare tactics and rumormongering among the Filipino populace about the Japanese "threat."

In this context, then, up to the beginning of the Commonwealth, Japan's diplomats in the Philippines acted generally with care and circumspection. From 1935 on, in contrast, the Japanese readily accepted the new facts of international life which portended, in effect, the elimination of American power from the Philippines and consequently from the Western Pacific. Accordingly, they became far more active politically, economically and culturally in the Philippines and significantly helped raise "Japan consciousness." Quezon himself, in addition to his extensive local contacts with Japanese businessmen and consular officials, visited Japan twice: January 31–February 2, 1937 and June 29–July 10, 1938.[2]

Quezon's flirtation with Bushido seems to have resulted from a variety of factors. Of crucial importance was the growing predominance of Japanese power in Asia. In addition, the image of the Japanese people as diligent, disciplined, and patriotic was not only given the widest publicity by official Japanese pronouncements but was reinforced by observation of Japanese who lived and worked in the Philippines. On several occasions, Quezon himself had seen in Japan at first hand the apparently unstinting devotion to work and to country that the Japanese citizenry exemplified. With independence scheduled for 1946, Quezon deplored what he termed the "eroding" effects on the national Filipino character of four centuries of Spanish and American colonial rule. Quezon committed himself to revitalize and to refurbish Filipino ethics and morals in order to articulate a new national identity, and in this context what he believed to be the Japanese ethos was to play a central role.

Of course, he also found that Bushido, as officially propagated by the Japanese in the 1930s, could be utilized to reinforce the increasingly authoritarian Quezon presidency. Quezon probably also understood how potentially flattering to the Japanese it would be for him to call for a Philippine version of Bushido—whether, in fact, one existed or not. Or Quezon may have considered none of these factors. He may simply have proclaimed the need for an indigenous Bushido with no rationale at all. In his characteristically unpredictable, mercurial way he may have called for a Philippine Bushido on a whim with no specific, long-range plan.

As has been generally recognized, Bushido is essentially a relatively modern term that encompasses certain rules of conduct which evolved among the samurai or warrior class in Japan. Bushido came to be a collection of precepts with elements of Buddhism, Confucianism, Shinto, and Japanese folk traditions. It emphasized ethical and practical personal concerns such as honor, loyalty, and frugality. In a larger sense, Bushido sought to codify the ideal of total self-discipline and of unquestioned commitment to one's duty. After the Meiji Restoration in 1868, a kind of national Bushido was propagated through ethics courses in the new national public school system. In the twentieth century, the government sought to utilize Bushido to inculcate nationalistic, patriotic values and to mold a totally loyal citizenry.

The earliest Philippine advocate of Bushido seems to have been Jorge Bocobo, Dean of the College of Law in the University of the Philippines in 1934 and Secretary of Public Instruction in 1939. He is described by one author as "an almost fanatical *independista* and a political innocent"[3] and identified by another as "Bushido Bocobo."[4] Bocobo had been interested in Japan at least since his attendance, as a member of the Philippine delegation, at the Kyoto Institute of Pacific Relations conference in 1929. There Bocobo met Nitobe who chaired the Japanese delegation. Bocobo's favorable personal impression of Nitobe seems to have reinforced his desire to make Filipinos more familiar with the Bushido Nitobe had described.

Perhaps Bocobo's major public statement on Bushido is contained in an address he gave to the Philippine Association for Oriental Affairs, June 24, 1936, some seven months after Quezon's inauguration as Commonwealth President. In that speech[5] Bocobo began by calling Bushido "the inspiration of Japanese life" and "the source of Japan's strength as one of the great powers of the modern world." Then, in a lengthy quotation from Nitobe, whom Bocobo called "the greatest authority on this subject," Bocobo explained that Bushido was a remarkable unwritten code of moral principles which the samurai had been required to observe and which had evolved through the course of Japanese history.

Bocobo then emphasized what he believed to be the significance of Bushido for the Filipinos: "the secret of the strength and power of the great neighboring empire." He also exhorted his audience on the need to understand Japanese institutions because of "the close ethnical relations between the Japanese and the Malay races." According to Bocobo, these "relations" were evidenced by the facts that the Japanese "race" was of Malay origin, that the Japanese house was suited to a tropical climate, and that Japanese and Filipinos shared similar physical characteristics and traits.

In more detail, Bocobo analyzed the respective contribution of Shinto ("ancestor-worship" and "worship of nature"), Buddhism ("serenity in the face of tragedy or death"), and Confucianism ("family solidarity") to Bushido. He followed this with a discussion of the essentials of Bushido: honor, loyalty, bravery, calmness and courtesy. He again freely quoted Nitobe and also Lafcadio Hearn as he illustrated his points with appropriate examples: the suicide of General Nogi and his wife; the hara-kiri of the Forty-seven Ronin; and the suicide of a young man at the U.S. Embassy in Tokyo to protest the American Immigration Act of 1924. Interestingly, too, he equated Bushido's self-restraint and self-discipline with "resignation to the decrees of fate," and he argued that such "fatalism" was "an ancient Malay characteristic which is still seen among the masses of the Filipino people." He also contended that a significant aspect of Japanese courtesy was never to "give an unpleasant answer or make an outright refusal," a custom which he found very much analogous to Filipino "circumlocution."

The concluding section of Bocobo's lecture dealt with lessons Filipinos could learn from a study of Japan's Bushido. He found two overriding needs which it might meet. The first was the "urgent and imperative need of intensely cultivating social discipline" among Filipinos, and the second was the concurrent and equally urgent necessity to develop national loyalty. In both instances Bocobo stated that American-style individualism had corroded traditional Philippine values and must be suppressed in favor of greater state control which would result, as in Italy, Germany and Japan, in the "supreme good of the entire people."

Bocobo's comments can be interpreted in a variety of ways. Undoubtedly he had been deeply impressed by contemporary Japan as he knew it, both from his own observations and from Nitobe's writings. Moreover, with the significant growth of Japanese interest in the Philippines as independence neared, it must surely have seemed prudent to Bocobo that the islands draw closer to Japan both economically and culturally. Too, Bocobo was by no means alone in his disparagement of the Filipino "lack of social discipline," a phenomenon frequently noted by both native and foreign observers. Perhaps more significant than any of these factors was the support in Bocobo's speech for greater state control and implicitly, therefore, for President Quezon. Here one can discern the real crux of Bocobo's message. It can be understood to combine a sycophantic touting of Quezon as "El Supremo" for the Philippines with a faddish attempt to equate Quezon with that peculiar authoritarian triumvirate of the 1930s—Hitler, Mussolini and Emperor Hirohito. Bocobo had already advocated the previous year a Filipino-style fascism and militarism. He seems, therefore, to have promoted Bushido with all of its Japanese allusions as a smoke-screen to facilitate a more dictatorial regime under Quezon's leadership.

In December 1936, Professor Sugimori Kôjirô of Waseda University arrived in Manila at the University of the Philippines as a short-term exchange professor.[6] Professor Sugimori lectured publicly in English on a variety of topics about Japan. If there was a single central theme to his presentations, it was that Japan's parliamentary system had become outmoded and now required a more rigid internal structure. Similarly, Sugimori suggested that the Philippines too needed a stronger, more centralized government to unify its people through patriotic nationalism. That Sugimori's words corresponded well with Bocobo's particular appreciation of Bushido was evident, and, after Sugimori left the islands, Bocobo himself expressed fulsome praise to the president of Waseda University for Sugimori's "admirable scholarship, profound thought and charming personality."[7]

From June 29, to July 10, 1938, President Quezon was in Japan, for the last, and longest, and perhaps the most important of his visits.[8] In addition to the complex diplomatic maneuverings which took up much of Quezon's time, the very inclement weather kept him in Kyoto from June 29 to the morning of July 7. During those eight days in the Kansai, the Philippine president had time to investigate contemporary Japanese life and to observe at first hand Japanese hotels, restaurants, factories, and neighborhoods. Quezon's reaction to all this was epitomized by a Japanese companion, a close friend, who attributed the following words to him:

> Over the past twenty years, I have gone back and forth between the Philippines and the United States some twenty times, and I have met and exchanged views with Japanese politicians and leading figures and have become intimate with them. But on these occasions, I have gone from Kobe harbor to Yokohama harbor and have had no opportunity to have contact with the general public. Nor have I seen any factories. This time I have achieved both purposes, and I have marvelled at the solid society of Japan. I have been surprised by the high level of the economy and the spread of education and culture. Outside of the social and economic tensions of activating a million soldiers, I have seen nothing out of the ordinary. Everyone is hard working.[9]

Quezon was also to comment later in Tokyo that after extensive contact with "both the middle class and the broad mass of the populace" he was "delighted and satisfied."[10]

Still later in Manila, the president told the press that he had "never made a more profitable trip to Japan than this one" since he had been able to see how the Japanese worked and lived. "This is not for publication, gentlemen. I am really an admirer of the Japanese more than ever." He commended their commitment to work and the way they went about it, and he raved about how they educated their population for "useful citizenship," to say nothing of their "gentlemanliness and courtesy." "I have been in

Japan a million times," he said, "but I have not known her people as I did in my last trip. "[11]

In the seemingly euphoric context of his very recent excursion to Japan, on August 19, 1938, the President of the Commonwealth of the Philippines himself publicly announced his own commitment to Bushido. It was his sixtieth birthday. Some fifty thousand students and teachers gathered for the occasion in Rizal Memorial Stadium heard him speak of the great need to revive the national spirit. Quezon bemoaned the loss of the ideals of such heroes of the Philippine struggle for freedom as José Rizal and Apolinario Mabini. He warned that a true national spirit could only develop from each man's character, and to that end he emphasized the need to rebuild the national character of Filipino citizens. According to Quezon, self-discipline, productive labor, a sense of responsibility, cooperation and civic virtue could only be instilled in the Filipino citizenry by the formulation and indoctrination of a social code of ethics and personal conduct, what he called "a written Bushido." In an emotional plea he called on all Filipinos to follow with him such a code and to work with him in its context to achieve national regeneration.

Japanese reaction to Quezon's call for a Philippine Bushido was, perhaps predictably, positive. Manila Consul General Kihara Jitarô was quoted in the local press as saying that it could indeed regenerate the Philippines.[12] Privately Kihara was even more enthusiastic; he told the Foreign Ministry in Tokyo that what Quezon covertly intended to convey was that "Japan's Bushido must be the basis of the education of Filipino citizens."[13]

Reaction in the Philippine press to the Quezon "Bushido speech" was generally unenthusiastic. *The Commonwealth*, a local organ of Catholic Action, objected to the President's reference to Bushido and suggested that the Ten Commandments and the Sermon on the Mount would be a sounder foundation for Filipino moral regeneration than "going back to the pagans of ancient Japan."[14] *The Commonwealth Advocate* criticized Quezon's allusion to Bushido as a "jarring note" in an otherwise "eloquent and effective speech."[15] The pro-American *Philippine Magazine* stated that "it is well to bring out how utterly foreign Bushido actually is to what President Quezon so earnestly wished for the people."[16]

In an editorial which condemned any attempt to impose Bushido on the Philippines, the same *Philippine Magazine* stressed the cruel and scornful samurai attitude toward the common folk in traditional Japan. As practitioners of Bushido, it said, samurai also felt contempt for all "bread-winning pursuits" and for any material enterprise and gain. Moreover, they gambled, brawled, engaged in "Greek friendship," and killed themselves pointlessly. The *Philippine Magazine* concluded pejoratively that contemporary Bushido had been the principal instrument in the "progressive enslavement of the disciplined and docile people of Japan to the new fascism."[17]

Apparently unmoved by such criticisms, Quezon once more focused on the need for a spiritual revival among Filipinos in a speech on August 24, 1938. In this instance he urged his fellow citizens to pay their taxes honestly and patriotically. He held up to them the shining example of the willing Japanese support of their government despite the painfully heavy burden it imposed on them.[18]

The following month, September 1938, Quezon announced the dispatch of Assemblyman Camilo Osias to learn about education in Japan, the United States and Europe. It was thought that Osias was being groomed as the next Secretary of Public Instruction, and the trip seemed designed to prepare him for that post. In particular, he was to spend his time in Japan immersing himself in Bushido. In his column "So It Seems" in the *Philippines Herald*, Salvador P. Lopez greeted the news of Osias's trip with the following pointed words:

> It is hard to place democratic American-trained Mr. Osias in any scheme similar to Bushido, but that I suppose does not matter. I was only thinking of inviting him, after he returns from Japan, to go with me back to Ilocos where we both came from, there to learn something about the fine old ways of our fathers.[19]

Osias was accompanied on his trip by Dr. Mauro Baradi, a long-time Pan-Asianist and Osias's former secretary when Osias had been Philippine Resident Commissioner in Washington. He was also accompanied by Marcelino Bautista, Assistant Superintendent of Schools in Manila. After one month in the Kanto and Kansai studying the Japanese educational system, Bautista wrote:

> While I was staying in Japan…my deepest impression was of the people's unbending and unremitting diligence. Viewed from the standpoint of patriotism and national progress, this is what has made Japan strong. Although this is a fact, one must know the culture of Japan for hundreds of years past and the educational system which has inculcated a spirit of national ethics into the Japanese people.[20]

In the course of his trip in December 1938, Camilo Osias himself addressed a lengthy letter marked "CONFIDENTIAL" to President Quezon from Reno, Nevada.[21] Osias reported that the culmination of his educational study tour would be to formulate for the Philippines a regenerated social philosophy which would be embodied in a proposed seventeen-chapter volume to be titled *The Pluralized Universe or the Filipino Way of Life*. In a specific reference to Bushido, Osias stated: "The Bushido, good as some of its features are, is unfit and inadequate for Filipino life. I am not saying it is not or has not been good for Japan, but many of the thinkers with whom I have discussed acknowledge its inadequacy even for Japan and Japanese life today."

In an attached outline of his proposed seventeen-chapter tract, Osias, perhaps for Quezon's benefit, listed Bushido and *kôdô*, (the Imperial Way) as a subtopic in Chapter II, "Pluralized Social Philosophy." In Chapter IX, "Spiritual Regeneration and Social Reconstruction," Osias included among the topics to be discussed "Studying the Spirits of Peoples" and "Examples of Other Peoples" as well as "President Quezon's Birthday Speech Stressing Spiritual Revival." Osias's previous education and experience made him uneasy with Japanese values; he appears to have wanted, however crudely, to work out a unique Filipino social philosophy which would neither derive from nor depend upon Japanese Bushido.

Bushido was once again a matter for public discussion in the Philippines when, on a visit to Manila in January and February 1939, Prof. Negishi Yoshitarô of Rikkyô University gave a series of lectures on things Japanese before both academic and non-academic audiences.[22] Perhaps the high point of his visit was a speech on February 21, 1939, at the University of the Philippines: "Japan and the Real Spirit of Bushido." Surely members of his audience remembered President Quezon's birthday address the preceding August, and it may not have been simply coincidence that Prof. Negishi held forth once more on Bushido at the University of the Philippines.

On his return to Tokyo, Prof. Negishi summarized his impressions of the Philippines in a talk on April 17, 1939, at the Pan Pacific Institute of Tokyo. In particular, Negishi praised President Quezon, saying that he was in the mold of Japan's Meiji leaders and that he should certainly be made president for life. According to him, Quezon truly understood Bushido and the spirit of Japan as the basis of Japan's strength. Moreover, Quezon in his great wisdom intended to give the Filipinos their own Bushido in order to try to achieve a similar spiritual quality among his own people.

On August 19, 1939, Quezon's 61st birthday and exactly one year after his call for a Philippine Bushido at the University of the Philippines, the president issued Executive Order No. 217 which provided for the establishment of a national ethical code. This document stated that it was being promulgated in accordance with Article 13, Section 5 of the Philippine Constitution which read in part:

> All educational institutions shall be under the supervision of and subject to regulation by the State. The Government shall establish and maintain a complete and adequate system of public education, and shall provide at least free public primary instruction, and citizenship training to adult citizens. All schools shall aim to develop moral character, and vocational efficiency, and to teach the duties of citizenship.

The new code sought to implement the last sentence by the creation of a kind of Philippine Bushido. It contained sixteen essential points:[23]

1. Have faith in Divine Providence that guides the destinies of men and nations.
2. Love your country, for it is the home of your people, the seat of your affections, and the source of your happiness and well-being. Its defense is your primary duty. Be ready at all times to sacrifice and die for it if necessary.
3. Respect the Constitution which is the expression of your sovereign will. The government is your government. It has been established for your safety and welfare. Obey the laws and see that they are observed by all and that public officials comply with their duties.
4. Pay your taxes willingly and promptly. Citizenship implies not only rights but also obligations.
5. Safeguard the purity of suffrage and abide by the decisions of the majority.
6. Love and respect your parents. It is your duty to serve them gratefully and well.
7. Value your honor as you value your life. Poverty with honor is preferable to wealth and dishonor.
8. Be truthful and be honest in thought and in action. Be just and charitable, courteous but dignified in your dealings with your fellow men.
9. Lead a clean and frugal life. Do not indulge in frivolity or pretense. Be simple in your dress and modest in your behavior.
10. Live up to the noble traditions of our people. Venerate the memory of our heroes. Their lives point the way to duty and honor.
11. Be industrious. Be not afraid or ashamed to do manual labor. Productive toil is conducive to economic security and adds to the wealth of the nation.
12. Rely on your own efforts for your progress and happiness. Be not easily discouraged. Persevere in the pursuit of your legitimate ambitions.
13. Do your work cheerfully, thoroughly, and well. Work badly done is worse than work undone. Do not leave for tomorrow what you can do today.
14. Contribute to the welfare of your community and promote social justice. You do not live for yourselves and your families alone. You are a part of society to which you owe definite responsibilities.
15. Cultivate the habit of using goods made in the Philippines. Patronize the products and trades of your countrymen.
16. Use and develop our natural resources and conserve them for pos-

terity. They are the inalienable heritage of our people. Do not traffic with your citizenship.

Many of the elements in this code reflected real and continuing problems in Philippine life. Consular Assistant Itô Take of the Consulate General in Manila chose, when he conveyed the document to Foreign Minister Matsuoka Yôsuke, to emphasize its dependence on Japanese precedence: "This national moral code has been established after the president's frequent visits to Japan over the years and his taking hints from Bushido which provides Japan's spiritual guidance."[24] Clearly, Itô was right. There are many clear evidences of influences from Nitobe's Bushido, or at least Nitobe's Bushido as understood by Quezon.

To describe the Philippines in patriotic proto-familial terms as in item number two was, of course, an attempt to transpose Japanese national proto-familism into a Philippine context. Stating that the citizen must at all times be ready to lay down his life for his country reflects the Filipino impression of both the pre- and post-Meiji essence of Bushido. That the citizen must pay taxes "willingly and promptly" (No. 4) evidences both the traditional Filipino failure to do just that and Quezon's reiterated belief that in Japan citizens did pay their taxes "willingly and promptly." The concept that citizenship encompasses obligations (No. 4) seems to come right out of the Imperial Japanese Constitution of 1889. The Confucian-based Bushido ethic of filial piety is surely one of the sources of the code's provision that one must "love and respect" one's parents (No. 6). Moreover, throughout the code such qualities as honor, fidelity, courtesy, frugality, duty and loyalty (Nos. 7, 8, 9, 10, etc.), which were integral to the newly proclaimed Filipino ethic, were all equally integral to Bushido.

In his analysis of these new ethics as promoted by Quezon, Consular Assistant Itô found two other elements of significance in the document in addition to its derivations from Bushido. First, he attributed the code's structure and promulgation to the individualism of the Filipino, to what he saw as the Philippine lack of a sense of responsibility, to what he described as the eroding moral effects in the Philippines of American-sponsored "freedom and hedonism"; and to a Filipino world of "indolence and pleasure."[25] Second, Itô depicted this new code of national ethics as the "premise for preparing a new national structure" by which he appears to have meant a much more authoritarian Quezonian state. Moreover, Itô understood the whole effort of the Philippine government on behalf of "national spirit training" to aim at the reform of the existing American-inspired educational system. For him, a "reformed" educational system was part of Quezon's growing tendency to reinforce his own total dominance of the government and of Philippine life. Both President Quezon and Consular Assistant Itô appear to have viewed Philippine-style Bushido as an essential ingredient to increase popular Filipino support for a more rigid, more centralized, and more authoritarian regime in the Islands, one that depended less on American democratic ideas.[26]

When one asks what role Nitobe's *Bushido* played in this little drama, it might be useful to recall the proverbial remark attributed to supporters of free speech: "No woman was ever seduced by a book." In like manner, no nation or its leaders were ever "subverted" by a book. I certainly do not hold that *Bushido* was intended as a textbook to create or reinforce authoritarianism, but the Philippine leaders in the particular political climate of the 1930s wanted to use it that way. In the context of Japan's increasingly active economic, political, and cultural activities, Nitobe's work importantly influenced their ideas.

Interestingly written, articulate and easily accessible, *Bushido* more than any other book explained Japanese "thought" to readers of English at the time. Nitobe's Christianity gave him a further patina of authority in communicating Japanese values to Filipinos, as did his frequent references to and quotations from a very extensive and impressive spectrum of Western sources in mythology, history, literature, and religion.

The Japanese propagation of Bushido as a quasi-philosophy to undergird an increasingly activist Japanese foreign policy developed significantly after Nitobe's death in 1933. For a nation which in Akira Iriye's words was handicapped by a "paucity of ideology," Bushido served a useful purpose. That the most useful expression of Bushido appeared in a popular and widely read volume written in English by a Japanese intellectual increased its appeal to Japanese officials.

As we have seen, this coincidence appeared equally fortuitous to the elite rulers of the Philippines, the first Asian colony scheduled for independence. Quezon and his supporters perceived that the departure of the Americans endangered the order and authority which underpinned their control of the Islands. Bushido could at least partially assure domestic control and international respectability.

The 1935 Sakdal uprising had already revealed the extent of agrarian unrest and frustration in the Philippines. That outbreak had been quickly contained and suppressed by the American-directed colonial constabulary. There was no assurance that after independence greater or more widespread unrest would not occur; nor was there any certainty that, if there were a recurrence of such phenomena, they could be stopped as quickly or as forcefully without an American presence. The major factor to consider after independence seemed to be Philippine economic growth via trade and investment as well as Philippine security. Both would intimately involve the Philippine relationship with Japan. Accordingly, in both respects the appearance of a so-called Philippine Bushido could serve the newly independent state extremely well: The central government would be given new strength by means of a national ethical code based on Bushido, and Japan would surely better tolerate and respect the first nation outside its own empire to give such stature to Bushido.

In such circumstances Nitobe's writings played only a coincidental role. Yet Philippine Bushido would probably have not developed as it did if Nitobe's *Bushido* had not been so popular and respected. It was the only source of Bushido which could either have inspired the new Philippine ethical code or could have laid the foundation for closer Philippine-Japanese diplomatic ties.

Thus, the real importance of Japanese Bushido to the Philippines, derived in large measure from the ideas of Nitobe, lies in Quezon's effort to utilize what he perceived to be its contribution to the authoritarian structure of Japanese governance and its potential similar contribution to the Philippines. We cannot know the true root of Quezon's interest in Bushido, yet Bushido seems to have provided one more among Quezon's many other efforts to reinforce his power after November 1935. He made no secret of his admiration for Mussolini, Hitler, Franco, *and* the Japanese. Since Quezon ruled a country still officially under the American flag and dependent on American support, he could not blatantly take up fascism or Nazism. Bushido, with its less obvious political character, with its Asian origins and with its uniquely Japanese history and quasi-philosophy was far more attractive. Given the realities of the international scene in the late 1930s and the concurrent desirability for both a stronger Philippine national identity and strengthened Philippine leadership, a new Filipino ethical and spiritual code derived from Bushido was not then perhaps as strange or as obscure as it may seem now.

Notes

1. See my "The Problem of Philippine Independence and Japan: The First Three Decades of American Colonial Rule," *Southeast Asia: An International Quarterly* 1, no. 3, (Summer 1971):164–90; "Manuel L. Quezon in Tokyo, 1937," *Bulletin of the American Historical Collections* 10, no. 2 (39), (April–June 1982): 60–71; "Manuel L. Quezon's Visit to Japan, June 29–July 10, 1939," in *Four Aspects of Philippine-Japanese Relations, 1930–1940* (New Haven: Yale University Southeast Asia Program, 1967), pp. 195–237; "Consistency Is the Hobgoblin: Manuel L. Quezon and Japan, 1899–1934," *Journal of Southeast Asian Studies* 14, no. 1, (March 1983): 79–93.

2. These visits are described in detail in my "Manuel L. Quezon in Tokyo, 1937," and "Manuel L. Quezon's Visit to Japan, June 29–July 10, 1938."

3. J. R. Hayden, *The Philippines: A Study in National Development* (New York: Macmillan, 1950), p. 349.

4. Otani Jun'ichi, ed., *Philippine Yearbook* (Kobe: Tanaka, 1937), p. 240.

5. "Bushido" An address before the Philippine Association for Oriental Affairs, June 24, 1936 by President Jorge Bocobo. Papers of Jorge Bocobo, Library of the University of the Philippines, Quezon City, Philippines.

6. For details see my "Philippine-Japanese Professorial Exchanges in the 1930s," *Journal of Southeast Asian History* 9, no. 2, (September 1968): 229–40.
7. *Ibid.*, p. 234.
8. For details see my "Manuel L. Quezon's Visit to Japan, June 29–July 10, 1938."
9. *Ibid.*, p. 209.
10. *Ibid.*, p. 215.
11. *Ibid.*, p. 229.
12. *Philippines Free Press*, September 3, 1939.
13. Japan, Ministry of Foreign Affairs, A.6.0.0.1.-33, August 20, 1938 (hereafter cited as *JMFA* plus the number, date, and classification if given.)
14. Quoted in *Philippine Magazine* 25, September 9, 1938, p. 415.
15. *Ibid.*
16. *Ibid.*
17. *Ibid.*, p. 416.
18. *JMFA*, A.6.0.0.1-33, August 25, 1938. In code.
19. *Philippines Herald*, September 28, 1938, p. 4.
20. *Hirippin Jôhô* 23 (January 27, 1939), p. 59. The involvement of the Commonwealth leadership with Bushido was even apparent to a visiting member of the Tokyo Giants baseball team who quoted Executive Secretary Jorge B. Vargas as telling him: "We intend to base our new Bushido in the Philippines on Japanese as teachers." Ichioka Tadao, "Philippine Impressions," *Hirippin Jôhô* 33 (February 28, 1940), p. 62.
21. Contents of letter found in Papers of Manuel L. Quezon, National Library, Manila, Philippines.
22. See my "Philippine-Japanese Professorial Exchanges," pp. 235–36.
23. Quoted in Hayden, *The Philippines*, pp. 926–27 and found in Japanese in *JMFA* A.6.0.0.1-33, October 23, 1940.
24. *JMFA* A.6.0.0.1-33, October 23, 1940.
25. In August 1939, concurrent with the promulgation of the new code Paul Rodriquez Verzosa, Professor of Ethics, Centro Escolar University, spoke at Far Eastern University to the students of Philippine History and Culture. According to Verzosa, "Japan is unconquerable because she has a mighty spirit of endurance, patience and sagacity which her people have inherited from their great knights of chivalry known in history as the wonderful samurais." Verzosa contended that the spirit of Bushido produced in Japan "cohesive nationalism and patriotism" and exhorted his young audience to "hold in esteem the influence of the Bushido, at least in its Filipino version, for its moral power is already tested...and in consonance with Bushido let us try to build up the structure of a Filipino code of ethical standards, call it anything, so long [as] we can have a virile youth, a powerful race, a country of which you and your children will be proud, a radiant Philippines." Paul R. Verzosa, *Our Moral Code in the Light of Bushido* (Manila: 1940), pp. 5, 8, 11.
26. Quezon's borrowings from Japan in order to reinforce his personal rule were not limited to Bushido. Just before Christmas of 1939, in front of a specially invited audience of his cabinet members, their families and other dignitaries at Arayat, Pampanga, the president ceremonially harvested rice which had been planted the preceding July. Having been in Japan the first week in July when the Emperor ceremonially planted rice, Quezon was so impressed by the panoply and symbolism

that he sought to develop a similar ritual for himself. As with the Emperor of Japan, the purpose of such a ceremony for the president of the Philippines, in his own view, was to force him to think of and identify with the toiling masses. The Japanese-owned O'Racca Confectionary Co. of Manila printed as its 1939 Christmas calendar for 1940 50,000 copies of the picture of Quezon ceremonially laboring in the rice fields. The legend under the picture read: *THE DIGNITY OF LABOR.*

7

Toward Remaking Manliness

Donald Roden

Whenever and wherever it occurred, the industrial revolution produced a crisis of masculine identity, particularly among the members of social elites. In the pre-industrial world, the validation of manhood was inseparable from the validation of hereditary status. It was clear, absolute, and, to a varying extent, based upon physical prowess. Physicality, of course, was of paramount importance in defining the role of the peasants and other manual laborers; but among aristocrats as well, the skillful use of arms complemented the literary sensibilities of the ideal man or "gentleman" as he was defined by Castiglione, Richard Brathwaite, and, for that matter, Yamaga Sokô. In both Tokugawa Japan and old-regime France, the gentlemanly ideal represented a convergence of the "nobility of the sword" and the "nobility of the robe." The industrial revolution robbed the late-feudal aristocracies of their traditional sources of political authority and masculine validation. For the privileges that went with the sword, the ultimate emblem of manhood in preindustrial societies, and hereditary status were forfeited by the middle of the nineteenth century to make way for a new middle class of self-made men. Their claims to status and manhood rested squarely on an amoral quest for academic degrees. The question thus arose: If the ideal of manliness served a useful moral and social purpose, and if those young leaders who had once been entrusted with its preservation had now disappeared, then how could a group of middle-class achievers stand for an ethic of manliness without the aid of sword or benefice? This was a question that concerned a number of late Meiji and Taishô intellectuals, but few approached the problem with the breadth of understanding, the deeply personal intuition, and, yes, the frustrating inconsistency of Nitobe Inazô.

Here we examine Nitobe's conceptions of manliness and femininity as reflected in writings from his school-day letters to the "editorial jottings" of his twilight years. Of course a conception of sex role is inseparable from the sexuality of the person who is doing the conceiving. Accordingly, I propose to consider first the problem of manliness in Nitobe's own youthful development. Here our attention will embrace the murky realm of the unconscious about which my evidence is far from conclusive. In the second section, emphasis will shift to Nitobe's cognitive understanding of manliness from his perspective as an educator or moral ideologue. Nitobe the educator was primarily interested in promoting an "ethic of character" among new-middle-class youth, and his metaphors for this task presumed a bipolar view of manliness and femininity. Nitobe's fundamental concern as a late-Meiji moralist with character building did not prevent him from a less strident exploration of personality. Section three considers the tensions between Nitobe's "masculine" ethic of character and his "feminine" interest in personality. Finally, I consider some of the broader implications of the masculine/feminine dialectic in Nitobe's thought, especially as it relates to an evolution in history.

Nitobe's Early Years of Maternal Influence

Writing on the basis of his own experience, Nitobe's *Bushido* later defined the largely unconscious and intuitively inherited code of ethics representing "the apotheosis of strong manhood and of all manly qualities."[1] The irony of Nitobe's "Bushido upbringing" was that the "manly qualities" of the samurai emanated more from his mother than from his father. Not that the latter lacked hardness. Nitobe's father and grandfather were men of courage and foresight, who, in their devotion to opening new lands and enterprises in northeastern Japan, radiated a pioneer spirit. Jûjirô, Nitobe's father, is described as a man whose "restless energy outran the thought and comprehension of his generation," and indeed, on at least two occasions, he was placed under house arrest for exercising unruly independence.[2] Unable to collaborate with any superior, Jûjirô opened his own martial arts academy on the grounds of the Nitobe home. There, according to Inazô, he taught his students the importance of swordless combat, for "a true warrior should by sheer strength of will...so strike terror into his opponent as to subdue him without striking a blow." Thus Inazô's earliest childhood was spent in a fearful environment of "ear-rending grunts and uncanny gestures and grimaces of hypnotic intent."[3]

For all of his robust spirit, Jûjirô's influence on his youngest son was minimized by his premature death in 1867. Moreover, even during his final years, Jûjirô's awesome presence coupled with his erratic and sometimes explosive temperament apparently intimidated young Inazô, who clung to his mother, Seki, while his father grunted and groaned in the judo hall next to the house. From earliest infancy until the age of four or five, Nitobe rarely left his mother's side. He slept next to her and seemed especially possessive when, for example, a younger niece threatened to usurp his cherished spot.[4] Even by late Tokugawa standards, Fujinaga Tamotsu notes, Nitobe was weaned at a late age, perhaps not until he entered school.[5] The all-consuming relationship between Inazô and Seki was further intensified by the sudden loss of Jûjirô, although the thrust of that relationship changed significantly. Now Seki took it upon herself to perform the active role of father to Inazô, a role which Jûjirô had never really fulfilled. When Nitobe turned six, the year for initiation to young manhood and samurai status, Seki presented her son with his first sword. "She presided over this masculine ceremony in the absence of my father," Nitobe explained, and she impressed upon her son the supreme importance of the sword and the values of honor, courage, and righteousness that it symbolized. So much did she impress Nitobe that, when he was forced to relinquish his sword in 1872, he admitted that "not only did my loins feel lonely, but I was literally low in spirit."[6] Three years after Inazô's investiture, Seki sent him with his elder brother Michirô to Tokyo. Just before their departure, she warned her sons that, as Mary Nitobe put it, "unless they lived worthily of their father, they could not see her face again." Though Seki's stoic air, her intolerance for whining and her single-minded dedication won her a reputation as a woman who was "more than a man,"[7] her qualities of love and affection did not suddenly disappear. A close reading of her letters to Inazô reveals an unceasing maternal warmth, accompanied by an equal determination not to let her personal attachment interfere with her son's academic achievement.

Although Nitobe lived apart from his mother for the remainder of her life, she continued to be the most important person in his own life. In his reminiscences of study in Tokyo in the 1870s, Nitobe confided that his "frequent epistles from Mother" constituted the one source "of all my inspiration." "From the age of 8 to 18," he later explained, "my mother's heart somehow pressed upon me." Not surprisingly, then, that when Seki died in 1880, Nitobe, who was already prone to mental letdowns, fell into what Takagi Yasaka calls a state of "depressive psychosis."[8] The boundaries of identification between mother and son had become so intermeshed and for such an extended time, that for Nitobe, Seki's death was tantamount to the death of his vital spirit. The failure to see his mother since his original departure from Morioka nine years earlier weighed heavily on Nitobe, and for the remainder of his life, he berated himself for missed opportunities.

The severity of Nitobe's depression after his mother's death is suggested in several letters from his close friend, Uchimura Kanzô. In one dated August 3, 1880, Uchimura counseled:

> Be not, brother, overwhelmed with grief, because it is a great injury to your health.... Your deceased mother cares for your health [more] than she did for

her own body. Be courageous and try to become a strong and healthy man, and endeavor to please your departed parents by good and serviceable works for your country.

In another letter to a mutual friend, Uchimura confided that time spent with Inazô was extremely trying. "His gloomy and reflecting habits made him exceedingly sorrowful, and I was unable to console him with all my might."[9]

With the help of his friends and, according to Nitobe, a close reading of Carlyle's *Sartor Resartus*, Nitobe did finally break out of his first depression. But his mental health remained precarious for years to come, and a prolonged nervous breakdown in 1897–98 forced him to resign his professorship at Sapporo Agricultural College. The resurfacing of Nitobe's brooding tendencies often coincided with haunting memories of his mother and fears that he was not living up to her expectations. At least once every year he would take out a scroll which contained all of her letters to him and mentally devour them one by one. Reflecting on this ritual in 1905, Nitobe said:

> As I ponder her words, I become more and more aware of my shortcomings, for, without reproof, she ennobles me. As the scroll of letters unrolls, the five and twenty years that have elapsed since she last trod this earth merge into the living present and I feel her soft hand, hear her sweet voice, and listen to her step on the 'conscious floor.' The mysterious power of memory brushes away not only the present but the last quarter of a century, making me live again the time when I was still a boy and my mother in the prime of womanhood.... Such strange power has a mother's love![10]

This quite revealing passage underscores the depth of Nitobe's maternal attraction. Since he had never seen his mother after the age of nine, there were no adult or even adolescent associations to compete with childhood memories. These he lived and relived throughout his adult years, and no woman or man ever challenged Seki's psychological hold over his personality.

Granting Seki's extraordinary importance, we might explore further how the mother-son relationship affected Nitobe's perceptions of the masculine ideal. Critical to this issue is Seki's representation as two distinct, though at times overlapping, personality types: first, the tender loving mother of infancy, the mother referred to by Freud as the "primary love object" who nurses her child and envelopes her or him in dependent love; and second, the "phallic mother," who replaces the father as the symbol of patriarchal authority. In this latter role, for which Seki acquired the "more-than-a-man" epithet, Nitobe's mother exuded all of the qualities that social psychologists ascribe to a "traditional masculine ideal": the suppression of feelings, a stoic self-reliance, a belief that manhood is validated by achievement in the public realm.[11] Of course it is difficult to distinguish an actual transformation in Seki's role from Nitobe's own changing attitudes toward his mother and motherhood in general. To an extent, as Satô Masahiro has suggested, Seki exuded an air of manliness precisely because that is the way Nitobe wished to remember her in later years.[12] But clearly Seki wanted her sons to compete openly and fearlessly for academic laurels within the new social order. And Seki, together with her brother and Nitobe's adoptive father, impressed upon Inazô the importance of *character*, which is exemplified in both physical exertion and academic achievement.

As a student, at least until the age eighteen, Nitobe wholeheartedly accepted the Meiji character ethic, and in later years, the ethic often resurfaced in his pedagogical tracts. His adolescent obsession for good grades illustrates this attitude. At the end of each semester, it was not uncommon for early Meiji schoolboys to report their marks to parents or guardians; but Nitobe went far beyond the call of duty in his detailed reports to his uncle and mother. Proud of his own achievement and determined to put it in the best possible light, Nitobe would chart the grades of every class member from the top of the pack to the bottom.[13] This punctilious concern with grades and academic rank combined with a fierce asceticism. On at least two occasions during his teens, Nitobe signed pledges of abstinence. To an extent, Nitobe's denial of sex, liquor, and tobacco was prompted by his conversion to Christianity and, indeed, he was joined in his pledges by several fellow Christians, including Uchimura.[14] But asceticism is also a universal phenomenon of adolescence, and in Nitobe's case it might well reflect a fidelity to his mother and the puritanical, Bushido-inspired values she represented. It is more than mere coincidence, I believe, that he should begin his first extant letter to his uncle after his mother's death with an attack on prostitution. In mid-October of 1880, a famous brothel in Sapporo burned to the ground, and Nitobe wickedly rejoiced over the incident, explaining to his uncle that "pleasures of the flesh are for dogs and cats."[15]

Nitobe's drive for academic excellence, his interest in sports, his denial of sensual pleasure, and his refusal to admit weakness or disappointment were traits, inherited at least in part from Seki, that constituted what he recognized as his masculine character. Indeed, abounding with energy and unable to sit still for more than a minute, Nitobe earned the nickname "*Akuchibu*," or man of action, from his fellow students at the Tokyo Preparatory College. This nickname persisted until the age of seventeen, when Nitobe's identity as a compulsive doer or actor began to change. In 1877, Nitobe transferred to the Sapporo Agricultural College, where "I became a great reader and submerged myself in books everyday. Accordingly my friends began to call me 'monk,' the exact opposite of my earlier nickname."[16] Suddenly the outwardly gregarious, the fiercely competitive, and the dependably optimistic Nitobe turned reclusive, incommunicative, even sullen. The transformation of Nitobe the active into Nitobe the monk coincided, of course, with the illness and death of Seki and thus marked the onslaught of Nitobe's first prolonged bout of depression. The simplistic dictums of masculine achievement and character provided little comfort for Nitobe as he brooded over the meaning of life and death. Clearly Nitobe identified with his mother as strongly after her death as while she lived, but the image of mother after 1880 was of a more complex figure suspended between recent memories of stoic resolve and more distant memories of infantile dependence, between masculine *animus* and feminine *anima*. The tension between Nitobe's ethic of character and expression of personality which we will discuss in the pages ahead may have arisen from conflicting memories of Seki with the "soft hand" and "sweet voice," on the one hand, and Seki with the "more-than-a-man" directives, on the other.

Nitobe's "fixation" on mother and motherhood took numerous forms during his adult life. Besides cherishing all kinds of childhood memorabilia, Nitobe associated his mother with other women, from Mary Elkinton to the heroines of history, like Joan of Arc and Tôjin no Okichi. With the intention to write an historical biography of Saint Joan, Nitobe visited her birthplace and other sites of interest on two separate occasions in 1900 and 1921, collecting mementoes along the way. Among these were a marble bust and bronze statue of Joan, which he described with almost mystical reverence as "all precious and dear to me."[17] Similarly, Okichi's "martyrdom" so impressed Nitobe that he erected a statue of Jizô in Shimoda with the date of his mother's death on it. Thus, images of Joan of Arc and Okichi blended indistinguishably into Nitobe's mother-oriented, mystically inclined sense of femininity. The blending of religiosity and motherhood is evidenced throughout Nitobe's life, as in the case of his introduction to Quakerism through the auspices of the Women's Foreign Mission Association of Philadelphia as described by Furuya Jun.[18] Primordial ties to his own personal past may even have influenced his academic interest in the role of motherhood as presented in the social anthropology of Robert Briffault.

In strict Freudian terms, Nitobe's various preoccupations with mothers and motherhood can be interpreted as a form of psychological regression, notably a "failure" to smash œdipal attachments in the latency and adolescent years. One searches in vain for even a hint of œdipal antagonism toward Seki, either in her sweet, indulgent or stern, patriarchal roles. Such mother "fixations" or "complexes," according to Freud, stymie the achievement of manhood, inducing, instead, a passive syndrome which Freud, especially in his early writings, considered the psychological essence of femininity. Masculinity, which Freud associated with activity and the psychic strength and independence that femininity lacked, required a complete "dissolution of the Œdipus complex," a "renunciation" of submissive traits, and a bold defiance of parental authority. The restricted model of manliness as renunciation, uninhibited creativity, and bold defiance of authority (qualities which in Freud's view were exemplified in truly great men like Leonardo da Vinci) does not fit Nitobe Inazô. After 1880, and most certainly after 1895, he emerged as a man who *lacked* rugged independence, relentless drive, and combative determination. Yet it is precisely because Nitobe, from a narrow early Freudian perspective, fell short of the masculine ideal of renunciation and psychic independence that makes him so interesting, both as a proponent of "manly character" and "womanly personality." Nitobe's blended temperament also accords with Freud's later, and far more telling, recognition that in the twentieth century, at least, "pure masculinity and femininity" had become "theoretical constructions of uncertain content."[19]

Manliness as an Ethic of Character

To this point we have focused primarily on manliness as a problem of adolescent psychology and mother-son attachments. We now go on to consider manliness as social morality or a pedagogical ethic for character building. To be sure, the Freudian views of renunciation and bold action overlap in several respects with the social morality of manliness. But, whereas the Freudian paradigm is informed largely by unconscious drives, the social morality of manliness or femininity represents a thoroughly cognitive and systematized body of principles that serve specific pedagogical or ideological goals. A man of "character" is the embodiment of this social morality. He is defined not by his intrinsic temperament or his intrapsychic relationships, but by the extent to which he lives up to the extrinsically prescribed social norms of manliness. As an ethic of character, manliness is an artificial paradigm that is imposed upon the individual from outside; it is the product of education. An educator himself, Nitobe Inazô felt deep concern over character building and obliged, as a leading professor and administrator at several colleges and universities, to articulate his conception of the behavioral norm for educated young men. That these norms occasionally violated his own feminine sensibilities only underscores the tension between ideology and personality in his thought.

Nitobe's coming of age and rise as an educator over the last three decades of the nineteenth century coincided with a period of social and political upheaval in Japan. The liquidation of hereditary status and iconoclastic disavowal of Confucian learning for the new school system created a moral vacuum for the new generation of Meiji youth. While translations of Samuel Smiles, Daniel Defoe, and John Stuart Mill provided some guidelines, the "self-made man" of early Meiji lived in a relatively free-wheeling environment, uninhibited by any systematized code of social morality. Schools in the 1870s were, as Nitobe described them, "marts of information" and not in the business of building character or defining the masculine typological ideal. The laissez-faire attitude of educators in the 1870s changed frantically in the 1880s and 90s with the reorganization of the school system, the reintroduction of traditionalistic morality in the curriculum, and the proliferation of youth-oriented magazines loaded with advice on how young men should and should not make their way in the world.[20] The urgency to establish a moral ideology for young men was prompted by the convulsive changes in Japanese society, particularly the migration of young men and women to the cities. Character building at the end of the century helped to assure that the vital energies of Meiji youth were properly channeled toward "safe" and constructive ends.

Nitobe's own contribution to the prescriptive literature of late Meiji and prewar Japan falls under two related rubrics: the biography of great men and the principles of character building. Much of what Nitobe wrote, from *Uiriamu Pen Den* (The life of William Penn) (1894) to *Ijin gunzô* (Portraits of great men) (1931), represents a kind of prescriptive hagiography, whereby great figures of the past and present serve as behavioral models for contemporary youth. Thomas Carlyle provided Nitobe with the inspiration to write historical biography or biographical vignettes. As noted earlier, a reading of *Sartor Resartus* in 1880 "revived" Nitobe's spirit and convinced him that spiritual depression, far from an excuse for whimpering retreat, was a necessary stage in a man's growth and development.[21] Like many late Meiji intellectuals, Nitobe was much impressed by Carlyle's elevation of history over metaphysics, idealism over skepticism, and the spiritual prowess of the individual over the exigencies of fate and disorder. For Nitobe, like Carlyle, history embodied the acts of great men or heroes; and also like Carlyle, Nitobe greeted the modern age with an ambivalent fear that heroism might be going out of style. In a little essay written in the summer of 1906 and entitled "No Hero Among Us," Nitobe called attention to "a discouraging feature of our national psychology." He went on to identify this flaw as a "petty, peevish, and hypocritical trait" among people who had "no comprehension of greatness in the flesh or goodness in the concrete." "No hero is tolerated among us," Nitobe lamented, adding that "a nation that has no hero can never be a nation of heroes."[22] The remark resonated Carlyle's famous dictum from *On Heroes and Hero Worship*: "A nation which denies the existence of great men, denies the desirableness of great men."

To demonstrate that great men do make a difference in history, Nitobe, in 1894, completed his first and most comprehensive biography, *The Life of William Penn*. Nitobe's interest in the "founder of Pennsylvania" arose from his own commitment to the Quakers, his many associations with the Society of Friends in Philadelphia, and his interest in the problem of colonization and the possible analogies between the Pennsylvania and Hokkaido experiences. Yet even more important was Nitobe's attraction to Penn as a man who stood up for his convictions whatever the cost. For example in 1667–68, when he was still in his early twenties, Penn confronted a series of crises that led, first, to his incarceration (he was imprisoned for conscience's sake on at least five separate occasions) and, second, to his expulsion from his father's home. A lesser man would have buckled under similar circumstances, but the young Penn rebounded quickly and even convinced his father of the sincerity of the Quaker demand for direct and unmediated communication with God. In Nitobe's words, "The younger Penn's willingness to overcome all adversity, his dogged perseverance, his courage, and his expressions of the essence of manliness—these qualities greatly impressed the Admiral [Penn's father], who soon realized the integrity and pure character of his son's religion."[23] Much has been made of the mystical quality of Nitobe's religious faith and particularly his Quaker vision of intuition and inner light. But the biography of William Penn also underscores the muscularity of Nitobe's beliefs: the notion that self-reliance, boundless energy, and the capacity to make firm decisions of conscience are the true mark of a Christian leader. In this sense, Penn may be grouped with writers like Thomas Hughes and Charles Kingsley, also on Nitobe's list of idols, who realized that "Christian righteousness cannot be likened to the feminine love of cats" and that "power reverberates in the realm of ethics."[24]

Among the other notables who received verbal and written tribute from Nitobe were Abraham Lincoln, Saigô Takamori, and, above all, Nogi Maresuke, the general famous for his successes in the Russo-Japanese War. Nogi's Spartan style, his laconic speech, his self-possession and composure all struck a responsive chord when he and Nitobe got together on at least five occasions. So, too, did Nogi's ethic of fair play. No matter that 75,000 young men lay dead or maimed in the siege of Port Arthur. What impressed Nitobe was the grace and gentility the General displayed when receiving his Russian counterpart, General Stoessel, after the surrender.[25] As for Nogi's hara-kiri during the funeral of the Meiji Emperor, Nitobe could not contain his admiration. "To those who ask me about the impact of General Nogi's suicide," he wrote in *Chûô Kôron* just months after the event, "I reply that in every respect I think the impact will be beneficial." In Nitobe's view the suicide was an act of pure "altruism" as Durkheim defines it, firmly anchored in public responsibility (*sekinin*) and duty (*gimu*) and free of any hint of egoism or personal anxiety.[26] Two decades after Nogi's death, Nitobe returned to the issues raised by the incident, and though he acknowledged criticisms, both from within and outside Japan, Nitobe remained adamant in his esteem for the General. "Looking back at General Nogi's last act," he wrote in 1930, "we can say that it represents the model of the old *bushi* and that Nogi may have been the last *bushi*." And while moralists and theologians might decry such behavior as barbaric, Nitobe continued, "from the perspective of Japanese Bushido such action is, to the contrary, manly [*otokorashii*]."[27] Thus, unlike his more universalist praise for Carlyle, Penn, and Lincoln, Nitobe retreated to cultural relativism and his earlier conceptions of Bushido in his defense of General Nogi.

Not surprisingly, the men who occupied Nitobe's pantheon of heroes resonated certain values and experiences in the author's own life. William Penn's Quaker vision and Lincoln's struggle with depression are two obvious links. In other respects, one is struck by glaring discrepancies between Nitobe and his heroes. William Penn, for example, acted in bold defiance of social convention, political authority, and parental wishes. He spent considerable time as a *persona non grata*, outside and inside London's Newgate Prison. He epitomized what Nitobe called "*otoko ippiki*" (the male loner) whose sense of "moral courage" induces individual drive even in the absence of community or family support. Nitobe's warrior heroes, including Kimura Shigenari as well as Nogi and Saigô, seem somewhat out of place as well, given Nitobe's own proud declaration that he had never "crossed swords with another man."[28] On the other hand, it may have been Nitobe's self-conscious awareness that he did not fight, that he did not challenge his parents or uncle, that he did not defy the government and go to prison, which compelled him to admire men who did.

The problem of what might be called Nitobe's "compensatory manliness" receives further elaboration in his famous character-building tracts, *Shûyô* (Self-cultivation) (1911) and *Jikei* (Self-discipline) (1916). It should be recalled that the first volume and parts of the second were written during 1906–1913 when Nitobe served as headmaster at the First Higher School (*Ichikô*). His experiences there convinced Nitobe that a group of young men, regardless of social status, should not be left to their own devices. Nitobe was horrified by the stories of school bullies who sauntered through the dormitory halls preying upon weaker schoolmates. In Nitobe's view, there was nothing "manly" about a senior roughneck pouncing upon a sleeping freshman during a higher-school rite of initiation. "Today there are judicial institutions for settling disputes," Nitobe explained in another context. "[T]he blind resort to force is no longer permissible under any circumstances." Rather than to rely on brute force, he continued, "the hallmark of manliness" (*danseiteki kishô*) is described in such phrases as "Men nourish themselves on spirit alone" or "Spirit precedes manhood."[29] Clearly Nitobe's vision of manliness cannot be reduced to flexed biceps or a grunt, and indeed, as we shall discuss in the following section, Nitobe's soft, almost androgynous image aroused considerable controversy among students of the First Higher School.

Still, when writing about the "masculine spirit" in his character-building tracts, Nitobe usually adhered to a rigid bipolar view of sex role and sexuality. The meaning of phrases such as *danseiteki kishô* hinge on the meaning Nitobe attributed to the character *"ki,"* which he used in a variety of combinations (*kishutsu, kisei, kibun*). As Doi Takeo points out, "ki" may refer to spontaneous emotions or judgmental consciousness, and Nitobe made use of both connotations, but within certain guidelines. On the one hand, he took pains to distinguish men from women according to what he perceived as the judgmental intelligence of the former and the emotional uncontrollability of the latter. "When Tennyson wrote that women are small men," he explained in *Jikei*, "he was not referring to physical size but to the availability of intelligence." Continuing in the same vein, "The judgmental powers of women are extremely weak."[30] In other words, what makes men men is their "power of judgment" and, conversely, what makes women women is their deficiency of the same (although Nitobe did not rule out the possibility that some men can think like women and visa versa). Without saying so explicitly, Nitobe appeared to echo the early Freudian bias that women are endowed with relatively weak superegos. Yet at the same time that men are blessed with stronger moral fibers than women, they are also the beneficiaries of vaster reserves of instinctive energy. "Action distinguishes manhood," Nitobe wrote, "to work and to be active is masculine. Women are passive."[31] Elsewhere Nitobe referred to the distinguishing characteristic of men (*dansei no tokuchô*) as "a wild and combative energy." This he contrasted with the more passive emotionalism of women.[32] Thus, the masculine ideal lies somewhere between morality and instinct with the former providing a steering function for the latter. Or, again, the masculine ideal is achieved when a man exercises judgmental control over his abundant and easily activated energies. While Nitobe feared the instinctive reservoirs of young men, he never denied psychic energy or power as an emblem of manhood. For to do so would turn young men into "namby pambies" (*niyaketa danshi*). As an educator, or defender of the male superego, Nitobe urged his students and readers to control rather than deny their vitality through the pursuit of responsible social goals.

Nitobe's prescription for self-control reads like a page out of Benjamin Franklin's *Autobiography*. In a section of *Shûyô*, he lists the do's and don't's of "healthy" male adolescence. The first obligation for every young man was "preservation of stamina" (*tairyoku no chochiku*). Weakness of body, Nitobe inferred, was a major cause for the near epidemic of nervous depression among late Meiji youth. Considering his own melancholic tendencies, Nitobe had surprisingly little sympathy for the "anguished youth" (*hammon seinen*), whom he castigated in 1904 as "cowardly spirits who flee life's stern duties."[33] To stem the tide of existential retreat, Nitobe called for habits of good eating, sleeping, and exercise. The first order of the day, he explained, was to get out of bed at the crack of dawn and then submerge oneself in a cold bath, whatever the season.[34] Regularity, in every sense of the word, was important to Nitobe. So too were manners, which served as an "economy of force" and a way to insure "power in reserve." During the summer vacation, when "the body is disposed to lethargy and to all the temptations that lethargy brings," Nitobe advised students to "shake the dust of the city from off your feet...and forth into the country speed.... There is health in rural air," Nitobe explained. "There is vigor in rustic living. Cities sap manhood and manliness."[35]

Nitobe combined his call for "rustic living" with an ethic of struggle or combat. As we have seen already, the young "active" Nitobe was a fierce competitor in school, and the legacy of noble achievement (*risshin shusse*) never disappeared completely from his thinking. In later years Nitobe became a great admirer of Theodore Roosevelt, whom he once called an "old-fashioned samurai," and phrases like "strenuous life" or "spirit of struggle" became code words in his speeches. Nitobe's ethic of struggle required action, as opposed to passivity, but action on two distinct, albeit interrelated, levels. First, in the spirit of his younger days, Nitobe advocated intellectual and physical competition between individuals. Children become men through rivalry with their peers, either in examination halls or on athletic fields. The physical dimension of Nitobe's ethic of struggle is often overlooked, even though he was an avid participant in "athletic meetings" during his own schooldays. As headmaster at the First Higher School, he expanded the school's athletic facilities and urged student participation in both intra- and intermural sports. Furthermore, under the proper circumstances, that is, where the rules of "fair play" obtained, Nitobe was not completely adverse to a pair of antagonistic students who boxed or wrestled their ways through to solutions of their disagreements. One need only recall his unwavering admiration for Thomas Arnold and for Thomas Hughes' schoolboy novel *Tom Brown's Schooldays* to understand his:

> Fair play in fight! What fertile germs of morality lie in this primitive sense of savagery and childhood. Is it not the root of all military and civic virtue? We smile (as if we had outgrown it!) at the boyish desire of the small Britisher, Tom Brown, 'to leave behind him the name of a fellow who never bullied a little boy or turned his back on a big one,' And yet, who does not know that this desire is the corner-stone on which moral structures of mighty dimension can be reared?[36]

For Nitobe, it was not fighting *per se* that was good or bad, but the way the fight was fought. "Enemies can fight politely and end fighting with courtesy. Men can behave like gentlemen on all occasions. [I]t is the unwanted and untoward circumstances that are the best test of gentlemanship."[37] Thus, whereas a freewheeling brawl between roughnecks was a degrading experience, a supervised match between two gentlemen ennobled the combatants. Sportsmanship provided the litmus test of ethical manliness, and anyone who strayed from its standard won Nitobe's contempt. Yamato Takeru's slaying of the Izumo chief in traditional mythology, after exchanging his real sword for a wooden one, produced this expostulation: "What a tricky and unfair way of fighting! This story is too unsportsmanlike for the hero!"[38]

Clearly Nitobe Inazô was no pacifist. His heroic prototype for young boys was Momotarô, "the daring conqueror of Ogreland," not the shining Prince Genji. Still, fighting for the sake of fighting had no place in Nitobe's social morality. Moreover, the combat that most concerned Nitobe was not waged interpersonally on athletic fields or judo mats, but within the mind of the individual. To wage war against the "internal enemies" of the soul (jealousy, enmity, and, most importantly, sensual desire [*yokujô*]): this was a young man's greatest challenge. When young men "carelessly squandered their energies," when they indulged themselves in the fleeting pleasures of alcohol, tobacco, and consumer goods (fancy clothes, grooming aids, accessories), they rendered themselves incapable of facing the external challenges of life.[39] It was a student's solemn obligation, therefore, to be *on guard* against the darker instincts of self-indulgence. To assist in this task, Nitobe encouraged young men to follow the example of Benjamin Franklin and itemize on paper every personal foible, from a weakness for drink to a shortness of temper. Anger represented a violent eruption of instinct suitable to "wild boar warriors" and uncultivated roughnecks. Nitobe hoped that students would frequently consult their lists of private foibles, reflect on ways to correct each deficiency, and thus "conserve energy" for the public challenges of adulthood.

Of all the wasteful displacements of masculine vitality that concerned Nitobe, none ranked higher than masturbation. "On the question of preserving stamina," he wrote in 1910 or 1911:

> I call the attention of young men to this serious problem: the indulgence in fleeting pleasure by unnatural means. Out of every group of ten young men at least eight or nine have had this experience. But young practitioners say nothing, parents say nothing, doctors reserve comment, and teachers virtually ignore the problem. My readers, however, know full well to what I am referring.

Nitobe went on to explain that as a teacher in Hokkaido he never failed to call a "secret meeting" once a year to alert pupils to the dangers of this "odious habit." Self-arousal was the root cause, in Nitobe's view, of nervous breakdown, hysteria, and other such "diseases." Sooner or later, he warned, even the youth of abounding vitality would fall prey to mental disorder if he failed to control himself. Admitting that resistance to temptation was no easy matter, Nitobe offered these preventive guidelines: take cold baths, exercise frequently, eat properly and at regular intervals, maintain regular sleeping hours, sleep without "sinister intent," and get out of bed immediately when eyes open.[40] Nitobe's prescription for the avoidance of masturbation and his association of self-arousal with a sabotage of masculine energy has a familiar ring. A stream of late-Victorian commentators, both in the United States and Great Britain, made strikingly similar pronouncements. "Spermatic economy," to borrow the phrase of one American historian, was an apparent *sine qua non* for masculine character on both sides of the Pacific.

Finally, Nitobe's prescriptive view of manliness, especially his equation of character with self-control, required understanding and cooperation from women. We have already noted how Nitobe projected a conventional bipolar view of the sexes: the logical, active, and judgmentally capable man versus the intuitional, passive, and judgmentally incapable women. Still, for all their deficiencies, young women, Nitobe believed, bore a responsibility to support and uphold the ideals of manliness. As he explained, "Among my acquaintances, there are some who simply condemn women, saying 'women are enemies.' There is no justification, however, for making women the enemy. The enemy, rather, is the sensual desire that is stimulated by women."[41] The problem, as Nitobe explained elsewhere, was that since the turn of the century the influence of women, especially among middle-class urban youth, catered to the weaknesses of their male counterparts.

> I cannot escape the impression that the ideal man for most women today [1916] is what we used to call a 'softy,' that is a pale-complexioned, weak-willed, unsteady namby pamby. Women avoid sturdy, simple, sincere, and manly men; instead they are inclined to respect weak, fawning, and clever little men.

Consequently, young men felt obliged to compromise their "masculine essence" by accommodating the tastes of young women. The wearing of garish attire, the use of facial creams and hair oils, the patronizing of cafes: these and other trends in male fashion were symptoms of impure heterosexual relationships. Hence:

> The greatest challenge for women's education is, first, to cultivate respect for sincere and manly men, second, to elicit scorn for weak and effeminate men...and, third, to impress on the minds [of young women] the idea that tolerance of namby pambies casts shame on young men. If, on the other hand, young women develop respect for truly masculine men [*shin ni otokorashiki otoko*], the disposition of young men would become more virile.[42]

Thus women held one of the keys to the restoration of masculine character.

Between Masculine Character and Feminine Personality

As we have seen, Nitobe Inazô's prescriptions for how young men should and should not behave—how they should resist temptations of the flesh, take cold baths, and avoid foppish attire—were linked to an external ethic of character. To an extent, Nitobe mirrored these values of independence, hard work, and frugality in his own youth, but not consistently so. The Tom Brown prototype, who stands on his own and fights for his honor, bears little resemblance to "Nitobe the monk," whose tender sensibilities and severe melancholia forced a temporary withdrawal from school and society. Similar discrepancies exist between Nitobe and his pantheon of heroes. What we are faced with is an apparent contradiction between Nitobe's more general view of character as an externally imposed, institutional norm of manliness and the internal psychological realities of Nitobe's occasionally unsteady, delicate, indeed effeminate disposition. In this context, Nitobe's contempt for the "namby pamby" approaches self-denunciation. Of course, character, as a code of norms against which to measure individual behavior, and personality, as the intrinsic emotional structure of the individual, are inherently adversarial for all human beings. But the fact that Nitobe was a widely acclaimed ideologue for the former created special problems, especially when students became more familiar with his emotional disposition. Responding to the challenge and the attending charge of hypocrisy, Nitobe attempted to balance his pedagogy of manliness with the recognition that emotional self-expression was as much a personal right as masculine drive was an obligation.

During his tenure at Ichikô, the tension between character and personality in the behavior of Nitobe became the subject of controversy, both within and without the school. Before coming to Ichikô, Nitobe expressed qualified support for the notorious "roughneck style" of the higher school student as an example of his character ethic. In scattered references before and during his tenure, he spoke glowingly of students' "plain" and simple habits, their "unkempt hair," "shabby garb," and "careless" disregard of social convention. He also consistently condemned "dandyism" as "a heinous offence in the society of learning."[43] Yet for all of his admiration of the student roughneck, Nitobe increasingly wondered whether the masculine training in the higher schools had gone to excess. In his famous address of January 1907, Nitobe called upon his students to balance their "exclusive" tradition of "monasticism," "asceticism," and "self-restraint" with the freer, more "inclusive" values of self-expression, "culture," and "sociality."[44] In other addresses, he gently chided the extreme roughneck for his lack of "refinement," his untamed energy, and his brute appearance. "Animalistic vitality" (*dôbutsuteki genki*) or a "primitive level of energy" had rendered students gruff and laconic at the expense of their "cheerfulness" and sensitivity. As a remedy, Nitobe urged his students to break out of their procrustean shell of manliness and reconsider the world around them. Toward this end, Nitobe exposed himself to his students like no other headmaster at Ichikô. He talked with them about his favorite flowers and colors; he lectured on Joan of Arc and the importance of Marguerite in Goethe's *Faust*; and when he felt like laughing he laughed, and when he felt like shedding a tear, he did so in front of his students without apology or embarrassment. He even suggested that "gentlemanly" interaction with educated young women might restore the sensibilities of higher school students. Accordingly, he proposed the construction of grandstands around the school's athletic field as a gesture to female visitors.

Was this the same man who had earlier warned of the dangers of "dandyism?" Confused and frustrated, a group of Ichikô stalwarts led a vigorous protest that almost forced their headmaster to resign. In an extremely acrimonious school assembly on March 1, 1909, two student leaders called Nitobe a "*happôbijin*," a man of weak will who pleases everyone and stands for nothing. Moreover, one protester argued, striking at the heart of the issue, "The Western custom of showing respect for women at the expense of manliness will lead down the path of degeneration." According to Yanaihara Tadao, a significant number of students believed that their headmaster had infected the Ichikô community with "weakness" and a "feminine temperament" (*onna no kigen*). Nitobe responded to the furor with characteristic calm and gentility, suggesting that he was only thinking of his mother when he made the grandstand proposal. He then offered to resign.[45] Besides illustrating, once again, Nitobe's familiar obsession for motherhood, the incident demonstrated Nitobe's skill in avoiding head-to-head confrontation through retreat to neutral ground and self-deprecation. While the tactic worked, at least temporarily, to defuse the crisis, a minority viewed their headmaster's soothing qualifications as confirmation of his "*happôbijin*" or unmanly image.

But Nitobe's troubles at Ichikô did not end with the grandstand incident. Two years later, Nitobe lost the confidence of several of his most ardent supporters when he refused to respond boldly to criticisms from the Ministry of Education. The Ministry was annoyed by Nitobe's decision to allow Tokutomi Roka to speak at a student assembly. Nitobe accepted the government's position without a word of protest, and then, after brooding over the incident for several months, did in fact resign, suggesting that external pressures had made it impossible for him to remain in office. "Since my arrival here, there have been many criticisms to the effect that Ichikô has degenerated and fallen into a state of emasculation," he explained in his resignation speech of April 25, 1913. "As Headmaster, I cannot allow Ichikô's reputation to be spoiled."[46] In Kawai Eijirô's opinion, Nitobe's equivocation and submission to outside criticism represented a serious "weakness of will" (*ishi no yowai koto*). "Inadequately endowed with strength, seriousness, and solidity, our professor's character exuded a certain feminine weakness or shallowness. Professor Nitobe was not the strong man who presses ahead without worrying about society's criticisms."[47] Coming as it does from a devoted disciple, Kawai's misgivings are especially telling. Yet in expressing his disapproval of Nitobe's last days at Ichikô, Kawai accepted a bipolar view of masculine strength and feminine weakness that does not do justice to the complexity of Nitobe's situation. Ironically, it took real strength for a higher school headmaster to admit weakness and shed a tear in front of his students.

Between 1909 and 1913, the attack on Nitobe Inazô as a symbol of emasculation and feminine deception was by no means limited to the Ichikô students. Outside the school a number of social critics accused Nitobe of acting like the very "namby pamby" whom he had denounced in his own character tracts. As we have seen, there are numerous passages in works like *Shûyô* and *Jikei* that speak of manliness in terms of "combative energy" and muscularity of spirit, but there are also passages that suggest a far more gentle vision of the ideal man. However one explains the difference in emphasis, the books consisted of articles written over several years when Nitobe's own ideas were in flux, and the apparent contradictions created a furor. For example, in 1912 Nitobe published a sequence of articles in *Jitsugyô no Nihon* on the immorality of harsh verbal disputes. Fault-finding and abusive language (*warukuchi*), Nitobe argued, sowed "the seeds of anger" and returned man to an "animalistic" state of combat. Nitobe called upon his readers to seek out the good in other people, overlook their shortcomings, and refrain from self-congratulation. The seemingly innocuous advice struck a most unharmonious chord within the staff of a rival magazine, *Jitsugyô no sekai*, whose chief editor, Noyori Hideichi, immediately launched an ad-hominum attack on Ichikô's headmaster as the purveyor of pacifism and unmanly recoil. Unlike Nitobe, Noyori welcomed verbal attack and confrontation as a "righteous necessity." Anger, he argued, is cause for celebration not shame, and if young men should take Nitobe's advice seriously, they would soon turn into "spiritless errand boys" or "effeminate" nervous wrecks.[48] Noyori's attack was joined by Oshikawa Shunrô, among others, who characterized Nitobe as "a weakling...without bowels, firm beliefs, or masculine backbone."[49]

Such strong contempt is hardly justified on the basis of what Nitobe wrote, suggesting to this writer that Nitobe's mannerisms and life-style contributed greatly to the hostility. Instead of firing back at his critics, Nitobe would either talk around the problem (and thus exhibit an "effeminate" volubility that defied the masculine motto of "action before words" [*fugen jikkô*]), or he would ignore the matter completely.[50] In either case, he confounded his friends and further inflamed his enemies. But on this score, both supporters and detractors alike failed to grasp the key distinction, with which Nitobe was forever grappling, between "doing" and "being." The former referred to an extrinsic character model or the external actions of the individual while the latter referred to the inner spirit or personality. In all situations, Nitobe explained, "to be is more important than to do." In elevating being over doing, Nitobe seemed to suggest, on the one hand, that effeminacy of appearance by no means precluded an inner spirit of manliness. As he suggested in 1916, a feminine exterior often served to highlight the spirit that dwelled beneath the surface. "True strength lies within, hidden from the sight of man. It is often the possession of the meek and the humble."[51] Consider, for example, the case of Hashimoto Sanai, whose "appearance was so soft and mellow that most people could not perceive the burning enthusiasm that lay beneath the surface." Nitobe went on to explain that "Even men who appear like women, and are too soft to swat a fly, may have backbones of steel.... While the adjective effeminate (*memeshii*) often implies a weakness of will, I use the term womanly (when describing men like Hashimoto Sanai) to mean gentle and meek (*onwa jûjun*) in the best sense."[52]

Invoking the motto of "outer gentleness and inner fortitude" (*gaijû naigô*), Nitobe raised the complex psychological possibility of the most effeminate men also being the most manly. As illustrated by Hashimoto Sanai, a pale complexion and squeaky voice had nothing to do with the inner spirit of manliness. But Nitobe went even further than the "outer-gentleness-inner-fortitude" model when speaking of himself. For in his own case, femininity, which he defined as gentleness, meekness, and tender sensibility, penetrated beneath his delicate exterior to the inner reaches of his soul.

Nitobe's awareness of his own femininity was hastened by his departure from Ichikô. Now free from the stern posturing required of a higher-school headmaster and believing himself more comfortable in the company of women than men, Nitobe became a major contributor to the women's magazines *Fujin gahô* (Women's illustrated) and *Fujin sekai* (Women's world); and in 1918, he accepted an appointment as President of Tokyo Women's Christian College. In these capacities, he quickly emerged as one of Japan's most popular spokesmen on women's issues, ranging from higher education to family problems. He criticized conventional instruction that, in the name of preparing "good wives and wise mothers," reduced women to "male accessories" or household supports.[53] He also called for an expansion of women's rights in the public realm, but he stopped short of endorsing those "militant suffragettes" whose aggressive assertions violated the gentle essence of femininity. Given, in addition, his mystical reverence for motherhood and the code of chivalry, Nitobe hardly qualifies as a political feminist. Yet among middle-class housewives, Nitobe's popularity was probably unexcelled by any contemporary writer. The readers of *Fujin gahô* and *Fujin sekai* deluged his mailbox with letters of inquiry as if Nitobe were the champion of their hopes and aspirations. Herein lies the secret of his journalistic success. In his articles, Nitobe projected himself, not as a political feminist, but as a man who could empathize with the feelings of his readers. He attacked the hollow rituals of patriarchy and especially the insensitive husband, whose masculine facade prevented any conscious recognition of either his wife's psychological hardship or his own marital dependence. Nitobe denounced such men as "weaklings."[54] Nitobe's inversion of the conventional ethic of patriarchy and manliness was made all the more convincing by his own behavior and self-disclosures. "Our teacher was a man of tears," recalls Kawai Michiko, a man who was not afraid to sniff peonies or distribute chocolates to little girls.[55] What's more, he made no effort to hide his emotions and confided in his readers. "I have something to share with you about which I feel deeply," Nitobe wrote on the eve of World War I:

> That is, I am nervous and emotional, and I think my temperament takes on feminine qualities. When I try to fathom the origins of these traits, I think of the proverb, 'the soul of the three-year-old lingers until the age of one hundred'. Since my youngest days I have been under the influence of [feminine] emotions, and even now they form a strong behavioral inducement.[56]

Equating femininity with an outpouring of feeling uninhibited by the "masculine restraints of reason or logic," Nitobe made the remarkable admission that for him, the meaning of "to be" was to be like a woman.

Nitobe's willingness to write about himself emboldened his readers to do likewise. Beginning around 1915, young housewives turned to Nitobe for personal advice on how best to handle relations with their husbands and children. The most frustrated of these women made appointments to visit the "good doctor" who, in the quiet of his living room, listened and counselled for hours on end. Nitobe did not sympathize with every woman whose problems were brought to his attention, especially those who submitted to lust. But for the majority of "sincere" women, whose fate had been tarnished by insensitive, boorish, sickly, or deceased husbands, Nitobe abounded with sympathy and warmth. He cherished their letters, their photographs, their visits and referred anonymously to their situations in his writing. Few men before World War I were eager to act as "Ann Landers," and Nitobe's willingness arose from a recognition that the problems of womanhood were inseparable from his own personality, his own being. The more Nitobe studied the personal problems of his readers, the better he understood his own persona in a world where the lines between manliness and femininity had become blurred.

Gender and the Future

Nitobe's growing fascination for feminine personality over masculine character raises certain questions in regard to his well-known public record in the late 1920s and 1930s. If femininity is equated with tender feelings and sensitivity, as Nitobe argued on numerous occasions, then there is nothing particularly feminine about Nitobe's statement in 1932 that the actions of the Kwangtung Army deserved "the gratitude and respect of the nation." "If Japan lost in her reputation as a peace-loving nation," Nitobe continued, "the world gained an insight into *the fundamental weakness of Chinese manhood....*"[57] Clearly aspects of Nitobe's earlier ethic of character—of aggressive competition between men and nations—resurfaced in early Shôwa and blended indistinguishably with the popular nationalism of the day. Does this mean that Nitobe's psychological pendulum simply oscillated back and forth from manliness at the turn of the century to femininity in the late teens and early twenties back to manliness on the eve of world war? Not really. One can argue, for example, that much of Nitobe's tough rhetoric in the wake of the Manchurian Incident formed part of a defensive strategy to win the confidence of politicians. They tended to view him as a delicate and effeminate cosmopolitan of suspect patriotism. In this sense, the more Nitobe admitted to his own feminine sensibilities, the more he felt compelled to compensate for his personality with bellicose statements. As we noted earlier, compensatory manliness underlined much of what Nitobe said about character. One can also argue that certain values which he ascribed to femininity—such as "sacrifice" and "service," the motto for Tokyo Women's Christian College—were quite compatible with the official, manly ideology of state. Moreover, Nitobe believed that just as men like himself could exude feminine virtues, so too could women exude masculine virtues. Manliness and femininity transcended physiology. Still, these arguments do not resolve the paradox of a man who, on the one hand, appealed to his fellow men to unlock their "feminine" feelings of tenderness and, on the other, warned that peace "has often sapped, worse than war ever did, the sinews of a nation; sucked its blood and ruined its character."[58] To make any sense out of this dichotomy, we must reconsider Nitobe's broader view of history and the role of manliness and femininity in historical evolution.

A great admirer of Thorstein Veblen, Robert Briffault, Franklin Giddings, and above all Herbert Spencer, Nitobe was a confirmed believer in the social implications of evolutionary theory. His frequent invocation of such categories as "savagery," "barbarism," "militarism," "industrialism," and "civilization" reflect his view that stages of growth or progress apply equally to periods of history and the development of the human organism. In the spirit of Veblen and Spencer, Nitobe regarded Japan's prehistoric or mythic age as a time of primeval tranquility under the feminine domination of the

Sun Goddess. Like the child, Japan's early history was "moulded in womanly qualities," which explained why "there is at the bottom of Japanese character a feminine trait." With the passage of time, "The child whose soul is moulded in womanly qualities is made to admire masculine strength."[59] A harsh and competitive world requires the acquisition of manly strength and valor, and the developing child's recognition of this reality was represented historically in Japan by the rise of the "wild boar warrior"—"a rude race, all masculine with brutish strength"—in the fourteenth, fifteen, and sixteenth centuries. Significantly, Nitobe identified the military ethos of this early feudal age as "infantile Bushido" (*yochi naru bushidô*). It was "the apotheosis of strong manhood and of all manly qualities," yet it also reflected an "unconscious and irresistible power" of instinct reminiscent of a "primitive age" and immature mind. After 1600, the childish, primitive, purely instinctive qualities of Bushido were transformed into a more cultivated or codified ethic of character. This domesticated Bushido corresponded to the bureaucratic demands of a late feudal society in which the cult of primitive manliness coexisted with the sedentary values of learning and mutual cooperation. Thus began a process of feminization from, using Spencer's terms, a "wholly militant" age under the domination of the early feudal samurai to a more peaceful, less physically active age of commerce and industry. "What Spencer gives as the characteristics of a militant type of society may be said to have been exclusively confined to the samurai class," Nitobe explained; but during the Tokugawa period the samurai gradually lost "the awkwardness of the boar" and tempered their "brutish and overbearing ways" with "intellectual pursuits." The most refined of the samurai gentlemen, together with the lower-class merchants and tradesman, who dedicated themselves completely to "the arts of Peace," emerged as forebears of Spencer's "industrial type."[60] The seeds of sedentary industrialism were sown in the Tokugawa, although they would not flower until after the Meiji Restoration. Thus Nitobe accepted Spencer's view that modern Japan, like Europe and the United States, was evolving inexorably from a stage of violent "militarism" to a stage of peaceful "industrialism," wherein the man of arms, serving no useful purpose, would disappear from the social landscape. With the completion of the Meiji reforms, he noted that his countrymen could look forward to "the next step of our progress as a nation—that is to say, in our coming stage of economic evolution as a commercial and industrial people."[61] Nitobe realized that the road from "militarism" to "industrialism" was neither straight nor easy. He knew that a society at the threshold of complete industrialization often reverted to an ethic of manliness and valor in order to reduce the tensions wrought by social and psychological change. This atavistic impulse, which Spencer condemned as "rebarbarization," produced a rather sympathetic response from Nitobe, as we have seen in his elegiac praise for Bushido and his qualified support for imperial expansion. For Nitobe, like his contemporary Western economists Joseph Schumpeter and Thorstein Veblen, the persistence of atavistic, masculine values presented Japan with a rare "opportunity" both to hasten and ease the transition from "militarism" to "industrialism." But once the transition was completed, the military ethos would dissolve into memory. Regarding "the future of Bushido," Nitobe wrote, "If history can teach us anything, the state built on martial virtues—be it a city like Sparta or an Empire like Rome—can never make on earth a 'continuing city.'"[62]

Linked as it was both to the military tradition of the samurai and to the aggressive "rebarbarized" tendencies of a society in transition, Nitobe's ethic of masculine character represented, using Schumpeter's phrase, an early-twentieth-century "social atavism." His culture of feminine personality, on the other hand, represented the wave of the future. Looking beyond the "rebarbarized" crises of the present, Nitobe optimistically anticipated a wholly industrial society, the acme of social evolution, where men *and* women replaced "physical battles" (*wanryoku no tatakai*) with "economic battles" (*keizaiteki no tatakai*). As men and women worked together in the new industrial era, the old sex-role distinctions would disappear. Nitobe put it this way: "With the progress of culture, the necessity for the old masculine spirit of hardiness diminishes remarkably, and without further development of judgmental or conceptual powers, the male loses any justification for his superiority over women."[63] Accepting the mental and, to an extent, physical convergence of the sexes, Nitobe believed men must prepare themselves for the acquisition of more delicate personality traits, traits that were first evidenced in history, although never completely developed, among the "highest type" of samurai in the late Tokugawa period. In my view, Nitobe recognized the prototype of the twentieth-century man among the most refined and erudite of samurai gentlemen. About the latter, he wrote: "Here dwells and greets you, a gentler race of men—they are unsoldierlike and almost feminine in appearance and behavior.... Affection beams from their eyes and quivers on their lips."[64] Such men are far better adapted to the needs of an industrial as opposed to a military society. But what of those reactionaries who refused to accept feminization as an evolutionary inevitability? Nitobe understood full well that, compared with women, men were far more resistant to social and psychological change. In the name of masculine vigor and purity, some men would stand up and fight any accommodation with feminine sensibilities. But in so doing, these diehards merely consigned themselves forever to the level of "animalistic men" (*dobutsuteki dansei*).[65] "Gentleness," Nitobe wrote in 1933, "is the essence of civilization."[66] Gentleness was also the essence of Nitobe's personality. The utopian vision of the androgynous man was no idle abstraction. With some immodesty, but also with insight and even courage,

Nitobe connected the tenderness of his feminine personality with a teleological view of history.

Notes

1. *Works* 1: 414.
2. *Works* 4: 559.
3. *Ibid.*, p. 510.
4. *Ibid.*, p. 485.
5. "Nitobe Inazô ni okeru jinkaku keisei," in *NIK*, p. 96.
6. *Works* 4: 508.
7. *Works* 4: 487; Kitasawa Sukeo, *The Life of Dr. Nitobe* (Tokyo: Hokuseidô, 1952), p. 7.
8. *Works* 1: xii and 4: 530; Nitobe Inazô, *NIZ* 7: 151–52.
9. *UKZ* 20: 7, 22.
10. *Works* 1: 263–64.
11. Marc Fasteau, *The Male Machine* (New York: McGraw-Hill, 1974), pp. 2–11; Alice Sargent, *Beyond Sex Roles* (St. Paul: West Publishing Co., 1977), p. 190.
12. From Professor Satô's comments on an earlier draft of this essay of May 25, 1984, Nitobe-Ohira Memorial Conference.
13. See especially *NIK*, pp. 405–6.
14. *Ibid.*, pp. 17, 397.
15. *Ibid.*, p. 430.
16. *Ibid.*, p. 84; *NIZ* 7: 213.
17. Mrs. I. Nitobe, "Jeanne d'Arc and Dr. Nitobe" in Maeda Tamon and Takagi Yasaka, eds., *Nitobe hakushi tsuiokushù* (Tokyo: Nitobe hakushi kinen jigyô jikkô iin, 1936), p. 481.
18. See pp. 66–67 in this volume.
19. Sigmund Freud, *Sexuality and the Psychology of Love* (New York: MacMillan Company, 1963), p. 193. In writing this paragraph I have also benefitted from reading Judith Van Herik, *Freud on Femininity and Faith* (Berkeley: University of California Press, 1982), especially chapters 1 and 6 On the distinctions between "character" and "personality," I owe much to the late Warren Susman's *Culture as History* (New York: Pantheon, 1984), esp. pp. 271–85.
20. Earl H. Kinmonth, *The Self-Made Man in Meiji Japanese Thought* (Berkeley: University of California Press, 1981), especially chapter 5.
21. *NIZ* 5: 158 and 167.
22. *Works* 1: 312–313.
23. *NIZ* 3: 302
24. *NIZ* 7: 423
25. *NIZ* 5: 580.
26. *NIZ* 4: 450–51.
27. *NIZ* 5: 586–87.
28. *NIZ* 8: 159.
29. *NIZ* 7: 424.
30. *Ibid.*, pp. 426–27.
31. *Ibid.*, p. 427.

32. *Ibid.*, p. 425.
33. *Works* 1: 188; *NIZ* 7: 196–203.
34. *NIZ* 7: 96–7, 133–34, 200.
35. *Works* 1: 179–80.
36. *Ibid.*, p. 27.
37. *Works* 5: 330.
38. *Works* 4: 663.
39. *NIZ* 7: 196–99, 8: 146–47.
40. *NIZ* 7: 199–200.
41. *Ibid.*, p. 129.
42. *NIZ* 11: 15–16.
43. *Works* 2: 176–77.
44. Nitobe Inazô, "Rôjôshugi to soshiariichi to ni tsuite," *Dai Ichi Kôtô Gakkô Kôyûkai Zasshi* 163 (January 30, 1907), pp. 13–16.
45. "Dai Jûkyûkai kishikuryô sôritsu kinensai kiji," *Dai Ichi Kôtô Gakkô Kôyûkai Zasshi* 185 (March 31, 1909): 91,96; Yanaihara Tadao, *Yanaihara Tadao zenshû* 24 (Tokyo: Iwanami shoten, 1965): 668–90.
46. Quoted in *Yanaihara Tadao zenshû* 24: 657.
47. Kawai Eijirô, *Gakusei seikatsu* (Tokyo: Nihon hyôronsha, 1936), p. 354.
48. Noyori Hideichi, *Seinen no teki* (Tokyo: Jitsugyô no sekaisha, 1913), pp. 17, 44–45. My thanks to Yuzo Ota for calling attention to this source.
49. *Ibid.*, appendix, p. 10.
50. Nitobe's talkativeness as a source of student irritation and misunderstanding at Ichikô is discussed in *Yanaihara Tadao zenshû* 24: 665.
51. *Works* 5: 300.
52. *NIZ* 7: 451–52.
53. *NIZ* 11: 194.
54. While Nitobe seems to be suggesting this in pp. 38–43, he is far more explicit in later essays and speeches. See, for example, Katei Heiwakai, *Katei Heiwa ni okeru Nitobe Inazô hakushi kôenshû* (Sendai: Katei heiwakai, 1935) pp. 60–70. My thanks again to Satô Masahiro for this source. Also, *Works* 5: 97–98.
55. Kawai is quoted in *NIK*, p. 86.
56. *NIZ* 11: 19.
57. *Works* 5: 299 (italics added).
58. *Works* 1: 267–68.
59. *Works* 2: 104–05.
60. *Works* 1: 26,115,283, and 414; *NIZ* 7: 459.
61. *Works* 1: 304.
62. *Ibid.*, p. 137.
63. *NIZ* 7: 427–28.
64. *Works* 1: 284–85.
65. *NIZ* 7: 428.
66. *Works*, 5: 456.

FOUR

Japan in the World

8

Colonial Theories and Practices in Prewar Japan

Miwa Kimitada

While Nitobe taught his students in Ichikô, he continued active as a consultant to those in charge of Japan's colonial policy. His position at Tokyo University, to which he gave full time when he left Ichikô, included the responsibility to develop policies for colonial administration. These policies grew in part out of a tradition of Japanese attitudes toward the countries nearest to them which had their roots in the centuries of Edo rule. Our purpose here is to study Nitobe Inazô as a colonial theorist and practitioner. The substance of his colonial theories will be found in his works on colonialism, principally his *Shokumin seisakukôgi oyobi rombun shû* (Colonial Policy: lectures and essays)[1] edited from his lectures of 1912–17 by Yanaihara Tadao, a student of Nitobe's at Tokyo University. Nitobe began a lecture course called "Colonial Policies" in 1908 and continued it through 1919, when he left Japan to join the League of Nations in Geneva. The course was resumed by Yanaihara in 1924 and ran through 1937, when he resigned under pressure from the militarist government of Japan after its renewed aggression against China.

From the beginning, Japanese colonial thought had emphasized national defense. Nitobe and Yanaihara continued this tradition but did not emphasize it. They also made no significant reference to the military and strategic benefits that could result from colonial policies.

Rather than deal with colonial policies as a function of national defense, we will examine Nitobe's beliefs and theories about how a colonial nation could best civilize less fortunate tribes and "races" under its beneficent guardianship, his concept of colonial control. In this respect, it will serve our purpose to start with a brief survey of traditional Japanese colonial thought.

Colonization for National Defense

Western colonial thought seems to have started in writings such as Francis Bacon's "Advice to Sir George Villers" (1616), "Of the Plantation in Ireland" (1606), and "Of Plantation" (1625). The primary concern expressed in these articles was population, the excessive growth of which would be solved by an appropriate policy of overseas colonization. In the same vein, Thomas Hobbes called a colony an offspring of a nation. In contrast, premodern Japanese colonial ideas in the Tokugawa period emphasized not population but national defense. Japanese worried about Western colonial activities near their borders, especially in reaction to the Russian expansion which resulted from the eastern policy of Czarina Catherine II. For their national survival, independence and development, the Japanese thought they had to cope with these developments through a defense-oriented colonial policy.[2] One example of such thought appears in Hayashi Shihei's *Sangoku tsûran zusetsu* (Illustrated survey of three countries) (1785–86). In it, Hayashi urged the Japanese to cultivate and gain the confidence of the natives (Ainu) in Ezo, now Hokkaido, through a policy of honesty and benevolence. Should the Japanese continue to deceive and exploit those naive natives, he continued, the natives might select the Russians if asked whether they wanted to join Russia or Japan, for the Russians had befriended them rather than subjugating them.[3]

Though the Japanese also recognized the economic benefits of colonial overlordship, their concerns for security lead them to stress what they called "benevolence" toward the natives in a new-found colony. They hoped to express noblesse oblige toward the barbarians on their borders. Satô Nobuhiro (1769–1850), a student of *kokugaku* (national learning) elevated this traditional Confucian virtue to the level of national policy. In *Udai kondô hisaku*, (Mixed secret tactics for the country) (1824), Satô advised the Japanese to bring Korea under their control after first conquering the local natives to the north of Korea. Then, having won the enduring confidence of the natives through the benevolent gift of abundant free Japanese rice, Japan should attack Korea from its vulnerable northern end.[4] Here the principle of benevolence became a tool for conquest. And after the conquest, a derivative of the principle was to be Japanese assimilation of the conquered peoples to make them fully Japanese.

Although slight differences separated the various proponents of colonial theory in pre-Meiji Japan, they all felt concern for national security in response to Western expansion and advocated benevolence as a means for the eventual assimilation of native peoples.

Like Satô, many other Japanese colonial theorists found references to "benevolence" in Japanese classical sources like the eighth-century *Kojiki* (Record of ancient matters). This emphasis resulted from the search for something Japanese in place of the Western nations' Christianity to win the minds of the natives under their colonial control; economic concerns were understated, if mentioned at all. The Western powers developed colonial ideas based on their experiences with voyages of exploration and later explicit policies of conquest, but twentieth century Japanese colonial theories derived from Western ideas without the experience which formed them.

These theories found justification in religious and humanitarian ideals. Some emphasized agricultural development, others the growth of industry and trade, and yet some others the importance of civilizing the natives. Theorists after the Meiji Restoration shared one common feature, or so it seems: they expressed little interest in national defense or security. How did this change come about, if Japan's international environment remained the same? Or had it actually changed: had Japan's position in East Asia been established, and its relations with major powers in the area stabilized?

In terms of geopolitics, the Japanese felt less threatened after the successful foreign wars with the Chinese (1894-95), with the Russians (1904-05), and especially after World War I. They could afford to assign themselves a "world" mission and also view their new colonial empire as a source of economic aid. Now the Japanese had to implement the moral principles behind their policies by applying a derivative of their principle of benevolence to assimilation. They had the duty to bring the peoples of the new colonies into full Japanese citizenship. It was against this setting that Nitobe made his debut in 1908 as professor of colonial policies at Tokyo University's newly formed Department of Economics. His administration of Japan's first colony, Taiwan, had given him practical experience. He had started the tradition which would lead to courses on colonial theory at Japanese universities during the Meiji-Taishô periods.

Study of colonial policy began at the Sapporo Agricultural College under Nitobe's friend Satô Shôsuke. Nitobe continued the course when he succeeded Satô. In his lectures Nitobe built on his German study of agricultural settlements. But Nitobe was not all agronomist. He and Yanaihara Tadao, his successor at Tokyo University, shared another concern. Their theories of colonial control and the civilization of natives found inspiration in their Christian beliefs. The "Nitobe heritage" in modern Japan's colonial theories reflected two concerns: economic and ethical. It lacked any concern for military strategy. At Tokyo, Nitobe, and more especially Yanaihara, preached a practical "gospel": colonization as a way to civilization and world peace, with clear moral obligations for the colonizers.

Such was the way feudal benevolence was combined with modern scientific knowledge and perhaps given added vitality. As a result, students of Nitobe and Yanaihara, though in theory pacifist, generally condoned and sometimes supported expansion in the very name of "Imperial benevolence."

More explicitly opposed to Western imperialism was the theory of Nagai Ryûtarô, whose course on colonial policies was first offered at Waseda University in 1907. When Nagai spoke of the "yellow peril" as a defense against the solidly existing "white peril" from the Western imperialist nations, he repeated the themes of Tokugawa pioneer colonial theorists. Yamamoto Mitono at Kyoto Imperial University fell in line with Nitobe's successor at Sapporo in his book *Shokumin seisaku kenkyû* (A study of colonial policies) (1920), which relied heavily on German sources and their concern with agricultural settlements. A postwar offshoot of this mixture of agrarian orientation and national mission is found in *Nôgyô takushoku gaku* (Colonial agriculture) (1964) by Sugino Tadao of Takushoku University. Sugino studied under Yanaihara in the mid-1920s. Sugino also had a chance to talk with Nitobe when the latter visited Tokyo University from his post in Geneva. He reflects in his own curious way what Nitobe and Yanaihara taught and preached.

Attitudes Toward Natives

The policy of benevolence toward the natives on the frontiers and their eventual assimilation into the Japanese nation reflects Japanese experience. It may be said that the Japanese people themselves developed from a core tribe in Yamato which conquered and assimilated surrounding tribes. In this respect, what happened in Hokkaido was merely a final phase of this historical process, though it occurred while Western nations were building empires.

In its initial efforts to build a modern nation, the Meiji government first had to mark its national borders. After the Treaties of Shimoda (1855) and of St. Petersburg (1875) with Russia finally determined the northern boundaries, the Japanese intended to treat the Ainu in the northern territories with benevolence. This "benevolence" consisted in theory of distributing farmland and imparting civilization through Japanese schools. Whatever the stated policy, the Ainu increasingly lost control of their lands as immigrants from the south squeezed them out. At the other end of Japan, the Meiji government gradually integrated the inhabitants of the Ryûkyû archipelago and Tsushima into the mainland. The next step was to deal either directly with Korea as a full-fledged modern nation state independent of China or to handle it in the same manner as the Ryûkyûs, reducing it to an appendage of, or even a component of, the emerging modern Japanese state and empire.

When Nitobe studied in Sapporo, Hokkaido had until very recently been the exclusive preserve of the Ainu who lived by hunting and fishing. It is recorded that when he entered the college in 1878, there were about 17,000 Ainu. This figure remained stable while the Japanese in Hokkaido grew from less than 200,000 to almost 2,500,000 in 1924. When Nitobe studied in Sapporo he must have seen many Ainu, but one looks in vain in his letters or those of other students at that time for mention of them. The newly arrived Japanese neglected the Ainus' presence in their enthusiasm to build a new nation along Western lines. They must have thought much like William Smith Clark, the man whom they admired as the founding president of their College and who shared American attitudes toward the natural environment, including its inhabitants. American developers felt they must exploit natural resources and bring civilization to the less fortunate races who inhabited a territory. Uchimura Kanzô's valedictory with Nitobe in the audience brought this representative attitude into a sharper focus. It promised hard work and even death if need be for the development of Hokkaido.[5] Replete with this sort of determination and devotion, his words totally neglected the pitiful state into which these innocent natives had already fallen as a consequence of Japanese ambition.

Such was the attitude of Nitobe and his classmates and of contemporary Japanese in general. This does not mean that no one considered the fate of the Ainu. On the contrary, distinguished people, both Japanese and foreign, wept as "civilization," whether benevolent or malevolent, disrupted Ainu culture. Nitobe himself later compared the Ainu to American Indians, and he systematically discussed their place under colonial rule at Tokyo University. Therefore, it is useful in this paper to introduce some early commentators on the Ainu, and then compare their ideas with Nitobe's.

Matsuura Takeshiro (1818–1888) made a trip to Ezo on the eve of Japan's modernization. There the Japanese merchants' exploitation of the Ainu appalled him. He produced a detailed account of the life of the Ainu which, if published as intended in 1858, would have exposed all these abuses, but authorities permitted publication only in 1912. Second, Nakae Chômin (1847–1901), a leading spokesman for enlightened nationalism and parliamentarianism, had opposed discrimination against the *burakumin*, Japan's outcastes. In 1891, Nakae travelled in Hokkaido and wrote an essay which denounced his well dressed compatriots who duped ragged but innocent Ainu. He could not get it published. Both of these Japanese observers expressed natural humanitarian reactions. Matsuura had been trained as a Zen monk, while Nakae knew Western egalitarian literature well. In a way, their views represented a Japanese tradition of philanthropy reinforced by Western theories and beliefs.

The third person who concerned himself with the fate of the Ainu was not a Japanese but an Anglican missionary from Great Britain, John Batchelor (1854–1944). In the spring of 1878, he saw Ainu men in the streets of Hakodate for the first time. He had always wanted to evangelize this "lost" tribe of Japan. But when he said so, a Japanese student suddenly became "frantically arrogant" and said:

> The Ainu are not human. They are a cross between dog and man. That's why they are as hairy as bears. They don't have a language except for a few words, very bad ones at that. They eat everything uncooked; and everything else they do is so barbaric that it is extremely dangerous for you to go into them.[6]

Batchelor could hardly believe his ears. These remarks, he recalled, convinced him to go into villages and work for them rather than remain in the midst of those "civilized and powerful Japanese."

While Batchelor met conditions like these in Hakodate, Nitobe studied as a freshman less than a hundred miles to the north at Sapporo. There he came under the influence of the American, W. S. Clark, who had set up the school. Clark taught the boys to "strive to prepare yourself for the highest positions of labor and trust and consequent honor in your native land."[7] A few months later he modified this exhortation to worldly success with his famed farewell: "Be ambitious not for money or for selfish aggrandizement, not for the evanescent thing which we call fame. Be ambitious for the attainment of all that a man ought to be."[8] Though he phrased his ideas in the pieties of nineteenth century America, Clark's basic frame of reference for success in life was the frontiersman's life of the United States. Applied to conditions in Hokkaido, it may be summarized as follows. As the Japanese moved north the Ainu suffered as did the Indians of North America. The Ainu were expected to accept "civilization" and fade away. When Nitobe had a chance to mention philanthropic work for these disappearing natives, he did not refer to Batchelor in relation to the Ainu, but rather to Helen Jackson (1830–1885) and her services to rectify the "sin of omission" in the handling of Indians.[9] When Nitobe spoke of the Ainu to his students, he was articulate enough. Here are some samples: The Ainu are "barbaric," and have no notion of making a living from working; their capacity for work is very poor. "They may spend three or more days without sleep when they go hunting bears, but if they are made to work with the plough, they will not stand even a couple of hours of labor."[10] This reflected Nitobe's belief in the agrarian way of life as the basis of civilization and peace. The Ainu, too, had to be made civilized farmers. He called for assurances that the Ainu could retain their title to properties, yet he believed in the biological difference of "races." He called the Americans "optimistic but absurd" when they upheld the notion that there was no racial superiority or inferiority. Their hopes for republicanism in China and their efforts to make the Philippines independent were cases in point. "They are trying to make those peoples, who have never been nations, independent nation-states."[11] Thus Nitobe assumed that biological differentiation disqualifies some races from political equality. At the same time, he endorsed others' rights to exercise colonial control and regretted that the Japanese did not emulate the Spanish rule in the Philippines by "bringing under the bell [of the church] the Ainu in Hokkaido to a way of civilized community life."[12]

Development of Colonial Policy

Before 1885, the Japanese undertook the colonization of Hokkaido. They developed this colonial policy in opposition to the Russian threat to Japanese territorial integrity. The nation that the Japanese most wanted to emulate was Britain, with its overseas empire. They acted just as Western nationalism began to turn into imperialism. Japanese felt that to become a leading Western-style power included the possession of overseas colonies. Yet somehow the word "colonial" or "colony" had a sinister ring as the Japanese discovered after they signed the Treaty of Shimonoseki to end the First Sino–Japanese War. It took Taiwan away from China and gave it to Japan. The immediate response of Japan to its acquisition of Taiwan was to apply its time-tested policies of assimilation of natives and to extend domestic law to make Taiwan a full-fledged part of the Japanese nation. This is what it had done in the Ryukyus.

An official report of 1895 by Hara Takashi Kei (1856–1921), a member of the Taiwan administrative committee, to Itô Hirobumi (1841–1909), who had signed the Treaty of Shimonoseki, illustrates this view. Hara strongly opposed the use of the term "colony" with regard to Taiwan. Instead, he recommended gradual but total assimilation into Japan proper. He equated the status of Taiwan to that of Alsace-Lorraine and Algeria, inasmuch as the Governor-General of Taiwan should enjoy power similar to the German and French administrators. Hara went further to insist that "the institutions for Taiwan should eventually be made indistinguishable from those of Japan proper."[13] Nitobe agreed in part. He advised against a rash application of the principle of "Liberty, Equality and Fraternity" to backward natives, while Hara reasoned that the time-tested traditional policy of assimilation would also benefit an expanding Japan.

Between 1901 and 1903, Nitobe served as a colonial civil administrator in Taiwan. During these years the status of Taiwan within the Japanese empire remained vague. But by 1905, the Russian threat had been removed after the Russo-Japanese War, and Japan had more territories and overseas rights. The Japanese then turned to the Taiwan question again. At the twenty-first session of the Imperial Diet, Takekoshi Yôsaburô (1875–1950), who would form the Colonial Studies Association with Nitobe in the same year, argued that Taiwan should be handled as a "colony," for otherwise Tokyo would have to accept parliamentary representatives from Taiwan. To this, Premier Katsura Tarô responded, "My answer to whether it should be made the same as Japan proper is of course that it should be considered a colony. I believe it cannot be made the same as Japan proper." Another representative of the Diet, shocked to hear the word "colony" for the first time with regard to Taiwan, asked "what could be more weird than this?"[14] Katsura's attitude reflected the reality of Taiwan. It had already been masterfully administered as a colony and yielded substantial profits with the promise of more to come. These encouraging results flowed almost entirely from Gotô's civil management with Nitobe's assistance. Before Gotô became the Civil Governor for Taiwan, there had been no clear vision for its future: there had even been talk that Taiwan should be sold. Gotô was convinced, in contrast, that his government in Taipei must emphasize economic development leading to financial independence. Nitobe was suggested as the best qualified man to implement this policy. When Nitobe's plans were put into practice, they produced quick results. Sugar production grew rapidly, reaching 60,000,000 pounds in 1912, six times the size of the 1901 crop.[15]

When the Japanese began to rule Taiwan, they sought the expertise of Western colonial nations. A British consultant, Montague Kirkwood, advised that the British adopted a benevolent attitude toward the natives in their colonies, and the Japanese should do likewise.[16] Nitobe agreed. In his lectures at Tokyo University, he argued that no colonial nation intentionally and as a matter of policy maltreated natives.[17] Only adverse circumstances in the alien environment of a colony would lead a colonial administrator or police officer to inhumane treatment of natives. Yet, in fact, Japanese authorities had brutally suppressed members of the Takasago tribe in the mountains of Taiwan. Nitobe felt he owed an apology or at least an explanation for these Japanese actions to Western colonial observers. He told his students that Worcester, an English scholar, had claimed that the Japanese had wanted to exterminate the head-hunting tribes of Taiwan. Nitobe called for a critical self-examination on the part of the Japanese. As he saw it, one apparent shortcoming of the Japanese was their disinterest in matters of the soul. To illustrate his point, he noted that two Spanish priests and two American missionaries had gone into the mountain villages to save the souls of these individuals, but that only one Japanese Buddhist monk had lived among them.[18]

The Korean Question

So far we have analyzed Japanese colonial theories and policies as they related to the natives of Hokkaido and Taiwan. The last area on the outskirts of traditional Japan for which there was no "definitive" solution was Korea. It was true that the Japanese-Korean treaty of Kanghwa (1876) mutually recognized Korea's "independence," a stipulation which China was forced to endorse after its defeat by Japan in 1895. But the position of Korea in the minds of Japanese nation- (or empire-) builders was anything but stable. In their minds, they still heard the arguments of Saigô Takamori who had wanted more than twenty years earlier to conquer Korea. The "three countries" Hayashi mentioned as the frontiers of Japan were Korea, the Ryukyus and Hokkaido. By the early twentieth century the Ryukyus and Hokkaido had been redefined as "outer lands" (*gaichi*) of modern Japan. To some Japanese, the annexation of Korea in 1910 was a foregone conclusion, since they hoped to use the traditional East Asian concepts of Hayashi to adapt their nation to the needs of the new international environment suddenly thrust upon them.

Nitobe, though a leading Japanese intellectual, had nothing specific to say about Korea and Koreans in his lectures at Tokyo University. Is it possible that he did say something, but Yanaihara edited out the words when he prepared the lectures for posthumous publication in 1943? I prefer this explanation to account for the lack. What sort of thing might Nitobe have said? He might have repeated something similar to earlier comments when he visited Korea in the fall of 1906. Two essays, "Bôkoku" (Lost nation) and "Koshi koku Chôsen" (The aging and dying nation of Korea), formed a part of his *Zuisôroku* (Essays) of 1907. In these he compared the Koreans to the peoples of the Iberian peninsula. Their glories had faded, and they had practically no future.[19]

Also, he might have said something similar to the reference in his principal's address to newly admitted students of the First Higher School in the fall of 1910. The student Yanaihara Tadao records, in *Yo no sonkei suru jimbutsu* (People I admire)[20], that Nitobe at this time rejoiced over the annexation of Korea which had taken place during that summer. "All of a sudden Japan had acquired a vast expanse of territory, bigger than Germany, France or Spain," he said. "The number of people you can reach with your speeches or essays in Japanese has also increased by ten million." Then he urged the students to shed their "insular mentality," for Japan today had become a "great country," and the small Japan of a month before existed no more. Especially noteworthy is the sense of finality as he commented on the direction and extent of the Japanese expansion. This he did in terms of concentric circles. With Korea under Japanese control as a starting point to rethink Japan's future territorial limits, he suggested a circle of outer limits into which would fall not only the Liaotung Peninsula, Southern Manchuria, and the southern half of Sakhalin, but even Northern Manchuria as far as Chichihar (Romanized as "Qiqihar" in the final years of the twentieth century) and Harbin.[21] This concentric projection of the outer limits of growing Japan did not originate with Nitobe. A contemporary of his, Tokutomi Sohô (1863–1958), was one of the most influential publicists of modern Japan. He had already warned the Japanese on the eve of the Sino-Japanese War that the nation which does not grow is destined to perish and that the United States, which was expanding in a concentric circle, would inevitably collide with Japan. Japan, in reaction, would also have to expand if it were not to perish.[22]

If Sohô preceded Nitobe in his sense of a determined and concentric Japanese expansion, it is not so farfetched to call Kita Ikki (1883–1937) a successor. Kita, in his *Nihon kaizô hôan taikô* (An outline plan for the reorganization of Japan) (1923), proposed a circular territorial limit for the Japanese Empire into which the Maritime Province of the Russian Far East would fall, while Korea would be called Saikaidô (Western seaboard region), as opposed to Hokkaido (Northern seaboard region), the former term being an ancient regional administrative designation for Kyushu. His justification for the integration of Korea into the Japanese Empire resulted in part from his understanding of the origins of the Japanese people. He emphasized the Korean contribution to the formation of the Japanese "race" and especially Korean consanguinity with the Japanese aristocracy, as many Koreans had entered the early Japanese Imperial court.[23] He elaborated the theory, advanced by Shiratori Kurakichi (1865–1942), that Japanese and Koreans had descended from the same ancestors. A later development of that theory would justify the Japanese "return" to the ancestral land of Manchuria as the Japanese and the Koreans were of the same stock and so, like the Koreans, came from Manchuria.

It is quite likely that Nitobe agreed with this interpretation of Japanese origins and its relevance to Japanese overseas expansion. During the academic year of 1911–12 he produced a book, *The Japanese Nation: Its Land, Its People, and Its Life*.[24] Here, he noted the clear Korean imprint on the early Japanese people and their civilization: "Tribes allied with the Koreans crossed the Sea of Japan and, being much more advanced in civilization, made themselves masters of Ainu territory.... [T]here is some ground to believe that it is the tradition of Korean tribes which largely formed the beginnings of our chronicles."[25] Nitobe made the most of the folklore of Momotarô, the Peach Boy, to excite the Japanese imagination and to encourage development in Southeast Asia. Nitobe had already published his first treatment of the Momotarô tale in 1907. He wanted to enlist tradition to increase national vigor and wrote:

> I believe that the folklore of Momotarô's overseas expedition represents correct Japanese interest in the outside world, and their marching spirit. The Island of Ogres is the general name for south sea islands.... With the southward advance of the Japanese, what is signified by the Island of Ogres moves southward too. In 1895, Taiwan was the Island of Ogres. Over a decade later today, Japanese in Japan proper still look upon it as the Island of Ogres.... In five or ten years, this name will become incorrect. Momotarô of today will expand to conquer toward the Island of Ogres further south."[26]

It must surely have been more than a mere coincidence that in the year Korea became part of the Japanese Empire, Nitobe launched what would turn out to be a long-lasting contribution to the systematic recording and studying of Japanese folkways. This was the inauguration of the *Kyôdô kai* (Home country association) in 1910. Yanagita Kunio (1875–1962) and Kindaichi Kyôsuke (1882–1971), among others, joined Nitobe. Studies of folkways would map out a zone of cultural affinity beyond the limits of Japan's national territories. This would help the people, who still believed that Japan was in the process of "nation building," to back the rationality of the earlier formal integration of the Ryukyus and now of Korea. Nitobe's associates in this study seemed to have shared a conviction in the inevitability of progress. Kindaichi recorded the Ainu language, not to encourage native speakers to use it but rather to record it before it died; Yanagita studied a variety of other local cultures. Both men felt committed to the Japanese nation and chose to nationalize divergent cultural groups rather than conserve ethnic distinctions.

Another expression of nationalism was the foundation of the Tokyo Geographic Society in 1879 which helped Japan redefine its border with Russia. The Dai Ajia Kyôkai (Greater Asia association), established in 1932, and the Shôwa Kenkyû Kai (Shôwa study group), of 1933, both responded directly to the inauguration of Japan's puppet state, Manchukuo. Furthermore, in anticipation of southward expansion, the Nihon Chisei Gakkai (Japan geopolitical association) was inaugurated less than a month before the Pearl Harbor attack. It was followed by the Nihon Takushoku Gakkai (Japan colonial association) early in 1942. Takaoka Kumao, professor of colonial policies at Hokkaido University, became its president "because he was considered the highest authority" in the field.[27] Takaoka had studied under Nitobe at the precursor to Hokkaido University, the Sapporo Agricultural College, in the early 1890s.

The Return of Old Ideas

The fratricidal war in Europe in 1914–1918, with its accompanying Bolshevik Revolution in Russia, led the Japanese to reconsider their course of modernization. The thesis of Oswald Spengler's *The Decline of the West* (1918–1922) struck a receptive chord in Japan and reinforced some nativist thinkers' ideas about how to restructure their homeland. Tachibana Kozaburô (1893–1974) represents those thinkers. He recommended a reorientation of colonial agriculture which eventually took form in Manchuria after the Mukden Incident of 1931.

Japanese ideas toward China also changed slightly but significantly as a result of World War I. Nitobe seems to have been influenced by this trend. In *A New Map of Asia* (1919), H. A. Gibbons (1880–1934), who acknowledged contact with the Japanese delegation to the Versailles Peace Conference, declared that China was not a state but merely a civilization. One may assume that Matsuoka Yôsuke (1880–1946), the Foreign Ministry's Press Secretary, suggested this notion to Gibbons. Yano Jun'ichi (1872–1970), professor of Chinese history at Kyoto Imperial University, expanded this thesis on the basis of his professional expertise. Naitô Konan (1866–1934), another Sinologist at the same university, furthered this line of historical interpretation. Oda Man (1868–1945), a professor of Chinese legal history at Tokyo University, would do likewise later on. Even the president of Japan's foremost ultranationalist organization, Uchida Ryôhei of the Amur Society, said the same thing. He sounded neither more nor less respectable than these tycoons of the academic and journalistic worlds.

It was against these ideas that Kita Ikki proposed a new trans-Sea-of-Japan empire for Japan in his *Nihon Kaizô Hôan* (Outline plan for the reorganization of Japan) (1923) which slowly gained currency during the interwar years. This included his unique emphasis on the consanguinity of the Japanese Imperial family and the Koreans. Encouraged by Woodrow Wilson's proposal for the self-determination of nations, the Koreans had risen against Japanese colonial rule in 1919. In response, the relativistic nationalist Shiga Shigetaka (1863–1928) had said that a practical way to cope with this development was to let the Koreans have the right of parliamentary representation first, and then as promptly as feasible they should be allowed autonomy, for it seemed a fool's act to try to stop this irresistible force in the history of human development.[28] Although Nitobe did not comment, we may conjecture that he would not have liked this resolution of the problem. He would rather have criticized the Japanese colonial administration for its failure to practice Imperial benevolence, for to him the nationalization of the Koreans as part of the Japanese nation was a more natural development of human history. Nitobe came from an undeveloped part of Japan. Villagers in his own home province had acquired a semblance of nationalism through their newly cultivated sense of loyalty to the Emperor after 1868. He would have seen the making of Koreans into Japanese in a similar light.

Nitobe's and Shiga's scenarios for the future of Korea reflected opposed attitudes toward the modern nation-state. Both differed from a tradition-inspired outlook toward East Asia common to the Japanese in the 1920s. In the spring of 1921, the *Taishô Nichi Nichi Shimbun*, an Osaka daily newspaper with a circulation of 40,000, proposed a new state called *Dai Kôrai Koku* (Great Korea). This state was to be more or less coterminous with the ancient state of Koguryo. It would include most of Manchuria and the Maritime Province as well as the Korean peninsula.[29] The proposal resembled a Korean irredentism with the noteworthy feature of complete independence from Japan plus a resettlement for Koreans throughout the newly acquired territory. A later variation of this idea proposed a political system based on agricultural communities with maximum local autonomy. It included some of the most idealistic elements in the Chinese tradition of government. In practice it would have approximated Lao-Tsu's worldview.

This important strain in the intellectual currents of the 1920s, coupled with the heritage of such men as Hayashi Shihei and Satô Nobuhiro, would lead even the most rational minority among the Japanese to accept Japanese the occupation of Manchuria after 1931. The less educated, in contrast, would justify it more readily in terms of the 100,000 Japanese lives lost in Manchuria during wars with the Chinese and the Russians. In the context of this analysis of Nitobe's colonial theories, this much can be said of the "Manchurian Incident:" although most Japanese approved of the Japanese Army's advance, it was an unforgivable blunder. In the occupation of Manchuria, Japan exceeded the limits of traditional East Asian inter-state relations. In this system, the Chinese Emperor stood at the apex of a hierarchical inter-state system. He commanded with his Imperial benevolence, at least in theory, lesser states like Korea and Vietnam. The Japanese saw themselves as a miniaturized version of the "Middle Kingdom," and Japan found a certain persuasion in the adoption of this pattern as to their own experience, but they had no detailed plans, a fact which became apparent as Chinese nationalism grew.

But by the mid-thirties, a new policy science was taking form. It arose from Japanese interest in Eastern Siberia and Manchuria after the Japanese intervention (1918–1922) in the Russian Revolution, and it incorporated geopolitical thought imported for the most part from Germany. This theory recommended and justified, in the name of a regional economy, economic integration of lands outside the Japanese Empire.[30] This policy science preoccupied itself with the growth and security of the particular nation concerned. The most influential exponent of these ideas, Rôyama Masamichi (1895–1980), was professor of political science at Tokyo University. He had earlier formed a group of scholars with Konoe Fumimaro (1891–1945) and others to study the problems of Japanese farming communities. They included Nitobe. Another student of Nitobe from the First Higher School, Gotô Ryûnosuke, a classmate of Konoe, organized the Shôwa Kenkyû Kai (Showa study group). Rôyama helped develop a strategy to make Konoe a prime minister with a credible, positive policy and nationwide support which even the extreme militarists would not reject.

Needless to say, these personal connections did not mean that Nitobe agreed with the others on all counts. Even though he endorsed the Shôwa Kenkyû Kai which would do much of Konoe's thinking for him, Nitobe had his own ideas about a Manchurian state which differed distinctly from those of Rôyama. Nitobe sounded like Carlyle when he lamented the absence of a great personality in Manchuria who could symbolize the nation-state of Manchukuo. In contrast to Nitobe, Rôyama spoke little if at all of such intangibles as hero-worship or close blood relationships among East

Asian peoples. He advised the Japanese government to foster economic compatibility, co-operation and complimentarity among East Asian nations, with Japan's contribution its studied leadership.

Nitobe must have experienced much difficulty in his formulation of policy since the military invasion of Manchuria severely tested both his reputation as a university professor of colonial policies and as a moral educator for the masses. In a curious way, he expressed a concern for national defense reminiscent of the Edo colonial theorists. One clear implication of "A Far-Eastern Fable," which he published in the *English Osaka Mainichi* of September 30, 1931, is that the threat of their gigantic northern neighbor justified Japan's invasion of China.[31] Since the "independent state" of "Manchukuo" had already been proclaimed, Nitobe's statement seems to express unusual sarcasm if he was not fully convinced or blind in the face of reality. He wrote in the *Mainichi* of February 19, 1932 that Manchukuo represented a form of national self-determination as preached by Woodrow Wilson. Such a development had long been awaited in this part of the world. "Nothing would have pleased Mr. Wilson more than...the Mongol-Manchurian state." It was "to uphold the doctrines of Open Door, Equal Opportunity, and Racial Equality," among other things. China would become proud of this independent state just as "Great Britain is now proud of the United States." He concluded his short essay with the words, "No people can be prouder of any achievement than of being 'the Mother of great nations'"[32]

This last remark is of exceptional interest to us, for in its ambivalence, it suggests what Nitobe thought of Japan's position in Manchuria. The "mother" country here could mean Japan, the framer of "independence." It becomes credible only as a utopian day-dream from the harsh reality with which he could not grapple: Japan, aggressor; China, aggrieved. But this colonial control could be made tolerable and even rewarding. Through their judicious application of the age-old Japanese principle of Imperial benevolence for winning the trust and respect of the people under colonial control, the Japanese had the duty to erect a truly independent state.

Even at this juncture, Nitobe did not speak about the right of national self-determination for the Koreans. His logic required him to talk about Japan, a "mother," rejoicing in Korea's independence in due course, but he did not do so.

These were the differences between Nitobe and Rôyama. Japanese policy pronouncements of the late 1930s and early 1940s became progressively more traditional in their attitudes toward the peoples under Japanese occupation. They in a way merely extended what used to be a domestic policy of Imperial benevolence and assimilation. This even suggests that the Japan of the 1930s and later never had a "foreign policy" apart from a mere extension of domestic policy toward minority groups like the Ainu and the

Takasago, along with the Okinawans and Koreans. Japan's relations with China and the variety of peoples in South and Southeast Asia reflected the same attitude, starting with the New Order in East Asia proclamation of 1938 and continuing with the Greater East Asia Co-prosperity Sphere pronouncement of 1940 and the Greater East Asia Joint Communique of 1943.[33]

In other words, the Japanese formed their policies for the natives of their new territories out of their domestic experience with minority groups. Not much new was added during "the Greater East Asian War." Nakajima Kenzô (1903–1979), then a French instructor at Tokyo University, urged Japanese military men to instruct local natives in the occupied countries of Southeast Asia in the "correct, strong and beautiful Japanese language."[34] As they learned to use Japanese, these people would qualify for the same benefits as the Japanese themselves under the benevolent rule of the Japanese Emperor.

Conclusion

We have come a long way in the discussion of Nitobe and his colonialism. We have probed the rather obscure area of "influences" and "connections" between men's ideas and their public lives. Several things have become clear enough, and another has come to light. It suggests further investigation is necessary.

Among those things that have been made clear is the relation between tradition and modern developments in Japanese colonial thought. Another was a continuing preoccupation with particularistic national values centering around the Emperor and Imperial practices as valid for all, once the principle of Imperial benevolence had been judiciously applied. A third was Nitobe's concern for national defense which surfaced in his support of Japan's position in Manchuria after it had proclaimed the "independent state" of Manchukuo. Also, Japanese policies and attitudes toward China and peoples of Southeast Asia might be construed as an extension of Japanese thought and policies toward other colonies. Finally, the results of our investigation so far invite us to assess the relations between men like Nitobe and Yanaihara and those directly responsible for the official policies of the Japanese government in the 1930s and early 1940s.

Such a study would help those still confused by the contrast between Nitobe's ideals and the brutality which characterized Japanese aggression. Nitobe is frequently criticized because he did not lay his reputation on the line to condemn Army atrocities in China, yet his student Yanaihara gave up his position as Nitobe's successor in Tokyo University over the issue. One of the best ways to seek a solution to this contradiction would be to study what those who made the decisions to advance into Asia thought of Nitobe's writings.

Notes

1. *NIZ* 4: 5–389.
2. Kuroda Ken'ichi, "Hikaku shokumin shisô shiron," in *Dai Nihon takushoku gakkai nempô* (Tokyo: Nihon hyôronsha, 1943), pp. 36–37.
3. *Hayashi Shihei zenshû* (Tôkyô: Seikatsusha, 1944): 662.
4. Tokita Keikichi, ed., *Satô Nobuhiro senshû* (Tokyo: Dokusho shimposha, 1943) pp. 364–67.
5. *Shiga Shigetaka zenshû* (Tokyo: Shiga Shigetaka zenshû kankô kai, 1928): 3.
6. *Jon Bachiyera jijoden* (Tokyo: Bunrokusha, 1928), p. 114.
7. The Hokkaido Imperial University, *The Semi-Centennial of the Hokkaido Imperial University* (Sapporo, 1927), p. 10.
8. Quoted in Inatomi Eijirô, *Meiji shoki kyôiku shisô no kenkyû* (Tokyo: Fukumura shoten, 1956), p. 103.
9. *Nitobe Inazô hakushi shokumin seisaku kôgi oyobi rombunshû* Yanaihara Tadao, ed., in *NIZ* 6: 148.
10. Yanaihara, *Nitobe Inazô hakushi*, p. 143.
11. Yanaihara, *Nitobe Inazô hakushi*, p. 139.
12. Yanaihara, *Nitobe Inazô hakushi*, p. 150.
13. Referred to in Gotô Shimpei, *Nihon Shokumin seisaku ippan, Nihon bôchô ron* (Tokyo: Nihon hyôronsha, 1944), p. 6
14. Gotô, *Nihon shokumin*, p. 7.
15. To Shaw-en, *Nihon teikoku shugi ka no Taiwan* (Tokyo, University of Tokyo Press, 1975), pp. 49–50.
16. Memorandum of Montague Kirkwood addressed to Count Shigenobu Okuma, Foreign Minister, dated July 12, 1898, "The Position of Taiwan and the Constitution" file number 1, 5, 3, 8. Japanese Foreign Ministry Archives of Diplomatic Papers.
17. Nitobe, *Shokumin seisaku*, p. 136.
18. Nitobe, *Shokumin seisaku*, p. 147.
19. Quoted in Tanaka Shin'ichi, "Nitobe Inazô to Chôsen" *Kikan: Sanzen ri* 34 (Summer 1983): 94–95.
20. In the popular paperback series Iwanami Bunko edition, originally published in 1940. From its fifth printing published after the war in 1948, this diary portion is completely deleted without explanation. The full text was restored in volume twenty- four of the *Yanaihara Tadao Zenshû*, published by the same company in 1965.
21. In the original as mentioned in note 20, pp. 93–94, and in the *Zenshû* volume, pp. 136–137.
22. Tokutomi Sohô, *Nihon bôchô ron* (Tokyo, Min'yûsha, 1894).
23. Miwa Kimitada, "The Rejection of Localism: An Origin of Ultranationalism in Japan," in *Japan Interpreter* 9, no. 1 (Spring 1974).
24. (New York: G. P. Putnam's Sons, 1912).
25. *NIZ* 13: 88.
26. Nitobe Inazô, *Nitobe hakushi bunshû*, Yanaihara Tadao ed. (Tokyo: Ko Nitobe hakushi kinen jigyô jikkô iin, 1936), pp. 408–9.
27. See my *Kyôdôtai ishiki no dochaku sei* (Tokyo: San'ichi shobô, 1974), Chapters 2 and 3.

28. *Nihon ichi* (June 1919), in *Shiga Shigetaka zenshû* (Tokyo: 1928): 267.
29. Hasegawa Yûichi, "Taishô chûki tairiku kokka e no imeiji," *Kokusai Seiji 71* (1982): 94–100.
30. See my "Japanese Policies and Concepts for a Regional Order in Asia," *Sophia University Institute of International Relations Research Papers*, Series A–46 (1983), pp. 14–19.
31. *NIZ* 16: 271–72.
32. *NIZ* 16: 318–19.
33. Miwa Kimitada, "Nichi Bei Higashi Ajia kan no sôkoku, " in Miyake Masaki, ed., *Shôwa shi no gumbu to seiji* (Tokyo: Dai ichi hôki, 1983), pp. 225–26.
34. Moriyama Kôhei and Kurisaki Yutaka, *Dai tôa kyôei ken* (Tokyo: Shin jimbutsu ôraisha, 1976), p. 60.

9

The Geneva Spirit

Thomas W. Burkman

Everyone who worked in the League of Nations knew well what was meant by the "Geneva spirit." The full poignancy of this ethos cannot be apprehended by those who have never lived by the shores of Lac Leman. Sir Eric Drummond, Sugimura Yôtarô, Ayusawa Iwao, and William Rappard understood the ease with which the nationals of diverse countries interfaced in their routine professional and social activities. Hand-in-hand they worked hard, with religious devotion, to make international organization efficacious and to nudge the nations of the world into harmony with League ideals. In Geneva, the spirit of the peace enterprise was inseparable from the serenity of the natural setting: the mountain-framed lake, the greenness of the grass, the flowers, the quaint antiquity of the city. In the world viewed even today from the Palais des Nations, the state of nature and humanity seems totally incompatible with the state of war. The possibility of aggression seems remote. To the Japanese in the League Secretariat in the 1920s, Mukden, Shanghai, and Vladivostok were very far away.

Such a creature of good will as Nitobe Inazô internalized the Geneva spirit quickly; such an expressive communicator made it infectious to others. Addressing assembled delegates of the Institute of Pacific Relations (IPR) in 1929 on the advance of world order in his day, the retired League Under-Secretary General asked, "Do we not find the spirit of the hills and the lakes...conductive to fellowship and interdependence? The Locarno spirit is such, and it is admitted that this was nurtured on the shores of Lac Leman, surrounded by its hills, the Jura and the Salève." Nitobe devoted much of his League career to the spreading of the ideas of the organization in Europe, but there were two special mission fields where he longed to transplant the Geneva spirit. The first was his homeland, Japan. He genuinely believed that the terrain of Japan was as hospitable to the spirit of international understanding as that of Switzerland. Hence he lifted the eyes of his IPR audience to the Kyoto around them: "Here we meet in this ancient city, called in olden times Heian, the City of Peace and Ease, at the foot of the Hiei range and with Lake Biwa close by. Thus does Japan provide...the geographical requisites for the peaceful discussion of international relations."[1] The other special target of his endeavors was North America, his second homeland to which he repaired nine times during his life. Nitobe might just as well have applied the mountain-and-lake imagery to the Canadian Rockies and Lake Louise near Banff, the site of his last international conference. Nitobe never lost faith that a true spirit of tolerance and sympathetic understanding of his beloved Japan could flourish in American hearts.

Nitobe loved the League. He called it "the greatest achievement of the human race."[2] Inazô's service as Under-Secretary General was indeed the crowning point of his distinguished career, and the study of his life is incomplete without treatment of the Geneva years. At the League his established reputation for understanding and communicating with the West was tested in the crucible of formal international duties. After he left Geneva, acrid disputes involving the League and Japanese vital interests exposed the paradoxes inherent in the character of the bridge-builder. The League crisis over Manchuria brought Inazô's internationalism into sharp confrontation with his nationalism. In a study of Nitobe's League connection we move beyond the man himself to discover much about Japan's role in international organizations in the critical interwar years. We see demonstrated at Geneva important realities of the international power structure which were of vital concern to Japan in the 1920s and which account in part for shifts in the nation's diplomatic posture in the 1930s. In exploring Nitobe's embodiment of the Geneva spirit, lovers of peace can meditate upon one humanist's sincere efforts to build a structure to prevent war. They may also inquire whether a person of letters can find an audience in the councils of professional diplomats and international power brokers.

The Making of an Internationalist

Nitobe's posture toward the League of Nations in the 1920s and 1930s was conditioned by a complex background of ideas, moral convictions, international experience, and personal ties. From his Quaker cultivation and world travel, he acquired a passion for peace and mutual understanding. From his career as an educator sprang his sense of need for international intellectual cooperation. As a student in New-Manifest-Destiny America, an administrator in Taiwan, and a professor of colonial policy, he embraced notions of enlightened overseas hegemony. His nationalism was honed by a fixation for Japan's past and immersion in the heady patriotism surrounding the Sino-Japanese and Russo-Japanese Wars. Among his early contacts were Woodrow Wilson, James Bryce, Makino Nobuaki, Gilbert Bowles, and Takagi Yasaka. Their names would also be associated with the causes of the League and internationalism.

When Inazô undertook graduate study at The Johns Hopkins University, one of his classmates was Woodrow Wilson, whose name outshines all others as a founder of the League of Nations. Wilson at age twenty-eight was six years Nitobe's senior and had entered The Johns Hopkins program a year earlier. He was already married, held a law degree, and had completed the opening chapters of his later published *Congressional Government*. Though shy, Wilson displayed a sophisticated maturity. His opinion was often solicited by Professor Herbert Baxter Adams in the midst of heated seminar discussions. Nitobe later recalled that Wilson possessed the air and appearance of a man of the world, a "Southern Gentleman" not unlike the former samurai Nitobe admired.[3] When Nitobe revisited Hopkins in 1912, he took his traveling companion and former student Tsurumi Yûsuke to the seminar room and proudly showed him the places where he and Wilson, then governor of New Jersey and presidential aspirant, had sat during two years as students together.[4] Did schoolmate ties to the American architect of the League favorably predispose Nitobe to the cause three decades later? It is hard to say. No correspondence between them remains, and Nitobe never publicly attributed his views on the League to Wilson. Yet among Japanese, *sempai-kôhai* (junior-senior) ties lay a basis for affinity which persists despite decades of nonintercourse. Tsurumi may have been acting for his mentor Nitobe when in July 1912, he temporarily took leave of the latter's entourage, irresistibly drawn to the Democratic convention in Baltimore. There, thrilled at Wilson's nomination for the presidency, Tsurumi noted in his diary, "The time comes at last when character and conviction carry, over the tactics of trained politicians."[5] When teacher and pupil returned to Japan, Tsurumi organized a Wilson Club to promote the president's ideals in Japan. Wilson wrote Tsurumi of his delight that "the club should bear my name and should devote itself to the spreading of ideas which personally I feel to be essential to the peace of the world."[6]

Other noteworthies who drank from the same Johns Hopkins' intellectual font were John Dewey and Frederick Jackson Turner. Dewey left Adams' tutelage a month before Nitobe arrived, to teach at the University of Michigan. In 1918 this exponent of liberalism and pragmatism would fully endorse Wilson's program of fourteen points for ending the World War, especially the President's call for an "association of nations." In February of 1919, while the Paris Peace Conference was hammering out the League Covenant, John Dewey traveled to Japan to lecture at Tokyo University, carrying with him the League cause. For three months the philosopher and his wife lodged in the Nitobe home. After the peace treaty was finalized, Dewey would become disillusioned by the vindictive nature of the settlement and denounce the fledgling League as a device to perpetuate the old imperialist order. But his disfavor did not crystallize until after he and Nitobe parted in the spring of 1919, Dewey moving on to Shanghai and Nitobe setting out for Paris.[7]

Frederick Jackson Turner entered Adams' seminar a year after Nitobe departed for Germany in 1887. While at Hopkins both Nitobe and Turner were influenced by progressive economist Richard Theodore Ely, who introduced his students to social Darwinism, to an economic interpretation of political and social change, and to a nascent "economic internationalism." In the respected *Chautauquan*, Ely cited scientific enterprise, the labor movement, and the spread of international weights and measures as evidence of an increase in "social solidarity" which transcended national boundaries.[8] There is a remarkable resemblance between Turner's famous Frontier Thesis (1893) and Nitobe's "Momotarô Doctrine" (1907). Both saw frontier regions as incubators of national character. According to Nitobe, "Frontier life rejuvenates the human nature which we are apt to forget and lose. For human life there must always be a frontier. If it were not for it, man would be reduced to a trifling existence, under the pressure of the customs and traditions of society."[9] For Inazô the frontier was Taiwan and beyond. This is part of the intellectual baggage which he brought to Geneva and which may have influenced his response to the 1931 spread of Japanese power into the new Manchurian frontier.

Nitobe encountered Makino Nobuaki in 1906 when the latter, as Minister of Education, prevailed upon him to accept an appointment as Principal of The First Higher School in Tokyo.[10] Son of elder statesman Ôkubo Toshimichi and soon to be a foreign minister, Makino would be the major proponent of the League of Nations among government leaders in critical foreign policy debates at the end of World War I. As de facto head of Japan's delegation to the Paris Peace Conference, he would have the crucial voice in recommending Nitobe for the League Secretariat. While on a lecture tour of the United States in 1912, Nitobe made the acquaintance of other international figures whose names would be closely associated with the League movement in the United States and Great Britain. In Washington he met President William Howard Taft, who would lend his prestige to the League to Enforce Peace as its president from 1916; and British Ambassador Lord James Bryce who after 1914 headed the so-called Bryce group of British parliamentary and public League advocates. At a Johns Hopkins reception he was introduced to Theodore Marburg, soon to be a founder of the League to Enforce Peace and tireless campaigner for Japanese participation in the League enterprise. The League to Enforce Peace and the Bryce group provided the Japanese government with valuable reports on the League movement prior to the Armistice.[11]

Well before World War I, we can observe in Nitobe's mind the crystallization of important ideas on international order, concepts that eventually would bring Nitobe into conflict with the League over Manchuria. One was his belief in the irrepressible, onward march of superior civilizations. This social Darwinian view had helped inspire the New Manifest Destiny in the United States in the 1890s and the naval theories of Alfred T. Mahan. To Nitobe, Japan was "in the forefront of the civilization of the East." He had personally helped Japan civilize Taiwan. His Momotarô Doctrine, to which Miwa has already alluded,[12] expresses it best. It linked Japanese contemporary colonial ambitions to an appealing folk tale: "Today's Momotarô will expand to conquer the Island of Ogres further south."[13] It would be easy to transfer this concept from Taiwan to Manchuria in 1932, when he wrote, "Japan's advance..., in search of a life-line, is as irresistible an economic force as the westward march of the Anglo-Saxon empires." If Nitobe's expansionist ideology had a liberal component, it was his concern for the interests of the colonized. Here we see a Japanese counterpart of the "White Man's Burden" sentiment so prevalent in America at the turn of the century. In Nitobe's lectures on colonial policy at Tokyo University from 1906 on, he urged the improvement of colonists' living conditions, advocated assimilation policies, and reminded his compatriots that "the natives can teach us, too."[14]

A second concept, a reverse image of the first, was Nitobe's conviction that China could not govern itself in accordance with twentieth century standards. During China's Republican Revolution, he expressed pessimism over the viability of centralized government on the mainland:

> I do not believe a republic can survive in China, do not believe the people are prepared to govern their country so. They are fitted to govern it in small local governments. If China could be divided into many different States, each with its local government, it could live as a republic, but there remains the problem of forming a confederation.[15]

Skepticism over China's ability to govern itself was a common sentiment in Japan and major world capitals in 1912, and would influence even supporters of the League of Nations during World War I.[16] Internal affairs of the next two decades would do little to refute the allegations of Chinese political incompetence. Nitobe would repeat the theme in 1932 to vindicate Japan's policy in Manchuria.

Third, Nitobe believed that lack of understanding was the prime cause of international conflicts. In 1912 he told an audience at The Johns Hopkins University:

> If it is sometimes knowledge that brings the sword, it is still better knowledge that keeps the sword away. If this country and mine can come to a better knowledge of each other, to a fuller and deeper understanding of the missions and aspirations of each other, that will be a great stride toward the

advancement of the human race, a long step toward the fulfillment of a prophecy...:

> When the war-drum throbbed no longer
> and the battle-flag was furled;
> In the parliament of man, the federation
> of the world.[17]

Confident as he was that true knowledge would uncover human commonality, Nitobe tended to blur the specific differences between nations and their interests. His lifelong theme song was, *there are no real bases for Japanese-American animosity*. War-talk, he told his audiences in the United States in 1911-12, had no foundation in fact. It was stirred up by selfish people on both sides who profited from marketing munitions and newspapers. At Brown University he assured the students that there was no absolute distinction between East and West.[18] International ill-will and conflicts were, in short, misunderstandings, resolvable when each side was willing to view the situation through the eyes of the other. Nitobe pressed this assumption to his dying day, certain that intellectual cooperation was the key to peace, confident that Japan could explain its Manchurian policy to the League, and sure that he could lead Americans to accept Manchukuo.

A fourth idea was the necessity of national defense through armed force. Despite his ties to the Society of Friends, Nitobe did not oppose the Sino-Japanese and Russo-Japanese Wars. In the latter instance he parted ways with Sapporo Band colleague Uchimura Kanzō, and only painfully explained his position to Philadelphia Quaker in-laws. As Japan besieged Port Arthur, he and his wife Mary were drawn to embrace "Japan's sense of the importance of her mission in the development of the Far East...." In 1931, Inazō reiterated the lesson of the Triple Intervention, that "only in armament lay security."[19] His later rationalization of the Manchurian invasion as a defensive act was facilitated by his prior affirmation of armed defense and war for a noble cause.

Destination Geneva

A League of Nations movement was slow to form in Japan, and when a few public leaders voiced support for the League at the time of the Armistice in 1918, Nitobe was not among them. He had, however, clearly identified himself with liberal optimism during World War I, a high point in Taishō Democracy. He believed that democracy was the wave of the future and that no place on the earth could avoid its influence—an idea prominent in Woodrow Wilson's academic writings. Nitobe saw this trend as one component of an equally inevitable Americanization sweeping the world. In 1917, he argued in the magazine *Jitsugyô no Nihon* that Japan was not immune to the spread of influence from America, "the world's greatest democratic country:" "Even with regard to the increase in the power of the masses, we must reject the notion that our Japan alone is an exception.... This is a world-wide phenomenon, and it will be impossible for this nation or that nation to exempt itself." Appealing to the premium Japanese placed on domestic tranquility, he warned that "nations which promote democracy will easily achieve public peace, while those hostile to democracy court instability."[20]

Japanese liberal intellectuals began to take notice of Woodrow Wilson when he undertook the task of peacemaking in 1916-17. His reform program at home, his peace initiatives abroad, and his gentleman-scholar likeness were often cited in contrast to the unimaginative, "bureaucratic" leadership of Japan's government figures. Just before the American entry into the war when Wilson's popularity was at its peak, *Chûô Kôron* carried a symposium in which speakers praised the president. Nitobe's contribution was a short reminiscence of their days at Johns Hopkins together. He praised Wilson's gentlemanly character and predicted that the president would "go down in history for all ages." As Miwa Kimitada correctly notes, this was the last extended written comment by Nitobe on Wilson.[21] Nitobe had few heroes, and Wilson's parrying of Japan's racial equality demand at the Paris Peace Conference did not endear the president to his Japanese classmate. Moreover, American entry into the war a month after this symposium was published removed much of the glitter from the image of Wilson in Japan. The United States attracted more Japanese attention as the builder of a new battle fleet and as a competitor in Siberia than as a crusader for peace and democracy. By the time of the peace conference, the League of Nations impressed Japanese realists as a device to perpetuate Anglo-American predominance rather than a mechanism for international harmony.

Among vitriolic critics of the American president and his vision for world order were some of Nitobe's students and close associates. Washio Shôgorô, a student at The First Higher School under Nitobe who went on to a Harvard Ph.D., questioned Wilson's commitment to democracy in view of the dispatch of troops to Siberia without Senate authorization. In *Chûô Kôron* he labeled the president "a dictator unparalleled in the world." Another former First Higher School pupil, Konoe Fumimaro, warned of Anglo-American economic imperialism and condemned the League as a scheme to keep late-developing nations in a subordinate position. Gotô Shimpei, civilian governor and Nitobe's superior in Taiwan in 1901-03, was a hawkish, impulsive advocate of Greater Asianism who was known in the Diet as *wasei Ruzuberuto*—"Roosevelt made in Japan." In a 1918 memo to the prime minister, he pictured Wilson as a hypocrite and American ideology as indistinguishable from German militarism. Meanwhile, Nitobe's friend and fellow Christian Uchimura Kanzô had abandoned the faith in human progress which underlay Wilson's and Nitobe's optimistic world views. After World War I, he derided the League of Nations as a "tower of Babel," and preached that only the Second Coming of Christ would save the world from its predicament.[22]

Some Taishô democrats did not waver in their faith in the proposed League of Nations as the touchstone of human progress. Among them were Tokyo University professors Yoshino Sakuzô and Anesaki Masaharu along with pioneer labor organizer Suzuki Bunji. When President Wilson articulated his Fourteen Points in January 1918, Yoshino was one of the few Japanese writers who took notice of the all-important Point Fourteen which called for the formation of what became the League of Nations. The professor expressed to readers of *Chûô kôron* his hope that the president's proposal for a general association of nations would be "one of the controlling ideas of the peace conference.... So long as this task remains unaccomplished," he said, "eternal peace cannot be guaranteed." When the peace conference opened in January 1919, he continued the campaign, urging that no creditable reason existed why Japan should not follow the trend of the times and fall into step with the League movement. Even when public sentiment toward the project grew hostile and Japan's racial-equality provision was defeated, the Tôdai professor steadfastly defended the League Covenant as an agent for world reconstruction.[23] Pro-League intellectuals like Yoshino agreed with Wilson that the organization was the international expression of the irresistible trend toward democracy. Japan's participation in a reformed global political system would, they hoped, encourage at home the expansion of suffrage, the recognition of organized labor, and the reduction in arms expenditures they so deeply desired.

Among officials, Makino Nobuaki was the boldest proponent of Japan's membership in the League of Nations. This career diplomat's wide travels began as a child in 1871 when he accompanied the Iwakura Mission and remained in Nitobe's beloved Philadelphia to attend middle school. He served as foreign minister immediately prior to the World War. Makino promoted Japanese membership in the League to mend the fissures in international relations caused by the indiscretions of the autonomous policy Japan had pursued toward the continent during the war. He stated his views before the Gaikô Chôsakai (Diplomatic Advisory Council) on the eve of his departure for Paris with the delegation to the peace conference. In order to refurbish a world image tarnished by a China policy of "selfish action and intrigue," Japan should devote serious attention to the League of Nations. The League proposal, he argued, reflected the world trends of pacifism and internationalism. The establishment of some kind of postwar international peace organization was inevitable, and Japan would be wise to assume the role of an active promoter rather then sideline observer.[24] Makino's views in the Gaikô Chôsakai were greeted with a barrage of volatile objections voiced by the War Minister Tanaka Giichi, Privy Councilor Itô Miyoji, and Kenseikai Party leader Inukai Tsuyoshi. Disarmament and sanctions could interfere with exercise of the Emperor's constitutional prerogatives and circumscribe the elevation of Japan's international position. The League could undermine or displace the Anglo-Japanese Alliance which for nearly two decades had formed the backbone of Japanese security. Itô spoke for many Japanese realists when he warned Makino that "A league of nations will be an international political union to preserve the status quo for the Anglo-Saxon race and check the ascendancy of other powers."[25]

It is important to note that neither Yoshino nor Makino, the League's most vocal proponents in Japan, disavowed continental expansion. Yoshino believed very strongly in Japan's "special interests" in China and openly approved the Twenty-One Demands. For Makino, it was the image and not the integrity of Japan's China policy which caused him concern. In a Gaikô Chôsakai meeting on the eve of Makino's departure for Paris, Inukai reacted to the plenipotentiary's fervent advocacy of the League by asking point blank if he was opposed to Japan's territorial expansion. Itô, who openly regarded Woodrow Wilson as a honey-mouthed hypocrite, compounded the attack by asserting that "a policy of conformity to world trends does not sufficiently take into consideration Japan's expansion needs." Makino replied that while territorial expansion was natural and necessary for Japan, the nation must work to erase a German-like image.[26] Neither the professor nor the diplomat regarded the League system as opposed to the realization of Japan's natural territorial expansion in East Asia. At best it would moderate Japanese methods of growth and give Japanese positive diplomacy an air of international respectability. An understanding of the secure place of expansionism within Japanese mainstream internationalism is important in comprehending Nitobe, whose love for the League and vindication of Manchukuo are too easily pictured as incongruous.

After months of sometimes acrid official and public debate over the League's preservation of the status quo and racial discrimination, pragmatism dictated that Japan affirm the League of Nations despite its drawbacks. Crucial were the considerations that Japan retain title to wartime territorial acquisitions and economic rights and avoid diplomatic isolation. Accommodating the world program of the major powers was particularly important to the Seiyûkai Cabinet of Prime Minister Hara Kei, the business community, and the Anglo-American faction which dominated the Foreign Ministry. Had it spurned the League, Japan would have raised further suspicions among the powers and forfeited the prestige of permanent Council membership. To remain aloof while China joined might have placed world sympathies and international economic sanctions at China's disposal for use against Japan. In short, the alternatives to League membership were less palatable. Itô Miyoji summed it up:

Our nation's action of joining the League of Nations was not, of course, taken with total satisfaction. This course was followed simply in consideration of Japan's future self-interest and the necessity of avoiding the disadvantageous circumstance of international isolation that would accompany refusal to participate in the League.[27]

Nitobe did not publicly participate in these debates. New responsibilities as president of Tokyo Women's Christian College after March 1918, absorbed his energies, and the educator's temperament was not that of a crusader. Moreover, he was out of the country when Japan was rebuffed on racial equality. That issue, however, did not escape his notice. A few years later he wrote, "I am acquainted with the details of the case, and my guess is that, regrettably, Wilson discarded his religious and scholarly conscience for the sake of politics."[28]

Once the League was launched, no time was lost in organizing and staffing its Secretariat. This task was guided by both internationalist ideals and big-power politics. Unlike the professional diplomats who would hold seats in the Assembly and Council, members of the Secretariat were not to represent their governments but to be servants of the League, responsible to it alone. The Secretariat was envisioned as an international civil service—a wholly novel concept at the time—compromised of impartial lay persons whose duties were not national but international. They were to be recommended by their governments, but appointed by the Secretary General and confirmed by the Council. Nevertheless, major Secretariat appointments throughout the period of Japan's membership reflected political realities. The Secretary General, Sir Eric Drummond, was British; the Deputy Secretary General was commonly a Frenchman; and the three or four Under-Secretaries General were chosen from such middle powers as Italy, Japan, and after 1926, Germany. Typically, the Section Directors were nationals of major countries. Jockeying for positions began even before the Covenant was signed. When it appeared that an Italian would receive a high post, Japan—one of the peace conference Big Five and proposed permanent member of the Council—demanded equal treatment. The Japanese delegation was then asked to nominate an Under-Secretary. Japanese diplomats in Paris sought someone fluent in English and French, a pleasing personality of high reputation in Japan and abroad, and someone neither a diplomat nor a politician. Not only was Nitobe Inazō eminently qualified; he was also at the right place at the right time.[29]

Prominent Japanese were not hard to find in Paris in the spring of 1919. The diplomatic entourage alone included a past and three future premiers, along with two former and nine future foreign ministers! Non-officials of varied ideologies were drawn to Paris to be present when the new world order was born. Among them were labor leader Suzuki Bunji, theologian Ebina Danjō, educator Tagawa Daikichirō, religious historian Anesaki

Masaharu, future fascist Nakano Seigo, and pan-Asianist Gotô Shimpei. Baron Gotô was en route around the world to see for himself the state of affairs in the wake of the Great War. With him he took the Nitobes to help when he needed people fluent in English. The story goes that Marquis Saionji and Baron Makino were gathered with others at the Japanese Embassy in Paris, wrestling with the question of whom to nominate for Under-Secretary General. Several names had been discussed and rejected, when Nitobe walked through the door with Gotô. Makino looked at Nitobe and exclaimed, "Here is a splendid candidate." True or not, it is a fact that Gotô pushed for Nitobe, and that plenipotentiaries Makino and Chinda Sutemi were enthusiastic. When Nitobe sought Gotô's counsel, the Baron gave his former Taiwan subordinate his full blessing and pressed the nomination with Sir Eric Drummond.[30] As for Makino, no Japanese understood more poignantly the reluctance of Japanese leaders to acquiesce in the League program. The appointment of a former colonial administrator with ties to the nationalistic Gotô could allay conservative fears that Japanese vital interests would be compromised in the new organization. At the same time someone with genuine internationalist views could serve the Secretariat wholeheartedly. Moreover, to make conspicuous a Japanese so cultivated and well-traveled could help to refurbish the atavistic image of Japan which so dismayed Makino.

Though the nomination and subsequent appointment took Nitobe by surprise, he regarded the opportunity as no less than providential. Writing to Anna H. Chace, a Quaker friend in Providence, Rhode Island, he announced:

> I have been most unexpectedly and unsoughtly appointed Director of a Section, and one of the four Under-Secretaries General. When I think of the change in my career, I feel afresh that there is a Guiding Hand above me. I confess I do not trust in my ability but the cause which I serve is certainly deserving of all my energy. When the offer was pressed upon me by Viscount Chinda and Baron Makino, our Peace delegates, and by Baron Gotô and by my younger friends, Tsurumi and Tajima, they were absolute in their assertion that this is the career for which my past experience and my domestic life have been pointing.

In later life Nitobe would write that the motive guiding his acceptance of the appointment to the Secretariat was the dream of his youth "to be a bridge across the Pacific Ocean, over which the ideas of the West and those of the East could travel back and forth unimpeded." After the Paris conference, Nitobe chanced to run into his former pupil Konoe Fumimaro on a London street. Nitobe shared the news of his appointment. The young noble noted that he had never seen his former teacher so happy.[31] Without returning to Japan, Nitobe went to work immediately with Drummond in London and Paris setting up the machinery for the League.

Lac Leman

Appointment to the League of Nations Secretariat enabled Nitobe to apply two of the principles that guided his life: international understanding and intellectual cooperation. When the Secretariat moved to Geneva in late 1920, the Nitobe home overlooking Lake Geneva became a place of hospitality for men and women of goodwill and intellectual curiosity. To a host of observers, Nitobe epitomized the spirit of the League and became one of the most effective communicators of its ideals.

It is important to reiterate that Nitobe served the League as a layperson and not as a governmental representative. He never sat in the Assembly or the Council as a delegate or cast a vote in any committee under instructions from the Japanese Foreign Ministry. Nor did he publicly voice opinions on the many political questions that confronted the League. We search in vain for his position on the Model Treaties, the Geneva Protocol, and the Geneva Arms Conference. Nitobe was not incapable of speaking out on issues of policy and power apart from the League—as indeed he did with regard to the 1924 U.S. Immigration Act—but in matters handled by the League he carefully adhered to the bounds of his position as an impartial, international civil servant. He also found that his job as an Under-Secretary General afforded causes large enough to absorb his full energies and passions.

The permanent contingent of League-related Japanese in Europe was not large. Japan never supplied its quota of Secretariat personnel. In 1928, for instance, there were five Japanese, compared to 143 Britons, 100 French, 126 Swiss, and 23 Italians. Japan also sent no clerical staff to Geneva.[32] The distance from Japan, the French-English official languages of the League, and the Euro-centered nature of Secretariat business probably account for this paucity of Japanese. The Foreign Office established a Japan Office of the League of Nations (Kokusai Remmei Teikoku Jimukyoku) in Paris in 1921. The head of the Office held the rank of minister and was assisted by six foreign service officers. Japan was typically represented at League meetings by members of this Office and ambassadors drawn from nearby capitals, and atypically—as in the case of Matsuoka Yôsuke in 1932–1933—by special envoys sent from Tokyo.[33]

Japan attached great importance to its membership in the League and took pains to assume that it played the role of a major power. The League provided an entree to Europe broader than that enabled by the Anglo-Japanese Alliance. As Marquis Saionji declared to the Emperor on his return from Paris in 1919, "Japan ranks among the five Great Powers of the world and has passed the threshold which allows it to take part in the affairs of Europe." As the only permanent member of the Council among Asian members of the League—the others were Siam, India, Persia, and China—Japan could claim to represent Oriental interests before the world, continue to press the issue of race equality, and speak with impartiality on European questions. In 1920, after conferring with Japan's Ambassador to London on the mechanics of League representation, Secretary General Drummond noted that the Japanese were eager to know what other governments were doing with regard to permanent envoys and living accommodations in Geneva. "My impression," he recounted, "was that the Japanese Government were showing considerable interest in League of Nations affairs."[34] Japan regularly sent to meetings of the Assembly and Council its ranking diplomats in Europe. Ishii Kikujirô (Ambassador to Paris) and Hayashi Gonsuke (Ambassador to London) represented the Empire at the First Assembly in September 1920. Assignment to the Japan Office of the League of Nations apparently helped one's foreign service career. All four chiefs who served while Japan was a member of the League—Matsuda Michikazu, Sugimura Yôtarô, Satô Naotake, and Sawada Setsuzô—later served as ambassadors to major capitals. Japan was unable, on account of distance, to be represented in the Assembly by its foreign minister or premier, a practice common among European members of the League. The customary journey from Tokyo to attend a two-week session in Geneva took four to five weeks one way. Troubled by this handicap, Japan actually sought, without success, the adoption of a biennial Assembly schedule to enable the attendance of a more prestigious delegate.[35]

Though Japan sent outstanding men—both lay and professional—to the League, the representatives of the Empire did little in Geneva to erase the "Silent Partners of the Peace" epithet earned at the peace conference. William E. Rappard, a Swiss who served as Director of the Mandates Section during Nitobe's years in the Secretariat, remarked that "I do not feel that I know, nor that I understand the Japanese. Never having visited their country, I can judge them only by what they say, and they say uncommonly little!" Nitobe himself lamented the weakness of the Japanese on their feet: "Reticent by training, and handicapped by the very meager linguistic talent vouchsafed to them by nature, the Japanese cannot win the confidence of nations by word of mouth. How inferior we are in this respect to the Chinese!"[36]

Nitobe's immediate assignment as Under-Secretary General was to direct the Section of International Bureaux. He held this directorship without respite until his resignation from the Secretariat in 1926. In this capacity he helped produce a "Handbook of International Organizations." To his nephew in Philadelphia he wrote, "It is through voluntary organizations, in which men and women of like minds scattered all over the world take part, that the real international spirit is fostered."[37]

Most celebrated was his contribution in the founding of the International Committee for Intellectual Cooperation (ICIC), the forerunner of today's UNESCO. After the First Assembly mandated the Committee's formation in 1920, Nitobe undertook to secure the participation of savants with international reputations. In May 1922, the Council appointed twelve as the first Committee, and their first meeting was held in August of that year. The members included Henri Bergson, Albert Einstein, Hendrik Lorentz, Madame Marie Curie, and Gilbert Murray. The ICIC always included an American representative. Bergson, the most distinguished French philosopher of his generation, became president. Nitobe was especially drawn to this thinker, and the two enjoyed several friendly and unhurried private conversations in the early years of the Committee.[38]

The philosophy underlying the Committee came naturally to Nitobe: the world of knowledge knows no national frontiers. Léon Bourgeois, also a moving force in its establishment, stated that the Committee's purpose was "to afford each country the opportunity of developing vigorously and abundantly by drawing upon the common fund of knowledge, methods, and discoveries."[39] It purposed to facilitate contacts between teachers, artists, scientists, and authors; to establish ties between universities in different countries; to foster the protection of intellectual property; and to encourage the development of international bibliographical facilities. Nitobe viewed the enterprise of world intellectual cooperation with mixed pessimism and hope. When the first Committee was announced, he commented that:

> the problems that lie before them are so vast, and it is not impossible that what they can accomplish under present circumstances is very little to the world desiderata; but I believe they owe it to their own names to do something towards bringing at least the intellectuals of different countries a little closer together.[40]

An additional purpose of the ICIC was to strengthen the League's influence for peace. In carrying out its projects, the Committee transcended differences of race, religion, and language. This, in the minds of some observers, constituted a demonstration to the larger League and to the world of a genuine internationalism that could prevail in political issues as well. Intellectual workers were seen by the Committee's instigators as an untapped reservoir whose influence in support of international political cooperation might be very great. Hitherto foreign policy had been the sole purview of politicians, diplomats, soldiers, and bureaucrats. Poets, historians, and scientists had entered the enterprise only as apologists or propagandists for the ideas of others. The Committee intended to make of intellectuals instigators of policy. In this goal, as in all its purposes, the resources available to the ICIC fell far short of its visions. For all the tasks it proposed to undertake, it was granted by the Assembly an annual budget of less than five thousand pounds. Evaluating its impact, historian of the League F. P. Walters concluded that:

The Organization not only failed to achieve the ambitions of those who first conceived it, but seemed in some of its undertakings, to be fanciful and impractical. In many others it produced results which were useful, but which fell so far below its real potentialities that these were soon forgotten by all but a few.... Although the Intellectual Co-operation Committee rendered many useful services to intellectual workers,...it failed completely to bring them into a common front against the dangers of national hatreds and national ambitions.[41]

Many of the Committee's tasks were assumed by an International Institute of Intellectual Cooperation, established in Paris in 1924 with French government support. Upon reflection, the incapacity of the Committee on Intellectual Cooperation to translate lofty goals into concrete achievement bears striking similarity to the ultimate frustration of the League as peacekeeper, and to Nitobe as bridge builder.

One project of the Committee in which Nitobe played a direct hand was the publication of a series of twenty-two booklets on intellectual life in various countries. The purpose of the series, as stated in the booklets' preface, was to "draw attention to the questions of organization and intellectual cooperation which arise in relation to each of the subjects dealt with." Nitobe wrote one of the booklets, "Use and Study of Foreign Languages in Japan: A Study in Cultural Internationalism." In it he treated the history of Chinese linguistic influence on Japan and the state of the study of Western languages in his home country.[42]

A secondary but nonetheless important role of Nitobe in the Secretariat was publicist for the League. As a writer and lecturer he conveyed the goals and spirit of the organization to audiences in Europe and Japan. When Ambassador Ishii asked Drummond why he so often tapped the Japanese Under-Secretary to speak on behalf of the League, the Secretary General explained, "because Nitobe is the most highly qualified. He is not only a good speaker, but he gives audiences a deep and lasting impression. In this respect no one in the Secretariat can excel him." Ishii at first took Drummond's praise as an attempt to flatter Nitobe, but after years of close observation of the latter's eloquence declared, "I discovered that it was just as the Secretary General has said; my admiration was as strong as his."[43] An Asian's appearance on behalf of the League lent credence to the myth of the organization's universality. The first product of Nitobe's public relations work was a lecture given September 13 and 14, 1920, at International University, Brussels. It was entitled "What the League of Nations Has Done and Is Doing." In its translated and published form, this work served as a basic primer on the league for French-, English-, and Japanese-speaking audiences. Delivered when Nitobe had been with the Secretariat barely a year, and before the First Assembly convened, this piece provides insight into Nitobe's ideas regarding international organization at the outset of his League career.

Nitobe expressed a Wilsonian confidence in the future of the "world parliament." Its member-nations encompassed three-fourths of the world's population. The eight meetings of the Council so far had enabled representatives to sit around a common table and discuss freely and in private the questions before them. From this, Nitobe drew inspiration:

> Few things afford a more encouraging prospect for harmonious co-operation, a more hopeful earnest of universal peace, than the sight of the leading statesmen of the foremost countries of the world coming together in close personal relations, holding different views and expressing them with utmost freedom, yet in the spirit of mutual understanding and concord. They come agreed to differ and differ to agree.[44]

In the Secretariat, reported the Under-Secretary, there was an *esprit de corps* in which "the members are actuated by a spirit of idealism, and spurred on by a strong sense of responsibility in this new venture of world reconstruction." He did not find in the Secretariat the cynicism and personal jealousy he had observed in bureaucracies at home and abroad.[45] Through the mandate principle, the Covenant had dealt imperialism a fatal blow. Twice in the essay Nitobe referred to the freedom for women to participate fully in the machinery of the League. As for the upcoming First assembly, for which 100 delegates from forty countries were expected, Nitobe anticipated "a holy experiment in world politics," and hoped for "a day of Pentecost with tongues of fire each understanding the other." Even should tangible results not be forthcoming, the "moral gain accruing from the mere personal contact of national leaders coming from the ends of the earth" would in itself make the conclave worthwhile. "In the realm of ideas, to *come* and to *see* is to *conquer*, and it is on the broad field of humanitarian ideals that the League of Nations desires to outrival the conquests of Julius Caesar."[46]

In describing the League, the Under-Secretary was not blind to its deficiencies. The United States, one of the institution's leading organizers, was missing from its rolls, as were Germany and the Soviet Union. This state of affairs had contributed in part to the postponement of the First Assembly. The League peace machinery was designed to prevent war and was powerless to restore peace once armed conflict started. While Nitobe pointed glowingly to progress in seventeen projects initiated by the Council and the Secretariat, he lamented the League's lack of power to intervene in an existing state of war in the Hedjaz and lack of financial and manpower resources to accept a mandate over Armenia. The system of apportioning financial contributions, he added, was inequitable and in need of revamping. He warned against false hopes for the League. It could not sweep away atavistic institutions at once, but over time would remold them into instruments of universal cooperation. As a true liberal, Nitobe thus asserted his preference to work through existing institutions to effect gradual change. He assured his readers that, despite its defects, the League of Nations was "the organization most compatible with existing conditions." He concluded with a Nitobe-like plea to refrain from premature judgments, confident that patient observers would see fruits that vindicated the League's existence.[47]

Nitobe did not ignore his home country in his publicity efforts for the League. His essays were published in Japanese journals and circulated in Japan by the government-subsidized Japan League of Nations Association. He spent eleven weeks in Japan from December 1924, speaking on behalf of the League to audiences the combined attendance figures for which exceeded more than 50,000 and giving twenty-five press interviews. "Thus," he summed up this exhausting mission, "nearly the whole of my sojourn was taken up with League propaganda. As this was entirely in accordance with my intention when I left Geneva, I was only thankful that the way opened so readily for my task." Due to his cultivation of the public while on furlough, the number of local branches of the Association rose from nine to nineteen. His schedule included a lecture before Prince Regent Hirohito, during which the future Emperor was more than a passive listener. The Prince's first question concerned America's attitude toward the League, in answer to which Nitobe reported American participation in committees of the League and voiced the belief that the United States would enter the organization. Several gatherings of dignitaries heard him in closed session. They included a group of individuals associated with the Court, a session with members of the cabinet and the Privy Council, a group of Lower House Dietmen, and a large meeting of bankers and industrialists. Nitobe felt that he was warmly welcomed as a spokesman for the League.[48]

Upon his return to Geneva, Nitobe presented to Secretary General Drummond an in-depth report on his Japan travels in which he analyzed prevailing Japanese attitudes toward the League. He had found that no one stridently opposed the organization. Foreign Minister Shidehara Kijûrô had told him that the Diet willingly budgeted Japan's annual apportionment. Genuine *zeal* for the League, on the other hand, was limited to "educated youth" and the 2,300 members of the League of Nations Association. Otherwise, "the older generation as represented in the Higher governmental service, the parliament, the larger business circles and the professions, is lacking in enthusiasm except in a few instances." Though the press had dutifully reported debates in Geneva on the Protocol and Opium questions, "the League looked so far off, and its work touched the country so lightly.... Many studied the League, but few knew it."

Among the specific complaints Nitobe encountered at home and reported to Drummond was the allegation that the League had failed to achieve universality. Some Japanese viewed the League as Eurocentric, and asked whether participation was profitable for Asian nations. Nitobe confessed that the question of universality was the hardest to answer. His reply to Japanese questioners concerning the practical value of League membership is a classic statement of international accommodationism:

> Japan will find in a few years that the wisest course for her to pursue in her diplomacy is to bring it in line with the world's public opinion as mirrored in the League. Such a course, far from being a passive obedience to a supernational body, as some ultra-nationalists fear, can rightly be viewed as an active utilization of the League on the part of Japan.

The position of permanent membership of the Council was adequate return on Japan's investment. "This position," he said, "is not only highly honorable, but very valuable in ordinary times and priceless in extraordinary times." To any suggestion that Japan should vacate Geneva, Nitobe's response was clear:

> Japan is in, and she must stay. If she leaves, that will not improve her relations with America. On the contrary, it is more likely they will worsen. It seems the noblest, and in the long run the wisest thing for Japan to do is so to conduct herself within the League as to prove herself above suspicion, and thus even pave the way for America's entry.

In Japan, Nitobe found a "glum silent look of disavowal" of the League on the part of the educators. The former Tôdai professor observed that the educational system was thoroughly grounded in the theory of the absolute sovereignty of the state and the exalted position of the Throne, and "the educational authorities are exceedingly jealous of any doctrine or opinion that may possibly infringe upon their sacred dogmas." While the textbooks proudly represented the League as a "quasi-philanthropic 'Parliament of man'" to which Japan adhered of its own accord for the welfare of the world, the official mind was afraid that "the interest and dignity of the nation may be compromised by affiliation with a super-national organization." Nitobe was conscious that a struggle between nationalism and internationalism in Japan—"The World" versus "The Country"—could be fraught with peril. He regretted that the authorities distrusted people who philosophically upheld the claims of the world in opposition to those of the state. Nonetheless, he took heart in signs that leading educational institutions had recently opened their doors to the activities of the League of Nations Association.

The Under-Secretary ended his report with an appeal for better communication from Geneva. Japanese in the Secretariat should write more frequently for the Japanese press, if only to offset such false rumors as the one that the League had classified the institution of the *geisha* as "traffic in women and children." He called for the dispatch of League functionaries to the Far East, and for the holding of some League-sponsored, international conference in Tokyo. Secretary General Drummond responded warmly to Nitobe's report, going so far as to state a desire of his own to go to Japan, and pledging his efforts to send League officials to East Asia.[49]

To foster internationalism and the "Geneva spirit" in Japan, Nitobe believed that it was necessary to establish a permanent League presence in his homeland. To this end he formally proposed, in May 1925, the establishment of a branch office of the Information Section in Tokyo. Similar branches already were operating in London, Paris, Rome, Berlin, and Washington. Nitobe insisted that the office be headed by a Japanese with experience in Geneva and on good terms with the Foreign Ministry and the Japan League of Nations Association.[50] Secretariat leaders endorsed, and the Sixth Assembly approved, Nitobe's proposal in full, including a Fr20,000 annual appropriation for a Correspondent's salary and funds for his travel to Geneva every other year. Aoki Setsuichi, a secretary of the League of Nations Association stationed in Geneva, accepted the position. The Office opened in May 1926. Nitobe considered this a major personal accomplishment and a major step in the promotion of the League in Japan. The Association took this move as "concrete evidence of the League's interest in the Far East and in Japan in the particular," and predicted "added zest and increasing sympathy" from the people of Japan. The Office grew to employ five assistants by 1933. Its functions were curtailed in 1935 when Japan's withdrawal from the League took effect.[51]

Before he went to Geneva, Nitobe's reputation as an internationalist and a Christian thinker was well established in Japan and the United States. Service in Geneva made him a citizen of the world, respected in Europe as he was in America and in his homeland as an apostle of ideals and as exemplar of Christian character. The gracious charm which had endeared him to his Ichikô students two decades earlier now won friends for the League and led men and women otherwise prone to cynicism to believe that international order was viable. The reputation of the League was enhanced by his personal magnetism, and stereotypical images of Japanese as humorless, unprincipled pragmatists were countered by humane example. Satô Naotake testified that all Japanese in Geneva benefitted from Nitobe's reputation for integrity.[52]

Personality and character to Nitobe were not traits passively acquired, not mere by-products of heredity, life circumstances, or religious experience. Personality was rather a quality to be developed through learning, self-reflection, and discipline. His book *Shûyô* (Self-cultivation) influenced a generation of Japanese youth in quest of selfhood. In his educational program at First Higher he emphasized character building. He admonished the students to be cheerful and sociable, not cynical and gloomy, and to display democratic spirit. From his example they learned how to laugh and enjoy jokes. He preached the virtues of idealism and humanitarianism to counter the naturalism which flooded his nation after the Russo-Japanese War.[53] Nitobe was a keen observer of persons in the League and shrewd judge of their character. He once said there were four kinds of delegates— those who understood nothing and kept silent; those who understood nothing and spoke; those who understood everything and kept silent; and those who understood everything and spoke on appropriate occasions. He added that even among the commendable fourth group were bad men. After returning from Geneva he would write an essay on the power of personality as expressed in elocution, drawing inspiration from prominent orators heard in the League Council. He believed in national character and distrusted the French. He was known for humorous references to national traits: "One Pole, charm; two Poles, quarrels; three Poles, three political parties!"[54] There were many testimonials to the popularity of the Nitobes in Geneva. The Nitobe home with its large collection of Japanese *objets d'art* was a center of urbanity. Harriet Newman, an English Quaker living in Geneva, recalled that "They were most hospitable over a large circle and spent themselves most liberally. Their home was always open to me and I valued it very much. It was delightful to see Inazô Nitobe with little children.... They were unsparing in the time they would give to show visitors what the work of the League was." Ayusawa Iwao, member of the secretariat of the International Labor Organization during the Nitobe years in Geneva, later reminisced about the scene by Lac Leman:

> The Nitobes selected a residence on the west side of Lake Geneva in the village of Bellevue. The mansion overlooked the pure waters of the lake, which lapped the edge of an expansive lawn. From time to time a flock of swans floated by to accent an elegant picture. Beyond the lake rose the glistening white cap of Mont Blanc amidst a thousand mountains and ten thousand peaks of the Alps. Here and there in shady spots across the lawn were small white tables and chairs. On weekends one could observe seated there sipping tea and engaging in friendly conversation such world-renowned authorities of philosophy and science as England's classicist Gilbert Murray, Germany's Albert Einstein, and France's Madame Curie, along with various musical geniuses. Had it been a century earlier, no doubt the faces of the English poets Shelley and Byron would have been counted as well.

In Ayusawa's estimation, the international interaction within the Nitobe home was the starting point for the Geneva peace experiment.[55]

The Under-Secretary General's warmth also extended to persons of no reputation. Avoiding the ritzy restaurants in Geneva, he preferred to hobnob with his subordinates in basement cafes. The clerks and typists who worked under him loved him for it. When opera was on, the Nitobes would buy ten tickets and invite friends to join them. His student research assistant, Blanche Weber Schaffer, recalled his knack of drawing others into conversation. He would say, "Oh, on this subject Ayusawa knows a delightful story," and Ayusawa would tell his vignette and for a while be the center of interest. Even those who knew the Under-Secretary through correspondence remarked about his gracious, intelligent ways.[56] Henry F. Angus, of the Canadian Institute of International Affairs, gave a memorable character portrait:

> We were attracted from the outset by Dr. Nitobe's simplicity, by his gentleness, and by his sincerity. We were attracted, too, by his playfulness in conversation and by his power of seeing the amusing side of men and things. We should call these very human qualities, and by that term we mean qualities which made a direct appeal to all mankind. It is a great achievement for a man to make his personality felt by people of a different race, a different language and a different culture. If Dr. Nitobe was able to do this, it was partly because of his complete mastery of our language and by his scholarly knowledge of our letters, but mainly because he had a distinctive and, indeed, a great personality.[57]

Personal warmth enabled Nitobe to be an effective apostle for the League and international understanding.

One virtue which Nitobe conveyed by both word and deed was tolerance. Takagi Yasaka recalled that in the ethics class at Ichikô, the principal taught the boys not to prejudge anyone by outward appearances. James T. Shotwell, an organizer of the International Labor Organization and officer in the Institute of Pacific Relations, summarized Nitobe's message as, "there should be more thoughtfulness in the judgment which we make concerning others." This attitude, said the Columbia University historian, "was one which he held towards life in all its manifestations. It was the source of broad tolerance, of his ready appreciation of what the Western nations have been striving to attain in such organizations as the League of Nations...." A sympathetic nature was, to Nitobe, the essence of the Geneva spirit. It was this attitude which he tried to evoke in Western hearts toward Japan in the last years of his life. The difficulty of that task became his final frustration.[58]

One might expect that seven years in a major world center of international relations would have turned such a versatile mind as Nitobe's toward political science. The Secretariat, the context of his daily activity, was constantly humming with issues of national power and national interest.

During the annual meetings of the Assembly and the more frequent convenings of the Council, Geneva teemed with diplomats, foreign ministers, and heads of state. Despite these stimuli, the Japanese Under-Secretary remained very much a humanist. Said James T. Shotwell, "International understanding meant to him...sympathetic study of all those varied expressions in the fields of art and literature as well as of politics in which a nation reveals its complex personality." Ambassador Ishii recalled the comprehension of his vision, the richness of his cultivation. More than a scholar of broad knowledge, he was "something of a philosopher,...a spiritual man [*seishinka*]."[59] If anything, his humanist bent became even more pronounced during his Geneva sojourn. He found common cause in Bergson's assertion that human survival in the machine age requires a decision to strive for the growth of the human spirit.[60] Herein lies a crucial key to understanding the man, his concept of internationalism, and his dealings with League issues.

Nitobe took time amidst his Secretariat chores to continue his scholarly task of introducing and explaining Eastern culture to Western readers. Among his writings in this period are his *Japanese Traits and Foreign Influences* and his unfinished translations of the classics the *Lao-Tzu* and the *Kojiki*. In *Japanese Traits* he explained the doctrine of universal human commonality which lay at the heart of his internationalism. He believed that "fundamentally human nature is identical," and "if one be scratched only deep enough he will show common humanity." This commonality applied in intellect, morals, religion, and art. He wrote of universal genius, of "the global character of the moral world," and of the demise of religious barriers in the face of modern scholarship. Christ, his chief mentor, was an example of the "universalism of spirit." He tried to bridge the gap between Oriental thought and Christianity by relying on the mysticism so prominent in Quaker experience. "All art deserving of the name," he explained, "is international." People everywhere can appreciate it because of a "universal standard of beauty, transcending all technical canons of national aesthetics." Hope for man lay in "his growing more universal in knowledge and in sympathy, in broadening his education so as to embrace the East and the West."[61] Thus, for Nitobe, internationalism was cultural internationalism, not political or systemic internationalism, and was to be furthered through a slow but effective process of education. Nitobe talked no more about *international relations* after Geneva than he did before Geneva: his field was *humankind relations*. The stuff of his discourses was not the issues facing the League, but rather the eternal sentiments common to humanity. The illustrations he used to buttress his arguments came, on the whole, not from current events but from classical literature and philosophy of both the East and the West, and most markedly from the Bible. As a thinker, Nitobe was never a Tachi Sakutarô, a Konoe Fumimaro, or even a

Yoshino Sakuzô. Miwa Kimitada has underscored this trait in Nitobe's earlier career as well. Despite his studies in economics at Johns Hopkins and agricultural administration at Berlin and Halle, the professor of colonial administration never said anything about petroleum but rather taught the importance of the imperial nation's human attitude toward colonized peoples.[62] The Japanese humanist's message was profoundly appreciated in the salons by Lac Leman. Would it communicate in the tense air of an international crisis?

By the time Nitobe resigned from the service of the League in December 1926, the Secretariat had grown in prestige and power, and Japan had elevated its international reputation considerably through its deportment in Geneva. League officials attested to the importance of Nitobe's contribution in this welcome development. Joseph A. Avenol, later Secretary General, noted "the good fortune for the League as well as for Japan that Inazô Nitobe should become one of the highest officials in this creative task...." Historian F. P. Walters called Nitobe one of the "brightest spirits" of the Secretariat's "old team" which included Jean Monnet, William Rappard, Salvador de Madariaga, and Bernardo Attolico and which, with Sir Eric Drummond, had established the Secretariat's respectability. Japanese delegates to League meetings had, said Walters, "set a standard of courtesy, industry, and thoroughness which no others surpassed and few equalled," and were valued for their dispassionate impartiality with respect to the quarrels of Europe. Symbolic of Japan's appreciation of the importance of its role in the Secretariat was Ambassador Ishii's nomination of a rising diplomat, Sugimura Yôtarô, to succeed Nitobe. Symbolic of Japan's rising prestige in the League was Sugimura's subsequent appointment by the Secretary General to head the crucial Political Section.[63]

On the scene for seven years since the League's inception, Nitobe occupied an ideal vantage point from which to evaluate the progress of universal order. Germany's admission to the League in 1926 pleased him, but the continuing aloofness of the United States was troubling and belied his earlier predictions that America would join. Moreover, with the Soviet Union a nonmember, it was obvious that the League was not universal in scope. Despite conscientious Japanese involvement in its activities, the League remained very much preoccupied with Europe. When Nitobe's Japanese colleagues in the Secretariat returned home on furlough, they found frequent references in the press to the League as a European club. Anti-Japanese discrimination in California, capped by the U.S. Immigration Act of 1924 which so vexed the Under-Secretary, called into question the efficacy of universal morality. Japanese in Geneva feared that the discriminatory Act would fire reactionary sentiment in Japan against internationalism and the League of Nations.[64]

Events Nitobe observed in Europe gave strong evidence that the powers were prone to circumvent the League in matters of vital self-interest. The 1923 Corfu Incident involving League members Italy and Greece was settled by a conference of ambassadors rather than League machinery because Italy refused to accept League jurisdiction in the case. In 1925, a set of significant political, military, and territorial accommodations with Germany was concluded by Britain, France, Italy, and Belgium at the Locarno Conference. Though elaborate efforts were made to incorporate the Locarno Pacts into the League system, it was obvious that the European powers were presenting the League with a *fait accompli* and using the organization to give legitimacy to understandings forged elsewhere. The League was clearly secondary in the European power game. The model of Locarno-type regional understanding drew a positive response from Japanese. In a speech to the League, Council Ambassador Ishii praised the Pact as a regional entente, more effective for peace than the Versailles Treaty. Foreign Minister Shidehara saw a brighter future for the League in the light of Locarno. The *Hôchi* newspaper voiced the feelings of many observers in calling the Pact "an epoch-making diplomatic document far more forceful than the Versailles treaty of peace." Locarno pleased many Japanese as a supplement to the League order because it was concrete rather than idealistic, and regional rather then universalistic.[65] Though such notions did not mesh with Nitobe's assertion of universal humankind, he too would voice them later when his country's regional interests were threatened by the League.

As Nitobe's Geneva years drew to a close, his support for the League remained strong. Yet one can detect a loss of the earlier assurance. He was more willing to admit the League's failings and limitations. His affirmations tended toward the line that "Japan has no acceptable alternative." Writing in July 1926, to a young Quaker acquaintance in Philadelphia, he contended that:

> the League seems to be the only hope of the world at present. I do not mean by that, that it is doing everything expected of it. I mean rather that it has shown itself to be the right kind of institution to deal with international troubles, and I do earnestly wish that the time may speedily come when America will see it right to join it.

Back in Japan, he summed up a lengthy defense of Japanese membership: "The League of Nations has now been in operation for eight years. In these years Japan has lost nothing by her membership. The imponderable advantages she has gained more than justify her presence in that parliament of the world."[66]

Forty-Two to One

Even before Nitobe left Europe in 1927, he learned of new assignments. For the sixty-five-year-old former Under-Secretary General, the post-Geneva years would not afford retirement. A seat in the House of Peers and appointment to the Imperial Academy awaited his return. He was named Advisory Editor by the *English Osaka Mainichi* and *Tokyo Nichi Nichi* newspapers. In announcing this appointment, the *Nichi Nichi* described Nitobe as "Japan's foremost savant and humanitarian," and stated that "for most learned people both at home and abroad the mere mention of his name is copious introduction." His column of "Editorial Jottings" appeared daily on the back page, keeping his ideas before the international community in Japan. Through this mouthpiece he called on Japan to take a more active position in the League of Nations and to comply more fully with the resolutions of the International Labor Congress. Moderating social Darwinian views expressed earlier in his career, he drew from the animal world examples of "cooperation of the tenderest nature" to illustrate that "competition was not the whole process of development." In editorials he applauded the Kellogg-Briand Pact and criticized the policy of Prime Minister Tanaka Giichi to delay Japan's signing until the other governments announced their intentions. Nitobe chided, "would he were as modest in his dealings with China!" The League of Nations appointed Nitobe to the International Committee on Intellectual Cooperation; though he accepted the honor, he never returned to Europe for a meeting.[67] In 1929, he was named chairman of the Japanese Council of the Institute of Pacific Relations (IPR). In this capacity he served for four years on the Pacific Council of the IPR and headed the Japanese delegations to the Kyoto (October 1929), Shanghai (October 1931), and Banff (August 1933) conferences. As in the case of his Secretariat appointment, Nitobe's scholarly background, world experience, and reputation as a bridge builder made him the obvious choice to represent Japan in the IPR.

Two biennial conferences of the Institute, held at Honolulu in 1925 and 1927, predate Nitobe's involvement. At these, Japan was represented by Sawayanagi Masatarô, a member of the House of Peers and former trustee of the Japan League of Nations Association. The proceedings reflect little interest in the League of Nations at these meetings. This feature changed noticeably in 1929 and markedly in 1931 and 1933. The entry of a former Under-Secretary General had something to do with the shift, for Nitobe himself introduced the subject at Kyoto. But even without Nitobe the IPR could hardly have ignored the subject of the League. The phenomena of world depression, Chinese nationalism and political reunification, the strengthening of the Soviet Union, and—from the very eve of the Shanghai convocation—the Manchurian Incident were destabilizing power relations in the Pacific region and compelling creative minds to assess all available options for international order.

In his opening address at the 1929 Kyoto gathering, Nitobe referred to Geneva as "that world capital, the Mecca of international peace and cooperation," and called the League of Nations "indispensable for the future of our species." He was gratified to report to the IPR that this "moral institution" was gaining in size and power. His words of praise began a fitting welcome to those in the audience who were sent by the Secretariat as observers—fulfilling Nitobe's desire as Under-Secretary that the League dispatch officers to meetings in the Far East. But more significant was Nitobe's call for a regionally-based mechanism to supplement the Geneva order:

> As the League grows in membership and geographical dimensions, it will presumably be compelled to conduct some of its business in regional congresses. For, though theoretically and ideologically the concern of one nation is the concern of the whole world, there are, in practice, international questions that affect only restricted areas. Questions of this character can be best discussed by the parties interested in a regional gathering, under the general direction or oversight of the central body.

Nitobe believed that the IPR could provide the model for such a regional institution.[68] Round-table discussions among the IPR delegates scrutinized in depth the notion of peace machinery for the Pacific, and in the discussion the Versailles order as then constituted came up wanting. The Chinese delegation articulated widely-held views when it expressed frank suspicions about the fairness of League procedures and the relevance of the system to Asia. China had received both injustice and neglect; the League was too much under the domination of the great powers. Other delegates added that, with its successes mainly in Europe, the League might in fact be regarded as a European regional organization. In the Pacific, practical advance had been made mainly by regional conferences outside the League.[69]

Thus, the suggestions advanced by the keynoter were sustained in conference discussion. The League had a positive role to play, but in its present form it could not be the instrument for order in East Asia. The Kyoto Conference is evidence that, well before Mukden, Nitobe's political universalism was wearing thin. The principle that "the concern of one nation is the concern of the whole world" was now relegated to the realm of the ideal, and regional schemes for international order were gaining approval. It is no mere coincidence that Nitobe's *Japan*, published in 1931, lamented the termination of the Anglo-Japanese Alliance in 1922.[70] Woodrow Wilson, who had promoted the League as an alternative to such regional ententes, was turning in his grave!

On September 18, 1931, an explosion on the South Manchurian Railway near Mukden set off a series of events which would permanently separate

Japan from the League of Nations and confront Nitobe with the most frustrating dilemma of his career as an internationalist. Three days later, China appealed to the League to intervene. A League Council resolution on October 24, asked Japan to withdraw its troops to the railway zone. Three days before this resolution, on October 21, the Fourth Conference of the IPR was scheduled to open in Shanghai. At first there was doubt that the meeting could transpire at all and that the Chinese hosts could assure the safety of the Japanese delegation.[71] Shanghai in the fall of 1931 was no Lac Leman. Chinese nationalism, communism, and anti-imperialism were in the air. No lofty ideals of universal humanity would satisfy the demands of the hour.

As in Kyoto two years before, the question of diplomatic machinery for the Pacific was the central political issue, and the immediacy of the Manchurian crisis made the discussion all the more poignant. Nitobe's direct input on this question is not recorded, but Takayanagi Kenzô, a professor of the Law Faculty of Tokyo University, made a formal presentation of the Japanese delegation's position in which he tackled the universalism-regionalism problem head-on:

> It seems to me that the conception of universalism—the League as a universal organ, to deal with all disputes arising throughout the world—is a very valuable one. There should not be too many competing organs. There is much justification for that argument. But that conception may well be reconciled with an attempt to set up here in the Pacific an organ to investigate in a realistic way the conditions in China and Japan, and ultimately to solve the international difficulties in the Pacific area. Arrangements may be made in such a way that such an organ will not do away with the idea of the universality of the League.

Takayanagi then took up the issue of Manchuria, contending that a League without American and Soviet representation could not deal adequately with such complex matters as Chinese nationalism and Soviet designs on the region. His conclusion was a clear challenge to existing League machinery:

> My main thesis tonight is that Geneva is too far away to appreciate the complex conditions obtaining in the Far East. Members of the League Council may fall into the error of judging things by superficial observation of events and the mere study of the provisions of the treaties contained in MacMurray. A permanent body, either a part of the League, or an independent unit affiliated with the League, and with America and Russia co-operating, is highly desirable for dealing, not only with the Manchurian question, but with questions relating to the whole international situation in the Orient.

Not unexpectedly, the Chinese delegation reversed its Kyoto position and argued that the mechanisms of the League were indeed adequate for the present situation.[72] The question of the League and Pacific order was not to be resolved at Shanghai.

These were difficult days for Inazô and Mary. As though uncontrollable events, soul-searching, and constant danger of assassination in Japan and China were not enough, Inazô was suffering from a crippling back ailment. While her husband was at the IPR conference, Mary wrote that she felt "as though I had lived through a life-time in the past month." Her frustrated assertion in a letter to her nephew that the League in its initial response "went off half-cocked" does not contradict Inazô's later criticisms of League action, although they were more subdued.[73]

It now seems clear that the deep, dark night of the soul brought to the surface all the impulses that had at any time moved the heart of Nitobe. Some moral imperatives which had been supplanted for years reawakened to tug at his conscience. Among these passions were the sense of honor that flowed in samurai veins, love for the Emperor, the nationalism of the turn of the century, the Momotarô Doctrine, Christ's universality of spirit, the craving that Japan be understood and accepted by the outside world, the serenity of Lac Leman. It should not surprise us that Nitobe acted and spoke in 1931–33 in ways that seem contradictory and out of character. Inazô himself prayed for patience. In retrospect, it might have been better had he retreated from public view to sort things out and find solace. But he chose instead dutiful action, at risk to himself and his reputation abroad and at the price of violating a public vow. He decided to undertake a personal mission to the United States and Canada.

An invitation to tour under the auspices of the Institute of Pacific Relations enabled him to travel as a private citizen, though before departing Tokyo he consulted with War Minister Araki Sadao on the policy of the military.[74] In late April 1932, he disembarked in California in his first visit to the United States since 1919. He would remain in North America until March 1933 and return for the last time the following August. He came impelled by his life-long conviction that correct knowledge brings understanding and peace. He sought, he said, not to justify Japan's behavior, but to explain why Japan had followed its course of action in Manchuria. He believed that someone had to tell the American people, in language they could understand, Japan's side of the story. He did not deny that his government deserved criticism, but resolved to give advice to Japan at home and not abroad.[75] He tried to place Japanese policy in perspective—not only the perspective of the real circumstances of Asia, but also the perspective of the expansionist and regional hegemonic impulses which had shaped the historical development of the United States. For this task Nitobe—Quaker Christian, Johns Hopkins–educated student of America, retired League official—was as qualified as any Japanese could be. By public and private talks, radio addresses, and personal conversations, Nitobe took his message to a broad spectrum of the American people. Into this mission he poured all his arts of articulation and persuasion. His efforts were not well received or understood. Even some of his friends regarded the trip as a mistake and his message as defensive and nationally self-serving. His closest in-law, J. Passmore Elkinton, concluded that Nitobe sublimated his pacifist convictions to loyalty to his government.[76]

Nitobe headed directly for the East Coast, telling reporters along the way that he had come to study American opinion, correct misinformation, and confront American prejudices with regard to Japan's China policies. He denied any Japanese intent to colonize Manchuria and expressed confidence that knowledge of the truth would cause Americans, "with their common sense and idealism," to moderate their judgment of Japan.[77] While in New York he went on the air to address a nationwide audience on "Japan and the League of Nations." In this, the first of several radio speeches, he listed three fatal drawbacks to the Japan-League relationship: 1) the absence of a stated principle of race equality; 2) the nonmembership of America and the Soviet Union; and 3) the lack, until the current case, of issues involving Japan as a principal party. Drawing upon a theme he had played two decades earlier in the United States, he depicted a China which "does not or cannot function as a sovereign state, in the modern sense of the term." He warned that if the League refused to "recognize the justice of our claim which involves our honor and our very existence as a nation," Japan would withdraw and "carve out, unaided and alone, her own destiny."[78]

Self-confident enough to engage the highest levels of government, he traveled to Washington for a polite interview on June 1 with President Herbert Hoover and a more substantive conversation with Secretary of State Henry L. Stimson. Five months earlier Stimson had articulated the non-recognition doctrine which bears his name as a warning to Japan. Nitobe assured Stimson that the Japanese occupation of Manchuria could not be permanent, and explained his hope that the Chinese there would learn elements of order and government from the Japanese presence for the benefit of all China. Stimson spent a great deal of energy during their "long and friendly talk" lecturing Nitobe on the Nine-Power Treaty and, with copious references to English history, on the principle of subordination of military authorities to civil authorities.[79] As a Japanese liberal who had long been on public record against chauvinism, Nitobe did not need Stimson's tutoring on authority. The Secretary of State apparently did not convert Nitobe, for in an August 20, radio speech Nitobe lashed out against the Stimson Doctrine as a "hair-splitting legal interpretation" of the Kellogg-Briand Pact. Nitobe instead called for forbearance: "Triumph can come only as a moral suasion...." Nitobe's line of argument ran that the ideals of the Peace Pact could not be implemented immediately, but only incrementally over time. To rush that day by imposing the treaty provisions rigidly on a nation whose self-preservation was at stake would destroy the treaty. "Nations will not offer themselves for martyrdom for an interpretation of a pact," he said. Citing the cases of Panama, Outer Mongolia, and the Nanking Government in China, Nitobe tried to vindicate the helping role of an outside power in the birth of Manchukuo. Why, he asked, should such action be right in one place and wrong in another? The American Secretary of State's non-recognition policy was, he contended, a replay of the hated Triple Intervention of 1895. Should he carry it forward, America too would suffer through loss of economic opportunity in Manchuria.[80]

In his lectures and radio speeches, Nitobe pleaded that the West not relegate Japan to the company of the condemned. He warned that an ostracized nation whose honor was challenged might take even more extreme actions. He foresaw that non-recognition would result in an autonomous policy for Japan, a policy deaf to the restraints of the League, Peace Pact, or any other multilateral mechanism. Matsuoka Yôsuke similarly would urge the League not to pillory and isolate a great nation when the Assembly was about to vote to accept the Lytton Report.[81] Matsuoka and Nitobe both also charged North American missionaries with creating misunderstanding of the situation in China. "My advice to missionaries," Nitobe told a Toronto audience, "is to keep their hands off Chinese internal politics and international questions. They are sent out to teach the gospel to the Chinese people as men, not as politicians."[82] The only solution to the crisis was to let China and Japan work out their differences without third-party interference, be that third-party missionaries, the United States, or the League of Nations. A consistent thread in his talks was the implication of American hypocrisy. How do *you* respond to disturbances in Nicaragua and El Salvador? he asked. How did you win the West? You sent gunboats to Haiti in 1915 when there was a faint rumor of German interference. You build tariff walls, because you can produce anything you need; yet you deny Japan the right to reach out to Manchuria. He chafed, "We have learned many things from America, especially in dealing with neighboring unstable governments, and when we put the lesson into practice we are severely criticized by our teacher."[83]

The former Under-Secretary General seemed to have recaptured some of the Geneva spirit when he addressed the Twelfth Annual Institutes of Politics in Williamstown, Massachusetts, in July. There, a more subdued Nitobe called the League of Nations "the greatest organ of international cooperation as yet devised by man," and expressed the "sincere hope that Japan will not leave the League and America will join it." With the absence of the United States and the Soviet Union from Geneva, however, "the twelve years Japan has sat there she has largely been a spectator of European events that concerned her little." Muting an earlier threat, Nitobe assured his audience that Japan would not isolate itself from the world, even if it withdrew from the League.[84]

When in 1925 no vital interest of Japan was at issue in the League, Nitobe had told his countrymen that the stature of a permanent Council seat was adequate reason for adhering to the League of Nations. Now in 1932 when a perceived lifeline was challenged by the organization, he was saying, in effect, that no amount of international favor was worth capitulation to League directives. Nitobe spoke in North America as though Japan's fate hung in the balance. He also spoke as from the heart, not as a mere dutiful mouthpiece of the Japanese position. His speeches at home and his correspondence give no cause to believe that in addressing the North American public he was anything less than sincere.[85] That Japan was not allowed to become the predominant power in East Asia and remain in the League too was a painful frustration.

Nitobe's mission was doomed to failure, precisely because it ran counter to the higher wisdom he had articulated in Geneva. His message there had been that we should exercise more thoughtfulness in our judgements of others. He repeated this plea in America in 1932. But in Geneva he had also taught that the attitude of sympathetic understanding must be cultivated through a long process of education in the ideals, spirit and human accomplishments of other cultures. Nitobe, out of a sense of duty to his nation and to its right-wing politicians, offered Americans in 1932 a crash course in Japanese motives, but it was too late. The crisis for which that understanding was required was already at hand. His sound arguments came at the wrong time. His American audience showed little empathy for the exigencies that moved the burglar once he was discovered at work in the Chinese house.

A long-standing problem in Nitobe's internationalism was the difficulty of applying his humanistic universalism to the political world of Japanese international relations. Japanese liberal intellectuals who supported the League in the 1920s spoke of lofty ideals of shared human sentiments. They displayed little concern or expertise when it came to questions about the concrete national interests and security needs of Japan in East Asia. Nitobe, and Sugimura Yôtarô after him, used metaphors and references to classical literature to build their case for the League. Nitobe compared the Covenant to the Magna Carta and likened "world-conscience" to the still, small voice which moved the prophet Elijah.[86] This praise of cooperation was lyrical and ritualized. Such a foundation is airy and transitory, effective for celebrating peace when it exists but impractical for creating goodwill in the midst of strife. Except in rare moments—like the post-World War I months which gave birth to the League—when a tide of idealism sweeps the world, the humanist summons evokes little response in the halls of government, diplomacy, commerce, and the military. Nitobe could not communicate the League in practical, enduring terms to Japan in the 1920s; nor was he any better suited for communicating understanding to the American people in 1932.

On February 24, 1933, the League of Nations Assembly, by vote of forty-two to one, accepted the Lytton Report which labeled Japan an aggressor in Manchuria. The Japanese delegation walked out, never to return to Geneva, and so signified Japan's challenge to world order. Nitobe Inazô acquiesced in Japan's withdrawal, believing that it was the League that had failed Japan. Small powers had induced the League leadership to apply the Covenant "like lawyers" in a narrow and technical way, violating the broad and tolerant intentions of the statesmen who drafted it. To the Japanese public he confessed the conflicting impulses which tore his conscience:

> I am one of those inconsistent and self-contradictory people who believe that while Japan is justified at the present moment to leave the League, still believe that the League is the greatest hope for the future welfare of the world. I still insist upon looking at the League as the greatest achievement of the human race, and it is a pity that we have had to leave it.

He urged his countrymen to renew their commitment to international comity: "Whatever rights we may have lost by our withdrawal from the League, we must make good by further attention to the family of nations." When in August he addressed the Inaugural Dinner of the Fifth Institute of Pacific Relations Conference in Banff, he assured the delegates that Japan was still part of that family. At the same time he issued his final warning about "the dark forces of intolerance born of ignorance."[87] When he reached the Pacific Coast a few days later he was gravely ill. Death in Victoria mercifully removed him from the scene before the full fruits of Japan's autonomous diplomacy and America's intolerance cast their pall on the world.

Conclusion

It would be unfair to judge the accomplishments of Nitobe Inazô solely on the basis of reverses during his lifetime. The foundations for international order and understanding among peoples which he helped lay could by design come to full fruition only with the passage of time. Were Nitobe to return to life today, he would be gratified to see that wholehearted participation in the United Nations is one policy on which divergent political factions in Japan agree. He would take particular pride in the achievements of UNESCO and its active support organizations in Japan. In the U.S.-Japan Security Treaty and ASEAN ties he would affirm mechanisms for regional security and cooperation supplemental to the U.N. He would be elated to know that Oriental exclusion was terminated by the U.S. Congress in 1952. Most rewarding would be the awareness that Western peoples today look to Japan for models of human organization and spirit for the sake of a better life. The ascendancy of liberal internationalism rests upon groundwork which Nitobe helped to erect. But on his return, the bridge builder would not bask in the pride of accomplishment. Rather, Nitobe Inazô would attend to the still unfinished task of spreading the Geneva spirit.

Notes

1. Nitobe Inazô, "Opening Address at the Kyoto Conference of the Institute of Pacific Relations," October 28, 1929; in *Works* 4:359; also published as "Japan's Preparedness for International Co-operation," in *Pacific Affairs* 2, no.1, (January 1930).
2. Quoted in *Tokyo Nichi Nichi* (English edition), April 12, 1933, p. 7.
3. Miwa Kimitada, "Crossroads of Patriotism in Imperial Japan: Shiga Shigeta (1863–1927), Uchimura Kanzô (1861–1930), and Nitobe Inazô (1862–1933)," Ph.D. diss., Princeton University, 1967, p. 361.
4. William Robert Carter, "With the Nitobes in America, 1911–12," (chapter of unpublished thesis draft), p. 45.
5. *Ibid.*, p. 83. Quotation from Tsurumi's English diary.
6. Tsurumi to Wilson, November 15, 1918, Wilson to Tsurumi, November 18, 1918: Woodrow Wilson Presidential Papers, Library of Congress, Reel 249.
7. Charles F. Howlett, *Troubled Philosopher: John Dewey and the Struggle for World Peace* (Port Washington, N.Y.: Kennikat Press, 1977), pp. 31, 45; George Dykhuizen, *The Life and Mind of John Dewey* (Carbondale: Southern Illinois University Press, 1973), pp. 182–85.
8. John Higham, *History* (Englewood Cliffs, N.J.: Prentice-Hall, 1965), p. 174; Richard T. Ely, "Economic Internationalism," in *The Chautauquan* 10 (February 1890):538–42; Miwa, "Crossroads," pp. 86–87.
9. Miwa, "Crossroads," p. 345, quoting from Yanaihara Tadao, ed., *Nitobe hakushi shokumin seisaku kôgi oyobi ronbun shû* (Tokyo: Iwanami shoten, 1943), p. 66.
10. Miwa, "Crossroads," p. 278.
11. Carter, "With the Nitobes," pp. 47, 53; George W. Egerton, *Great Britain and the Creation of the League of Nations* (Chapel Hill: University of North Carolina Press, 1978), p. 8; Shidehara heiwa zaidan, ed., *Shidehara Kijûrô* (Tokyo: Shidehara heiwa zaidan, 1955), pp. 136, 137. On Marburg, see Thomas W. Burkman, "The Campaign of Theodore Marburg to Recruit Japan for the League of Nations," in Virginia Consortium for Asian Studies, *Occasional Papers*, 3 (Spring 1986) pp. 51–60.
12. See p. 168 in this volume.
13. Yanaihara Tadao, ed., *Nitobe hakushi bunshû* (Tokyo: Ko Nitobe hakushi kinen jigyô jikkô iin, 1936), pp. 408–9.
14. *Baltimore Sun*, 12 January 1912, p. 8; Miwa, "Crossroads," pp. 276, 345; Nitobe, "Japan, the League of Nations, and the Peace Pact," radio broadcast, May 8, 1932, *Works* 4:247.
15. Nitobe interview in *Baltimore Evening Sun*, January 13, 1912, p. 2.

16. Theodore Marburg, a founder of the League to Enforce Peace, described China in 1916 as "a backward country which is unable to maintain law and order at home," and believed that "a Japanese hegemony in China" was preferable to the prevailing chaos. Marburg to Gulick, June 20, 1916: John H. Latane, ed., *Development of the League of Nations Idea: Documents and Correspondence of Theodore Marburg* 1 (New York: Macmillan, 1932):128; Marburg To Taft, July 12, 1916, Taft Presidential Papers, Library of Congress, Reel 168.

17. Nitobe quoted in *Baltimore Sun*, January 12, 1912, p. 8.

18. Carter, "With the Nitobes," pp. 22, 26.

19. Mary E. Nitobe to Joseph Elkinton, January 6, 1904, Nitobe Papers, Friends Historical Library of Swarthmore College (hereafter NP-S), RG 5, Ser. 2; Nitobe, *Japan: Some Phases of her Problems and Development* (London: Ernest Benn Limited, 1931), p. 131.

20. Nitobe, quoted in Mitani Taichirô, "Taishô demokurashii to Amerika," in Saitô Makoto, ed., *Demokurashii to Nichi-Bei Kankei* (Tokyo: Nan'undô, 1973), pp. 143–44; see also *New York Times* (hereafter *NYT*), April 6, 1919, 2:2.

21. Miwa, "Japanese Opinions on Woodrow Wilson in War and Peace," in *Monumenta Nipponica* 22, no. 3-4, (1967):380.

22. Washio Shôgorô, "Ôshû sensô no motarasubeki sekaiteki kakumei," in *Chûô kôron* 33, no.11 (October 1918):3; Konoe Fumimaro, "Ei-Bei hon'i no heiwashugi o hai su," in *Nihon oyobi Nihonjin* 746 (December 15, 1918):23–26; Gotô Shimpei, "Terauchi shusô ni teishutsu seru Gotô naimudaijin no ikensho," in Kobayashi Tatsuo, ed., *Suiusô nikki* (Tokyo: Hara shobô, 1966), pp. 806–11; Uchimura Kanzô, "Seisho to gensei," in *Seisho no kenkyû* 224 (March 1919):3, 4; *UKZ* 24:488.

23. Yoshino Sakuzô, "Beikoku daitôryô oyobi Eikoku shushô no sengen o yomu," in *Chûô kôron* 33, no.2, (February 1918):16–20; "Nanzo kokusai renmei ni ka'nyû suru o chûcho," in *Chûô kôron* 34, no. 1, (January 1919):154; "Jinshuteki sabetsu teppai mondai ni tsuite,"in *Chûô kôron* 34, no.5, (May 1919):96, 97.

24. Gaikô Chôsakai meeting of December 8, 1918, Kobayashi, ed., *Suiusô nikki*, pp. 333–44.

25. *Ibid.*, p. 339.

26. Shumpei Okamoto, "Ishibashi Tanzan and the Twenty-one Demands," in Akira Iriye, ed., *The Chinese and the Japanese: Essays in Political and Cultural Interactions* (Princeton: Princeton University Press, 1980), pp. 184, 185; Gaikô Chôsakai meeting of December 8, 1918, Kobayashi, ed., *Suiusô nikki*, p. 337.

27. Gaikô Chôsakai meeting of October 29, 1919, Kobayashi, ed., *Suiusô nikki*, p. 709.

28. Nitobe, *Ijin gunzô* (1931), *NIZ* 5:525.

29. Matsushita Masatoshi, *Japan in the League of Nations* (New York: Columbia University Press, 1929), pp. 37, 115–17; Martin David Dublin, "The League of Nations Secretariat—A Preliminary Excursion," unpublished paper presented at the International Studies Association, Cincinnati, 1982, p. 21. Nitobe was fluent in English and skilled in German, but his French was poor.

30. Kitasawa Sukeo, *The Life of Dr. Nitobe* (Tokyo: Hokuseido, 1953), p. 64; J. Passmore Elkinton to Catherine Bruning, January 3, 1941, NP-S, RG 5, Ser. 2. Nitobe confided by letter to his friend, U.S. Ambassador to Tokyo Roland S. Morris, that "one of the chief reason[s] why I consented to accompany our mutual friend [Gotô]

was the expansion of his views on some points. I have reasons to believe that that object is largely, at least partly attained. If you meet him on his return you will notice some changes." Nitobe to Morris, August 20, 1919, Roland S. Morris Papers, Library of Congress, Box 2.

31. Nitobe to Anna H. Chace, August 12, 1919, NP-S, RG 5, Ser. 2; *Tokyo Nichi Nichi shimbun*, April 2, 1929, p. 2; Miwa, "Crossroads," p. 378.

32. Matsushitô, *Japan in the League*, p. 119.

33. Gaimushô manual, 1935, Foreign Ministry Archives, Tokyo; Satô Naotake, ed., *Kokusai remmei ni okeru Nihon* (Tokyo: Kajima kenkyûsho shuppankai, 1972), pp. 441–42.

34. Saionji report to Emperor, August 27, 1919, in Kobayashi, ed., *Suiusô nikki*, p. 692; Drummond memo, April 28, 1920, League of Nations Archives, Geneva (hereafter LNA), Box 572.

35. Matsushitô, *Japan in the League*, pp. 48–50.

36. William E. Rappard, *International Relations as Viewed from Geneva* (New Haven: Yale University Press, 1925), pp. 202–3; Nitobe, quoted in *International Gleanings from Japan* 3, no. 10–11, (October, November 1927):1, 7.

37. Nitobe to J. Passmore Elkinton, June 2, 1922, NP-S RG 5, Ser. 2.

38. On the International Committee on Intellectual Cooperation, see F. P. Walters, *A History of the League of Nations* (London: Oxford University Press, 1952), pp. 190–94; Charles Hodges, "The World Union of Intellectual Forces," in *Current History* 24, no. 3, (June 1926):411–15; and Unno Yoshirô, *Kokusai renmei to Nihon* (Tokyo: Hara shobô, 1972), pp. 107–13. Takagi Yasaka, "Introduction," in Works 1:xviii.

39. Bourgeois, quoted in Hodges, "World Union," p. 412.

40. Nitobe to J. Passmore Elkinton, June 2, 1922, NP-S, RG 5, Ser. 2.

41. Ayusawa Iwao, "Nitobe Sensei no kokusaiteki kôken," in *NIK*, p. 331; Walters, *A History of the League*, pp. 191, 193.

42. Nitobe, *"Use and Study... :"* Swarthmore Peace Collection, Swarthmore College, CDG-B, Box 146.

43. Drummond quoted in Kitasawa,*The Life of Dr. Nitobe*, p. 66; Ishii Kikujirô, *Gaikô zuisô* (Tokyo: Kajima Morinosuke shuppankai, 1967), pp. 182–83.

44. Nitobe, "What the League of Nations Has Done and Is Doing," in *Works* 4:378.

45. Nitobe, "What the League...," p. 381.

46. Nitobe, "What the League...," pp. 375–76, italics his. The "holy experiment" rhetoric is borrowed from Quaker and Philadelphian William Penn.

47. Nitobe, "What the League...," pp. 382, 399, 400.

48. Nitobe, "The League of Nations Movement in Japan (A Report on the Trip to Japan)," April 9, 1925: LNA, Box R1573.

49. Nitobe, "The League...in Japan," with attached Drummond comment.

50. Nitobe to Drummond et al., May 26, 1925, with endorsements: LNA, Box R1342; *Kokusai Chishiki* 5, no. 12, (December 1, 1925): 6–7.

51. *International Gleanings from Japan* 2, no. 5–6, (May–June 1926): 1, 2, 8. "Report on the Activities of the Tokyo Office during the Year 1933;" Tsuchida to Azcarate, June 27, 1935: LNA, Box R5383. The Tokyo Office was abolished in 1938, and its files were subsequently destroyed. An interesting question of conflict of interest involved the Secretariat's Tokyo Office and the government-subsidized Japan

League of Nations Association. Since office space in Tokyo was scarce in the wake of the 1923 earthquake, the Association found quarters for the Office in the building which housed its own headquarters. It also paid the rent and opened the pages of its organ, *Kokusai chishiki*, to advertise League activities. The Foreign Ministry supplied a telephone and free telegraphic service to Geneva. Correspondent Aoki disclaimed any compromise of the policy that Secretariat activities be free of government attachment, but Secretariat General Drummond objected to any subsidy. When the Tokyo office moved to new quarters in Marunouchi in late 1927, the matter was apparently laid to rest. Close association between the two agencies persisted nonetheless. Aoki Setsuichi, "the First Year of the Tokyo Office of the League of Nations," January 18, 1927; Drummond to Okayama, June 24, 1927; Sugimura to Drummond, June 27, 1927: LNA, Box R1342; Tsuchida to McKinon, May 29, 1933: LNA, Box R5383.

52. Greg Gubler, "The Diplomatic Career of Satô Naotake (1882–1971): A Samurai in Western Clothing," Ph.D. diss., Florida State University, 1975, p. 90.

53. Kiyoko Takeda Chô, "The Christian Encounter with the Traditional Ethos of Japan: A Study of Nitobe Inazô's Ideas," in International Christian University, *Asian Cultural Studies* 5 (October 1966):131; Kitasawa Sukeo, "Memories of Dr. Nitobe Return at Azalea Time," in *Nippon Times*, May 1, 1948.

54. Richard R. Wood to J. Passmore Elkinton, August 10, 1939: NP-S, RG 5, Ser. 2; Nitobe, "Yûben to jinkaku no chikara,"in *Tôzai aifurete* (Tokyo, 1928), in *NIZ* 1:201–5.

55. Newman to J. Passmore Elkinton, September 7, 1939: NP-S, RG 5, Ser. 2; Ayusawa, "Nitobe Sensei no kokusaiteki kôken," pp. 329–31. Ayusawa was a protégé of Nitobe and a graduate of Quaker Haverford College.

56. Ishii Mitsuru, English summary of Nitobe biography, ms. p. 20: NP-S, RG 5, Ser. 2.

57. H. F. Angus, "A Canadian Farewell," in *Pacific Affairs* 6, no. 8, (November–December 1933): 548.

58. Takagi Yasaka, *Toward International Understanding* (Tokyo: Kenkyûsha, 1954), p. 172; James T. Shotwell, "An Appreciation," in *Pacific Affairs* 6, no. 8, (November–December, 1933):547; Gilbert Bowles, "The Foundations of Dr. Inazô Nitobe's Character," ms.: NP-S, RG 5, Ser. 1.

59. Shotwell, "An Appreciation," p. 547; Ishii, *Gaikô zuisô*, p. 183.

60. Takagi, *International Understanding*, p. xix.

61. Chô, "Christian Encounter," p. 125; Nitobe, *Japanese Traits and Foreign Influences* (London: Kegan Paul, Trench, Trubner, 1927), pp. 9, 175, 189–206.

62. Miwa, "Crossroads," p. 399.

63. Avenol, quoted in Kitasawa, *The Life of Dr. Nitobe*, p. 65; Walters, *A History of the League*, pp. 419,496; Matsushita, *Japan in the League*, pp. 113–14; Rappard, *International Relations*, p. 203; Ian H. Nish, "A Japanese Diplomat Looks at Europe, 1920–1939," in Nish and Charles Dunn, eds., *European Studies on Japan* (Tenterden: 1979), p. 136.

64. Furukaki Tetsurô, "Le Japon et la Société des Nations," March 21, 1927; Harada Ken, "The Visit to Japan," October 9, 1924: LNA, Box R1573. Nitobe stated publicly that he would not visit his second homeland again until the United States repealed the offensive immigration legislation.

65. Ishii speech in League Council, October 30, 1925, in *Official Journal* 6, no. 2, (November 1925): 1715–16; Shidehara speech to Diet, January 21, 1926, in Gaimushô 2, *Nihon gaikô nenpyô narabi ni shuyô bunsho, 1840–1945* (Tokyo: Hara shobô, 1955): 87; *Hôchi*, December 4, 1925, p. 6; Furukaki Tetsurô interview, May 26, 1978.

66. Nitobe to Richard R. Wood, July 10, 1926, NP-S, RG 5, Ser. 2; Nitobe in *Japan Times*, quoted in *International Gleanings from Japan* 3, no. 10–11, (October–November, 1927):8.

67. J. Passmore Elkinton to Catherine Bruning, January 3, 1941: NP-S, RG 5, Ser. 2; *Tokyo Nichi Nichi*, March 31, 1929, p. 1; Nitobe, "Japan in International Cooperation," in *English Osaka Mainichi*, August 30, 1929; "Are We Ready?" in *ibid.*, April 21, 1929; Takagi, *International Understanding*, p. xix.

68. Nitobe, "Opening Address at the Kyoto Conference," pp. 355, 356. Interestingly, the two Japanese who presented papers at the meeting, Rôyama Masamichi and Matsuoka Yôsuke, would later become advocates of an East Asia order to *displace* the Versailles system in the Orient.

69. J. B. Condliffe, ed., *Problems of the Pacific, 1929* (Chicago: University of Chicago Press, 1930), pp. 227, 241.

70. p. 160.

71. Yokota Kisaburô, *Watakushi no isshô* (Tokyo: Tokyo shinbun shuppankyoku, 1976), pp. 124–25. The delegates included Suzuki Bunji, Tsurumi Yûsuke, Maeda Tamon, Matsumoto Shigeharu, and Yokota Kisaburô.

72. Takayanagi Kenzô, "The Application of Existing Instruments of Policy," in Bruce Lasker, ed., *Problems of the Pacific, 1931* (1932; rpt, New York: Greenwood Press, 1969), pp. 233–36. "Mac Murray" refers to the standard compilation of China treaties, published in 1921.

73. Mary E. Nitobe to J. Passmore and Anna Elkinton, October 22, 1931: NP-S, RG 5, Ser. 2.

74. Memo, "Dr. Inazô Nitobe," June 1, 1932, Far East Division, U.S. Department of State: Stanley K. Hornbeck Papers, The Hoover Institution, Box 258.

75. J. Passmore Elkinton to Dorothy Gilbert, December 15, 1948: NP-S, RG 5, Ser. 2.

76. Gilbert Bowles, "The Peace Movement in Japan," pamphlet reprinted from *The Friend*, November 23, December 7 and 21, 1944, p. 21; Sharlie C. Ushioda, "Man of Two Worlds: An Inquiry into the Value System of Inazô Nitobe (1862-1933)," in Hilary Conroy and T. Scott Miyakawa, eds., *East Across the Pacific: Historical and Sociological Studies of Japanese Immigration and Assimilation* (Santa Barbara: ABC-CLIO Press, 1972), pp. 199–200; Elkinton to Gilbert, December 15, 1948.

77. "Dr. Nitobe Arrives: Pleads for Japan," *NYT*, May 7, 1932, p. 4.

78. Nitobe, "Japan and the League of Nations," radio broadcast, May 8, 1932, in *Works* 4:234–39.

79. H. L. Stimson, "Memorandum of Conversation between Secretary Stimson and Dr. Inazô Nitobe," June 1, 1932: Hornbeck Papers, Box 258. In his briefing before this interview, Stimson was reminded of the March 4, 1932 incident when Nitobe was taken from his hospital bed to the Reservists Association headquarters to apologize for the remark that militarists were more of a threat than Communism. This incident had been reported in the American press. When Stimson published his book, *The Far Eastern Crisis* in 1936, he cited this incident as evidence of a "reign of

terror" to drive Japanese moderates into hiding. Stimson, *The Far Eastern Crisis: Recollections and Observations* (New York: Council on Foreign Relations, 1936), p. 88. On the Hoover interview, which lasted seven minutes, see "Japan's Savant Meets President Hoover," *English Osaka Mainichi*, June 4, 1932.

80. "Japan and the Peace Pact," radio broadcast, August 20, 1932, in *Works* 4:240–50.

81. "Japan and the League of Nations," p. 239; "The Manchurian Question and Sino-American Relations," November 21, 1932, in *Works* 4:221–33, quoting *English Osaka Mainichi*; Hugh R. Wilson, *Diplomat between Wars* (New York: Longmans, 1941), p. 279.

82. Nitobe, quoted in "Nitobe Blames Missionaries for Political Unrest in China," *NYT*, September 7, 1932, p. 11.

83. Nitobe, "The Manchurian Question," p. 232; *NYT*, August 14, 1932, 8:2; "Japan and the United States," November 28, 1932, in *Works* 4:256; "Nitobe Calls Japan Spectator in League," *NYT*, July 29, 1932, p. 11.

84. Nitobe, quoted in "Nitobe Calls Japan Spectator in League," *Ibid*.

85. On his Shikoku speaking tour in February 1932, Nitobe sympathized with the Japanese occupation of Manchuria. Miwa, "Crossroads," p. 414.

86. Nitobe, "Japan and the League of Nations," p. 235; "Retrospect and Prospect," in *English Osaka Mainichi*, November 16, 1929.

87. "How Geneva Erred," in *Tokyo Nichi Nichi*. April 12, 1933, p. 7; Nitobe, "Text of the Address as Actually Delivered…at the Banff Conference, August 14, 1933," in *Works* 4:301–3.

FIVE

Evaluation

10

Journalism: The Last Bridge

Satô Masahiro

In his final four-and-a-half years, Nitobe served his country and its people as a journalist. In 1929 he accepted an invitation from the *English Osaka Mainichi* and *Tokyo Nichi Nichi* to serve as their Advisory Editor. When Nitobe accepted the invitation, the two newspapers were controlled by Motoyama Hikoichi who had owned the latter for twenty-three years and started the English language *Osaka Mainichi* in 1922. *The English Osaka Mainichi* had a wide circulation of at least fifty thousand.[1] When Nitobe came back to Japan on a short leave in 1924, his disciple Ishii Mitsuru, then a part-time staff member of the *Tokyo Nichi Nichi*, advised the editors to carry essays by his venerable teacher. Nitobe did not accept the invitation until five years had passed.

Nitobe had come home in 1927 after seven years at the League of Nations. Chinese tradition through Lao-Tze holds that the Way of Heaven is to retire after one has distinguished oneself and become famous. But at age sixty-seven, when most ordinary Japanese men enjoy their retirement, Nitobe took on an arduous new assignment in the world of journalism. He had come back from Geneva with many projects to finish. They included revisions to his two youthful theoretical works on agriculture and a novel on Joan of Arc.

Nitobe had loved the traditions associated with Joan of Arc ever since his student days in Sapporo. In his youthful diary he listed as his spiritual leaders the names of Christ, Buddha, Mohammed, and Joan of Arc, instead of the commonly accepted "four saints"—Confucius, Lao-Tze, Buddha and Christ. Inclusion of Joan of Arc in the list shows two elements of Inazô's spirituality that would linger throughout his life: his deep interest in the mystic, and his high respect for women. In 1920, as Nitobe served in Geneva with the League of Nations, Joan of Arc was sanctified. Nitobe admired her loyalty to God and to her country and made pilgrimages to places associated with her—Auxerre, Chinon, Orleans, Compiegne, Rouen. And he bought many books about her which included biographies, poems, portraits, and songs. With these materials in hand, he had long wanted to write a novel about this maiden saint of France.

But he never found time to finish any of these works. Instead, he took on added tasks and other responsibilities. He wrote, for example, a book on Japan in the *Modern World Series* by Ernest Benn and Company in England. This was published in 1931 as *Japan: Some Phases of Her Problems and Development*. He also accepted in 1929 the Chairmanship of the Japan branch of the Institute of Pacific Relations (IPR). Both of these duties had, in Nitobe's heart, a close relation to the promotion of mutual understanding and world peace.

Here we take up his work as a journalist. It is a subject not yet dealt with in any depth. New sources on Nitobe were required to do this study. Fortunately, I found microfilm back-issues of the *English Osaka Mainichi* which contained a large number of his articles unknown to scholars. It is with great joy that I introduce them here.

Debut as a Newspaper Editor

The *English Osaka Mainichi* proudly announced, on the last day of March 1929, Nitobe's appointment as advisory editor. The statement reads:

> The Osaka Mainichi Publishing Company is extremely pleased to announce that henceforth Dr. INAZO NITOBE will participate in editing and supervising the Osaka Mainichi and Tokyo Nichi Nichi, English Edition, as the ADVISORY EDITOR.... A lengthy presentation of so highly honored a scholar and statesman as Dr. Nitobe would be superfluous. For most learned people both at home and abroad the mere mention of his name is copious introduction.... With his mellow point of view exalted by notable experience as a scholar and internationalist, and above all as a man, Dr. Nitobe will now address himself wholeheartedly to the mission which has been his life-long ideal, and of which his past career has been a partial fulfillment—the promotion of sympathetic understanding between East and West.... There is cause for general felicitation in the fact that their perfect concurrence in this pertinent ideal led to the collaboration of the Mainichi and Japan's foremost savant and humanitarian. It is an event in the journalism of Japan, which enhances the effort of the English Mainichi and Nichi Nichi to stand as a truly great English language newspaper and dependable spokesman of the Far East.

The circumstances required Nitobe's appearance on the stage of journalism. These were hard times indeed. The anti-Japanese movement had increased in intensity in America; China looked at the military power of Japan as extremely dangerous; at home, the corruption of the political parties and the failure of the government's economic policies brought extremists from the right and left to the foreground. "The bridge across the Pacific," which Nitobe had painstakingly constructed throughout his career, had begun to weaken. Dark war clouds gathered on the horizon. The world and Japan needed Nitobe's services in the press.

On April 2, Nitobe wrote his first article "Let Us Take Counsel Together—A Word to the Foreign Readers." A photograph taken during his years at the League was printed above the editorial. In this article, Nitobe calmly wrote:

> Man learns but slowly; it is only through tribulation that he attains wisdom. For centuries, philosophers thought that competition was the law of progress, and nations and races have vied with each other in a ruthless struggle for existence and for a place in the sun. Only since the World War, have they come to realize that, after all, the word of St. Paul was true—that individuals in nations are but parts of an organic whole, members of one body. Of countries, as of individuals may it be said that wants, frailties, passion, closer still ally the common interest or endear the tie.

Nitobe stressed the importance of international cooperation as a fundamental principle in uniting nations. He recollected the great ambition he harbored in his youth, his desire to bridge the Pacific. Setting his sights firmly on this ideal, he insisted that the surest way to world peace was for the Japanese to strive to communicate their thoughts to the world in English. He writes:

> Shall the consciousness of an imperfect knowledge of an exotic tongue deter us from so needed a task as that of disseminating abroad correct information about our own land and of acquainting alien people with the real sentiment of our own nationals? We consider it a duty not only to our country, but to the world at large, to overcome the shyness so characteristic of the Japanese to speak a foreign language. The course of world peace and cooperation is too dear to our heart to be barred by jingoistic reticence. Come, my foreign readers, let us take counsel together, you in your own tongue and we in yours!

All mankind, for Nitobe, consists of not just brothers and sisters, but rather many members of one body as Paul says in First Corinthians 12:12. On this eternal Biblical truth, he erects his platform for peace.

It seems strange that such a splendid writer of English as Nitobe had no typewriter at home and appears to have been unable to type. He lived in Tokyo, and the *English Osaka Mainichi*, of course, was set in type in Osaka. Sixty years ago, there was no telex or other electronic device to transmit written messages over hundreds of miles in an instant. The quickest means was the telephone. Nitobe handed his beautifully hand-written manuscript to a reporter at the *Tokyo Nichi Nichi* who then read the draft over the telephone to a staff member at the *English Osaka Mainichi*. The staff member painstakingly wrote down the telephoned report, sentence by sentence, and verified it by re-reading it to the Tokyo transmitter. Then it was sent to the typesetter. Mistakes could not be avoided. They may perhaps be called 'mistransmissions' rather than misprints.

Besides a few minor errors, there was one serious mistake near the conclusion of the article. It reads: "The course of world peace and cooperation is too dear to our heart to be barred by jingoistic reticence." In the original manuscript, Nitobe wrote "linguistic reticence" instead of the strange expression "jingoistic reticence." "Jingoistic" and "linguistic" sounded very similar, nearly the same, over the telephone of that day.

Nitobe took up this mistransmission as a rare opportunity to make public his view of true patriotism. On the next occasion, April 16, he wrote an editorial entitled "'Jingoistic' Reticence" which demonstrated his extraordinary good sense as a journalist: "The jingoist is the loudest of forward patriots, the reticent the timidest of the retiring. Is there no happy medium between these two extremes? Is there not a lover of his country who is not forever singing its praises or who never opens his mouth? Surely there must be a golden mean."

To him who is called by the Will of the God of Peace, all things work for the good. Nitobe's admirable rhetoric resulted from the fine training in speech he received fifty years earlier at the Sapporo Agricultural College. He combined this with his polished sense of humor, which looked upon life, however hard and burdensome, with cheer and a light heart.

With these first two articles, Nitobe strongly grasped the affections of readers everywhere. He visited Osaka monthly on his editorial chores and used these opportunities to relax. His many duties as a public man did not follow him on these trips. Fortunately too, there was no bullet train. He could relax in a way that he could not in Tokyo. Free from the pressures of work, he enjoyed the company of the staff at the *Osaka Mainichi*. The *Soganoya-Gorô-Geki*—a kind of modern popular tragi-comedy—gave him great pleasure, and he laughed like a child at the comic scenes; when the curtain fell after a sad act, he wiped his glasses and let out a deep sigh of relief. Life in Tokyo seldom afforded him such leisure.

The Writings

The enormous number of Nitobe's writings in the *English Osaka Mainichi* may be grouped into five categories:

1. *Editorials*. Written a few times a month soon after his appointment, the editorials include the first, "Jingoistic Reticence," dated April 16, 1929. A little more than a year later, on April 24, 1930, the "Kanebo

Incident and Social Justice" was the last piece in this genre to be published. The editorials number twenty; none of them are included in the *Nitobe Inazô Zenshû* which is used by most scholars as the main source for the study of Nitobe.
2. *Essays.* Printed during the summer months of 1929, from July 10 to September 11, the essays were all chosen from another work of Nitobe's originally published twenty years earlier, *Thoughts and Essays.* They were reissued under three headings: (a) "Drift and Mastery"; (b) "Life and Opinion"; and (c) "Faith and Truth." Fifty-nine of them were published.
3. *Editorial Jottings.* These were short pieces written for a special column. All were printed with Nitobe's portrait, which was frequently changed. They appeared almost daily, from June 1, 1930 to the day of his death on October 15, 1933. There are 730 articles in all, of which 691 were later collected and published in two volumes by Hokuseidô Press in 1938. 39 were omitted.
4. *Miscellaneous Articles.* These include "Let Us Take Counsel Together"; as well as various lectures and reviews. The last of these is his address to the Tokyo Pan-Pacific Club on April 12, 1933. There are some twelve articles in this category, printed over 27 days. Four of these articles are reprinted in later books.
5. *"Great Men I Have Met."* These are selections from a book of the same title, published on November 1, 1931, by the *Jitsugyô no Nihon sha.* Many of these articles had originally appeared in Japanese in the *Osaka Mainichi* and *Tokyo Nichi Nichi.* They were later translated into English by Ikeda Satoru, a staff member of the *English Osaka Mainichi.* They were printed at intervals from October 27 to December 30, 1931, and from February 21 until April 20, 1932. The first person mentioned is Count Gotô Shimpei with whom Nitobe had worked closely.

The articles in categories one to four and excluding the translations of category five, number 827 items. Nitobe served as Advisory Editor for the *English Osaka Mainichi* for about four and a half years. This amounts to approximately 1400 days. Omitting those days when the paper was not printed, we see that Nitobe wrote at an average of more than once every other day—that is, over 59 percent of the days.

While serving as journalist, he also wrote his book *Japan;* he lectured in various parts of the country; he went abroad on a thorny lecture trip to the United States in 1932; and during the whole period he led the Japanese Institute of Pacific Relations. He also entered a hospital several times for medical treatment. We cannot but admire his hard work and fervent activity. The spirit of "taking counsel together"—of promoting mutual understanding and cooperation—left him with few leisure hours.

We here take up the writings of this period, one after the other, and so study the concerns closest to his heart in those trying times. But before we set out on our inquiry, we must answer one important question: Why did Nitobe's writing form—first, editorials, then essays, then editorial jottings—change? The editorial is no doubt the most important article in a newspaper. Nitobe took it upon himself to write twenty editorials on subjects which included politics, economics, internationalism, education and patriotism. But I suppose that he thought it more desirable to communicate with readers more often and more freely than to write infrequent editorials. He struggled to find the fittest mode of expression for his ideas, and discovered the form "editorial jotting." Any other form would not have allowed him to express himself so freely, to cover so wide a range of subjects, or to discuss complex problems so elegantly. We feel gratitude when we read the mature thoughts and feelings of Nitobe in such a clear style.

Editorials

The political instability of Japan sets the stage for all twenty of these pieces. These include the final months of the Seiyûkai cabinet of Tanaka Giichi, its resignation and the formation of a new government under the Minseitô cabinet of Hamaguchi Osachi on July 2, 1929. Scandals plagued the Governor-General's Office in Korea; in Japan the government went off the gold standard, retrenched its expenses, and faced a general election on February 20, 1930. Abroad, the Great Panic of October 24, 1929, led to increasing hardships throughout the world, and the London Naval Disarmament Conference opened in January of 1930.

If we were to classify the twenty editorials, they would fall under seven major headings: Peace (5); Economics (5); Politics (3); Education (2); National Character (2); Newspapers (1); and General (1). We shall list the titles of the editorials and briefly mention something of their content. This is especially important because, unlike many others among Nitobe's writings, they have not been previously republished.

Those under the category of Peace include: "Jingoistic Reticence" (April 16, 1929); "Are We Ready?" (April 21); "Japan in International Cooperation" (August 30); "Retrospect and Prospect—Kyoto Conference of Pacific Relations" (November 16); "Japan's Training in Internationalism" (November 20).

"Are We Ready?" exhorts readers to prepare for peace and to broaden our views of it. "Japan in International Cooperation" insists that cooperation, rather than competition, should form the future basis of international relations. Nitobe advises his readers to take concrete measures for peace:

> In joining the League of Nations and by signing the Pact, Japan has pledged herself not only to refrain from war but to help to bring peace on earth. She

has promised voluntarily, under no duress, to abide by the principle of peace in her dealings with other nations. It is not enough that she stands for peace. She must not make it her bed. She must work for it. She has been suspected long enough of harboring aggressive designs. Now we have an opportunity of giving the lie to this suspicion. We can show our sincerity by changing that pernicious superiority complex in our negotiations with China, by abolishing militaristic training in schools, by ostracizing military men from politics, by taking an acquiescent attitude in naval conferences, by reducing our armies, by making a clear declaration against war, by positive proposals regarding the method of making the Non-War Pact effective, by conforming more closely to the resolutions of the International Labor Congress, and finally by taking a more active part in the work of the League of Nations.

Nitobe's resolutely anti-militaristic attitude was probably the reason he ended writing editorials.

"Retrospect and Prospect" expresses Nitobe's thanks as the Chairman of the Kyoto IPR Conference. He lauds the supra-national concept of the conference, which unites all people into a harmonious whole. Nitobe feels convinced that to lend an ear to the voice of the world's conscience will help find a solution to difficult problems.

"Japan's Training in Internationalism" seeks Japanese internationalism in the "Charter Oath of Five Articles," the policy statement which set guidelines for the new Meiji government in 1868, particularly in the last two of the five which read respectively: "To do away with mean usages and to follow the just ways of Heaven and Earth" and "To seek knowledge throughout the world and uplift the foundations of the Empire." He affirms that the right means to secure peace is cooperation with England and America, as illustrated in the Washington Disarmament Conference.

The five editorials which deal with economics are: "Retrenchment or Bankruptcy" (July 11, 1929); "Dismal Economy" (August 24); "Two Government Campaigns" (September 27); "The Use of Home Products" (January 9, 1930); and "Continuation of the Thrift Campaign" (January 16).

In "Retrenchment or Bankruptcy," Nitobe agrees with the economic policies of the Hamaguchi cabinet. Himself a man of rectitude, he abhorred the earlier Tanaka government. In reaction against it, he admired the new Minseitô cabinet, among whose ministers was his respected friend, Inoue Junnosuke, who had been the Chairman of the Japanese IPR until his appointment as Finance Minister.

"Dismal Economy" is a denunciation of the ex-Tanaka cabinet for its waste of taxpayer's money and bureaucratic corruption. Nitobe expresses his desire for a reconstructed national economy under a new government.

The next editorial, "Two Government Campaigns," acclaims the "National Educational Mobilization Campaigns" and the "Retrenchment in Public and Private Life" campaign initiated under Prime Minister

Hamaguchi. Nitobe attributes a moral basis to these campaigns, and hopes that they will not become associated with party politics. He stresses the close relationship between the economy and social morality.

Likewise, in "The Use of Home Products," Nitobe demonstrates his knowledge of economics and statistics. He points out that 63 percent of Japan's imports consist of raw materials which cannot be replaced by other domestic materials. Furthermore, he argues, 10 percent of imported materials are inferior to those available at home. We should, he concludes, shake off our sense of inferiority which results in admiration of imported products and neglect of homemade things as well as work diligently together to revive the sagging national economy.

In the "Continuation of the Thrift Campaign," Nitobe reports a curious phenomenon that he has observed over the past half year: a reduction in the incidence of stomach diseases. Thrift, he goes to point out, is not only a virtue for suppressing one's desires, but also has a positive effect in that it preserves things for future generations. Individual frugality, he argues, prevents political corruption. Throughout these editorials which deal with the economy, Nitobe stresses the moral significance inherent in the economic life of a people and attacks corruption from that point of view.

The three editorials on Politics are: "Arithmetic and Politics" (May 5, 1929); "Why British Politics Interests Us" (June 1); and "What is a Dangerous Thought?" (October 12).

The first deals with the First General Election which had been held the year before. Nitobe, uncharacteristically, is harsh. He accuses the Tanaka government of tampering with the vote-counting and even suggests that the ruling party may have used bribery to obtain votes.

The second editorial sharply contrasts with the first. Nitobe idealizes the election in England, which was held on May 30, 1929. The Labor Party won by a narrow margin, and the Conservatives gracefully handed over the reins of power. To Nitobe, this was an example of democracy in action, and he praised the steadfastness in the English people, who unlike the Japanese, he felt, practice a high standard of political morality.

The third political editorial has the most interest for us. It discusses the three major scandals under the Tanaka administration—the selling of decorations, the private railway bribery, and the Wakayama Prostitute Quarters Bribery. From this corruption in high circles, Nitobe draws a connection with "dangerous thoughts," the word government leaders used to describe leftist opinions. Nitobe sees all these cases as examples of degraded political leadership. He says:

> The nation feels as though the very ground were giving way under its feet. The weaker brethren get giddy, the stronger resentful. The young lose the sense of right and wrong. The thoughtful despise the authorities. The anar-

chists become confirmed in the belief that the state itself would better go. 'Woe unto them by whom the offense cometh.' Which is the greater sinner, the one who steals or the one who vitiates the whole atmosphere and robs theft itself of guilt? Which idea is more dangerous, the one that casts a doubt on the existence of the government or the one that furnishes good reasons for such a doubt?

Six decades after Nitobe wrote the above, we face identical problems, and we still have a great deal to learn from the wisdom of these words! Nitobe confessed that he always voted for the Proletariat parties. His act can be considered a symbolic criticism of the lamentable political situation in Japan at the time.

The two editorials on Education are: "The Need of Civic Education" (February 23, 1930); and "Civic Education and Kokutai" (March 20). Both are concerned with the Second General Election held on February 20, which returned the government to power with a landslide victory. In the first of these articles, Nitobe emphasized the need for civic education to clean up shady election practices; Japan needed it in particular, he said, because it has known no spiritual authority like that of the church in the West. In the second article, Nitobe insisted that, with universal manhood suffrage which the Japanese had been granted in 1925, loyalty to the Emperor has become implicit in one's duties as a citizen.

Two editorials take up the subject of National Character: "Cultural Melting Pot" (September 6, 1929); and "Kanebo Incident and Social Justice" (April 24, 1930). The former reflects Nitobe's view of Japanese history. He sees in history the 'Invisible Hand of God' guiding a nation's destiny. Isolation in the seventeenth century had saved Japan from Catholicism, he says. And the declining influences of the Catholic Church, if they had affected Japan, could not have helped reform the Ancien régime; only by an independence of personality and the self-consciousness of individuality, as manifested in the Anglo-Saxons, Nitobe stresses, can Japan complete her national character.

Nitobe's views on society are presented in the "Kanebo Incident" editorial which was the last that he wrote. To him, this incident illustrates the contradiction inherent within the Japanese family. Good will, he points out, does not work effectively within the old paternalism, for it is without a modern sense of justice. Nitobe declares that the time-honored family system does not meet the needs of the industrial age, and that new modes of social relations are necessary.

Nitobe's lone editorial on the subject of Newspapers, "What Will American Journa lists Say?" (June 1, 1929), was occasioned by a visit of American journalists to Japan. Nitobe urges, in this editorial, that Japanese newspapers pay more heed to public interest, particularly the pressing problem of political morality, by taking American journalism as their model.

"Hopes and Desires For the Year 1930" (January 1, 1930) looks back on the previous year of panic and unemployment. Then he expresses his hopes for the new year. Foremost among the concerns are: greater use of domestic products, an improvement in agriculture, a reform in the election system, and mutual disarmament.

These, then, are the twenty editorials that Nitobe wrote in his first year as a journalist. Although he touches on many themes, lofty aspirations and noble ideals run throughout all of them: internationalism, world peace, social justice, economics grounded in morality, and the meaning of true patriotism. Many germs of everlasting truth are embedded in these editorials.

Essays

Our comments will be brief, for all of these essays have appeared in Nitobe's earlier book *Thoughts and Essays* (1909). He utilized three topic headings for the essays: "Drift and Mastery," twenty-one pieces from July 10 until July 25, 1929; "Life and Opinion," twenty-five pieces from July 26 to August 24; "Faith and Truth," with thirteen pieces from August 25 to September 11. There are 59 essays in all.

These essays were originally written in 1909 for students of English. Nitobe decided to republish them for a new generation of young readers, with whom he wished to share his deepest feelings and thoughts. The essays abound in Nitobe's profound learning, his warm sentiment, his broad and firm faith, his deep sorrow and his refined sense of humor. Even after a lapse of twenty years, they retained all their vital essence and reflected the core of Nitobe's ideas on life.

Editorial Jottings

Approximately 88 percent of Nitobe's writings in the *English Osaka Mainichi* consist of these 730 editorial jottings. Often they were written down hurriedly, in pencil: sometimes as he sat in a train, or a rickshaw, with no reference materials. These jottings provide the best understanding of Nitobe's thoughts and feelings in his advanced years. The newspaper located them in the upper half of the page, in a special column enclosed in a frame, accompanied by his portrait. These continued to appear, regularly, for three years and four months. The editorials, when they appeared, and the essays were printed on the same page of the newspaper: the editorial in two columns on the left-hand side, and the essays on the right-hand side in smaller type.

Nitobe loved these columns so much that he ignored the warnings of his doctor as he lay dying in Victoria, and continued to write them. Several of them arrived at the *English Osaka Mainichi* office after he had passed away. I rank these jottings among the "three great diaries of modern Japan"—the other two being Uchimura Kanzô's *Hibi no shôgai* (Life day-by-day), and Nagai Kafû's *Danchôtei nichijô* (Diary of a broken heart). All three were written with the public in mind, and all commonly express a great concern for contemporary events. These writings give me insight into the problems of modern Japan and an intimate knowledge of each individual author. Nitobe's jottings differ from the others in two important respects: they were written in English, and they addressed an audience of thousands. Also, they had an immediacy about them—they were written and published with no time lag. Uchimura's diary, on the other hand, appeared in his *Seisho no kenkyû* (The Biblical studies), published monthly. Kafû's diary was published some years after he wrote it.

Throughout the jottings, there appear some 290 names, famous and infamous, Eastern and Western, philosophers and politicians, authors and doctors, painters and poets, marshals and historians, religious leaders and emperors. Mussolini, Hitler and Lenin make their appearance with Plato, Confucius, Carlyle and Shakespeare; the latter four are mentioned most often.

The topics touched upon are as many-sided as life itself, and as wide as the cosmos. They include nature, faith, religion, death, love, Bushido, taste, medicine, old age, humor, language, nursing, and solitude.

But the most emphasized subjects are those that relate to peace and society. On peace alone, there are some 193 items. We note such diverse themes as diplomacy, disarmament, national interest, transgressions of a state, internationalism, the League of Nations, the world economy, war, colonies, mutual understanding, and race. Under the category of society, we find an even greater number: some 208 pieces in all, or 28 percent of the total. These relate, in various ways, to the politics, economics, and the social thought of Japan.

Topics relating to science and technology are discussed, including, for example, gene improvement. Those jottings on education touch upon civic education, military training, women's education, and the Imperial Rescript on Education. Discourses on youth, the professions, labor, the Emperor, agrarian villages, newspapers, and the Diet are also found. The main theme, however, under which many others are subsumed, is political thought. Nitobe evaluates in turn communism, militarism, liberalism, democracy, individualism, nationalism, and fascism. He also speaks out strongly against terrorism, political falsehood, corruption, dictatorship, and the worship of money.

In the spring of 1931, while Nitobe travelled to Hokkaido on his holidays, other writers filled his column. From June 11 to 17, for example, selections from Bertrand Russell's *Why I am not a Christian*, and on July 2, a piece written by Dean W. R. Inge, took his place.

Nitobe visited America in 1932, after a thirteen-year interval, and delivered more than a hundred lectures over ten months. He met President Herbert Hoover and made three radio broadcasts. While in America, the "Editorial Jottings" column in the newspaper took the title "What I am Learning in America." The trip caused him great difficulty. American opinion had become hostile to the Japanese. Intellectuals who had earlier sympathized with Japan now criticized it. Nitobe could have no expectation of any success at changing American opinion.

Nitobe gave lectures on Japanese history, national characteristics, the arts, social life, and economic problems. Most important, he discussed the conspicuous Manchurian problem and Japan's relations with China and how they affected U.S.-Japanese relations. He sat up through many long nights preparing the drafts of these lectures after frequent interviews and meetings during the day. The jottings reflect these hardships, though Nitobe viewed them as an education for himself. As his title implied, he visited America, not so much to enlighten or teach, but to learn. We recognize his characteristically modest and tolerant frame of mind.

The Omitted Editorial Jottings

The American lectures of 1932 were collected, after his death, and published in a book *Lectures on Japan* (1936). Also published two years later were the Editorial Jottings in two volumes. The editor of this latter project, Satô Kennosuke, a writer for the *English Osaka Mainichi*, followed the advice of Mary E. Nitobe to omit some of the jottings from these volumes.

In 1938, war had already broken out between China and Japan; public opinion in the United States overwhelmingly supported the Chinese cause; Japanese party government had died—in large measure due to the terrorist activities of the early and mid-thirties—and army members had entrenched themselves in key positions. To select articles to be reprinted required extreme care. Some thirty-nine jottings were excluded for some reason or another. Two were repetitions; four contained inaccuracies. The remaining thirty-three jottings were omitted for the following seven reasons.

First, five articles were omitted because of Nitobe's harsh criticism of Japan and the Japanese. "Servility" (June 14, 1930) concludes that the Japanese are as servile as the Malays. "Barbarians" (July 3, 1930) warns against the stupidity and pettiness of Japanese in judging foreign ideas and manners. "Home versus Foreign Goods" (July 4, 1930) comments that foreign products are better than Japanese. "Nursing Discipline" (July 16, 1930) laments that Japanese nurses are badly disciplined, that they are "rough, noisy, careless and rude." "Lack of Manners" (July 25, 1930) points out the lack of courtesy in the behavior of Japanese gentlemen in public transportation. Nitobe's eyes sharply identified the defects of his fellow countrymen.

Second, some jottings were left out because of their sensitive political nature. "Future of the Privy Council" (August 21, 1930), "A Humorous State" (October 1, 1930), "Blind Leadership" (October 2, 1930), and "What Weakens a Nation" (March 11, 1931) strongly denounced party interests and tactics in the ratification of the London Naval Treaty. The concluding passages of the last jotting, which warns the Privy Council against taking steps towards its own self-destruction by descending into the arena of party politics, reads as follows:

> We shall make our country more vulnerable by rapid speech than by scrapping battleships. Machines are not the only weapons we fight with nowadays. We may girdle our coasts with submarines, but beware lest we expose the nation to foreign ridicule and contempt by empty talk and vacant minds!

Third, a few jottings were removed because they were considered incompatible with state policy and the changed situation of Japan. "A Cosmopolitan Patriot" (June 30, 1931), exhorts us to open our eyes to the best in the life of every nation, remembering the beauties of our own land and people. "Responsibility For Our Handiwork" (December 12, 1931) stresses Japan's responsibility to the League of Nations as an important member of it. "Generosity to Enemies" (January 16, 1932) relates that Japan's Bushido spirit teaches generosity, which is the child of justice and mercy. "Fair Play in Trade" (January 23, 1931) declares that modern commerce must be conducted on the Bushido principles of fair play and mutual respect.

Fourth, two jottings were not reprinted because of Nitobe's strong insistence on disarmament. The trend in international affairs was in the other direction. The two are entitled "Taxation for Armament" (January 4, 1931), and "Wearing of Swords" (February 2, 1932). The former concludes:

> But can this country or any other self-styled first-class power lower its taxes without reducing its army and navy? We cannot eat a pie and have it still. The heavy financial demands made upon us are the incense we burn at the altar of Mars. No hope of making them lighter without crushing the power of the god!

Fifth, those jottings on China and the Chinese are omitted, perhaps because the editor considered Nitobe's sources insufficient. Also his criticism of the Chinese mentality was too severe and his prophecy about China's future had not been fulfilled. "Historical Parallels" (July 16, 1932) states that China will be a federation of local governments. "Shanghai's Narrow Escape" (August 7, 1932) tells us that the 19th Route Army may sack and loot the city of Shanghai, where 65 percent of the entire movable wealth of China in 1932 is located. "Passing the Buck" (September 6, 1932) criticizes the Chinese for failure to accept responsibility. "Cessation of Hostilities" (September 18, 1932) speaks of Nitobe's hope for a Sino-Japanese peace. This appeared in print on the first anniversary of the Manchurian incident. "Old Chinese Influences" (November 1, 1932) concludes that Chinese customs had not penetrated into the core of the soul of the individual Japanese. In "Chinese Nationhood" (April 9, 1933) Nitobe wonders if China qualifies for the definition of a "nation" as postulated in the Covenant of the League of Nations. "Public Opinion in China" casts doubt upon the notion that the Nanking government is supported by the majority of the Chinese people. The seven jottings on China reflect Nitobe's views on China's politics, and in retrospect, we observe that he frequently did not know enough of Chinese problems. And, he fails to measure up to persons like Yoshino Sakuzô or Yanaihara Tadao in fairness of judgment.

Sixth, Nitobe's criticisms of America are excluded. They were written during his last visit, from April 1932 to March 1933. "A Curious Letter" (June 16, 1932) reproves an American scholar for his distorted slander of Nitobe. "The Missionary Mind" (July 8, 1932) and "Missionaries in Sino-Japanese Conflict" (September 21, 1932) say that American missionaries back from China are engaging in anti-Japanese agitation by scattering a most astounding "Gospel of Hatred." "A Christian" (July 9, 1932) argues that Christian journalists in America reflect the low level to which its Christianity has sunk. "A Moral Farce" (July 15, 1932) tells that American life is far less safe than in countries considered semi-barbarous. "Women and Love of Children" (October 1, 1932) comments that most American women long to be a wife but few care to be a mother. Nitobe puts forward this view after seeing so few children in parks, stores and in amusement places. "Clandestine Despotism" (November 24, 1932) reports the despicable means—threats and even terrorism—to which the American Legion covertly resorts on occasion.

These jottings on America reveal Nitobe's great anxiety about it. America, he saw, was seriously ill—the Great Depression, unemployment, anti-Japanese sentiment evidenced this. He felt sympathy for America, yet at the same time fear. He perhaps may have sensed the wind of war coming across the Pacific.

Seventh, two jottings on Korea are set aside—"Abuse of Hospitality" (8 June 1930), and "Assimilation of the Chosenese" (July 11, 1933). The former shows Nitobe's acute sense of justice for the innocent but ill-treated Koreans in Seoul. The latter blames the failure of assimilation on the Japanese, not the Koreans. I cite the former jotting, as related by Nitobe, on his experience in Seoul:

> I remember the time when my Japanese rickshaw man abused an innocent Chosenese quietly walking on the street in Keijo. It made me so angry that I

stopped the puller, and, jumping out of the kuruma—gave him a good thrashing.

I confess it was an unseemly sight, and I would rather not repeat the incident. But the rickshaw-man did not understand my motive. He rather thought I was not patriotic in so disgracing my own fellow-countryman in the presence of many Chosenese. He did not know that a patriot loves his country so well that he would not countenance any act which might reflect on the good name of his own people.

And last, "Sincerity in Diplomacy" (October 4, 1933) laments that expediency and not justice still guides statesmen in diplomacy.

Thus far we have traced all of the omitted jottings. As shown above, there are no differences of spirit between those omitted and those republished in the two volumes. Nitobe retained his faith in the final victory of peace, justice, liberty, internationalism and respect for personality. These convictions had their final expression in these works.

On his deathbed, in October 1933, Nitobe heroically continued to write the jottings. Holding a pencil in his weakened hand, he spelt out the words totteringly. As mentioned above, the last few jottings arrived at the *English Osaka Mainichi* after his death. In accordance with the wishes of his wife, they were not put into print. The final word of the last published jotting was "God." And the last words of the unpublished article are "more beautiful." I cite it in full:

> Who comes to hear news from a sickbed, unless it be about his friend? Doleful stories! There are plenty of moans and groans everywhere. Why should we harass you with news of more?
>
> Suppose, friend, suppose the news from a sick-room is neither moans nor groans, much less the yells and shrieks of pain.
>
> Suppose a poor man in his long confinement has found out that sickness is the distiller of the essence of his God-given nature; is that very dismal news?
>
> All that man is, is put in a retort. It is heated and cooled and the fluid which is the product is our nature—life itself—whatever be its character.
>
> In a sickroom we are subjected to this process, and when it is finished and we recover, we rise from our bed men truer, and more beautiful.

Can we not feel a noble yearning for resurrection between these lines? In all respects the *Editorial Jottings* are truly Nitobe's swan song.

Other Articles

Finally we take up his other articles. There are twelve in all, four of which have been republished. "The Intellectual Penetration of the West in Japan" (June 30, July 1, 3, 4, 1929) was revised and printed as "The Study and Use of Western Languages in Modern Times" in his *The Use and Study of Foreign Languages in Japan—Study in Cultural Internationalism* (1929).

"Some Basic Principles of Japanese Politics," which appeared as a series of five articles, from September 10, to September 15, 1932, is the text of an address presented before the Institute of Politics at Williamstown, Massachusetts in the summer of 1932. Here, Nitobe discusses the "Charter Oath of Five Articles" and its implementation. This article forms the basis for Chapter Six, "Magna Carta of Japan" in *Lectures on Japan* (1936).

"Japan and the Peace Pact," which ran in a series of four articles from October 7 to 11, 1932, became Chapter Sixteen, "Japan, League of Nations, Peace Pact," in *Lectures on Japan*. This originally was a twenty-six minute address read over the Columbia Broadcasting System in New York on the evening of August 20, 1932.

"Japanese Characteristics," printed from January 1 to 6, 1933, was revised and included as Chapter Nineteen, "National Characteristics of the Japanese People," in *Lectures on Japan*.

Let us now turn to those articles that have not been reprinted in Nitobe's later books. On the first, "Let Us Take Counsel Together," we have already commented. The next, "Political Pseudology" (August 18, 1929) gives a finishing blow to the Tanaka Cabinet which had resigned on July 2, 1929. The cabinet had spread false information about Manchuria. It resorted to bribery and terrorism, and it exaggerated the reports about "dangerous thoughts." Nitobe impeaches it as follows: "The Tanaka cabinet left the record of being the worst government this country has had since the Constitution came in force."

He compares Tanaka with the new Prime Minister Hamaguchi in a concise character sketch:

> Tanaka is a general who rose from the ranks, pushing and generous, good natured and jolly, ambitious and daring, thoughtless and irresponsible. The new premier, Hamaguchi, is a trained civil servant of the best type: quiet, sober, with very little sense of humor, businesslike, upright, sincere and earnest. His strong point is finance.

Nitobe uses strong words and urges upon the government the prayer: "Lead us not into temptation," and deliver us from "the sin of lying."

"Japanese Woman" (June 22, 1930) is his longest discourse on this subject in English. Nitobe tells us that women must play their part at this crossroads in Japanese history. To obtain complete equality of opportunity, they must sacrifice some of those qualities which have made them so precious in the past. Sections under "Japanese Woman" include: "Product of Preceding Ages," "Intellectual Advancement," "For Political Right," "Power of Mother," "Keeping Up With Men," "First Institution For Girls," "For Her Own Higher Evolution." These show clearly what is essential in Nitobe's view of women. From these subdivisions, "Intellectual Advancement," and "First Institution for Girls" were rewritten and reprinted as "Girls' Education and the New Women" in Chapter Five, "Educational Systems and Problems" in *Japan...* (1931).

In the opening passages of "Anti-Foreign Teaching" (November 26, 1931) which was written two months after the outbreak of the Manchurian Incident, Nitobe wrote:

> Peace is the normal condition of a well-organized community, whether of individuals or nations. When this condition is disturbed, the best efforts of its members should be directed toward the recovery of normalcy.
>
> We know that it is not just now the fashion of the day to speak of peace, and whoever does so in this country or China is maligned as a traitor or a malefactor. None the less, nobody can deny that a return to the normal habits of human existence should be the aim of every lover of his country.

Nitobe sympathizes with China for the invasion of its territory by foreign powers, yet he advises it not to sow the seeds of the "Gospel of Hate" in the hearts of its youth by filling its school books with anti-foreign lessons. These can never bear peaceful fruits.

"A Gift of Propaganda" (December 3, 1931) comments on shamelessly misleading Chinese propaganda and urges Japan to stand by its dignity and self-respect and to avoid such falsehoods.

Nitobe's meeting with President Hoover forms the basis of his signed article, "Japan's Savant Meets President Hoover—Dr. Nitobe Gives Account of His Visit to White House," which appeared on June 4, 1932. The President spoke of the May 15 Incident, where young army officers had assassinated Prime Minister Inukai; he remarked to Nitobe: "The recent assassination shocked and dismayed us all. In this respect America and the European countries are little better."

Nitobe gave a second radio speech "Japan's Hopes and Fears" over Radio Station WOR, New York, in a series entitled "Japan Today," sponsored by the New York Japanese Chamber of Commerce. This was printed on August 4 and 5. Nitobe spoke first about Japanese arts, next about economics, then politics, and lastly international relations—from the easier topics to the more difficult ones. Three fears, he emphasized, face industrial Japan: tariff walls, boycotts, and scarcity of raw materials. The world must not forget that Japan is a nation that has enjoyed 250 years of continuous peace and is not a warrior who brandishes his sword. In Manchuria, Japan seeks to exercise rights which are secured by treaties. Japan is afraid of Bolshevism, which is an enemy of her monarchial system. Already, a large part of China has succumbed. Manchuria serves as a buffer between Russia and Japan. Seen in this light, Japan's mission in the Far East is peace, order, and progress.

The last article that Nitobe wrote for the *English Osaka Mainichi* is "How Geneva Erred—Time Will Come When League Will Realize Its Mistakes: Is Not Japan Responsible for Geneva's Ignorance?" (April 12 and 13, 1933). This is the text of a speech delivered before an audience of over 100 people at a Tokyo Pan-Pacific Club luncheon in the Imperial Hotel on Friday, April 7.

Ten days before, Japan had left the League and become an outcast in the diplomatic world. How this pained Nitobe, who had worked so long and hard for the League's ideal of international cooperation! This grief is reflected in the following subdivisions of the article: "Admirer of U.S.," "Avocation not Abandoned," "Back into Darkness," "Japan also Erred," "U.S. is a Powerful Member," "Dawn Over Pacific." Nitobe sorrowfully says at this point in the passage that he is: "one of those inconsistent and self-contradictory people who believe that while Japan is justified at the present moment to leave the League, ... the League is the greatest hope for the future welfare of the world."[2]

Nitobe felt his heart torn to pieces, as did the Emperor, with whom he had a few days earlier discussed the future of the state. He tried to associate Japan with the rest of the world and stressed that it could not leave the family of nations, which was a natural institution, possessed almost with human emotions. The League, in contrast, was artificial. Nitobe endeavored not to lose hope:

> At present things look dark, but darkness will not last forever. The shouting and the tumult will die, and the captains and kings will depart. Then we shall gain cooler judgement, and I do not think the time is far distant when this cooler judgement will come back. Then we shall see that on both sides of the Pacific there are many earnestly interested in our good relationship—I see many represented here this afternoon.

He concluded this speech with the following symbolic words: "We meet like ships in the night, but we rarely forget the ship that we pass in the night." With "The Passing of a Samurai with a Pen," Nitobe fell at last in harness, holding not his sword but his pen, fighting bravely as a true samurai against the evil spirit of war that permeated the whole world. His last four-and-a-half years affirmed his love and devotion to his homeland and to mankind. Nowhere, except in these editorials, essays and articles of the *English Osaka Mainichi*, can we find more clearly the thoughts and beliefs, hopes and fears, griefs and joys, impressions and criticisms of the greatest internationalist of modern Japan. He dedicated his life to the great cause of reconciling peoples of different nations and uniting the East and West.

The *English Osaka Mainichi* inserted an eulogy by his friend, Dr. C. J. L. Bates, a Canadian Methodist missionary and first President of the Kansei

Gakuin University, which appeared a week after Nitobe's death. The eulogy, "The Passing of Dr. Nitobe," describes him as a "truly great man, a great scholar, a great patriot, a great internationalist, a great Christian." Dr. Bates lists the facts of Nitobe's matchless characteristics—an elegant speaker of English, a superb writer in the style of Carlyle, a great gentleman with fine courtesy and culture, a man of transparent honesty, a man with a samurai sense of honor burning in his bosom; a thoughtful, gracious, and entertaining guest at home. He was able to understand and appreciate the best in the spirit of the Western world and sought to unite it with the best elements in Japanese culture. He was a great architect bridging the wide gulf between nations. After praising Mrs. Mary Nitobe's faithful support of her husband, Bates concludes with the following warm words: "Farewell brave heart. You have done your best. You have played your part well. The world will not forget the service you have rendered, for your name will be written among those who have served it well."

On November 16, a month after his death, Nitobe returned to his motherland, embraced in the warm bosom of his wife, and followed by his younger friends. Two days later, at the Aoyama Funeral Hall, services were held in the manner of the Society of Friends. Some three thousand persons bade him farewell. The hymns sung were "Peace, perfect peace, in this dark world of sin" and "Till we meet again." Since the latter had been sung at the cremation of his old classmate Uchimura Kanzô three years before, Nitobe had requested that this hymn also be sung at his own funeral.

The *English Osaka Mainichi* published "Dr. Nitobe—Personal Recollections" by Satô Kennosuke, as a final tribute.

The Spirit of a Journalist

In ancient China, when decrees on cultural affairs were proclaimed, officials notified people by ringing a *bokutaku*. A *bokutaku* is a small bronze bell with a wooden clapper. Later on, it came to signify leaders of society who instructed people. In the *Analects of Confucius* (3:24), there is a story of a frontier official who, after meeting Confucius, said to people around him: "What are you worrying about? Truly it is long since the Way under Heaven became extinct. But Heaven will make of our Teacher a *bokutaku* [cultural innovator]. Indeed, a society where the clear ringing of a *bokutaku* is not heard for a long time is destined to perish."

The last four-and-a-half years of Nitobe's life embodied this ideal. He served as a "bokutaku of society." What social evils were there that he did not refer to? I can think of none. All were condemned, with militarism, political corruption, party self-interest, and defects in education the major ones. What injustice did he fail to notice? I can think of none. All were brought to light—racial discrimination, oppression, unequal distribution of wealth. What ways to peace did he not plead? I can think of none. Every possible way was pressed—mutual understanding, intellectual cooperation, disarmament, the abolishment of militarism and terrorism, and the removal of tariff walls.

Nitobe passed the last four and a half years on earth in the midst of utter darkness, fighting the powers of darkness with the inner light of his spirit. He rendered his last service as a builder of bridges to his motherland and to the world as a newspaperman. Not seated high and alone at the summit of Mount Olympus, not throwing down profound oracles from on high, he remained bravely below in this foul world of sin, smiling pure as a lotus flower in the mire, shining as bright as a beacon lamp in the dark roaring storm. He expressed his thoughts and feelings to the people at large in plain and lucid writing, seasoned with humor and irony.

The Quaker spirit of Nitobe, going above the boundaries of nations or races, arrived at the side of the throne of the Highest daily in his silent prayer. The petty minds which crept along the earth saw no truth beyond the narrow limits of their territory, and thus could not understand the true meaning of his words. Nitobe, like the Master whom he followed to the end of his life, rendered his last services slandered and misunderstood.

We have characterized him as bridge builder, as he described himself. He worked at bridging the gulf between nations of the East and the West, with all his mind and with all his strength. In the deepest sense, his bridge crosses the gulf between the visible and the invisible; it stands between the innermost recesses of our soul and the everyday life of the common people; ultimately, it bridges the love of God and the world that stands against Him.

This bridge, to which Nitobe devoted his life, we feel committed to make firmer, safer and more durable. We should strive to make this world and the men who inhabit it "truer and more beautiful," as he said on the day that he passed into eternity.

Notes

1. Mainichi Shimbun hyakunenshi kankô kai hen, *Mainichi Shimbun hyakunenshi 1872–1972* (1972), p. 622.
2. See also p. 208 of this volume.

11

Mediation Between Cultures

Yuzo Ota

At this point, let me focus our attention on Nitobe as a cultural mediator. The first thing to note is that Nitobe played this role consciously; he told his readers that he first voiced his intention to dedicate his life to cultural mediation during his student days in Tokyo.

The most important factor which induced Nitobe to take upon himself this role was probably his excellent command of the English language. Experts in such specialities as flower arrangement and *go*, the Japanese game of strategy, may be able to fulfil a cultural mission abroad without much verbal communication, but people who want to further mutual understanding between their own countries and foreign countries through lectures and publication must know the necessary languages. This is perhaps the reason why in *Jinsei dokuhon* (A reader on life) (1934) Nitobe referred to himself as an interpreter *(tsûyaku)*:

> I call myself an interpreter and write books and articles in English all the time, but I am afraid that none of them has lasting value. If you ask me if I write them for money, my answer is 'No,' although I appreciate it if they bring me money. As I regard my mission as that of an interpreter, I believe that my job is simply to explain the West in the Japanese language and to make foreigners understand Japan. I have done no research of my own, nor have I any original views superior to those of others. I simply convey what A says to B and communicate to A what I have learned from B. This is why I do not expect that my writings will be read by posterity and feel satisfied if they serve some useful purpose for the moment.[1]

It is generally believed in Japan that Nitobe contributed greatly as a cultural mediator to mutual understanding between Japan and foreign countries. It seems that almost everyone who has evaluated Nitobe's life and work includes encomia like "the author of *Bushido* which explained the essence of Japanese culture to the world," "a representative internationalist of Japan," and "a bridge across the Pacific." In contrast, let us here point out some of Nitobe's weaknesses as a cultural mediator.

To indicate the general direction of the investigation, let us begin with a quotation from the first of the course of lectures which Tsurumi Shunsuke gave, in English, from September to December 1979 at McGill University. Tsurumi later published these lectures as *An Intellectual History of Wartime Japan 1931–1945*. At the beginning of his first lecture, Tsurumi included remarks on the question of language. After proposing to use only English in his course, Tsurumi said: "[M]y use here of the English language creates a methodological difficulty. I have a hypothesis that in the majority [of] cases English-speaking Japanese are unreliable. This hypothesis tends to discredit whatever I might say in English about Japan."[2]

What has led to the quotation from Tsurumi is the striking contrast between his attitude and that of Nitobe. To anticipate a little, in my opinion Nitobe had a much stronger reason than Tsurumi to warn his audience to discount his words on Japan, but he never did. We will enlarge on this in due order.

In the first place, let us point out that in a sense Nitobe was an English-speaking Japanese par excellence. Very few people, before or since, who were born and brought up in Japan spent their life so immersed in English as he did. This was mainly because his boyhood coincided with a very special period in the history of education in Japan. Nitobe was one of those who "happened to receive an American-type education in a period of transition with no fixed governmental policy on education,"[3] as Miyabe Kingo, one of Nitobe's former classmates, put it. I used the phrase *"Eigo meijin sedai"* (The generation of masters in English) in my book entitled *Eigo to Nihonjin* (Use of the English language in modern Japan)[4] to designate people of Nitobe's generation who received a higher education. When specialists try to enumerate the Japanese whose English-language writings are best known, most name Uchimura Kanzô (born in 1861), Nitobe Inazô (born in 1862), and Okakura Tenshin (born in 1862). That they became fluent in English is no mere coincidence; it is closely related to their special education.[5]

Because of this education, it was almost the rule rather than an exception that the Masters in English at certain points in their careers, at least, read and wrote English with greater facility than Japanese. Nitobe recalled in *Naikan gaibô* (Looking inward and outward) (1933):

> When I entered Tokyo English School, the predecessor of the present Higher School, we studied every single subject in English. Mathematics, geography, history, etc.—all subjects were taught in English. Because of such education, it is very easy for me to read books written in English. It is somewhat differ-

ent nowadays, but in my twenties I read English books with much greater facility than Japanese books.[6]

During the year that Nitobe entered college, the concern of a highly placed education authority was not that students in university would not learn English but rather that, if nothing was done to redress the situation, "Those who boast themselves to be graduates of the University in Japan may be proficient only in English and incompetent in Japanese."[7] These are the words of Katô Hiroyuki, then the Head of the Faculties of Law, Science, and Arts of Tokyo University; he wrote them in his memorial of 1877 to the Ministry of Education.

If Nitobe was an English-speaking Japanese par excellence, was he then also unreliable? The degree of reliability or unreliability in question here does not refer to Nitobe's character or personality but only to Nitobe's utterances on Japan or Japanese culture. They, after all, represent what he said as a cultural mediator. Let us begin by considering in some detail the implications of the special education which Nitobe received as a member of the Generation of Masters in English. It is quite easy to see that people who received that kind of education must have been able to spend less time on Japanese history and Japanese culture and so knew less of it than those who studied nothing else. For example, Miyabe, Nitobe's former classmate, reminisced later:

> The students of my generation received a kind of abnormal education. We did not study Japanese and classical Chinese [kanbun] except as small children. All the instruction afterwards, including instruction in mathematics, geography, and history, was given directly by foreigners in English. Today I suffer great inconvenience due to my lack of basic culture in classical Chinese.[8]

Here Miyabe mentions only his lack of background in classical Chinese, but it is not difficult to imagine that such a person also lacked a basic understanding of Japanese culture.

Nitobe never acknowledged his ignorance of Japan in talks or writings for a foreign audience, but frequently he professed to Japanese audiences that he knew little of Japanese culture. For example, in a lecture given around 1929 and published in *Dokusho to jinsei* (Reading and life), he expands on his ignorance of Japanese and Chinese traditions in these words:

> To my shame, I cannot discuss with confidence literature of the East. I regret this very much. When I read books—when my appetite for reading was the strongest—Japanese literature was out of vogue. So was Chinese literature. When we were young, we virtually never heard of *Tsurezuregusa* (Essays in idleness). I was about twenty when I first learned of it and went to bookshops

to see a copy. I was told that all the copies of it had been put in storage because nobody wanted to buy them.[9]

In a letter of June 1, 1877, addressed to his family, Nitobe confesses his "total ignorance of Japanese and Chinese history."[10] There is every reason to believe that current attitudes toward tradition and the education Nitobe received made him extremely ignorant about Japan as a young student. And he never seems to have adequately made up for the deficiency of this early education. Apparently Nitobe remained to the end of his life able, for example, to discuss classical Greek literature much more confidently than the Japanese literature of the Heian period.

As a result, it was inevitable that much of Nitobe's English-language writings discussed Japanese culture with no real originality and depth. Albert P. Ludwig, in a review of Nitobe's *Lectures on Japan* (1936), wrote that "the reader looks in vain for new facts or new interpretations not already known to students of Far Eastern affairs."[11] "There are already in existence a number of excellent introductory works on the history and the culture of the Japanese. To these Dr. Nitobe adds very little,"[12] wrote K. S. Latourette in his review of Nitobe's *Japan: Some Phases of her Problems and Development* (1931). I agree with these reviewers.

In addition to the relative lack of originality in much of his English writings, I would like to point out that some of the views expressed in them may even run counter to his honest personal views. For example, in Chapter Six ("On Haiku") of his English-language *Japanese Traits and Foreign Influences* (1929), Nitobe presents haiku as a vehicle to express deep spiritual truths and what he calls "cosmic consciousness."[13] His evaluation of haiku in a Japanese-language work is different. In "Eigo to eibungaku no kachi" (The value of the English language and English literature), Nitobe discusses haiku. This evaluation dates from almost the same time as the passage quoted above, yet differs greatly from it. This becomes quickly apparent from such quotations as:

> The vogue of haiku which delights in clever casual ideas does not encourage one to think in earnest or to persevere to achieve some goal,"[14] and "I do not particularly intend to criticize haiku, but not everything can be handled after the fashion of haiku. Haiku itself may be a philosophy, but I believe that it can only be a very superficial philosophy, not worth Spinoza's little finger. Its worth is like the dirt under his finger nail.[15]

Those who have perceived elsewhere in Nitobe's writings his extreme sensitiveness to criticism directed against Japan and his constant endeavor to uphold the reputation of Japan before the foreigner,[16] will have no difficulty understanding which of the two views on haiku just mentioned is closer to his real belief. It is the one in Japanese. Here we can perceive Nitobe's tendency to "sell" an idealized image of Japan and things Japanese, even when it ran counter to his personal views. The tendency to idealize Japanese motivation is partly responsible for Nitobe's reputation as a propagandist for the Japanese military among many people in the United States after the outbreak of the Manchurian Incident in 1931. This question of Nitobe after the Manchurian Incident requires separate treatment and will not be dealt with here.[17]

We have pointed out that Nitobe's English-language writings on Japan were not particularly original, but not all of them show the same lack of originality. *The Intercourse between the United States and Japan: An Historical Sketch* (1891), Nitobe's first book in English, is quite original. When he wrote it, Nitobe was still in his twenties. His prose gives us the impression that the young man is voicing his honest opinions without inner impediment. He prepared it while still a full-time student in the United States and Germany. Accordingly, unlike his later works written when Nitobe, as a celebrity, was too busy to devote much time to study, it is in general well researched, although even here Nitobe betrays a superficiality in his basic understanding of Japan, which induced a reviewer to remark, "Dr. Nitobe's investigations in America have been thorough. Not so, apparently, investigations in his own country."[18]

As literature, too, *The Intercourse between the United States and Japan* is probably one of the best, if not the very best, of Nitobe's English-language writings. In his later works, Nitobe, probably motivated by his desire to appear the equal of Western readers, tended to show off his learning by too frequent allusions and quotations and the selection of unnecessarily difficult words. For example, the majority of Westerners for whom Nitobe's English-language writings were intended would not understand, without recourse to a dictionary, the following sentences, chosen from Nitobe's *Japanese Traits and Foreign Influences* (1931): "[I]n a matriarchate or a gyarchy...the object of filial duty and love is clearly defined;"[19] "'Drinking like an ox, eating like a horse' was the phrase applied to the physical act of deglutition and degustation;"[20] "Naturally, for singing purposes all degrees of epithesis and prosthesis, as well as of ecstasis and acopope, are permitted;"[21] "[W]as He [Christ] not using them merely for purposes of a synecdoche or metonymy?"[22] "To him, circumcision and sabbath and meat and drink were adiaphoron."[23]

The extremely difficult words in these examples seem quite uncalled for. It would almost appear that Nitobe was aware of the lack of solid research behind his later English writings and so tried to make them as impressive as possible by giving them high literary quality. In actual fact, however, they became artificial and inferior to *The Intercourse between the United States and Japan* even as English prose.

If *The Intercourse between the United States and Japan* is an original work, *Bushido: The Soul of Japan* seems a work of a very mixed value. Many people consider this work, first published in 1900, Nitobe's masterpiece. It may be an original work in the sense that, when he wrote it, he was not repeating or summarizing in English what he had read in Japanese secondary sources. Nitobe reminisced around 1930:

> I wrote about Bushido roughly thirty years ago. Around that time, the word 'Bushido' was seldom heard. The word apparently existed, but was not generally used. Chamberlain, a British Japanologist, and other people who were well informed about Japanese affairs, said that they had never heard the word 'Bushido' during their long residence in Japan and maintained that there had not been such a thing as Bushido even in Old Japan.[24]

That for a long time Nitobe thought he had coined the word "Bushido" is indicated, for example, by the following quotation from *Kigan no ashi* (Reeds of a returned goose): "I named it 'Bushido' or 'the Way of the samurai' because the culture to which it referred was most noticeable among the samurai class."[25] It was roughly thirty years after writing *Bushido* that Nitobe recognized that the word Bushido had apparently existed before he wrote that book. As he explained in *Naikan gaibô* (looking inward and outward), "The other day a person called Nakayasu who works for the *Nichi nichi* Newspaper Company informed me that he had come across this word Bushido several times while he was going over old books."[26] So when Nitobe wrote *Bushido*, he believed he was writing about a subject which nobody had dealt with before. In this sense, he was probably very conscious of the originality of *Bushido*. Another remark of his found in *Ijin gunzô* (Portraits of great men)(1931) also implicitly claims that *Bushido* was original and greatly influenced Japanese thought: "this noun [Bushido] came to be widely used even in Japan only with the publication of my Bushido."[27] In fact, to repeat, Nitobe knew very little about Japan. His few remarks about Bushido quoted above betray his ignorance.

In the first place, the word "Bushido" was by no means coined by Nitobe. It was used, for example, by Katô Kiyomasa (1562–1611), one of the famous generals of Toyotomi Hideyoshi and thus it goes back, at least, to the late sixteenth century.[28] Among Nitobe's contemporaries, Uemura Masahisa, another famous Christian of post-Meiji Restoration Japan, published an article titled "Kirisutokyô to bushidô" (Christianity and Bushido) in 1894, that is, six years before the publication of Nitobe's *Bushido*. Actually, the word "Bushido" had gained fairly wide currency before the appearance of Nitobe's *Bushido* in 1900. In 1898, even a magazine entitled *Bushidô* had appeared. This magazine, an organ of the Dai Nippon Bujutsu Kôshûkai (The society for promotion of martial arts of great Japan), counted among its contributors such prominent intellectual and political leaders as Fukuchi Gen'ichirô, Ozaki Yukio, Kataoka Kenkichi, Nakae Chômin, Ôi Kentaro, and Uemura Masahisa. These examples give us no room to doubt the relatively wide currency of the word *"bushido"* before the appearance of Nitobe's book.

Mikami Reiji's *Nihon bushidô* (Japanese Bushido), published in 1899, is another example of Bushido literature which preceded Nitobe's *Bushido*. Mikami would never have dreamed of claiming that he had coined the word "Bushido." On page sixteen of his book, we read, "The substance of Bushido was already in existence from the beginning of our country but the word 'Bushido' came into use in the medieval period."

Not only did Nitobe believe he coined the word "Bushido," he also wrongly ascribed great influence to his book within Japan. What caused a kind of mushrooming of books with the word Bushido in their titles was not Nitobe's *Bushido*. If Nitobe, with his erroneous belief that he was the inventor of the word Bushido, thought that people such as Inoue Tetsujirô, the author of *Bushidô* (1901); Kawaguchi Shûji, the author of *Nihon bushidô ron* (A Treatise on Japanese Bushido)(1904); and Ninagawa Tatsuo, the author of *Nihon bushidô shi* (A History of Bushido in Japan)(1907): That all of them had written about Bushido in imitation of him, his belief simply shows how out of touch Nitobe was with intellectual currents in contemporary Japan. These books were written in large part in response to the stimulus of the Sino-Japanese War and the Russo-Japanese War. Their authors perceived an urgent need for such works. Many of them aimed to prepare the Japanese for possible military service under the universal conscription law by instilling right military values and attitudes with the help of what we might call Bushido ideology. Others were stimulated by the stunning victories which Japan had scored during the Russo–Japanese War into a search for their "real" causes in the Japanese cultural tradition. "Since the Russo–Japanese War, the study of Bushido has become a great intellectual concern, attracting the attention of both Japanese and foreigners. No matter what they are—politicians, businessmen, scholars, military men—a great number of people want to study Bushido," writes Ninagawa in the preface to his *Bushidô shi*. These authors wrote for a number of reasons, but they did not include influence from Nitobe's *Bushido*.

We have referred to Nitobe's erroneous ideas about the word Bushido. His mistakes do not end there. His English-language publications actually betray his widespread ignorance about Japan, and especially its history. His special weakness in this area is probably related to the fact that, while one can absorb all sorts of information about contemporary Japan without conscious effort and as a result commit few grave blunders, things are different when one deals with Japan's past.

Let us cite several passages from Nitobe's English writings with my comments to point out how elementary some of his mistakes were. "The cultural penetration of China...was in full swing as early as the fourth century A.D., China being then under the rule of the famous Tang dynasty" (*Japanese Traits and Foreign Influences*).[29] China in the fourth century was not under the rule of the Tang Dynasty which began in 618 A.D. "Far otherwise with Buddhism, which, soon after its introduction into the country (7th century), supplied just what was most wanting in Shinto." (*Japanese Traits and Foreign Influences*)[30] "When Buddhism was first introduced, in the fourth century, there was some trouble as I shall describe in a subsequent lecture: but that did not last long." (*Lectures on Japan*).[31] These two quotations show that Nitobe was not sure about when Buddhism entered Japan; in one place he said "7th century," and at another place he said "the fourth century." Both dates differ from the usual date for the official transmission of Buddhism which is 538 or 552 A.D.

> The conflict that ensued between the Mononobes and the Sogas was embittered by the feud that had been fomenting between them. The former were badly beaten, and, as the latter showed further signs of inordinate ambition, they were in turn put an end to by a large *Uji*, subsequently called the Fujiwara, loyally devoted to the throne. Prince Shôtoku, who at the time was acting as Regent, having succeeded in confirming the legitimacy of the Royal House, established monarchism as the principle of Japanese nationality. As soon as he made secure the rights of the Crown, he pursued the policy of his former enemy, the Sogas, and espoused with open arms and more open heart the tenets of Buddha.(*Japan*).[32]

That Nitobe could actually publish such a fantastically distorted story as authentic history cannot help but amaze me. In this passage Nitobe obviously talks about two events, namely, the destruction of the power of the Mononobe family by the Soga family and their allies in 587 A.D. and the Taika reform which was started with the assassination of Soga no Iruka, the head of the Soga family, in 645 A.D. Prince Shôtoku (574–622 A.D.), who participated in the former event, was long dead when the second event occurred, but in Nitobe's account, he is made to play a leading role in the second event as well. "In the earliest census, which was taken early in the ninth century, it is surprising to see what a large proportion of aliens (Koreans and Chinese)—as many as 31 per cent—played their part as residents of the capital." (*Lectures on Japan*).[33] The earliest census in Japan goes back to the seventh century. This erroneous passage is very likely based on Nitobe's misunderstanding of the *Shinsen shôjiroku*, a book of genealogies completed in 815 A.D. It listed more than one thousand clans (*uji*) in the capital and in the neighboring areas.

> The Shogunate, which represented the actual governing power, passed, after the eleventh century, from one family to another in quite rapid succession until the beginning of the seventeenth century, when it fell to the lot of Iyeyasu, head of the Tokugawa house, in whose hand it was centralized and elaborately organized.*(Japan)*.[34]
>
> In the days when the *samurai* was all powerful—say from the eleventh to the twentieth centuries—even amusements and pastimes were so graded that some were considered proper for his rank and dignity, while others were despised *(The Japanese Nation)*.[35]

These two examples seem to indicate that Nitobe erroneously believed that the Kamakura shogunate was established in the eleventh century rather than toward the end of the twelfth century. The implication of the second quotation that the samurai was all powerful even in the twentieth century is also misleading.

> Thus was consummated by the founder of the Tokugawa family, the *exclusive* measures so jealously maintained by his successors for two and a half centuries. His policy did not stop here. It was as *inclusive* as it was exclusive. So rigorous was the Edict of 1637, that not only were foreigners forbidden to land on the Japanese coast, but the natives were prohibited from leaving it *(The Japanese Nation)*.[36]
>
> Even during the period of seclusion, when ship-wrecked people of a foreign nationality drifted to our shores, they were always treated with kindness. Even Iyeyasu, who initiated the policy, said that 'if devils from hell should come to my country, I will treat them as angels from heaven.' *(Lectures on Japan)*.[37]

These two examples show that Nitobe erroneously believed that Tokugawa Iyeyasu, who died in 1616, was the author of a series of seclusion edicts in the 1630s.

These errors may not be serious in themselves, but since individual facts furnish bases for large-scale interpretations and generalizations about Japanese culture and history, this rather shaky grasp of individual facts by Nitobe could lead to very serious misrepresentations. And it seems that this was largely what did happen in Nitobe's *Bushido*.

The majority of the Western reviewers of *Bushido* took it for granted that the author possessed a solid knowledge of his subject since he as a Japanese wrote about the culture of his own country. They erred in this assumption. Again, Nitobe did not conceal his lack of real expertise in this matter before a Japanese audience, as the following quotation from "Nogi Taishô no junshi o hyôsu" (On the Suicide of General Nogi) (1912) indicates: "Because I have published a book on Bushido, people tend to regard me as a student of Bushido or its propagandist. However, it would be a grave exaggeration if I claimed to have studied Bushido. Accordingly, such things as the secret of Bushido are beyond my comprehension."[38]

In my opinion, Nitobe's frequent careless generalizations in *Bushido* resulted from two factors. One is his failure to scrutinize whether the utterance of an individual could be deemed to represent his class or his age. When the so-called forty-seven *rônin* avenged the death of their late master in 1703, contemporary evaluations of their deed were not unanimous. Among the famous scholars of that time, Muro Kyûsô praised their action, while Dazai Shundai disapproved of it.[39] This is only one example which suggests how dangerous it is to regard a hasty individual opinion as an accurate reflection of majority values and opinions among samurai in feudal Japan, as Nitobe implicitly did so often in his English-language writings. Nitobe also often failed to distinguish samurai ideas and ideals from actual samurai behavior. For example, even though very few samurai would have openly repudiated loyalty as a virtue, a samurai's life was by no means dominated by the virtue of loyalty as Nitobe's *Bushido* would make us believe—especially not in the sixteenth century which is in a sense singled out by Nitobe. It is in fact rather curious that at the end of Chapter 2 of *Bushido*, Nitobe indicates that it is the pervading characteristics of the samurai of the sixteenth century that he proposes to discuss in the subsequent chapters. He does not seem to grasp the implications of the lasting peace after 1615 which radically altered actual roles of the samurai in the society and, hence, altered also their attitudes and values. What Nitobe wrote in *Bushido* is actually least applicable to sixteenth-century Japan, torn as it was by constant civil wars. That he did not notice this seems also to reflect his relative ignorance of Japanese history.

Uchimura Kanzô, Nitobe's former classmate at Sapporo Agricultural College and another Master in English, also often talked about Bushido as the following two quotations show: "Bushido is the finest product of Japan.... Christianity grafted upon Bushido will be the finest product of the world. *It* will save, not only Japan but the whole world."[40] "In our everyday life, in most of the cases, we Japanese Christians can safely conduct ourselves according to our Bushido, handed down from our ancestors without having to consult the Bible."[41] Ienaga Saburô, a noted intellectual historian of Japan, commenting on Uchimura's Bushido, said, "What Uchimura thought to be '*Bushido*' was merely an illusion created by projecting Puritanism, which he had learned from the West, on Japan."[42] The general tenor of Ienaga's comment seems relevant to Nitobe's Bushido as well. In both cases it was a relative ignorance about the real life and way of thinking of the *samurai* class which permitted their authors to describe what was largely a projection of their ideal as a historical reality.

What Nitobe wrote in *Bushido* is not all wrong. Component parts are sometimes good and interesting, but they are intermixed with numerous erroneous or misleading statements so that the whole picture which emerges can only be regarded, if not as completely illusory, at least as an excessive idealization of Japan's past. It is quite characteristic of Nitobe that, when he discusses "Sources of Bushido" in that chapter of Bushido, he immediately starts discussing Buddhism and Shintoism. Apparently it never occurred to him that the actual life of a samurai could be the most important source of his thought. Accordingly, Nitobe treated the samurai as unreal, abstract beings, scarcely paying any attention to the economic foundation and other concrete conditions of their life which were subject to historical change. Let us have a look at a characteristic statement of Nitobe: "In the precarious life led in times of constant fighting, property was naturally insecure and its value was lightly appreciated. The only permanent acquisition was a good name; that was immortality. 'Tigers, when they die, leave their skin behind.' How to leave his footsteps on the sands of time, was the care of every young samurai, and all his strivings and sacrifices had that single end in view."[43] This statement from the chapter on "Japanese Code of Honor" in *Lectures on Japan* is not completely false if given in the right context.

That many samurai placed a great importance on the acquisition of a good name is unmistakable. At the same time, the lord-vassal relationship of the Kamakura period, for example, usually provided substantial material rewards. They were based on the exchange of a favor *(goon)* from the lord and the service *(hôkô)* from a vassal. In return for his service, the vassal usually received a new plot of land or was confirmed in the ownership of a plot of land which he already held. Thus a samurai, contrary to what Nitobe says in the above quotation, normally placed great importance on his property (land) as the expression *issho kenmei* (to stake one's life on one's sole resource—his land received as a fief) indicates. While the samurai remained actual warriors, the pursuit of a good name or honor was seldom the only motive. They also expected material rewards. Unless one realizes this, the resultant picture will be inevitably onesided.

One of the most interesting reviews of *Bushido* was published in *The Athenaeum*, to which Powles has already referred on pages 114–115. The anonymous reviewer begins his discussion of *Bushido* with these words:

> Our first volume is the tenth edition of Prof. Nitobe's exposition of what certain latter-day Japanese and some of their well-intentioned Western admirers exalt as a particular quality or virtue which new Japan has inherited from the Japan of the Shogunate—Bushido. The book is a signal proof of the reaction—now, apparently, in full swing—from the ideas of the seventies and eighties, when the completest Westernization was the ideal, and the Tokugawa system the abomination of Japanese reformers. Time has brought about its revenge; the faith of the Shinto revivalists is abandoned, and it is to the mili-

tary caste of the Shogunate, to whose predominance Rai Sanyo, the one philosophical historian Japan has produced, ascribed all the evils of his country, that Japan is taught to look for the source of its national virtues. In a word, the *ishin* (restoration) government—if Prof. Nitobe's views are correct—is nothing more than the Shogunate enlarged by the abolition of the daimiates, and dignified by the presidency of the Mikado.[44]

The evaluation of *Bushido* by the reviewer as "a signal proof" of the reaction against the extreme Westernizing tendencies of the 1870s and 1880s seems quite accurate. As we have seen, Nitobe received a very Western education. He also remained to the end of his life basically a "Westernizer" who maintained the need to keep learning from the West. At the same time, he reacted quite vehemently against the type of Westernization symbolized by the Rokumeikan, a Western-style building erected by the Japanese in 1883 to impress foreigners with Japanese sophistication in Western ways. It must have appeared superficial or humiliating to him, as the following quotation from *The Intercourse Between the United States and Japan* indicates: "As to masquerades, frequently given in the highest circle of our society, no excuse is possible.... They are a violence to human dignity and nothing short of an abomination."[45] Nitobe was one of the numerous Japanese of the Meiji period whose patriotic sentiments had been roused and sustained by the sense that the very independence of Japan was still endangered. A reasoned recognition of the need for Westernization to strengthen Japan and an emotional desire for proud self-assertion of Japanese uniqueness must have created a considerable inner tension in many patriotic Japanese of the Meiji period, including Nitobe.

When, with the Perry expeditions to Japan, regular intercourse between Japan and the West resumed, the majority of the Westerners took for granted everything Western was superior to its heathen Japanese counterpart. In the face of demonstrated Western military superiority, many Japanese tacitly acquiesced to the Western claim of a general superiority, which led them to undervalue Japan's past at the beginning of the Meiji Period. Erwin Baelz is often quoted as saying in 1876:

> [T]he Japanese have their eyes fixed exclusively on the future, and are impatient when a word is said of their past. The cultured among them are actually ashamed of it. 'That was in the days of barbarism,' said one of them in my hearing. Another, when I asked him about Japanese history, bluntly rejoined: 'We have no history. Our history begins today.'[46]

Baelz's words neatly express a widespread feeling of self-abnegation held by many Japanese at the beginning of Meiji. This wholesale rejection of their past by many Japanese was certainly an overreaction. It was inevitable that, sooner or later, a more positive re-evaluation of their past should be undertaken, especially since their traditional culture did contain various admirable aspects which, for example, prompted Edward S. Morse who arrived in Japan in 1877 to remark, "A foreigner, after remaining a few months in Japan, slowly begins to realize that, whereas he thought he could teach the Japanese everything, he finds to his amazement and chagrin, that those virtues or attributes which, under the name of humanity are the burden of moral teaching at home, the Japanese seem to be born with."[47] Nitobe's *Bushido* was in a sense an attempt to rehabilitate Japan's past which had been rejected *in toto*. He shared the motives of those who initiated the movement for the preservation of the national essence towards the end of the 1880s.

Nitobe's *Bushido* was quite timely, too, since the Japanese victory in the Sino-Japanese War and other events had enhanced national self-confidence, and the Japanese were particularly receptive to such a work which would satisfy their latent emotional need to restore pride in their nation's past. This also explains why Nitobe's *Bushido* has not lost even today its power to move some Japanese. Even if one assumes such a motivation for writing *Bushido*, Nitobe in it goes beyond a balanced rehabilitation. Uemura Masahisa, who had a more solid grounding in traditional culture, was aware of the danger that "those who discuss Bushido conclude immediately from its idealized presentation by Confucian scholars that the samurai were really like that."[48] So, Uemura was critical of Nitobe's *Bushido*, too, and said, "I am sorry that Mr. Nitobe in his English language work *Bushido* assumed an attitude which was excessively advocatory."[49]

The reviewer of *Bushido* in *The Athenaeum* said immediately following the paragraph quoted above, "To our mind that whole thesis is singularly destitute of historical support." This judgment is basically correct, although the reviewer's evaluation of Japan's feudal past presented in the later part of the review may be too negative. His criticism of Nitobe's manner of constructing his arguments—"He makes out his case by partial statement and wholesale suppression"—is also quite valid in my view.

Another sign that Nitobe's *Bushido* is a kind of contrived work which engendered more misunderstanding than understanding is that Nitobe could not confidently maintain elsewhere what he had said in *Bushido*. For example, Nitobe who had so strongly defended Bushido in his English-language writings, especially in *Bushido*, wrote in a Japanese-language book titled *Fujin ni susumete* (Advice to women), first published in 1917:

> In my opinion our ancestors before the rise of Bushido lived in great spontaneity. Since the rise of Bushido in the Kamakura Period, however, it has become a practice not to admit to such feelings as hunger, pain, and sorrow, when one in fact suffers from them. This practice has done untold harm to us by curtailing our natural growth. In short, it is from this period that our coun-

trymen have been developing in an unnatural way, subjected to an upbringing which distorts us by suppressing our spontaneity.⁵⁰

It is evident that here Nitobe found Bushido to contain serious faults.

A cursory examination of Nitobe's writings soon reveals that he held basically to a universalistic position which tended to emphasize similarities rather than differences among the cultures of various peoples. This same universalistic stand can be seen in the motive for writing *Bushido* as explained by Nitobe himself in *Ijin gunzô* (Portraits of Great Men):

> As you see, what I wrote in *Bushido* were all elementary things which every Japanese knows. So, I did not intend it for a Japanese audience but for foreigners who seem to think that the Japanese are really a very strange people. I wanted to show in it that the Japanese are not really so different, that you can find similar ideas to those of the Japanese even in the West, though under a slightly different guise, and that there is no East or West as far as human beings are concerned.⁵¹

The result of excessive idealization of the samurai in *Bushido*, however, created, contrary to Nitobe's intention, an impression both in Japan and abroad, that the Japanese were really very special people. Bushido was later used, quite independently from Nitobe, as "evidence" for the Japanese superiority over other nations. Nitobe's *Bushido*, when it was translated into Japanese and was read by a fairly wide Japanese audience, tended to encourage the abuse of the Bushido ideology for the militaristic cause rather than prevent it. Some people recognized the dangers of reviving Bushido. We have already referred to Uemura's criticism of Nitobe's *Bushido*. Ôi Kentarô said, "In a civilized age ethics should be egalitarian, whereas Bushido is hierarchical; the social life should be closely knit, whereas Bushido is solitary; the ideas of people should be world-wide, whereas Bushido's horizons do not go beyond national boundaries. Where is the need to revive it?"⁵² Unlike Uemura and Ôi, Nitobe lacked the necessary objectivity and emotional detachment to make his discussion of Bushido an effective criticism of, and correction for, the Bushido preached by its militaristic exponents, but he wrote thirty years before the onset of their excesses.

To conclude, Nitobe's case seems to corroborate Tsurumi's proposition that English-speaking Japanese cannot be trusted. His case may serve as a lesson for those Japanese, including myself, who aspire to the role of a cultural mediator.⁵³

Notes

1. *NIZ* 10: 234. Nitobe was one of the few Japanese who had the necessary linguistic ability to explain Japan to foreigners. There were, and are, relatively numer-

ous Japanese able to interpret foreign and especially Western culture to the Japanese, but to interpret in the opposite direction is more difficult for the Japanese whose active skills of speaking and reading in a foreign language are generally less developed than their passive reading skills. Nitobe made the following remark in this connection during his later years. It was subsequently published in *Dokusho to jinsei*:

> While I stayed in the United States during the last year, I felt sorry that there were very few Japanese who could introduce Japan to foreign countries. The Japanese complain that foreigners are ignorant of, or indifferent to, Japan. The fact is, however, that we Japanese do nothing to help foreigners understand Japan and that we have no interpreters of Japan to foreigners among us.

NIZ 11: 414.
 2. (London: KPI Limited, 1986), p. 1.
 3. Miyabe Kingo Hakushi kinen shuppankankôkai, ed., *Miyabe Kingo* (1953), p. 76.
 4. (Tokyo: TBS Britannica, 1981).
 5. Those who wish specific details about the education of these "Masters in English," are referred to *Eigo to Nihonjin*. Members of this group received practically all their instruction in English after they had finished primary school or its equivalent.
 6. *NIZ* 6: 354.
 7. *Tôkyô Teikoku Daigaku gojûnen shi* (Tokyo: Tôkyô Teikoku Daigaku, 1932), 1: 473.
 8. Keiteki ryôshi hensan iinkai, ed., *Keiteki ryôshi* (Sapporo: Hokkaidô Teikoku Daigaku Keiteki ryô, 1933), p. 58.
 9. *NIZ* 11: 423–24.
 10. *NIK*, p. 419.
 11. *Pacific Affairs* 10 (June 1937): 220.
 12. *Annals of the American Academy of Political and Social Sciences* 161 (May 1932), p. 270.
 13. *NIZ* 14: 552–53.
 14. *NIZ* 6: 367
 15. *NIZ* 6: 368.
 16. See, for example, Kawanishi Jitsuzô, "Nitobe sensei ni kansuru tsuioku," in Maeda Tamon and Takagi Yasaka eds., *Nitobe sensei tsuioku shû* (Tokyo: Ko Nitobe Hakushi kinen jigyô jikkô iin, 1936), p. 254.
 17. See chapter fouteen in this volume which sheds light on this period of Nitobe's life.
 18. Gaillard Hunt, review of *The Intercourse Between the United States and Japan*, in *Political Science Quarterly* 6 (June 1891): 368.
 19. *NIZ* 14: 501.
 20. *NIZ* 14: 524.
 21. *NIZ* 14: 544.
 22. *NIZ* 14: 594.
 23. *NIZ* 14: 601. These examples are taken from my essay "Nihonjin no eibun ni

miru goi no mondai," in Terasawa Yoshio and Takebayashi Shigeru eds., *Eigo goi no shosô* (Tokyo: Kenkyûsha shuppan, 1988), p. 318.

24. *Naikan gaibô*, NIZ 6: 329–30
25. NIZ 6: 33.
26. NIZ 6: 330.
27. NIZ 5: 498.
28. See the section titled "'Bushido' naru meishô ni tsuite," in Ishida Bunshirô, *Nihon bushidô shi no taikeiteki kenkyû* (1944), pp. 5–8.
29. NIZ 14: 476.
30. NIZ 14: 566.
31. NIZ 15: 62.
32. NIZ14: 231.
33. NIZ 15: 36.
34. NIZ 14: 363.
35. NIZ 13: 75.
36. NIZ 13: 75–76.
37. NIZ 15: 63.
38. NIZ 4: 452.
39. As quoted in Kodama Kôta, *Genroku jidai; Nihon no rekishi 16* (Tokyo: Chûôkôronsha, 1966): 370. Excerpts from Muro Kyûsô's and Dazai Shundai's discussions of their deed are printed in Inui Hiromi, ed., *Kinsei II; shiryô taikei Nihon no rekishi 5* (Osaka: Ôsaka shoseki, 1978), pp. 92–93.
40. "Bushido and Christianity," UKZ 22: 161.
41. "Bushidô to Kirisutokyô," UKZ14: 647.
42. Ienaga Saburô, *Kindai seishin to sono genkai* (Tokyo: Kadokawa shoten, 1950), p. 149.
43. NIZ 15: 123.
44. *The Athenaeum*, No. 4060 (August 19, 1905), p. 229.
45. NIZ 13: 496.
46. Erwin Baelz, *Awakening Japan* (Translation of *Das Leben eines deutschen Arztes im erwachenden Japan*) (1932; reprint ed., Bloomington: Indiana University Press, 1974), p. 17.
47. Edward S. Morse, *Japan Day by Day 1* (1917; reprint ed., Tokyo: Kobunsha Publishing Company, 1936): 44.
48. Uemura Masahisa, "Bushidô," *Uchimura Kanzô shû, fu Kirisutokyô bungaku shû, Nihon gendai bungaku zenshû* 14 (Tokyo: Kôdansha, 1964): 285. (This article is partly a review of Nitobe's *Bushido*).
49. *Ibid*.
50. NIZ 11: 176.
51. NIZ 5: 435.
52. "Bushidô ni tsuite," *Bushidô* 3 (April 1898), p. 8.
53. Those readers who would like to see a fuller, more detailed examination of Nitobe's self-imposed role as a mediator between Japan and the West, including his advocacy of Japan in the United States after the Manchurian Incident, are referred to my *'Taiheiyô no hashi' to shite no Nitobe Inazô* (Tokyo, Misuzu shobô, 1986).

12

The End: 1929–1933

George Oshiro

As Burkman and Satô have indicated in part,[1] Nitobe did not slip quietly away into a meditative private life after his retirement from the League of Nations. In these golden years, he continued his diverse public activities and involved himself in some way or another with over a hundred organizations. Beside his work with the *English Mainichi*, he also rejoined the *Jitsugyô no Nihon* in the same advisorial capacity and wrote frequent articles for this popular journal aimed at young people. And from 1929 until his death four years later, Nitobe served in several prominent positions that made him again very visible to the general public. Here we focus upon these three aspects of these autumnal years: the facts of Nitobe's activities; the Institute of Pacific Relations (IPR) and its conferences of 1929, 1931, and 1933 in which Nitobe played a leading role; and lastly, the critical events and circumstances—in particular the Matsuyama Affair—that impinged upon Nitobe and drove him to his desperate American lecture tour and death.

The IPR, like the League of Nations, was conceived in the optimistic climate of internationalism after World War I.[2] First proposed by a group of community-minded citizens in Hawaii, the original idea evolved over a six-year period from a YMCA program to a visionary plan for a self-governing, self-directed organization of much wider scope.[3] The stated goal of the IPR was to "study the conditions of the Pacific peoples with a view to the improvement of their mutual relations."[4]

Organized as non-governmental bodies, the IPR national committees depended solely on contributions from individual memberships and private groups. This unofficial status, free from government ties, was seen as indispensable to independent research, frank sharing of information, and unimpeded discussion.[5] Three administrative bodies lent structure to the organization: (1) the Pacific Council, (2) a permanent Central Secretariat, and (3) the International Research Committee. The Chairmen of various National Councils formed the Pacific Council which controlled the IPR; the Central Secretariat administered the links between the various national groups; and the International Research Committee with representatives from each National Council met regularly to set research priorities.[6]

The first IPR organization emerged from a conference in Honolulu in 1925. Over the next two years, National Councils were formed in the United States, Canada, Japan, China, Britain, Australia, and New Zealand. And at a second conference, also held at Honolulu in the summer of 1927, a Constitution was drawn up and signed by representatives from the respective National Councils.[7]

The Honorary Chairman for the Japan National Council was Shibusawa Eiichi who was assisted by Saitô Sôichi, Secretary-General of the Tokyo YMCA (Honorary Secretary), Ishii Akira of the Pacific Life Insurance Company (Auditor), Masuda Meiroku (Auditor), and Takagi Yasaka (Research Secretary); Nitobe, before assuming the Chairmanship, acted as Research Director. The Board of Directors included Baron Sakatani Yoshirô; Professors Takayanagi Kenzô and Nasu Shiroshi of the Tokyo Imperial University; and two of Nitobe's closest disciples, Maeda Tamon and Tsurumi Yûsuke.[8]

With two hundred delegates, the Kyoto conference of 1929 became the largest among the thirteen held by the IPR.[9] The delegations for the various National Councils included some of the most prominent men in public affairs. Several independent groups, including the League of Nations, sent observers. The U.S. and Japanese governments, which had remained aloof from the two earlier conferences, sent goodwill greetings.[10]

On the bright and sunny morning of October 28, Nitobe, basking in the international limelight, opened the conference with an eloquent speech at the Kyoto Miyako Hotel. As Burkman has pointed out on pages 177–178, Nitobe drew a parallel between Geneva and Kyoto, each with its "spirit of the hills and lakes as conducive to fellowship and interdependence."[11]

Like his Japanese colleagues, Nitobe strove to make the conference a success. As the first of its kind ever held in Japan and with a large foreign press corps covering the daily proceedings, the Japanese were anxious that reports project a favorable image abroad. William Holland, Secretary-General of the IPR from 1946 until its demise in 1960, attended the Kyoto Conference as a newly appointed research assistant attached to the Secretariat. He recalls the meticulous care that the Japanese displayed to host the event. "They went out of their way to put on a very good show and to make it a major platform for presenting their case to the world...to make it a magnificent piece of organization...[with] magnificent entertainment as well."[12]

In what appears to have been a breach of rules against government support to the IPR, the Japan Council gave each delegate a first-class rail pass for unrestricted travel on Japan National Railways to any part of the empire. Holland recalls that he got his first glimpse of Korea and Manchuria by travelling "free all the way up to Mukden" on this pass.[13]

Of the six topics on the round-table agenda, the most contentious was the problem of Manchuria. Feelings of animosity between the Chinese and the Japanese delegates over this issue were so great, James Shotwell recalls, that "I have seldom, if ever, found myself in a more embittered atmosphere."[14] Both sides came to the conference prepared for the vigorous debate which occupied three days of discussions. The China Council presented two new studies. The first by Hsu Shuhsi outlined the recent politics of Manchuria and argued for complete Chinese sovereignty; the second by Chu Hsiao provided economic statistics.[15] The Japanese study by Rôyama Masamichi covered both politics and economics and stressed Japanese historical rights; his study was supplemented by a strong speech by Matsuoka Yôsuke on the developmental role of the South Manchurian railway.[16] Walter Young, a scholar attached to the American Council, and Sir Harold Partlett, of the British delegation, also presented data papers on the Manchurian question.[17]

Nitobe fully supported the Japanese position. Before the conference began, he received a message from Foreign Minister Shidehara and a briefing by Yoshida Shigeru, Vice Minister, on the various positions he expected the Chinese delegates to take.[18] He did not himself say much, though he followed the proceedings carefully. He later expressed his admiration for Matsuoka's oratory and his superb command of English.[19]

In addition to his role as conference chairman, Nitobe contributed a research paper, "Two Exotic Currents in Japanese Civilization," to the twenty-one cultural-related papers that the Japanese delegation had prepared for the conference.[20] Two years later, Nitobe edited these papers for publication under IPR auspices by the University of Chicago Press as *Western Influences in Modern Japan*.[21]

The Kyoto Conference ended well, and the delegates left Japan happy. Even the Chinese delegates who had feared attack from nationalistic zealots returned thinking generously of the hospitality shown them."[22] But the problems discussed at the session on Manchuria starkly revealed the completely divergent viewpoints of the Chinese and Japanese. The intractability of their positions prefigured, to a large degree, the later outbreak of hostilities between their two armies.[23]

The Fourth Biennial Conference of the IPR was scheduled to meet two years later in October 1931, at Hangchow,[24] but after the outbreak of the Manchurian Incident on September 18th, a wave of anti-Japanese sentiment swept throughout China and threatened to ruin the conference.[25]

The tactful leadership of Jerome Greene, Chairman of the Pacific Council, helped to smooth things over sufficiently for the Pacific Council to meet.[26]

On October 12th, its members decided to change the conference location from Hangchow to Shanghai. This would afford the delegates greater peace of mind. The Council also decided to modify the published agenda. Later, after the national delegations arrived and work began, it decided to go ahead as originally planned.[27]

Nitobe, suffering from lumbago and walking on crutches, left Kobe on October 9th, and arrived two days later in Shanghai in charge of the Japanese delegation.[28] At the Pacific Council Meetings, he represented Japan along with Maeda Tamon and Ishii Akira. He was less active than in Kyoto and even missed several executive meetings.[29] Nitobe stayed in Shanghai when the Council members briefly visited Hangchow. Five members of the Japan Council, Tsurumi, Maeda, Uramatsu, Iwanaga, and Matsumoto, made the one-day, two-night trip, and met Chiang Kai-shek, head of the Nationalist government, at Nanking.[30]

The Manchurian problem, though not originally listed among the nine main items in the round-table agenda, was included in the program at the last minute over the protest of the Japan Council representative.[31] At the general conference session on Diplomatic Machinery in the Pacific on the evening of the 27th, Takayanagi Kenzô read a paper: "Manchuria, a Case Problem" to which Burkman has referred to on page 203. The following evening, Hsu Shuhsi and Tsurumi Yûsuke each argued their country's case.[32]

Nitobe described the conference in an Editorial Jotting where "the sons of Japan and of China sit together in harmony of spirit," but he misled his readers with words about "peace and good will."[33] In actual fact, mutual suspicion poisoned the atmosphere as the Japanese and Chinese delegates stormed at each other. Nitobe himself took particular offense at a comment about Japanese militarism made by Hu Shih, the Chairman of the Conference, and demanded a retraction.[34] Hugh Keenleyside was the First Secretary at the Canadian Legation in Tokyo. Using diary entries from the time, he writes of Nitobe's actions at the Conference:

[T]he Japanese and the Chinese delegations had attacked each other with Nitobe leading the van for the Japanese. Next morning the senior Chinese participant rose in full conference and apologized. He said that he was sorry that he had let his nationalistic feelings get the better of him, admitted that China was far from blameless in the present conflict and that he personally had sinned against the spirit that should prevail among men of good will who were seeking solutions to difficult problems. Then Nitobe rose and everyone waited for him to make an apology of a like nature. Instead, speaking for the Japanese delegation, *he accepted the Chinese apology.*"[35]

Though the accuracy of Keenleyside's recollections is open to question, Nitobe's views of the Chinese and the Manchurian situation at that time are clear.³⁶ Mary sent a letter to the Elkintons in Philadelphia, while Nitobe was at the conference. It clearly stated their position on the current crises:

> Japanese troops were justified in what they did and would have been justified in doing much more—except the bombing at Chinchow....[I]t is scarcely more criminal, if as bad as the Chinese habit of lying and procrastinating and blaming the other party for every thing untoward that happens.³⁷

Nitobe analyzed the Manchurian problem a month before the conference in a succinct little tale in his "Editorial Jottings" column. Entitled a "A Far-Eastern Fable," the article reads:

> There was a rich man with a long line of ancestors. He had several sons, of whom the oldest [China] inherited the estate. An avaricious neighbor [Russia] got a large slice of this by threat and flattery. Before this thug the old man [Imperial China] cowered in abject fear. But when the giant neighbor strode down and tried to clutch the small and barren plot [Manchuria] which had fallen to the youngest child [Japan], the boy arose in anger and cut off the hand of the giant [the Russo-Japanese War] and asked his elder brother to let him till the ground vacated by the giant.
> The brother [Republican China], now grown old and in his dotage, far from rejoicing at the prospect of working with his own kith and kin, turned to him and said;— "I am too proud to own that you, who are younger and smaller than I, are stronger. I fear all strength. I admit I am by nature timid and calculating. But if I have to be beaten by anybody I wish to be beaten by a big fellow who doesn't look like me or you." At this insult the little man [Japan] stood up and smote his own brother [China] in the face. All that the poor man could do was to raise one piteous wail [appeal to the League of Nations], hoping that someone would come and chastise his kinsman.³⁸

In this passage, the square brackets reflect our interpretation of Nitobe's message.

For the next two years, until his death in October 1933, Nitobe's analysis of the Far Eastern situation would not vary much from this simplistic sketch. The Chinese, he would stress time and again, were the primary culprits for the problems in Manchuria. Even on the day he left for the Shanghai Conference, Nitobe wrote in his "Editorial Jottings" a harsh piece entitled "Premature Democracy" which condemned the Chinese Republic and its burgeoning nationalism. Critical of Chinese inability to govern themselves, he saw their leaders as "boys that 'lead' the nation." The "oft-repeated comparisons made by Chinese students between the American Revolution and theirs," Nitobe saw as without substance: "The young Republic is still dominated by a crude and text-book definition of Democracy, which does not distinguish it from Demagogy. Her college boys may discourse on republican principles in the classroom, but they identify them with mobocracy when on the street."³⁹ He declined an invitation to visit Chiang Kai-shek in Nanking after the Shanghai Conference and returned directly home on November 4th.⁴⁰ Several weeks later, in an article "Lessons of Manchurian Incident," he complimented the Kwantung army on its decisiveness and bravery in the field and noted that its members "have won the gratitude and respect of the nation."⁴¹

Though he agreed with the invasion of Manchuria, Nitobe did not admire the army blindly, nor did he condone the indiscriminate use of military force. He had warned earlier of the dangers of a "monopoly of soldiers" in the affairs of the state: "Precarious and unstable is the country whose greatest glory is military efficiency. Such a country is like a body with an arm and not a head at the top.... Armies cannot as yet be safely dispensed with, but they are not the only embodiment of loyalty or patriotism."⁴²

After the Manchurian Incident, further incidents escalated Japanese involvement. Nitobe was disturbed by the actions of the Japanese which led to the bombing of Shanghai in 1932. He felt that the Japanese had provoked the Chinese in this latest bloodshed. Though he had supported the Manchurian takeover, he could not accept the government's explanation of the Shanghai Incident. But he refrained from public criticism.

The Matsuyama Incident

On February 4th, Nitobe visited Shikoku at the request of a friend, Kunimatsu Toshio, Principal of the Ehime Prefectural Agricultural College, to address students and other groups.⁴³ He immediately gave three lectures, plus an interview with local newspaper reporters. The journalists wanted to hear his opinions on the outbreak of fighting in China. Conscious of the delicate nature of the subject, Nitobe did not want his views published, so he obtained the reporters' assurance that his statements were strictly off the record.⁴⁴ They agreed. But while he spoke, a reporter from the local *Kainan Newspaper* arrived late. He did not know that Nitobe's remarks were confidential, and his paper printed them the following day:⁴⁵

> Getting up every morning and reading the newspaper is depressing. Our country is being destroyed by the communists and the military clique. If one asks which one of the two is more dangerous, surely the answer must be the military. Communism will probably grow in proportion as the military expands. I believe that communist ideology will gradually spread as a result.⁴⁶

Nitobe also condemned the government's explanation of its recent actions in Shanghai and called it "sophistry." But he assigned the greater part of the blame to the military.⁴⁷

On February 6 and 7, the *Kainan Newspaper* published editorials which viciously denounced Nitobe for his statements.[48] It also printed several readers' letters which bristled with patriotic indignation. Nitobe, they charged, with his misguided internationalism, was leading the country to ruin. "Just what country is the Doctor from that he uses such intemperate language?" Instead of criticizing the government and military, they felt, all loyal Japanese should rally together in these hard-pressed times.[49] Nitobe thought it best to ignore the attacks. After the first editorial, he wrote the following in his "Editorial Jottings" column entitled "Canine Writers:" "The worst thing you can do is to reply to an editorial attack.... If you write a defence, that is exactly what is wanted, since it will show that you have recognized its existence and thought it worthy to speak to. A more philosophical attitude [is] to neglect it entirely."[50]

Nitobe returned to Tokyo with the hope that the commotion would die away, but it did not. At a local military reserve organization meeting in Matsuyama on February 20, the matter was brought up again, and the following proclamation adopted:

> Nitobe Inazô's statements to reporters on 4 February are extreme and show a lack of respect one expects from a learned man. Because he is a celebrity, his words will have far reaching influence. The result will be to mislead the public and break the united spirit of the people. This in turn opens the way to invasion by other countries. The responsibility is great. Japan faces grave prospects and must call for the cooperation of both high and low. We are alarmed over the future of our country. As Imperial subjects, we could not stand by, so a general meeting was called and it was decided that Nitobe Inazô should not be excused. We, the reservists who serve the Emperor and work for the public, urge Nitobe to reflect upon his words. If he does not, we must inform the people of Japan. We await his decision.[51]

The public furor in Matsuyama and the Local Military Reservists' censure brought the issue national publicity. Tokyo newspapers and magazines began to pick up the story.[52] On February 27, Nitobe was visited at his home by the Vice-Minister of the Navy, Sakoji Seizô, and the chief of Military Affairs Section in the War Ministry, Nagata Tetsuzan; they inquired about the charges. Later Sakoji met with the media and said that "the Doctor made clear that the newspaper article was at complete odds with his own personal opinions and that he regretted that some members of the public misunderstood his views."[53]

This statement by the Naval Vice Minister only added fuel to the fire. Feeling that stronger action was needed, the Military Reservists brought up the Matsuyama remarks again at a three-day conference at the National Headquarters in Tokyo in early March. They formed a committee of censure in order to extract a public apology from Nitobe.[54]

Nitobe, meanwhile, had been admitted into the St. Luke's International Hospital in Tsukiji with neuralgia.[55] He thought that the incident had blown over, but on the evening of March 3, three representatives from the Imperial Reserve Censure Committee visited his sickbed. They relentlessly pursued him about his statements in Matsuyama. Nitobe "defended himself by saying that the statements about military cliques and the downfall of Japan was not meant to imply the Japanese military clique, and that he had used the military cliques of China and the world in talking about this." But his defense was in vain. Uchikawa Eiichirô quotes the minutes of that meeting: "Each member attacked with proof, and Nitobe suddenly became confused and very bewildered and retorted, 'The fact that my words were not reported as I said them is my own fault. I will appear tomorrow at your meeting and apologize.'"[56]

At 11 A.M. the following day, Nitobe, with his grandnephew Ôta Tsunetoshi, a Lieutenant Commander in the Naval Reserves, at his side, appeared before the trustees at the headquarters of the Imperial Reserve Association[57] and spoke to the hostile veterans group. He related the details of his Matsuyama statements of the month before and tried to show that they were misinterpreted in the press; his talk finished, he tried to leave, but a trustee, not satisfied with Nitobe's explanation, angrily ordered him to "fulfill the promise you made yesterday." Nitobe, realizing that the group wished nothing less than to see him capitulate before them, complied without resisting: "Because my words were not sufficient, I have caused much trouble to society. I sincerely regret this. I apologize before you all."[58]

And with this, Nitobe bowed his head in apology to the triumphant reserve officers. Guarded by his grandnephew, he returned to St. Luke's Hospital where he remained for the next twelve days.[59] His apology attracted widespread attention, and his liberal reputation suffered a major setback when newspapers at home and abroad reported the event. The *Kainan Newspaper*, which had started the whole affair, ran large front-page headlines in its issue of March 7th: "Dr. Nitobe Takes Off His Hat in Defeat."[60]

Uchikawa Eiichirô, who has investigated this incident in great detail, writes that "Nitobe [apologized] for his personal safety."[61] Had Nitobe not done so, would his life have been in danger? Contemporary events suggest this possibility. An ultranationalist terrorist group, the *Ketsumeidan* (Blood brotherhood band), made a "hit list" of twenty prominent government and business leaders. Among them were friends of Nitobe. Members of the *Ketsumeidan* then murdered three of them.[62]

On February 9, a few days after Nitobe's Matsuyama statements, Inoue Junnosuke, a close acquaintance of Nitobe, was shot in the back; and on March 5, the day after Nitobe's apology to the Imperial Reserves, Baron

Dan Takuma, director of the Mitsui holding company was assassinated.[63] In the days after the Matsuyama Incident, Nitobe's home was guarded by policemen to ward off would-be attackers. And Ôta Tsunetoshi stayed by Nitobe's side for two whole months to protect him against violence.[64] One of the unforeseen repercussions of the Matsuyama Incident was Nitobe's reappearance in the international limelight, this time as a spokesman for Japan to the United States and Canada.

Emissary to North America, April 1932–March 1933

The first announcement of Nitobe's trip abroad "on behalf of the country" came after his February 28th meeting with the Navy Vice Minister Sakoji and Military Affairs Bureau Chief, Colonel Nagata. A statement to the press released immediately after the meeting quoted Sakoji to the effect that Nitobe agreed "to go overseas in the future to announce his views concerning contemporary problems."[65]

This was surprising news. Eight years earlier, Nitobe had stated in public that he would not step foot on American soil until the Immigration Act had been repealed. Though he had subsequently received "over a dozen invitations" to speak in the United States, Nitobe stuck to his vow. Nicholas Butler invited him to Columbia University in May 1931, to inaugurate the newly established Institute of Japanese Studies; Nitobe replied: "Nothing will entice me to enter the country where my own kith and kin are not treated on equal terms with the rest of mankind. I shall be ashamed to be treated with special consideration, as though I do not belong to the Japanese race."[66]

Nine months later, Nitobe's personal feelings on the immigration issue were overshadowed by larger and more pressing international concerns. Through the autumn and winter of 1931–32, the Japanese army continued to consolidate its gains on the continent, while the League of Nation's Council, to whom China had appealed, deliberated on what steps it should take to resolve the crisis.[67] Its delay in reaching a resolution was blamed on the stalling tactics of the Japanese representative. Finally on December 10, the Council decided to send a Commission of Inquiry, headed by Lord Lytton, to make an on-the-spot investigation of the Manchurian crisis and submit a report to the League.[68]

The American government did not have a set position on the Far Eastern Crisis. Secretary of State Henry Stimson wanted to take strong measures against Japan, and had issued the "Stimson Notes" in January. These called for non-recognition of areas Japan had acquired by force. President Hoover and Assistant Secretary of State William Castle, his influential advisor, opposed actions which might antagonize Japan.[69] The Japanese government tried to use American hesitation to its own ends by winning over public opinion.[70]

The American Press responded with hostility. Since the outbreak of the Manchurian Incident, leading newspapers and journals had carried many articles critical of Japan.[71] "Militaristic" and "aggressive" were commonly used adjectives to explain its actions in Manchuria and Shanghai. As part of an effort to curtail this ominous anti-Japanese sentiment, the Foreign Ministry appealed to Nitobe, well known in America as a liberal.[72]

By the middle of March, detailed plans to send him to the United States were taking shape. In a letter to his Matsuyama friend Kunimatsu, dated March 18, Nitobe, after apologizing for the Matsuyama Incident, mentions that "I have been asked to go abroad next month.... I am not completely happy about it, but it will be the last service I can offer my country, so I go willingly."[73]

Two days later, he wrote another letter to a young Buddhist nun in Yamagata Prefecture, Satô Hôryô, whom he had befriended five years before. It reveals he felt pressured to undertake the "disagreeable journey:" "I have been advised to leave for America soon and will probably be ordered by the Japanese government to do so."[74]

Nitobe pondered the chances of success for this difficult mission. The outlook was depressing, since the tide of American public opinion was running too strongly against Japan. He himself would be viewed "as an apologist of the militarists" and be accused of cowardice for seeking refuge in America from threats upon his life. Indeed "wild rumors" that ultra-nationalists had targeted him appear to have been one reason for Mary's desire to take the trip.[75] But whatever fears Nitobe himself may have harbored about assassination, he did not reveal them. Rather his statements at this critical point suggest that high ideals motivated him. Even if it cost him his international reputation as a liberal, he felt it a personal duty to explain to Americans Japan's case in Manchuria. In the "Editorial Jottings," he put his private struggles into a public confession:

> The country to which I was bound presented an appearance of utter darkness. I strained my eyes...to see some light to lead and comfort me. Failing to find any, my heart sank within me and I felt like giving up the mission. Then a Voice within me said—Go on, depending on the light that is within you! I felt greatly encouraged, because within me I harboured no thought of gain or ambition. I could say to myself that 'my strength was as the strength of ten because my heart was pure.'[76]

To guard against charges that he spread official propaganda, Nitobe chose to travel as a "private citizen" under the pretense of "studying American public opinion." The column that he wrote in the *English Osaka Mainichi* changed its heading from "Editorial Jottings" to "What I am Learning in America."[77] Other factors convince one that Nitobe did not act alone: his mission from the very first was conceived by, and had the complete support of, the Japanese government. The Foreign Ministry monitored his activities carefully as an apparent part of a general collaboration. On April 14, when he, Mary, and her nurse left Yokohama, among the crowd at the pier was the former Foreign Minister Shidehara Kijûrô, who had come to wish Nitobe success.[78]

The trip across the Pacific took thirteen days—five to Hawaii and eight to California. The Nitobes reached San Francisco on April 27. Nitobe made several quick calls around the city, including one to the Japanese Consulate-General, and left directly by train for the East Coast. He arrived in New York on the evening of May 6.[79]

Nitobe had worked out a careful strategy in advance: he would focus first on Americans at the very core of the Establishment. New York City, with its concentration of influential opinion leaders, was the logical place to begin. A second major reason for starting with New York was the headquarters of the major newspapers and broadcasting companies there. Statements released there reached a very large audience across the country through communications networks. With these considerations in mind, Nitobe began his painful campaign to shift American public opinion to Japan's cause.[80]

On May 7, the day after he arrived, Nitobe interviewed newspaper reporters at his hotel. The next day he made a radio broadcast entitled "Japan, the League of Nations, and the Peace Pact" over the new national network of the Columbia Broadcasting Company. In a report of his interview published in the *NYT*, Nitobe appealed to the American's sense of "fair play" and carefully explained that "Japan does not want anything in China except stability in that country." He emphasized that Japan does not want any Chinese territory. "I am sure," Nitobe concluded, "that when all the facts are before the people of the United States, they will agree that the Japanese want world peace."[81]

Reactions to his interview were quick and harsh. In an "Open Letter to Dr. Nitobe" in the *New Republic*, Raymond Buell, Research Director of the Council on Foreign Relations, challenged Nitobe's attitude on Japan in Manchuria. "It is heartbreaking for those who have followed your past career to believe that these statements accurately portray your views." After reminding Nitobe of his Quaker beliefs and his service to the League, Buell continued that "[i]n view of the present regime in Japan, we could understand a policy of silence on your part, but we cannot understand a policy which uncritically defends Japanese militarism."[82]

The *Christian Century*, in its June 1st editorial entitled "The Menace of Militarism," recognized that Nitobe's life "was imperiled" by his Matsuyama statements, but continued that "Dr. Nitobe was accordingly persuaded to disregard his previous scruples" to undertake the journey to America. The editorial concluded:

[Nitobe] made public the most sweeping and unqualified approval of everything that Japan has done in Manchuria and Shanghai, particularly Shanghai! It is incredible that the Dr. Nitobe of the Geneva days could have taken such a position. The Dr. Nitobe who has defended the sack of Chapei is a war casualty. He is a testimony to the ruthlessness with which militarism will bludgeon anyone who dares to stand in its path.[83]

These remarks hurt Nitobe, and he commented on both pieces in his *English Osaka Mainichi* column. Of Buell's letter, he wrote, "I would not have minded it if it had been written in a fair spirit: but it was an expression of hypercritical distortion."[84] Nitobe further responded to the second notice:

'The Christian Century'...has done me the honour of an editorial comment in which were some abusive allusions without any foundation upon which to base them.... As it has always been my principle not to care what others say, I shall not make any reply.... I look upon [the editorial] as indicative of the low level to which Christianity has sunk in this country.[85]

These two public attacks did not deter Nitobe. He remained in New York for the month of May and addressed various organizations on problems facing Japan. On May 20, he made a second radio speech over CBS radio entitled "Japan's Hopes and Fears." In this talk, which was part of a series sponsored by the New York Japanese Chamber of Commerce, Nitobe reiterated Japan's Manchurian policy and emphasized the treaty rights that she had won there at huge sacrifices. He also explained at length the Japanese attitude on the two crucial issues which lay behind the present crisis: first, the increasing tariffs erected against her by trading partners; and second, his country's imperative need for a stable supply of raw materials. Peace and order in the region, he stressed, is indispensable to Japan, for Manchuria is "Japan's life-line."[86]

The Japanese Consul in New York was pleased with Nitobe's public relations work and cabled the Foreign Ministry in Tokyo that "Nitobe is doing a good job."[87] In June, Nitobe was in Washington D.C. He continued to speak to different organizations and to meet privately with important decision makers. Accompanied by Ambassador Debuchi, he paid a courtesy call on President Hoover; afterwards he visited Secretary of State Henry Stimson. These activities in the nation's capital did not attract much attention from the media. His seven-minute meeting with the President was not even mentioned in the *New York Times*, the paper that Nitobe always read.[88]

He spent the rest of June and July in and around Philadelphia near Mary's family. Here he rested and received some private honors. Haverford College granted him an Honorary Doctorate of Law.[89] And shortly thereafter, he and Mary attended as distinguished guests another smaller graduation ceremony at Westown, a Quaker school for boys. Their seventeen-year-old grandnephew, David Elkinton, was among the graduates. While in Philadelphia, Nitobe gave speeches to Friends Meetings on the situation in the Far East. Howard Elkinton, a relative, later described Nitobe's difficulties to explain "Japan's militarism" to the pacifist Quakers.[90] After concluding a pleasant visit with the Elkintons, Nitobe, Mary, Mary's nurse Mori Futae and a *Tokyo Nichi Nichi* reporter drove north to Williams College for the Twelfth Institute of Politics. The young David Elkinton served as chauffeur and general helper. They arrived at Williamstown, Massachusetts on the evening of July 27, and checked in at the Williams Inn, where they spent the next four weeks while the Institute was in session.[91]

The Institute of Politics at Williams College ranked first among the some half-dozen groups started in the United States after World War I to study world affairs. Among its Officers and Board members were Walter McLaren, George Blakeslee, Walter Lippman, and James Brown Scott—men widely known for their expertise in international relations.[92] For the Institute's Twelfth Session, the agenda of which included six Round Table Discussions and two General Conferences, some three hundred people from many different countries attended. Nitobe, designated keynote speaker, gave an address on the opening day entitled "Development of International Cooperation."[93] Though his address was non-controversial since it dealt mainly with the growth and development of various international bodies and the need of "fostering the international mind," he did not skirt the problem of Japan and the League. Perhaps to the discomfort of some in the audience, he may have been a little too direct: "In [Japan's] foreign relations we have most to do with China, and the issues between us belong strictly to the two nations. We, therefore, prefer direct negotiations."[94]

Nitobe gave his second Institute talk, "Basic Principles of Japanese Politics," a few days later in the evening. And he participated actively in the Round Table Discussions on "Sino-Japanese Relations in Eastern Asia." Here, Nitobe freely expressed his opinions on the current crisis in Manchuria. The participants, as in the Kyoto and Shanghai IPR Conferences, divided sharply on the issues according to their nationalities. The Japanese, Nitobe, Roy Akagi, and Professor Obata lined up on one side, and the Chinese participants, V. Wellington Koo and Professor Kiang stood on the other. The participants from the other countries generally took positions somewhere between.[95]

During the final week of the Institute, Nitobe made a quick visit to New York City to give one more radio speech on CBS.[96] This time, he concentrated on the Stimson Notes. In his twenty-six minute address, Nitobe argued that the Non-Recognition Doctrine put forth by the American Secretary of State under the terms of the Kellogg-Briand Pact did not apply to Japan. The Pact, he noted, was signed on August 27, 1928; the Non-Recognition Doctrine originated three and a half years later. "Is it fair to bind," he asked rhetorically, "a signatory to a treaty by interpreting it in a way of which it was not warned and to which it may not have consented?" Though Nitobe affirmed his support of the Peace Pact, its application, he stressed, had to be considered in light of the actual conditions at hand: "I have faith in [the Pact's] ultimate triumph, but triumph cannot be forced by hairsplitting legal interpretation. Triumph can come only as a moral suasion befitting a real situation."[97]

In Nitobe's eyes, the political situation in China made the various peace institutions—as formulated in the League's Covenant, the Nine Power Treaty, and the Peace Pact—irrelevant. Only after certain fundamental conditions had been met could Japan realistically rely upon these covenants. Among these, three stood out: (1) that China attain political unity and "renounce anti-foreign diplomacy as a means of national policy;" (2) that Japan be allowed access to vital food and industrial supplies; and (3) that Russia be checked from encroachment on Chinese soil. Until the time when these conditions were met, Japan would have to take matters in her own hands and defend her interests as she saw fit.[98]

In late August, Nitobe went north to Canada to study Canadian public opinion. In Ottawa, through the introduction of Ambassador Tokugawa Iesato, he met many of Canada's leading politicians and welcomed their generally favorable views regarding Japan and the Manchurian problem, while, as Burkman has pointed out on page 206, he criticized the one-sided support given China by Canadian missionaries to East Asia.[99]

After his trip to eastern Canada, Nitobe crossed the continent to California. He had extended his original six-month plan when he received an unexpected invitation to lecture at the University of California, Berkeley.[100] He delivered nineteen lectures over the next two months. Much in the same vein as his Carnegie Exchange Professorship lectures of twenty years before, Nitobe treated various facets of Japan and the Japanese in a comprehensive but popular fashion. In contrast to their general tenor, two of the lectures dealt with matters of crucial contemporary significance. One treated Japan and the League. In it he reiterated the points he had made in his New York radio broadcast. The other one on Manchuria expounded in greater detail the earlier arguments mentioned above.[101] After he completed his Berkeley lectures on December 2, Nitobe went south to Riverside, California to attend the Tenth Institute of World Affairs which was meeting there from December 11th to 16th.

The Institute of World Affairs had been founded seven years earlier on the model of the Institute of Politics at Williamstown. Its aim was "to give the people of the far west a first-hand acquaintance with diverse views on current international questions."[102] Nitobe was one of ten lecturers for the Special Evening Lectures Series. He gave two addresses; on December 13, he spoke on "Japan's Place in the Family of Nations," and, two days later, dealt with the subject, "Blending of the East and West in Japan."[103] Though the latter talk did not deal with substantial matters, the former dealt explicitly with the Lytton Report which had been announced two months before.[104] Nitobe's primary disagreement with the report was that it had failed to consider Japan's legitimate right of self-defense.

> [The report] is not fair when it states that Japan exceeded her rights of self-defence when she took the course that she did in Manchuria. Common sense should convince one that drastic and speedy action be taken when a small army of 10,000 had to defend itself against an army of 200,000—and that on foreign soil. No third party can define self defense. As Mr. Kellogg remarked repeatedly, it must be left to each sovereign state. We may recall the definition of it given by Mr. Elihu Root, as 'the right of every sovereign state to protect itself by preventing a condition of affairs in which it will be too late to protect.' The American government has maintained the Monroe Doctrine under this definition of self-defence.[105]

After the end of the Institute of World Affairs, Nitobe rested for the remainder of the month in California. Then, in early January 1933, he began an intensive lecture tour in the Northwest. After covering Oregon and Washington, he left Seattle on the morning of the 18th for Vancouver. Along the way, he lectured at noon at the Teachers College in Bellingham before he crossed the border into British Columbia. His two-day visit to Vancouver involved five speaking engagements; they included speeches to the Canadian Club, to students at the University of British Columbia, local Japanese groups in Steveston, and a thirty-minute radio broadcast. The contents of his speeches were essentially the same as his earlier ones. On January 21, he left for Los Angeles.[106]

Nitobe spent the next two months speaking mainly to Japanese-American groups in Southern California. His last major appearance to a wider audience was an address to the Institute of International Affairs at Pasadena. Here he gave an address entitled, "A Japanese Tribute to Abraham Lincoln." For his work with the Institute, Nitobe was honored, on March 1, 1933, with an Honorary Doctorate of Law—his fourth—from the University of Southern California. In early March, he prepared to return to Japan.[107]

Mary had suffered a heart attack in December and could not travel. So Nitobe, pressed with many commitments back home, left her in Pasadena in care of her nurse Mori Fusae. It was agreed that he would return in late summer.[108] The Fifth IPR Conference would meet in Banff, Canada at that time. He had thought at first he would not go; he wanted to turn the Institute's work over to younger people. But now, with Mary in California, he changed his mind and decided that he would make the trip after all.

Thus with firm plans to return to North America in a few short months, he left alone from Los Angeles on the *Kirishima Maru* and arrived in Yokohama on March 24. He had been away almost a full year.[109]

The Final Months in Japan and Death in Canada

Ten days after his return home, Nitobe visited the Imperial Palace and spent an hour briefing the Emperor on his mission.[110] Eight years earlier, while Hirohito had still been Crown Prince, he had asked Nitobe whether the League of Nations could be effective without participation by the United States. This time, it seems, the Emperor wanted to know about current Japanese-American relations.[111]

In the eleven months of Nitobe's absence, public sentiment in Japan had shifted from the internationalism Nitobe symbolized to increasing nationalism. Many Japanese now saw the League as hostile. While Nitobe lectured in California, the League had formed a Committee of Nineteen to study the findings of the Lytton Report. The Committee's recommendations, which refuted Japan's claims, were accepted on February 24, by the General Assembly.[112]

Three days after Nitobe had returned to Japan, on March 27, the Saitô government sent the League a formal notice of withdrawal. Most Japanese agreed with the decision. They felt indignation over the League's condemnation of Japan and considered that Japan had no alternative but to take its foreign affairs into its own hands.[113]

Nitobe agreed. A week after his meeting with the Emperor, he addressed a luncheon of the Tokyo Pan-Pacific Club at the Imperial Hotel. As Burkman has pointed out on page 208, his multinational audience of over a hundred heard him express his ambivalence over Japan's departure from the League. The small powers serving on the Committee of Nineteen, Nitobe felt, misguided the debate on the Manchurian question by interpreting "the Covenant not in a broad and statesman-like manner, but like lawyers, in a cheap way." But the blame should not only lie with them nor with the League as a whole. Japan too, he felt, had erred; she had failed to enlighten the League's members on the complexities of the Manchurian problem: "We have committed a grave error in being too reticent and uncommunicative, and I may also say unsociable, and the sooner we find out that error, the better for our future relations with the rest of the world."[114] Though the future appears dark, the "darkness will not last forever. The shouting and the tumult will die, and the captains and kings will depart. Then we shall regain cooler judgment."[115] Nitobe clung to this faith that men were good hearted and rational enough to find peaceful resolutions to their differences.

The usual hectic pace continued during Nitobe's final months in Japan. Though his popularity as a lecturer had declined with the new political climate, he still received requests to support various groups.[116] The Morioka Production Corporation, which he served as President, asked him to assume yet another role—President of its Youth Association. Nitobe willingly complied. He travelled to Iwate Prefecture on May 4, to attend a meeting of it; he then gave a number of speeches. In his few free hours, he paid his respects before the family graves at the Zen monastery outside the city.[117] Then he crossed the mountains to the coast to observe the damage caused by a devastating tidal wave two months earlier. His next stop was Sambongi, the town his grandfather had founded. Then he returned to Tokyo to prepare for the upcoming IPR conference.[118]

This conference had attracted the interest of General Mutô Nobuyoshi, Japanese overlord in Manchuria. Mutô wanted Japan's delegation to know the latest developments there. On July 7, Mutô requested the Foreign Ministry to have the "man in charge" of the Japanese delegation view Manchuria in person. This would, the general reasoned, "give authority to his statements."[119] Nitobe flew to the continent for a quick inspection tour that lasted only a week, during which time he saw a great deal and even spoke with the puppet ruler, Henry P'u yi.[120]

Upon return to Japan, on July 16, Nitobe made the trip to Shimoda where he erected a jizô statue to the memory of his mother (see pp. 46–47).

Death, Nitobe intuitively suspected, approached. He wondered, putting the words into the mouth of Okina, his alter ego, will the "Good Angel"—his term for Death—visit?[121] On July 15th, he wrote:

> During my life of three score and ten years, I have been three or four times on the point of dying.... While swimming in a small river in Hokkaido, I was suddenly taken ill,... No thought of eternity or of the loved ones at home, troubled me.... *I was simply annoyed at the probability of being drowned in such an insignificant stream. Whether it was from idle vanity or not, I wished my end to be in a larger river.*[122]

Nitobe also discussed in his newspaper column a fundamental concern that had driven him all his life: had he lived up to his mother's expectation? How would people judge his work? What was to be his place in history? Several months before his Shimoda visit he reveals his deep concern:

> I am proud of my mother as every boy and girl, young and old should be. I shall never forget her saying:— 'You must grow up to be a great man. If you don't, people will say that you are like your mother; but if you do, they will say you are like your father.' In the three-score years that have passed, I have often pondered these words—words, that show the modesty becoming a woman and her pride in her husband and her hopes for her child.[123]

At the end of this piece, Nitobe evaluated himself: "her son fail[ed] to attain any measure of distinction." This strange remark could be dismissed as mere false modesty, but it seems that he was lamenting his inability to accomplish more. Perhaps he feared that his life's work had been in vain. The jizô he had erected commemorated Seki's death to Inazô the internationalist, who now would sacrifice himself, as Okichi herself had done eight decades ago, to secure Japan's place in the world.[124]

On July 31, two days before he departed for Canada, an old friend of his student days, Saeki Riichirô visited Nitobe. During their conversation, Nitobe confessed that he was "tired of life."[125] The following day, after breakfast with Jôdai Tani, a disciple whom he had known for many years, he lunched with the Foreign Minister.[126] The next day, August 2, accompanied by eight other Japan Council delegates, Nitobe embarked for Canada.[127]

The group arrived in Vancouver on the 13th at 5 A.M. After a newspaper interview and a luncheon hosted by the Japanese Consul, they entrained for the five-hundred mile journey to Banff Alberta and the Fifth Biennial IPR Conference.[128]

En route, Nitobe was struck by a violent pain in his abdomen,[129] but he rested well, and the pain subsided after arrival at the Banff Springs Hotel; by evening he had recovered enough to give his speech before the 137 delegates at the inaugural dinner.[130] The delegates were curious to hear what Nitobe would say now that Japan had announced its withdrawal from the League. Nitobe completely skirted the issue of the merits or demerits of the decision and instead focused on the contents of an Imperial Rescript that had accompanied the announcement of withdrawal. "Japan's traditional policy to co-operate with the world," Nitobe emphasized, "is not affected by this [decision to withdraw] at all." Japan would remain active in the "family of nations.... Japan is proud to think that she is still an inseparable part of the great world. Her eager participation in all international gatherings of this kind as the Institute is the eloquent evidence of this national feeling."[131]

The Japanese delegation hoped to avoid a repeat of the 1931 Shanghai Conference with bitter disputes between Chinese and Japanese delegates. Though Nitobe had prepared himself with his quick trip to Manchukuo, he told the delegates there was "no reason to deal with the Manchurian issue at the conference." He also noted that "Hu Shih [Chairman of the China delegation] is a gentleman. I do not think he will touch on the difficulties between Japan and China."[132]

As the result of careful forethought, the conference did not include the Manchurian problem in its agenda. Rather, the discussions focused on various aspects of the theme "International Economic Conflict in the Pacific Area: Its Control and Adjustment."[133] The planners of the Conference, moreover, had taken pains to avoid the conditions which had made the earlier meetings "too preoccupied with outstanding events of the moment." They now hoped to throw light on "slow moving and often invisible social and economic forces" and show their "relationships to the outstanding political issues of the day."[134] Indeed the Pacific Council Chairman's appeal to participants that they act first "as individuals" and secondly as members of particular national groups helped the conference off to an auspicious start. The confrontational mood of the proceeding two conferences was markedly absent.[135]

In contrast to the 1929 and 1931 meetings, Nitobe played a much less conspicuous role. He did not prepare a data paper for the round-table discussions, and he lacked his usual enthusiasm, an acquaintance later recalled.[136] Though he stoically refused to inform the others of his physical condition, he appeared to suffer greatly. The group portrait, taken at the hotel on the final day of the conference, shows Nitobe seated at the center in the front row with a strained expression on his face, his body awkwardly bent, as if to alleviate pain.[137]

After the conference, he returned to Vancouver. Henry Angus, professor of economics at the University of British Columbia, traveled back with Nitobe's group. He recalled half a century later that Nitobe had great difficulty in the descent from the Banff resort area, so that "they had to rest along the way for his sake."[138]

He proceeded to the Oak Bay Beach Hotel in Victoria where Mary awaited his arrival.[139] She had recovered sufficiently to move there with her nurse from Pasadena in late July, to avoid the heat of the southern California summer. Nitobe, refreshed, decided to rest a while before embarking on another public-speaking tour in the United States. He seems to have received instructions from the Ministry of Foreign Affairs to help "organize local Japanese groups" and received funds for this purpose.[140] On September 8, he returned to Vancouver for a reception hosted by the Japanese Consul. Here he gave his final speech. Back in Victoria, four days later, he collapsed in his hotel after attending a local fair. He entered the Royal Jubilee Hospital where he spent his remaining days.[141]

His illness did not seem at first serious and so did not attract media attention. The Foreign Ministry, oblivious to his difficulties, planned yet another major assignment: the Japanese representative to the Committee for Intellectual Cooperation in Geneva.[142] The current incumbent had returned to Japan from his six-year term in July, so the position was vacant. In spite of its withdrawal, the government appears to have desired to maintain cultural ties with the League. Nitobe could take no more. Mori Futae, Mary's nurse, recalls that he told Mary that "now they are asking me to go to Geneva, but I said I do not want to go."[143]

Though Nitobe's physician said on September 21, that Nitobe was "improving considerably," he continued to weaken. In addition to the persistent abdominal pains, he had contracted pneumonia. By the second week of October, surgery was recommended, in spite of the obvious risk. Mary after much deliberation consented.[144]

Four doctors operated for an hour on the morning of October 15. Nitobe regained consciousness around 4 P.M., but he quietly passed away at 8:34 P.M. with Mary and several others at his side.[145]

An autopsy revealed that he had pancreatitis, pneumonia, and diabetes.[146] A short memorial service was held in Victoria on October 16th. Then the remains were taken to Vancouver to be cremated. Takagi Yasaka, who had just arrived that morning after a long plane journey from New York, accompanied them.[147]

Two days later a large funeral service was held in downtown Vancouver at the St. Andrews Wesley Church. After the service, the urn containing Nitobe's ashes was taken to Mary in Victoria. On October 23, she left Victoria with her nurse Mori and her niece, Mary Duguid, for San Francisco. There, after another memorial service on November 4, the three of them returned on November 16, to Japan with the urn. At the harbor in Yokohama on the dark grey morning, "some 1000 [people]...came especially to meet the ashes."[148]

Nitobe was accorded a hero's funeral. He received the posthumous Order of the Sacred Treasure, First-Class. A special messenger brought Imperial condolences to his home to join the nearly two hundred other expressions of sympathy from all over the world. Prime Minister Saitô and other leading officials joined representatives from foreign legations and hundreds of other leaders to pay their respects. After the services, the urn returned to the Kobinata home for a few days, to be buried after the events described earlier by Howes on page 48, beside those of Nitobe's infant son, in Tokyo's Tama Cemetery.[149]

Though Nitobe's efforts to gain acceptance of Japan's case abroad were acclaimed by the Japanese public immediately after his death, the rapid developments after 1933 quickly made his work seem irrelevant. Japan's deepening involvement in China led to full-scale conflict after 1937 and then war with the United States in 1941. Nitobe was forgotten.

Notes

1. See chapters nine and ten.
2. The IPR initiated and supported a whole range of academic studies dealing with the Pacific and Asia, so that its publications and other title listings number more than 1200, yet surprisingly little has been published on the organization itself. A good summary account of the IPR is Paul Hooper, *Elusive Destiny* (Honolulu: University of Hawaii Press, 1980), pp. 105–36. Another study of the organization with focus on the post-war period is John N. Thomas, *The Institute of Pacific Relations: Asian Scholars and American Politics* (Seattle: University of Washington

Press, 1974). Also, Katagiri Nobuo, "Taiheiyô mondai chôsakai no kiseki," in *Gunma kenritsu joshi daigaku kiyô* 3(March 1983):92–110.

3. Hooper, pp. 107–25.

4. "Handbook of the Institute of Pacific Relations," in Bruno Lasker, ed., *Problems of the Pacific, 1931: Proceedings of the Fourth Conference of the Institute of Pacific Realations, Hangchow and Shanghai China, October 21–November 2* (Chicago: University of Chicago Press, 1932), p. 522. (hereafter *Handbook*).

5. *Handbook*, pp. 524–25.

6. *Handbook*, p. 525, 531.

7. Proceedings of both Honolulu Conferences were published. See *Institute of Pacific Relations: Honolulu Session, June 30–July 15, 1925* (Honolulu, 1925); and J. B. Condliffe, ed., *Problems of the Pacific: Proceedings of the Second Conference of the Institute of Pacific Relations, Honolulu, Hawaii, July 15 to 29, 1927* (Chicago: University of Chicago Press, 1928).

8. Institute of Pacific Relations, *The Third Biennial Conference of the Institute of Pacific Relations, Kyoto Japan* (pamphlet prepared for the conference, Second Announcement, July 1929), p. 18. The members of the Conference Preparation Committee as well as the officials of the various National Councils are also listed; see also J. B. Condliffe, ed., *Problems of the Pacific: Proceedings of the Third Conference of the Institute of Pacific Relations, Nara and Kyoto, Japan, October 23 to November 9, 1929* (Chicago: University of Chicago Press, 1930), pp. 626–27 (hereafter *Kyoto proceedings*).

9. *Kyoto proceedings*, pp. viii–ix. Appendix I of this volume lists the names of conference members, observers, and staff.

10. James Shotwell, *The Autobiography of James Shotwell* (New York: Bobbs-Merrill, 1962), p. 248.

11. *NIZ* 15:359. Nitobe's opening speech at Kyoto was printed as "Japan's Preparedness for International Co-operation," in *Pacific Affairs* 2, no.1, (January 1930).

12. Transcription of a two-hour taped interview with William Holland conducted by John F. Howes, Vancouver, B.C., July 1980 (in the private possession of William Holland).

13. *Ibid*.

14. James Shotwell, *Autobiography*, p. 250.

15. Hsu Shuhsi, "The Manchurian Question;" Chu Hsiao, "Manchuria: A Statistical Survey of its Resources, Trade, Railways and Immigration." See *Kyoto proceedings*, pp. 466–523, 380–422.

16. Rôyama Masamichi, "Japan's Position in Manchuria;" Matsuoka Yôsuke, "An Address on Manchuria." See *Kyoto proceedings*, pp. 524–93, 594–607.

17. Walter Young, "Chinese Colonization and the Development of Northern Manchuria," in *Kyoto proceedings*, pp. 423–65; Sir Harold Parlett, *A Brief Account of Diplomatic Events in Manchuria* (London: Oxford University Press, 1929).

18. *Bannen*, p. 55; Newton, p. 42.

19. *Bannen*, p. 60; Newton, p. 47.

20. *Kyoto proceedings*, p. 634. This paper is not included in *NIZ*.

21. Inazô Nitobe et al., *Western Influences In Modern Japan* (Chicago: University of Chicago Press, 1931).

22. Shotwell, *Autobiography*, p. 250.

23. See Katagiri Nobuo, "Taiheiyô mondai chôsa kai (IPR) to Manshû mondai," in *Hôgaku kenkyû* 52, no. 9, pp. 49–81.

24. See Bruno Lasker, ed., *Problems of the Pacific, 1931: Proceedings of the Fourth Conference of the Institute of Pacific Relations, Hangchow and Shanghai China, October 21–November 2* (Chicago: University of Chicago Press, 1932), p. v. (hereafter "Shanghai proceedings").

25. Many studies are available on various facets of the Manchurian Incident. For a study from the standpoint of the Japanese army, see Ogata Sadako, *Defiance in Manchuria: the Making of Japanese Foreign Policy, 1931–1932* (Berkeley: University of California Press, 1964). Other works include Yoshihashi Takehiko, *Conspiracy at Mukden* (New Haven: Yale University Press, 1963); Sara Smith, *The Manchurian Crisis* (New York: Columbia University Press, 1946).

26. Matsumoto, *Shanghai jidai 1*, p. 44.

27. "Place and form of conference," in *Pacific Council Minutes*, Monday, October 12, 1931, 9:30–11:55 p.m.; *Shanghai proceedings*, p. v; see also Matsumoto Shigeharu, *Shanghai jidai 1* (Chûô shinsho, 1974), pp. 44–45.

28. Those accompanying Nitobe included Maeda Tamon, Nasu Hiroshi, Saitô Sôichi, Takayanagi Kenzô and Tsurumi Yûsuke. See Matsumoto, p. 45; also *Bannen*, p. 116, Newton, p. 88. The latter mentions that nurses had to help Nitobe board ship.

29. *Pacific Council Minutes*, October 15, October 16, 10:30–11:00 A.M., October 16, 2:00–3:30 P.M.

30. Matsumoto, *Shanghai jidai*, p. 52. The Pacific Council held one session on 26 October at Hangchow; see "The Conference Program," in "Shanghai proceedings," p. 513.

31. Matsumoto, p. 47.

32. See Shanghai proceedings for Takayanagi's address (pp. 23–26); the same volume also contains Hsu Shuhsi's rebuttal to Tsusrumi along with a summary of the round-table discussions (pp. 236–42).

33. *NIZ* 16: 278.

34. *NIZ* 16: 278.

35. Hugh Keenleyside, *Hammer Out the Golden Day* (Toronto: McClelland and Stewart Ltd., 1981), p. 406.

36. Other statements made by Keenleyside about Nitobe in his book are either exaggerated or false. An interview with Mr. Keenleyside at his home in Victoria, B.C. on March 28, 1984, has revealed that his information rests on part on secondhand sources or hearsay.

37. Mary Nitobe, Letter to Passmore and Anna Elkinton, October 22, 1931, *FHLNP* and reprinted in *NIK*, pp. 509–11.

38. *NIZ* 16: 269–70.

39. *NIZ* 16: 272–3.

40. *Bannen*, p. 128; Newton, p. 98.

41. *NIZ* 16: 299.

42. *NIZ* 16: 269.

43. *Bannen*, p. 141; Newton, p. 107.

44. *Bannen*, p. 149; Newton, p. 112.

45. Uchikawa's research shows that the *Kainan Newspaper* was not only jingoistic, but also a rival of the local branch of the *Osaka Mainichi* for whose English-language edition Nitobe wrote. The attacks on him, therefore, may also have resulted from strategic business considerations (see pp. 147–49, 152–54; Newton, pp. 111–12, 114–15).
46. *Bannen*, p. 141–2; Newton, p. 107.
47. *Ibid*.
48. *Bannen*, p. 143; Newton, p. 108.
49. *Bannen*, p. 144; Newton, p. 108–9.
50. *NIZ*16: 312–13.
51. *Bannen*, pp. 146–47; Newton, p. 110.
52. *Bannen*, p. 150; Newton, p. 112.
53. *Bannen*, p. 151; Newton, p. 113.
54. *Bannen*, pp. 154–56; Newton, p. 115–16.
55. *Bannen*, p. 156; Newton, p. 116.
56. *Bannen*, pp. 158–59; Newton, p. 117.
57. *Bannen*, p. 159; Newton, p. 118.
58. *Bannen*, p. 160; Newton, p. 118.
59. *Bannen*, p. 163; Newton, p. 121.
60. *Bannen*, p. 161; Newton, p. 120.
61. *Bannen*, p. 162; Newton, p. 120.
62. For a description of the *Keitsumeidan*, see Richard Storry, *The Double Patriots* (Boston: Houghton Mifflin Co., 1957), pp. 100–7.
63. *Ibid*. Japanese historians refer to the assassinations of Inoue and Dan as the "Ketsumeidan jiken" and the Inukai murder as the "Go jû-go jiken." But Storry sees them as two stages of the same terrorist plot. See Storry, *Double Patriots*, p. 101.
64. *Bannen*, p. 159; Newton, p. 118. See also Nitobe Kotoko, *Kinen* 1: 95–96.
65. *Bannen*, p. 151; Newton, p. 113.
66. Nitobe Inazô, Letter to Nicolas M. Butler, July 6, 1931, in Central Administration files, Columbia University, New York City.
67. Henry K. Norton, "Sino-Japanese Relations in Eastern Asia," in *Institute of Politics: Twelfth Session* (Williamstown, Mass., 1932), p. 136. This volume contains the Proceedings of the Institute that was held at Williams College, from July 28, to August 25, 1932 (hereafter *Institute of Politics*).
68. *Ibid.*, p. 161.
69. James Hollingsworth, "William R. Castle and Japanese-American Relations, 1929–1933," Diss., Texas Christian University, 1971, pp. 150–76.
70. Talk of replacing Ambassador Debuchi in Washington because "he failed to dispel American misunderstandings about Shanghai" circulated in Tokyo just before Nitobe arrived in the United States. See *NYT*, May 4, 1932, p. 3.
71. For a detailed study of anti-Japanese articles in the American Christian press, see Alden Pearson, "The American Christian Press and the Sino-Japanese Crisis of 1931–1933: An Aspect of Public Response to the Breakdown of World Peace," Diss., Duke University, 1968.
72. Documents that link Nitobe directly to the Foreign Ministry are not available. Two recent researchers, Uchikawa Eiichirô and Sasaki Kô have searched the Foreign Ministry Archives for materials of this type to no avail. But, as will be

shown shortly, circumstantial evidence clearly suggests that Nitobe indeed worked on behalf of the Ministry.

73. *Bannen*, pp. 163–64; Newton, p. 121.

74. *Ibid.*

75. Rachel Read, Letter to Passmore Elkinton, March 29, 1932, in *FHLNP*.

76. "Cheering Advice to a Traveller" (May 1, 1932) in *NIZ* 16: 350.

77. I am grateful to Professor Satô Masahiro for photocopies of back issues of the *English Osaka Mainichi* that contain Nitobe's original contributions.

78. Matsumoto, *Shanghai jidai*, 2: 64; see also Jôdai Tani,"Nitobe sensei," in *NHTS*, p. 405. Jôdai refers to a luncheon that Nitobe had with the Foreign Minister in 1933 before his departure for Canada; this is one more example of Nitobe's intricate ties with the ministry.

79. "Dr. Nitobe Arrives; pleads for Japan," *NYT*, May 7, 1932, p. 4.

80. A week before Nitobe arrived in New York, a letter from the Mayor of Tokyo was printed in the *NYT* (May 1, 1932) outlining Japan's case in East Asia. Although no study of this kind has yet been attempted, evidence seems to indicate that Nitobe's efforts were part of a wider, more encompassing plan, perhaps under the auspices of the Foreign Ministry, to swing American public opinion to Japan's favor.

81. *NYT*, May 7, 1932.

82. Raymond Buell, "An Open Letter to Dr. Inazo Nitobe," *New Republic*, 71 (25 May 1932): 42–43.

83. "Editorial, " *The Christian Century* 49: 1 (June 1, 1931): 670–71.

84. "A Curious Letter," in his column "What I am Learning in America," *English Osaka Mainichi*, June 19, 1932. This article has been deleted from *NIZ* 16. See Satô, "Journalist," pp. 228–231 for reasons behind this omission.

85. "A Christian," in his column "What I am Learning in America," *English Osaka Mainichi*, July 9, 1932. This article is also deleted from *NIZ* 16.

86. The manuscript of the address "Japan's Hopes and Fears," is in *FHLNP*.

87. Telegram from Counsul Horiuchi to Foreign Minister Uchida, quoted in part in Sasaki Kô, *Amerika no Nitobe Inazô* (Morioka: Kumaya insatsu shuppan-bu, 1985), pp. 169–70 (hereafter Sasaki). This valuable book, full of rich material, was published after I had written this article. It illuminates many details about Nitobe's travels in the United States.

88. Nitobe describes his meeting with the United States' President in "Japan's Savant Meets President Hoover," in *Osaka Mainichi*, June 4, 1932.

89. Details of Nitobe's visit to Philadelphia are from an interview with David C. Elkinton, April 29, 1983; for Nitobe's Haverford Honorary Doctorate, see "Announce Hon. Degrees," in *The News*, (June 11, 1932), Haverford College, p. 1; on Nitobe's speech before the Quakers, see Howard W. Elkinton, Inazô Nitobe in *NHTS*, pp. 512–13.

90. David Elkinton, interview.

91. David Elkinton, interview; "Institute of Politics Opens Today; Japanese Statesman Initial Speaker," *North Adams Transcript*, July 28, 1932. Many newspaper clippings of this session of the Institute of Politics are on deposit in the Williamsiana Collection, Williams College. I express my thanks to David Elkinton for copies of them.

92. *Institute of Politics*, p. 1.

93. Reprinted in *NIZ* 15: 305–21.
94. Ibid., p 308.
95. Norton, "Sino-Japanese Relations," pp. 129–70.
96. "Japan and the Peace Pact," reprinted in *NIZ*15: 240–52.
97. *Ibid.*, p. 245.
98. *Ibid.*, pp. 246–52.
99. Interview with Nitobe reported in the *Tairiku Nippô*, Vancouver, Canada, January 18, 1932.
100. The offer to lecture at the university came in mid-July; Nitobe, after checking with the *English Osaka Mainichi*, wired the Vice-President of Academic Affairs, Monroe Deutsch, to accept the offer on July 27. The documents concerning his appointment are in the President's Files, University Archives, Bancroft Library, University of California, Berkeley.
101. The lectures are reprinted in *NIZ* 15; for Nitobe's views on Manchuria, see pp. 221–33; for his views on the League, pp. 234–52. These two lectures are the most controversial in the series.
102. Institute of World Affairs, *Proceedings of the Tenth Session, Mission Inn, Riverside, California, 11 to 16 December, 1932* (Los Angeles: University of Southern California, 1933), p. vii.
103. *Ibid.*, p. xii.
104. *Ibid.*, "Japan's Place in the Family of Nations," p. 112.
105. *Ibid.*
106. *Tairiku Nippô*, January 19–21, 1933.
107. Letter received from Paul Christopher, University Archivist, University of Southern California, March 19, 1985; "A Japanese Tribute to Abraham Lincoln," is in *NIZ* 15: 322–31.
108. "Dr. Nitobe Back Here After Year's Absence," in *English Osaka Mainichi*, March 25, 1933.
109. *Ibid.*; "Interview with Dr. Nitobe," *Tairiku Nippô*, January 19, 1932, p. 3.
110. Satô, p. 161.
111. See Burkman, p. 193, for Nitobe's first audience with the man who would become the Shôwa Emperor. Nitobe met the Emperor again in 1931 when he discussed his experiences at the League and the men he had met there.
112. Bannen, pp. 201–2; Newton, p. 145–46; Pao-chin Chu, V. K., *Wellington Koo: A Case Study of China's Diplomat and Diplomacy of Nationalism, 1912–1966* (Hong Kong: The Chinese University Press, 1981), p. 140.
113. Bannen, p. 201; Newton, p. 145.
114. *Ibid.*
115. *Ibid.*
116. Saeki, "Yonjûgonenkan kawaranu yûjô," *NHTS*, p. 42, mentions that Nitobe accepted many engagements because Mary was not there to temper his work habits.
117. Bannen, p. 203–10; Newton, p. 146–50.
118. Bannen, p. 210; Newton, p. 150.
119. Bannen, p. 224; Newton, p. 159. Uchikawa is in error here. He seems to think that Nitobe "made up" the story about going to Manchuria in an interview with the *Tairiku Nippô*. Uchikawa's reasoning for this is that Nitobe did not have

"enough time" to make the trip to the continent and back (Conversation with Uchikawa Eiichirô, May 21, 1985).

120. On Nitobe's trip to Manchuria, see his "Editorial Jottings" for July 7, 8, 15, 1933 in *NIZ* 16: 489–90, 492.

121. "Editorial Jottings," September 9, 1933 in *NIZ* 16: 521–22. Nitobe introduces his alter ego, the Okina, into his daily *English Osaka Mainichi* column first on February 7, 1931 (*NIZ* 16: 162); thereafter it appeared regularly for the next two-and-a-half years. See "Editorial Jotting" of December 29, 1931, (*NIZ* 16: 291) for a description of this alter ego whom Nitobe "visits" for advice and counsel.

122. "Editorial Jottings," July 15, 1933 (emphasis added), in *NIZ* 16: 492.

123. "A Mother's Humility and Pride," in *NIZ* 16: 452.

124. *Ibid.*; Miwa, "Crossroads," p. 423.

125. Saeki, "Yonjûgonen," *NHTS*, p. 41.

126. Jôdai, "Nitobe Sensei," *NHTS*, p. 403.

127. "Taiheiyô kaigi ni oite Nihon wa shômen kara ôsen," *Tairiku Nippô*, August 14, 1933, p. 3.

128. *Ibid.*

129. Takagi, "Nitobe sensei to Taiheiyô mondai chôsa kai," in *NHTS*, p. 490.

130. See Appendix III (p. 464) in *Problems of the Pacific 1933: Proceedings of the Fifth Conference, Institute of Pacific Relations, Banff, Canada, 14–26 August 1933* (London: Oxford University Press, 1934). (hereafter "Problems of the Pacific—1933").

131. "Address at Banff Conference," reprinted in *NIZ* 15: 303.

132. *Tairiku Nippô*, August 15, 1933; quoted in *Bannen*, p. 223; Newton, p. 159.

133. *Problems of the Pacific—1933*, p. v.

134. *Problems of the Pacific—1933*, p. 1

135. *Ibid.*

136. Takagi, "Nitobe sensei to Taiheiyô mondai chôsa kai," *NHTS*, p. 490.

137. See frontispiece to *NIZ* 15.

138. Interview with Henry F. Angus, May 2, 1984, Vancouver, Canada.

139. *Bannen*, p. 222; Newton, p. 158.

140. Mary Duguid, Letter to Passmore Elkinton, October 18, 1933, in *FHLNP*.

141. *Bannen*, p. 230; Newton, p. 165.

142. *Tairiku Nippô*, October 22, 1933; also *Bannen*, p. 232; Newton, p. 165.

143. *Bannen*, p. 232; Newton, p. 164.

144. "Nitobe hakushi tsui ni seikyo," *Tairiku Nippô*, October 16, 1933.

145. *Ibid.*

146. *Bannen*, p. 235; Newton, p. 167.

147. "Nitobe's Funeral Will Be Held Here," *Daily Province*, October 17, 1933. Nitobe's obituary was carried by newspapers across North America including the *NYT, The New York Herald Tribune*, and the *Philadelphia Inquirer*. The local *Victoria Daily Times* carried an editorial "A Great Japanese," on October 16.

148. "Santa Lucia Sails Today," *Victoria Daily Times*, October 23, 1933; "Nitobe Eulogized as Wise Prophet," *Japanese-American Courier* (Seattle, Washington), November 4, 1933; "Mrs. Nitobe Finishes Long Journey Home," *English Osaka Mainichi*, November 16, 1933.

149. Nitobe Yoshio and Mary Duguid, Letter to the Elkinton Family, November 19, 1933, in *FHLNP*; also reprinted in *NIK*, pp. 503–9.

13

Darkened Lanterns in a Distant Garden

Richard Eldridge Copley

The unexpected announcement in 1981 that his likeness would appear on the new five-thousand yen note brought the name of Nitobe before the Japanese public. By that time, the name "Nitobe" had been a household word in Vancouver on the West Coast of Canada for over two decades. Here a group of Nitobe's friends had erected a monument that in the metaphors of landscape architecture intoned a subdued requiem. Vancouver's Nitobe Memorial Garden seems to most visitors a quiet respite from the troublesome cares of daily life. Its beautiful greenery and shapes speak deeply to their own need for repose. The same garden has spoken very differently to the author of this chapter over several decades as he analyzed how the garden designer achieved his aims.

The Nitobe Memorial Garden at the University of British Columbia was created during a fifteen-month period in 1959 and 1960 by the distinguished Japanese landscape architect Mori Kannosuke (1894–1960). The garden stands in a wooded corner of the campus, near the edge of a high cliff which reaches westward above the waters of the Pacific. It is probably the finest Japanese garden outside Japan. Nitobe would certainly have enjoyed walks through a green gem like this, a quiet and peaceful strolling garden with teahouse. It is a magical three-sided world created on less than three acres of forest and lawn, pond and stream, and peopled with noble rocks and sturdy stone lanterns. Map 1 shows the plan of the garden and the different elements in it to which reference is made in this article. The names, with the exception of two lanterns to which we refer later, have all been assigned by me simply to facilitate the discussion.

The watercourse begins near the summit of a miniature mountain in the northern corner of the garden and disappears just beyond a three-sectioned iris pond in the southern corner. A large, rustic teahouse which contains several tatami-floored tea-rooms, including one of four-and-one-half mats, stands in the eastern or third corner. Just south of the four-and-one-half mat room is an exquisite little formal garden of rocks and moss. A *roji* or

Map One.

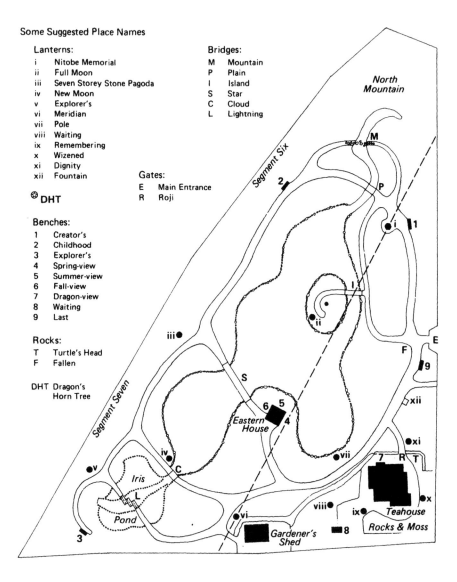

Some Suggested Place Names

Lanterns:
- i Nitobe Memorial
- ii Full Moon
- iii Seven Storey Stone Pagoda
- iv New Moon
- v Explorer's
- vi Meridian
- vii Pole
- viii Waiting
- ix Remembering
- x Wizened
- xi Dignity
- xii Fountain

⊕ DHT

Bridges:
- M Mountain
- P Plain
- I Island
- S Star
- C Cloud
- L Lightning

Gates:
- E Main Entrance
- R Roji

Benches:
1. Creator's
2. Childhood
3. Explorer's
4. Spring-view
5. Summer-view
6. Fall-view
7. Dragon-view
8. Waiting
9. Last

Rocks:
- T Turtle's Head
- F Fallen

DHT Dragon's Horn Tree

"dewy path"—a string of stepping stones—encircles the Teahouse. And dominating the western skyline and visible from many points in the garden is a very tall and ancient Western red cedar that actually stands outside the garden, even on the other side of the highway outside the garden, not far from the edge of the cliff over the ocean. This venerable tree demonstrates the principle of *shakkei* or "scenery borrowed" for the Nitobe Memorial Garden. It is a fine example of how the traditional garden-artist brings scenic items from a distance to complement views within the garden. This striking, spike-topped tree, which we refer to as the "Dragons' Horn Tree (DHT on map one)," also marks the fourth corner of an otherwise invisible earthly rectangle of land encompassing what appears to be, at first glance, a three-cornered garden space.

Dr. Mori began his work at the site in March 1959, having just retired from his position as Professor of Traditional Landscape Architecture at Chiba University—the only such chair in all of Japan. He was assisted by Dr. John Neill of the University of British Columbia's Landscape Architecture Department and by Mr. Roy Sumi, who became the first gardener when the garden opened in June 1960. Mori worked very carefully, as if he wanted to make this garden the masterpiece of his long career—as if he considered this his last garden and anticipated his death only a few months after his return to Japan. Professor Mori left behind thirty-five maps and architectural drawings of the garden, including a precisely-drawn map that was used as the base for the maps in this chapter; but these maps and drawings contain only a few clues that might help decipher Mori's design strategy for this garden, and there is no other record. If he had a special story to tell in this garden, he apparently did not share such ideas with John Neill or Roy Sumi; they claim that Mori had no ambitions for the garden beyond the wish to make it a beautiful place, one soothing the spirit and otherwise demonstrating the aesthetics of a traditional, strolling-type, Japanese tea garden.[1]

The Nitobe Memorial Garden certainly is a beautiful place, nicely illustrating the well-known canons of Japanese garden art. But my study of it since 1963 convinces me that Mori's masterpiece contains much more than just the widely known and standard arrangements of this sophisticated Japanese art form. Mori has also managed to weave these standard forms into what might be called a hidden matrix, a many-layered web of symbolic and esoteric references to the death of Nitobe Inazô. My thesis is that the garden is a sacred landscape preserving cosmic echoes of that death, and that in designing the garden Mori demonstrated a deep knowledge of Western, Chinese, and Japanese astronomy and astrology. Specifically, the structure of the Nitobe Memorial Garden precisely commemorates the moment of Nitobe's death, incorporating in the design not only emblems of Nitobe but also frozen-in-time observations of astronomical and astrological importance in both Western and Japanese traditions. If the secret garden plan is appreciated as a gigantic clock face, with hands showing centuries and years as well as hours and minutes, the hands would all be stopped and still at Nitobe's death at eight-thirty P.M., Pacific Standard Time, October 15, 1933. The trick for Mori was to marshal the skills to write the design, and the trick for us is to learn to read his secret landscape.

In a forthcoming book, which is based on ten seasons of field work at hundreds of sacred sites in China and Japan, I demonstrate that many of the gardens, pagodas, shrines, temples and cities of eastern Asia appear to have been designed based on similar astronomical principles. Angles which frequently appear in these sacred, man-made landscapes highlight significant angles of various astronomical observations that presumably were used by priests and royal astronomers to construct and monitor the lunisolar calendar, the civic calendar of traditional China and Japan.[2]

To discover whether the thesis stated above helps us understand the garden requires that one know Mori's career and motivation. Not much is known, but what little remains should be introduced before the garden itself is considered.

Photographs of the opening ceremonies for the garden in 1960 portray Mori as a typical man of his age and generation. Trim, bespectacled, hair closely cropped; he could have passed for any one of the Japanese businessmen then venturing out of Japan for the first time since the end of World War II. A young specialist on Japan studies on the University of British Columbia faculty at the time remembers Mori in retrospect as "extremely naive and simple," with nothing to suggest that he carried within him vast knowledge of Western and Chinese astronomy and astrology.[3] In contrast, a geography professor who enjoyed watching the garden being built remembers Mori on the work site as "listening to something I couldn't hear; he was painstaking in locating objects in the garden—and he would stand motionless for minutes just staring at and apparently lining up I-don't-know-what."[4] Whether he had special skills or not, he appears to have given much thought to the design.

A glance at Mori's curriculum vitae indicates that Mori had considerable experience with the way gardens are designed outside Japan. During his career he had spent about five years abroad, studying first at the University of Massachusetts, then in Germany; later he spent an extended period in wartime Jakarta and did sketches for a number of traditional Japanese gardens in India during a visit there in 1957–58. Within four months of his return to Japan from Vancouver, he had decided to visit Germany again. He died of a heart attack in an airport the following month.

A look at Mori's career reveals other patterns apart from what one would expect from a traditional Japanese garden designer. He had been trained in the traditional skills as a student, but shortly after World War II he designed a Shakespeare garden for a Japanese university. In Vancouver he sought out a Shakespeare garden and reported on it in Japan.[5] He published on sundials in the West, demonstrating expertise in spherical trigonometry, the basic mathematics of astronomy, first shortly after his study abroad and again a quarter of a century later.[6] In Chiba University the Department of Japanese Landscape Architecture, where he served as Professor and Head, trained for the most part bureaucrats who would administer Western-style urban parks.[7] Mori's Japanese training thus made him the repository of traditional skills, but his career took him far afield into comparisons with numerous other traditions. More than any other Japanese landscape architect of his generation, he had the opportunity to learn the techniques with which colleagues throughout the world approached problems common to garden design everywhere.

Finally, Mori in his own passage through life may have had a personal reason to commingle numerous traditions. He moved from his home in western Kyushu to study near Tokyo just at the time in his life when most thoughtful young men seek direction for their own futures. This coincided with the time when Nitobe started to publish his enormously popular works for such young men.[8] One supposes that if Mori had read such works at an impressionable age, he would have followed with great interest Nitobe's career until his death. For Mori then to receive shortly after his retirement a commission to commemorate Nitobe's death might have been seen to provide scope to implement all his experience while he expressed his personal regard for Nitobe.

Whether or not Mori tried to do this remains beyond the scope of research, for he never answered the question beyond what one may derive from the design of the garden itself. It is my conviction that he did use great sophistication in his design to unite Japanese and Western traditions. For this reason, I state as facts rather than hypotheses my conclusions on these points. The reader may draw whatever conclusions seem appropriate.

Time & Space and Myth & Science in East & West

Before I begin to review some among the many mythological and astronomical references to Nitobe Inazô that are hidden in the garden, let me briefly describe a few of the general concepts familiar to traditional Japanese artists that are apparent here. They will help us to appreciate the breadth of Mori's accomplishment. First, the master garden artist, like all the traditional artists of Japan, knows the old stories of folklore and religious teachings. They have included, since at least the thirteenth century, the teachings of Zen Buddhism and the difficult concept *yûgen*, which means mysterious or hidden or elegant or subtle. Arthur Waley said it means "what lies beneath the surface; the subtle, as opposed to the obvious; the hint, as opposed to the statement"; and he went on to describe some gates to yûgen: "To watch the sun sink behind a flower-clad hill, to stand upon the shore and gaze after a boat that goes hid by far-off islands, to ponder on the journey of wild geese seen and lost among the clouds."[9] A good garden like a good play or a good flower arrangement is rich in yûgen.

Secondly, to appreciate Mori's wizardry, we must remind ourselves that *scientific or quantitative cartography*, the basis of all modern maps, which in recent centuries has been so highly developed by geographers and landscape-makers in the modern Western world, including Japan, can be traced back to roots in the ancient East. There, priests and landscape artists, including those of Japan, formulated an emotionally potent *religious or symbolic cosmography*. Few of the modern scholars of Japan know the old cosmography; for most of them it is a dead issue. Well educated Japanese today, like their contemporaries everywhere, prefer to think that science is more valuable than myth, that science provides better explanations of natural phenomena than did ancient myths. Yet, except for the concerned specialists, the truth of the matter is that few people find much psychological satisfaction in scientific models of nature. Politically and psychologically satisfying myths are—and always were—in great demand and are eagerly welded into a society's belief system. The Japanese continue to respect, if not revere, the old myths. Certainly Nitobe did; in 1910 he founded with Yanagida Kunio an organization to study traditional Japanese ways.[10] The old myths are in the late twentieth century kept alive mainly by what might be called special interest groups, but these groups are entirely outside the academic world. The non-academic "schools" of flower arranging or tea drinking or sword making or mountain worshipping maintain myths that hold the world together—myths usually untouched by modern science.

In spite of the differences between traditional and modern sciences, this garden amazingly bridges the gap between the modern quantitative geographies and the ancient symbolic geographies. In this landscape full of both myth and science, Mori has brought the two together, old and new, East and West, and they enrich each other, just as Nitobe's life work joined the thought worlds of East and West. Here we discover manifestations of unexpected bridges and crossings-over: we find both a number-rich, quantitative and symbolic cosmography and a spirit-rich, scientific cartography. I have already mentioned one example of how the old cosmography is represented in this garden: that the apparently triangular garden space is more accurately described as a rectangle—though if one looks closely he will see that there are actually twelve sides to the garden. All are shown on Map 1. The long, western side has three segments, of which segments Six and Seven are labeled. Segment One is the broken line of the entrance gate behind "E." Segments Eight to Ten form the south side of the garden triangle. Segment Twelve is the very short line below "E." The twelve sides refer to the twelve months of the year, contributing to the already strongly developed sense of season that is gained in the garden. The garden becomes a living horticultural calendar, with winter captured—in all seasons and especially in winter—on North Mountain, and with the annual cycle of the seasons vividly presented as the visitor moves counter-clockwise around the garden. Every precinct of the garden blossoms or shows its colors at the appropriate time of the year—or, we could say, individual days and months have their own particular places in the garden. This seasonal show culminates in the colorful hues and somber scenes of autumn near the Teahouse. To the observer who comes regularly throughout the year, the garden becomes a very slowly turning, natural kaleidoscope. In the ancient Sino-Japanese cosmography, Earth was a square, a huge four-sided mountain, and Sky was a circle, a vast round dome of stars spinning slowly above the mountain. One can find that celestial circle superimposed over the garden.

The Grand Culmination in the Garden

The oldest and most pervasive symbol of natural organization in the Sinitic World is the Diagram of the Grand Culmination, usually called simply the yin-yang diagram. It is loaded with symbolic meaning, but it primarily describes the last stage in the creation of the world: the coalescence of primordial stuff into a polarized pair, yin and yang, female-spirited and male-spirited. Traditional Chinese philosophers thought that all things of nature were fashioned out of this theoretical, ideal, and harmonious world—parental yet inexplicable by ordinary means. Things tall, vertical, hot, dry, hard, angular, bright, active, or felicitous were considered rich in the male yang-spirit. Things low, horizontal, cool, moist, soft, round, shade-loving, quiet, or melancholy reflected the female yin-spirit. The sky and the sun were yang; the earth and the moon, yin. Most yin-yang diagrams rotate clockwise, a direction influenced by the movement of sun and stars as viewed from earth. But it is not uncommon to find yin-yang diagrams that rotate counter-clockwise. These leftwards or sinister diagrams also have an astronomical basis; they are lunar and yin-rich diagrams, since the moon is always slipping backwards or leftwards against its starry background—at a rate of about 13 degrees a night.

A lunar-type Diagram of the Grand Culmination has been superimposed on the garden plan in Map 2. The key points in its construction—the centers of the three larger circles or half-circles in the diagram—are the center of the major bridge in the garden, Star Bridge, the center of the one visible (yang) island in the garden, and the center of its invisible (yin) complement centered on the north shore of the Iris Pond. Just as the yin-yang

Map Two.

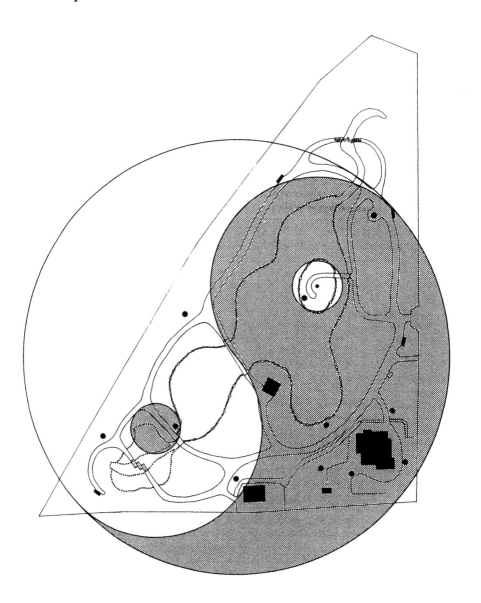

diagram represents the northern hemisphere sky in an occult understanding of the symbol, the perimeter of the outer circle in Map 2 represents the celestial equator in the secret astronomy of the garden. This means that the circle is ninety degrees from the celestial north pole. In the year 1933 when Nitobe died, Spica was 10.8 degrees south of the celestial equator—just 10.8 degrees outside the yin-yang diagram's perimeter and in the position where Dragon's Horn Tree stands. The celestial map represented in this yin-yang diagram shows this relationship.

The spike-topped Dragon's Horn Tree, prominent on the western skyline in many views from the garden, must have been the starting point and cornerstone of Mori's design. It is reasonable to assume that even before arriving in Vancouver and getting his first look at the boggy forest site he would transform into a garden he would have known the time of death of the man he would memorialize, and he would have begun to ponder how to represent it in the garden. Since the star Spica was behind the sun at noon on Nitobe's deathday, we can imagine that Mori, on first seeing the handsome tree on the western skyline, saw it as a heaven-sent opportunity for a celestial connection between the rude garden site and Nitobe's life and culture.[11] The Dragon's Horn Tree, which is the tallest of the many tall trees on this part of the North American coast, owes its spike-topped form to a calcium-deficiency in the local soils and a consequent loss of foliage on the uppermost four meters or so of the older trees. The Dragon's Horn star was the leading star in traditional Japanese star catalogs, where it was also known as *Tatsuta-hime* (literally, "Dragon Field Princess"), perhaps best translated as "Goddess of Autumn." The terms "Horn" and "Goddess of Autumn" are echoes of a theme sounded across the entire Eurasian continent. We realize their kinship with our own symbols and image clusters when we remember that the star the Greeks called Spica represents a spike of newly harvested wheat in the arms of The Virgin, a grand fertility figure in the night sky in the constellation we call Virgo.

The Dragon's Horn Tree bears a remarkable resemblance to a famous spike-topped katsura tree that graced the skyline of the Katsura Detached Palace garden in Kyoto. That garden, the first and most renowned of all strolling-type gardens in Japan, was built in 1620. It was designed in such a way that visitors on opening night were treated to a spectacular moonrise. An autumnal full moon, viewed from the teahouse, rose directly behind the katsura tree. Mori would have been familiar with the legacy of the moon-measuring katsura tree and would have delighted in the similarities and contrasts between these two spike-topped trees. The tree in Kyoto was inside the garden and southeast of the teahouse and was associated mainly with the moon; here in the garden the spike-topped tree, primarily a sun and Spica marker, stands outside the area that was available for the garden and is northwest of the Teahouse. Mori could not have known that the katsura tree in Kyoto was destined to crash to the ground soon after his garden for Nitobe was completed, but he may have known that the garden's spike-topped western red cedar was already over four centuries years old when the Katsura garden opened on that moon-washed autumn evening in 1620.[12]

Kasô in the Garden

Traditional gardens and important buildings were carefully located with respect to ancient rules that designated auspicious or ominous directions and recognized the supposedly powerful magic of numbers, directions, and local topography. The master builder would have to take into account what we would call an invisible landscape. This was a *landscape combined with skyscape*. It linked a *disciplined appreciation of the real world along with a commonly shared vision of the imaginary world* that was once well known and well respected by all educated persons in the traditional Orient. Those of them in Japan believed that the *kasô* or siting of a house foretold the fortune of its residents. The informed user of a traditional Japanese siting diagram would say, "We want to be well located between the Four Sky Palaces, the Four Gates, and the Twenty-Four Directions." The Four Sky Palaces are the heavenly quarters of the Black Turtle (or Dark Warrior) of the northern sky, the Green Dragon of the eastern sky, the Red Phoenix of the southern sky, and the White Tiger of the western sky. The Four Gates are the Mountain Gate in the northeast, the Wind Gate in the southeast, the Earth Gate in the southwest, and the Sky Gate in the northwest. Descriptions of the Twenty-Four Directions have been translated many times; a good one by Hirai Shirô is widely available.[13] The following examples from Hirai's translation provide us with the counsel given for several of the sectors or compass directions in a kasô diagram. Notice in Map 3—on which I have put the four cardinal directions indicated by dotted lines as well as the Four Gates and Twenty-Four Directions—how Mori honored the kasô rules when he laid out the major features of the garden and located the Teahouse. Mori created a safe, harmonious place for the commemoration of Nitobe:

16. "An excessive projection at this point means the predominance of feminine power; a pavilion or a storehouse [means] the master's early death; a recession [means the] ruin of the household." (The Gardener's Shed, which is close behind Meridian Lantern, is just out of harm's way.)

17. "A pond here causes deaths from drowning or the intemperance of the master of the house; a lavatory [causes] perpetual diseases; a garden or a wood does no harm." (The Iris Pond [surrounded by dots on the map] is just beyond sector 17 and therefore saved from disaster.)

Map Three.

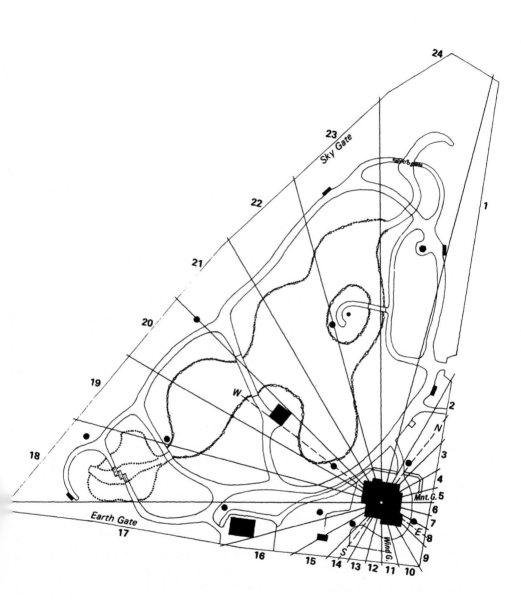

23. "A retreat built here for the elders gives longevity; a gate, watercourse or the like [gives] peace in the family." (Dragon-view Bench on the north side of the Teahouse along with the island and pond fit this requirement well.)

24. "A cooking stove brings wealth; a well gives good water and good luck." (The water enters the garden from this direction.)

The Zodiac in the Garden

The year 1933 was known in the Orient as the Year of the Rooster. An outline of a rooster, one of the twelve animals of the Japanese zodiac, appears in the garden plan when one holds Map 1 almost upside down, with the Iris Pond at the top. The majority of the earliest Japanese maps had south at the top of the page. The giant rooster in the garden is represented in a crowing, wing-flapping posture. He stands on North Mountain; his wings reach back toward the Teahouse; the Iris Pond outlines his head, including comb and wattles. The garden's rooster faces west, toward Japan. It is appropriate that this rooster is crowing because when the sun over Nitobe's room in the Jubilee Hospital in Victoria crossed in front of Spica in the fall of 1933 it was five A.M. in Japan. It is a striking image. Furthermore, this rooster can lead one to discover another zodiacal animal hidden in the garden. An imaginative student pointed out to me that if the garden plan is held with the Entrance Gate down, Teahouse left and North Mountain right, the water between Cloud Bridge and North Mountain resembles a puppy. I found this apparent coincidence curious but meaningless—until I discovered that Nitobe was born in the year of the dog.

The twelve animals of the zodiac and their conventional order of appearance are presented on the inner circle in Map 4. The ring of animals is carved under the light chamber of the huge Nitobe Memorial Lantern. It starts with rat, which we find on the north side; walking clockwise around the lantern we then see, in order: ox, tiger, rabbit, dragon, snake, horse, goat, monkey, rooster, dog, and pig. The animals are thus placed in the correct location to describe the direction to the sun in each of the twelve double-hours of the day in Japanese tradition. Midnight was the center of the double-hour of the rat; sunrise was the center of the double-hour of the rabbit; noon was the center of the double-hour of the horse; and so forth. Why the directional orientation of the zodiac on Map 4 does not fit the normal display, which is found on the Nitobe Memorial Lantern, will be explained later. Strolling through the garden, we next glimpse these animals at the Meridian Lantern where they again appear in carvings under the light chamber. These two zodiacal lanterns lie exactly north and south of each other and so accurately orient the garden.

Map Four.

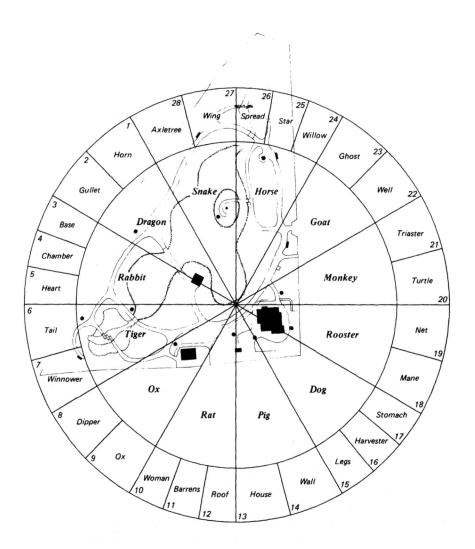

What we have called the zodiacal time system is a relatively recent and simplified version of a very ancient system. To make the zodiacal animals serve in a practical way as year markers it is usually necessary to identify the year in a longer cycle of years than the twelve zodiacal animals would make possible. The solution to this problem was found thousands of years ago when the sexagenary cycle was invented in China.

Two sets of terms—one of ten terms and the other of twelve—were used to enumerate years and other items. Each set, like a series of letters of the alphabet, could identify items in a series. The letter "C," for instance, is the third in the series of twenty-six letters in the Roman alphabet. The two Chinese sets or series, one of ten and the other of twelve, were combined to give a greater series of sixty items, for there are sixty possible combinations of the two sets of terms. The set of ten terms is known to the Japanese as *jikkan*, the Ten Heavenly Stems; the set of twelve terms is called *jûnishi*, the Twelve Earthly Branches. A year identified in the *jikkan-jûnishi* time system would locate that year within a span of sixty years—within a particular sexagenary cycle—which would usually be sufficient. It was, for example, a practical system to record the year of the birth of persons.

The complete name for the year 1933 in the *jikkan-jûnishi* time system was *kiyû* or *mizunoto tori*. Tori is Japanese for "bird," which, in the zodiac, is conventionally considered to be a cock or rooster. *Kiyû* describes it as the tenth year in a cycle of sixty, *ki* being the tenth *jikkan* and *yû* being what the Japanese call the "Chinese reading" for tori or rooster, the tenth *jûnishi*. The name *mizunoto tori* identifies this rooster year in relation to the ancient yin-yang and five element classification systems.[14] Of the five elements— wood, fire, earth, metal, and water—water was associated with the ninth and tenth *jikkan*.. So the year we call 1933 was associated with water, *mizu* in Japanese. What does the *-noto* of *mizunoto* signify? It tells us that 1933 was a younger or yin water-year. When Mori pondered the problem of how to portray the rooster in the Nitobe Memorial Garden, it was almost inevitable that he would choose to "write" the rooster in water—that readers of the landscape would find this vivid reference to the year of Nitobe's death in the figure formed by the stream and ponds of the garden.[15]

Noon Shadows in the Garden

We can admire the ingenuity with which Professor Mori marked the season, the year, and the day of Nitobe's death. He also marked both noon and death time on Nitobe's last day. For these, I believe he used two different garden "languages," one easily understood and one quite foreign to Western intellectual experience.

Everyone can read the "noon-shadow language." Every October fifteenth at noon at various places in the garden the shadows write. For example, at the Island Bridge, everyone notices on a first viewing how extremely low the bridge's two-railed hand rails are, but we miss the magic in this design until we see the shadows on the bridge floor when the noon sun falls to the altitude of the noon sun on Nitobe's deathday. At that moment, on this small bridge to the west, the shadows of the two rails on the south side longitudinally trisect the floor of the bridge. And the shadows are of similar width themselves, which is surprising because one of the rectangular cross-sectioned boards casting these shadows has its wide side up and the other has its narrow side up. This peculiar symmetry of shadow can be seen at noon on only two days of the year, when the sun is at this declination and altitude.

At the Roji Gate, the noon shadows cast by the Teahouse roof commemorate Nitobe's deathday. At noon the roof's shadow slants down to touch the top of the gate, to make a bridge across the gateway, open or closed. This shadow bridge, which would be the seventh bridge in the garden, stands gate-top high at noon only when the sun is exactly as high as it was on Nitobe's death day.

Equally amazing is the annual play of the Teahouse-roof's shadow on Turtle's Head Rock, which stands to the right of the Roji Gate as one leaves the Teahouse. In the sacred language of the garden, the turtle is a symbol of The North, The Armored Warrior, Darkness, and Longevity. To one aquainted with traditional East Asian symbolism, the associations are obvious. Turtles live extremely long lives, whether they are the large deep-sea varieties or the smaller, land-loving, winter-hibernating varieties. At the autumnal equinox, when the sun is fallen half-way to the winter low, the roof's noontime shadow draws a dark line exactly halfway between the bottom and the top of Turtle's Head Rock. Each subsequent noontide the shadow rises higher on the rock until finally, on October fifteenth, Turtle's Head Rock is just submerged. The rock will not see the sun again until spring. The best place to stand to watch these shadow dramas is on the large stone "porch" at the main entrance to the Teahouse. The turtle's head looks very realistic from this perspective. And it takes little imagination to discover the turtle's flippers and to realize that one is really standing on the back of a giant turtle. Mori used these stones to embody the creature that, according to Buddhist lore, will carry virtuous souls to the Island of the Immortals.

We also find noon on Nitobe's deathday marked by shadows at the Four-and-one-half-mat Tea-room on the other side of the Teahouse. Centuries ago four-and-one-half tatami mats became the popular size for small tea-rooms; this is the most intimate and "classical" room of the several tea-rooms in the house. A large sliding panel on the south wall of the room presents a remarkable view of the Rocks and Moss Garden. From inside the room one can see only fifteen of the sixteen rocks of this inner garden.

Does this suggest that from here Nitobe's death occurred on the fifteenth, but in another place—out of sight from here—it was the sixteenth? When we stand on the path outside this room and turn our backs on the sun in order to watch the shadows of October noontimes, we discover that the railing our hands rest on is casting a shadow on the wall of the Teahouse. At noon on the fifteenth the shadow is just a fraction of an inch below the floor level of the Four-and-one-half-mat Tea-room. On the sixteenth the shadow will lift into the room.

Regrettably, we can see today only faint traces of Mori's most ambitious manipulation of garden elements to mark the highest point of Nitobe's last sun. When the garden was built, a young Douglas fir tree a few yards south of the Rocks and Moss Garden was girdled. This tree stood exactly south of the central rock in the Rocks and Moss Garden. Girdling a tree involves making a belt-like cut around the trunk, cutting through the cambium layer. The wood above the cut soon dies. A spike-topped tree was thus created south of the Teahouse. It was a miniature version of the spike-topped tree on the greater garden's western skyline. If the big tree is "borrowed scenery," the young one was "cultured scenery." It produced a stunning effect, for it formed a marker on the southern sky designating noon exactly for some important points in the garden. It was, for example, exactly south of the nakabashira or "central post" of the Teahouse and exactly south of the central rock in the Rocks and Moss Garden. It was a marvel to see a miniature Dragon's Horn Tree here. But a strong wind in the fall of 1976 sent the top of the tree crashing down, tearing up moss in the Rocks and Moss Garden and landing heavily on the roof of the Teahouse west of the Crawling Entrance to the southwest corner of the Four and one-half mat Tea-room. Even in 1994 the moss remains patterned by this event. A scar high on the Teahouse—the six-foot-long section of obviously newer eaves-board—is another reminder. The altitude of the fatal cut on the tree was the altitude of the noon sun on Nitobe's deathday.

Lunar Mansions in the Garden

The garden "language" that is hard for Western students to comprehend has to do with an ancient system of astronomy imported from China over 1,000 years ago. Usually referred to in Japanese as the Twenty-Eight Lunar Mansions (*Ni-jû-hachi shuku*), it was an effective system for locating the position of the sun and moon among the stars. It was used to make calendars, to construct tide tables, and it could be used to identify any particular moment in time, to a fraction of a minute. The outer circle on Map 4 displays the lunar mansions and so becomes, if one considers the circle a map of the sky, a special kind of star chart. It represents with great accuracy the local sky at the exact moment of Nitobe's death. It also provides some of the most detailed and perhaps most convincing evidence of Mori's intent to celebrate Nitobe's death astronomically and in a Japanese way.

Various versions of the Lunar Mansion method to map the celestial sphere were once popular in many parts of the world. The Indians, the Arabs, Chinese, and Japanese all used Lunar Mansions. There are some important differences, yet, they all appear to be derived from a common source—Babylonian astronomy. All societies with a lunar calendar find Lunar Mansions useful. And conversely, as we can see in China and Japan today, societies that abandon the lunar calendar—Japan did so in 1873—soon lose the popular wisdom of moon-centered naked-eye astronomy.

The European system of astronomy, which was basically derived from Egypt via Greece, was very different, although the Oriental and Occidental systems were equally logical and useful solutions to a common problem—how to locate the sun among the stars. Both Babylonian and Egyptian traditions were born of the recognition that the sun determines the seasons and that it makes an annual journey around the heavens, though its daytime brilliance obscures the background matrix of stars against which its position at the moment might be plotted precisely. The Occidental astronomers solved the problem by observing risings and settings of stars just before sunrise and just after sunset. For example, when Sirius rose right before the sun, it warned the ancient Egyptians of the annual rising of the Nile. Attention concentrated on stars near the ecliptic, the path of the sun through the stars. The Western zodiac consists of the names of constellations of stars along the ecliptic. The ancient Western system did not require knowledge of the celestial pole, celestial equator, or celestial meridian.

The Oriental astronomers *indirectly* observed what star was near the sun; they paid little attention to direct observations of conjunctions with the sun. Their system focused on the pole star and the circumpolar stars that never rise and never set and on the utility of meridians—great circles in the celestial sphere stretching from the pole star to the sky directly overhead the observer, or from the pole star to the circumpolar stars and farther along the same great circle to other important stars. These stars pointed out the secret location of the hidden sun and they occupied, at the same time, points along invisible great circles used to measure the location of the moon in the night sky. The boundaries of the Lunar Mansions marked the astronomical longitude of important circumpolar stars. Reading familiar circumpolar stars and other visible stars, an observer could fix the location of the invisible sun or moon. At first sight, this system may seem less accurate than the Egypto-Greek system, but it had several advantages. For one, observations were not made inaccurate by smoke or mist or changing atmospheric conditions on the horizon.

Another characteristic of the Oriental system must be appreciated before we return to its expression in the garden: the principle of *opposability* dominated this astronomy. The celestial relations sought in the Oriental system were those of opposition (What, in the night sky, is on the meridian opposite the sun?) and not of conjunction (What is rising or setting with the sun?). For this reason we find what astronomers call the "interversion" of spring and autumn Lunar Mansions. Sectors of the sky visited by the sun in spring were, in accordance with this principle, associated with autumn in the minds of Oriental astronomers and poets. In the night sky exactly opposite the sun, where Full Moons would appear, "spring" Lunar Mansions would host Full Moons in spring and Lunar Mansions associated with autumn would display Full Moons at that season. The Lunar Mansions numbered 1 through 7 on Map 4 are known as spring mansions; those numbered 15 through 21—the Teahouse precinct in the Nitobe Memorial Garden—are called autumn mansions. The last seven, 22 through 28, are winter mansions. These seasonal associations are best seen in the garden if the diagram or sky chart is centered on Eastern House, but for most astronomical purposes it is better to center the diagram on Pole Lantern. Reference to Map 1 will show that Pole Lantern is at the convergence of the meridians on Map 4. Pole Lantern thus becomes the Pole Star on this secret star chart in the garden. The Pole Lantern is one of only two lanterns named by Mori on the thirty-five sheets of architectural plans he left behind, and the assumptions just mentioned hint at why he put this name on his map.

Map 4 thus becomes an old-style star chart of the heavens at the instant of Nitobe's death. It illustrates the traditional, stylized way to describe the spatial disposition of the Lunar Mansions and concordant zodiacal animals. This order gives form to Chinese astrology. Remember that this is an illustration of the sky at the moment of Nitobe's death; that is why the Zodiacal animals are not in their normal position with Rat at north and Horse at south.

We find that Mori did not mark the sun or moon on the garden's array of the Lunar Mansions—at least he did not mark them in a showy manner. An observer behind Remembering Lantern (ix on Map 1) who aligns it with the Pole Lantern (vii) is looking directly at the location of the sun below the horizon at the very minute of Nitobe's death. Remembering Lantern is an Oribe-type lantern, which makes this lantern an apt marker for Nitobe's sun. Named "Oribe Lantern" on Mori's blueprints, Mori gave it the name of its inventor, the famous tea master and garden designer, Oribe Furuta (1544–1615). It was and remains a popular style of stone lantern. Four centuries ago, when Japanese Christians were being persecuted for their faith, the distinctive shape of the Oribe-type lantern allowed them to worship secretly an image of the Madonna carved on the flat front surface of the long shaft which supports the lantern—on the part of the lantern buried under the ground. In the garden, about an inch of the Madonna's head is visible in this fine example of an Oribe lantern. Through this lantern, Mori may have been commemorating Nitobe's Christian faith.

A walk through the garden with Map 4 in hand will confirm that Mori planned the garden to display lunar mansions and zodiacal animals at the exact minute of Nitobe's death. A single glance at the zodiacal sectors in Map 4 presents some discoveries: Who cannot see Mori's fanciful shapes of the namesake animals in the zodiacal sectors called Horse and Snake and Ox? Where better to put a shed for a hard-working gardener than in the sector called Ox? And all western astronomers—and all modern Japanese who know their stellar constellations—know that across the sky from Spica and The Virgin is Cetus, The Whale, which Mori squeezes into the right-angled corner of the garden. The whale is raising Remembering Lantern on the tip of its tail, cradling the Teahouse on its back, and blowing water from Fountain Lantern.

In the garden, each one of the twenty-eight sectors on Map 4 is marked in some ingenious way. Rather than mention all of them here, let us look only at the final ones. At the moment of Nitobe's death, the garden's drinking fountain which takes the shape of a lantern and so has been called by me "Fountain Lantern" is in the center of Well, the 22nd Lunar Mansion. Last Bench and the Main Entrance of this memorial garden are enclosed by Ghost, the 23rd Lunar Mansion. I believe that Mori wanted to show both real/Western and stylized/Eastern knowledge of the stars. This may explain why we find the precise azimuth to delta Hydrae, the determinative star of Willow, at the nearest or first corner of Last Bench and alpha Cancri, a bright star just above the stars that mark Willow, at the exit from the garden.

Skywatching from Dragon's Horn Tree

Dragon's Horn Tree holds the key to the astronomical secrets of the Nitobe Memorial Garden. Imagine that you could stand atop Dragon's Horn Tree and observe sunrises, moonrises, and star rises over the garden at various important dates, including Nitobe's deathday. It would require some time-traveling, but what would you see? You would see that Mori anticipated your adventure and located the garden's features with great accuracy. He always put things within a few inches of where my calculations would put them. His maps and those which accompany this article are carefully drawn; their lines are usually accurate to within one-fourth of a degree.

To an observer in the top branches of Dragon's Horn Tree, sunrise on Nitobe's deathday rose directly over where Pole Lantern stands today, on a bearing that continues on to the crawling entrance of the most important room in the Teahouse, the Four-and-one-half-mat Tearoom in the eastern corner of the Teahouse. Viewed from the same vantage point, the moonrise on Nitobe's deathday appeared directly over the Main Entrance Gate, which despite its shape is a moon gate. The most northerly moonrises ever seen from Dragon's Horn Tree during any moonrise during the 18.6-year lunar cycle appear exactly over the north end of the eastern boundary of the garden; the lowest or most southerly moonrises appear over the southernmost path-junction on the western path of the garden. And perhaps the most beautiful sights of all—confirming that Mori planned the garden to glorify the big tree and tie it into the hidden matrix of the garden—are the solstitial sunrises: viewed from the top of the tree, on the longest day of summer the sun rises over the large, bright waterfall north of Mountain Bridge; on the shortest day of winter the sun rises over the small, dark waterfall south of Cloud Bridge. This means that sunsets are also marked in the garden with the aid of the Dragon's Horn Tree, which becomes on these occasions a foresight instead of a hindsight. An observer at the northern waterfall sees the setting sun fall to the base of the Dragon's Horn Tree on the winter solstice, while an observer at the southern waterfall, at the northern edge of the Iris Pond (where summer is so colorful), sees sunset of the summer solstice silhouetting the Dragon's Horn Tree.

When Nitobe died in 1933, war clouds were gathering. Professor Mori marked the rising and setting of Mars, the Planet of War, on the day Nitobe died: viewed from the Dragon's Horn Tree on the fifteenth of October 1933 Mars rose over the very center of Cloud Bridge. Standing on the center of Mountain Bridge, one would have seen Mars set exactly in the direction of Dragon's Horn Tree. Mountain Bridge, which is constructed of stepping stones as if broken in battle, sits amidst a stream bed covered with blood-red gravel. Mori seems to invite the viewer to remember Nitobe's pacifism.

Viewed from the top of Dragon's Horn Tree on the day of Nitobe's death, the sun rose 13.0 degrees south of east and Spica rose 16.7 degrees south of east, on the bearing which reaches to the Pole Lantern and the most uncomfortable entrance to the Tearoom. A bearing taken on the sunrise azimuth also hits Star Bridge at its north-most corner, and the Spicarise bearing hits the south-most corner of the bridge. At the eastern end of Star Bridge is the pavilion Eastern House. The deathday sunrise bearing from Dragon's Horn Tree that strikes the north corner of Star Bridge continues on to hit the northeast corner of Eastern House. The northeast corner is the corner that traditionally was so dreaded that special precautions were taken. The construction of the temple complex of Enryakuji on Mount Hiei at the northeast corner of Kyoto is a famous example.

The imaginary observer atop Dragon's Horn Tree who saw the deathday Spica rise over the south corner of Star Bridge would have noticed that this star rise was also on a line reaching over the Seven Storey Stone Pagoda. And now one can complete the series of angular relationships that tie together tree, bridge, pavilion, and stone pagoda. Another corner of Eastern House, the southwest corner, is sixteen degrees south of east from Seven Storey Stone Pagoda—and Dragon's Horn Tree stands sixteen degrees north of west from Seven Storey Stone Pagoda. Sixteen, the date of Nitobe's death in Japan, is what was popularly considered the "death number" squared. The association probably arises from the pronunciation for the word "four" which is a homonym for death in both Chinese and Japanese.

Since he dedicated his life to improve understanding between Japan and the Western world, Nitobe is said to have called himself a Bridge to the West. The dominant bridge in the garden, the Star Bridge, which reaches westward from Eastern House, could reasonably also be called Bridge to the West. And the center of this bridge is fifteen degrees south of east from the Dragon's Horn Tree—possibly another reference to the date of Nitobe's death in Victoria.

The Nitobe Memorial Lantern as an Anniversary Time-teller

The Nitobe Memorial Lantern presents some interesting noon shadows and a surprising flash of light every year on the anniversary of Nitobe's death. As the day approaches, visitors to the garden may notice that the noon shadow of this lantern is gradually reaching closer to the first post of a bamboo-rail fence that comforts the visitors as they climb the steep trail up North Mountain on the path between the Nitobe Memorial Lantern and Mountain Bridge. On October fifteenth, the shadow of the lantern touches the base of the first post. Later in the day, at 4:13 P.M., visitors seated at Creator's Bench will observe a rare sight. As the sun falls behind the light chamber of the stone lantern it transforms the cold, war-damaged lattice work of the Nitobe Memorial Lantern into a brilliant source of light, so brilliant that viewers are warned not to look directly at the sun. Why did Mori place the bench at a spot that will obtain the effect at about four P.M.? Was it simply the death number again? I don't think that explanation was all of it or even most of it. I think Mori was fascinated with the passage of the sun arching over the Pacific between Canada and Japan. This passage covered seven time zones, taking about seven hours and contributing to the richness of sevenness in the numerology of the garden. What is important here, I believe, is that every year a war-damaged lantern is lighted in this garden to memorialize one of modern Japan's eminent internationalists. This occurs just as the sun speeding toward Japan is passing directly over the International Date Line.

Another fact concerns the lantern itself. It was donated to the University of British Columbia by friends of Nitobe shortly after his death and originally sat about 100 meters south of where it stands today. Vandals tipped it over during the war and damaged the stone lattice work of the light chamber. During construction, Mori refused to have the lattice work repaired, indicating that he preferred to have the scars of war remain.[16] It is because of the damage that remains that the sun shines so brilliantly on the Creator's Bench. Mori thus transforms war damage into what appears to be redemptive light.

Nitobe's Deathmoon in the Garden

At Nitobe's death the shadow on the moon was not what Japanese poets refer to as the "curve of perfect shape," that crescent of the Third-Day Moon and a symbol of war and warriors. Nitobe's moon was a mirror image of the warrior's moon; it was exactly opposite. Nitobe's moon had reached an advanced age and was three days away from New Moon. The moon lay in Spread or Extended Net, Lunar Mansion 26, third from the last on Map 4. Nitobe's death moon was a 27-day moon, which may explain why Mori fit the garden's island into Wing, Lunar Mansion 27. In either case, such moons are so near their end that they come into view in the eastern sky tardily and only briefly in the quietest hour that summons the rising sun. Nitobe's mourners on the morning of the sixteenth could share the feelings of the twelfth century Japanese poet who wrote:

Hototoguisu	When I gaze towards the place
Nakitsura kata wo,	Where the cuckoo once sang,
Nagamureba	Nothing remains
Tada ariake no,	But greatness
Tsuki zo nokoreru	The moon in the early morning.[17]

Conclusion

The question of Mori's intent when he designed the Nitobe Memorial Garden can best be answered by reference to the complexity of the work itself. And this brief paper can only begin decoding its mysteries. In this garden the visible, day-time world—the "real world"—is mystified, maimed, magnified, and made supernatural; it becomes a stage for the performance of artful, evocative ambiguities. A hidden night-time world is disclosed to us in day-time. There is a science in this space, majestic and mathematical. And a spirit, too. It can be heard plainly in the garden at all times, and faintly wherever we listen to a dappled sky with the moon moving the trees.

Greatness in a garden is always marked by landscapes which, on viewing, bring more than beauty, for they possess a second, inner greatness by which we are being, almost unconsciously, touched. In the Nitobe Memorial Garden, Mori's art reminds us of the greatness of both men.

Notes

1. See David Morton with photographs by Alex Waterhouse-Hayward, "Signs of the Rising Sun: When is a Japanese garden more than a Japanese garden? When a man thinks he's discovered its celestial connections," *Saturday Night*, August 1988, pp. 42–28. The man in the title is me.

2. For a vivid demonstration of the artistic and scientific use in China of the ancient astronomical knowledge adopted in Japan and illustrated in the garden, see Edward H. Schafer, *Pacing the Void* (Berkeley: University of California Press, 1977).

3. Conversation between John F. Howes and Ronald P. Dore, July 29, 1994. I thank Howes for providing much of the biographical data on Mori. It comes from *Mori Kannosuke no gyôseki to sakuhin* (Tokyo, 1964), a compilation of biographical data and articles by and about Mori published by his students.

4. Conversation with Albert Farley, about January 1964.

5. *Mori Kannosuke no gyôseki*, pp. 41, 53–55.

6. *Ibid.*, pp. 66–69.

7. Conversation between John F. Howes and Miyagi Shûsaku, Mori's successor in garden design at Chiba University, May 28, 1994.

8. See p. 15 of this volume.

9. Authur Waley, *The Nô Plays of Japan* (New York: Grove, 1957), pp. 21–22.

10. *Encyclopedia Nipponica 2001* (Tokyo: Shōgakkan, 1988) 23: 197.

11. Using data from the *Nautical Almanac and Astronomical Ephemeris for the Year 1933 for the Meridian of the Royal Observatory at Greenwich* (Standard Edition) (London: His Majesty's Stationery Office, 1931), pp. 18 and 444, one can calculate that at noon on October 15, 1933, to an observer in Victoria, where Nitobe lay on his death bed, the center of the sun was only 2.1 degrees above Spica and 0.07 degrees to the right of it. If Mori did not have his own copy of an ephemeris, one was easily available in the university library.

12. I learned of the tree's age through conversation with Vladimir Krajina, the foremost expert on old trees of coastal British Columbia, August 28, 1987; Mori could have learned it from Dr. Neill.

13. Hirai's translation of the kasô points appears in Bruno Taut, *Houses and People of Japan* (Tokyo: The Sanseido Company, 1937).

14. Details on these systems and their pervasive influence on Japanese society from ancient to modern times can be found in Masayoshi Sugimoto and David L. Swain, *Science and Culture in Traditional Japan, A.D. 600-1854* (Cambridge Massachusetts: MIT Press, 1978).

15. According to Richard Seaton of the University of British Columbia's School of Architecture, Mori's preliminary plan of the garden proposed such a large area of water that the plan was rejected by the university's special garden committee. I

have not been able to find a copy of this early version of the garden plan. This conversation took place September 27, 1984.

16. Conversation with John F. Howes, August 24, 1994.

17. Henri L. Joly, *Legend in Japanese Art* (Tokyo: Tuttle, 1967), p. 116.

14

Conclusion

John F. Howes

Mori Kannosuke's thoughtful botanical tribute to Nitobe tells the observer, however uninformed he may be about the intricacies of Mori's design, that Mori felt a profound respect for the man he had been commissioned to honor. The integrity of the plan and the peaceful contemplation it inspires leaves the viewer refreshed and curious to learn about the man whose name the garden bears. In consequence, one who knows nothing of Nitobe other than the implicit tribute in the garden will learn with surprise that six decades after his death controversy surrounds the name of Nitobe almost to the extent that individuals know his life and works. When we ask what the contradictory judgments in the preceding pages add up to, it is wise to remember that in 1959 Mori, who lived through the events that so affected Nitobe's last days, felt a deep compassion and respect for Nitobe. We can, as a result, begin with this mute testimony to Nitobe's integrity when we seek to locate him in the history of his times.

One suspects that Mori would not have considered himself a deshi of Nitobe, but there seems to be little motive for the affection lavished on the garden design unless one assumes that Mori felt a personal gratitude toward the man his garden commemorated.

The truth about why Mori crafted his garden as he did makes little difference to those of succeeding generations. That an artist with personal memories of the events through which Nitobe lived accorded him unqualified respect spurs on the scholar who might otherwise lose interest faced with the ambiguities of the Nitobe legacy. Two points invite mention. They are, first, that those who study Nitobe find themselves sharply divided over his contribution to history; and next, that new institutions and developments have made a number of the ideas for which Nitobe struggled a part of mainstream thought in late-twentieth century Japan.

Controversy

The controversy over his historical contribution concerns the nature of Nitobe's character. Did this man who impressed those he met as transparently sincere and honest in fact knowingly deceive or try to influence opinion in a manner inconsistent with his professed aims? Mori seems to answer "no" to this question, though one can perhaps intuit a recognition that he knew of the controversy in the hint of melancholy in the garden. Nitobe failed in his final great endeavor, Mori seems to say, because events around him conspired to nullify the effects of his otherwise great accomplishments.

The authors in this collection have brought up two questions which challenge the attitudes that we have attributed to Mori. By far the most important is the question of Nitobe's relation to the Japanese piecemeal invasion of China which started in 1931 and eventually led to Japan's disastrous defeat in 1945. A second one, less insistent but still relevant, asks whether he succeeded in his professed ambition to become a "bridge." The editor owes readers some attempt to reconcile the differences.

In plain terms, the question of Nitobe's relation to the approach of World War II provokes questions like these. Was Nitobe in fact an international man as his actions otherwise proclaimed him? Or did he, when the chips were down, side not with international justice but rather with the narrow expansion of Japanese interests expressed by its military actions? The question begs an easy answer at the same time as it haunts one who seeks to understand Japan's expansionism in the first half of the twentieth century.

Satô refers to writings of Nitobe which have lain unseen since they were omitted from the first collection of his works shortly after his death. Satô points out that these articles provide further evidence of Nitobe's consistency and sincere attempts to resist the ultra-nationalism of his times. Satô further assumes that timid editors felt that what had passed censors in the early thirties might not pass them five years later and so did not reprint them.

None of the authors in this collection specifically disagrees, but Oshiro tells us of two authors who have emphatically disagreed. He alludes to Iinuma Jirô's attack in the *Mainichi* newspaper which concludes, largely because of Nitobe's attitude toward the occupation of Korea and Koreans, that Nitobe did not warrant recognition. Oshiro also mentions the memoirs of the Canadian diplomat Hugh Keenleyside who criticized Nitobe's reaction to the apology of the Chinese over their part in the Manchurian Incident. Both of these authors insisted in the 1980s that Nitobe is greatly overrated as a humanist, internationalist and pacifist. They urged us to conclude that Nitobe does not deserve the honor accorded him by those who put his likeness on the banknote. Both authors by their datelines draw attention to the length of time that has occurred between Nitobe's acts they criticize and their statements against them. Why, one asks, has it taken so long for those who criticize Nitobe to speak out? Keenleyside writes out of retirement as he reconsiders the events of a long and distinguished career, but the comments of Iinuma cannot be so easily explained. A historian, who himself has lived through many of the events of postwar Japan, suspects that Iinuma's delay may arise from a combination of the events themselves and Japanese reactions to them. Before we go on with this discussion, it is best to refer briefly to the second question posed here by the authors: Nitobe's ability as a mediator between cultures.

Ota's chapter has given us a number of examples which demonstrate that Nitobe, for all his unquestioned ability as a communicator between the Japanese-language world and the English-language world, simply did not convey accurate information about Japan in his English-language writings. This chapter repeats in part a fuller argument from Ota's *Taiheiyô no Hashi to shite no Nitobe Inazô* (Nitobe Inazô as a "Bridge across the Pacific").[1] The two essays in this book deal with Nitobe's works in terms of Tsurumi Shunsuke's dictum that Japanese speakers of English are not to be trusted. After he introduces the material also presented in his chapter of this book, Ota goes on to chart the development of Nitobe's nationalism through reference to his introductions to successive editions of *Bushido* and then to his final North American trip. In America, Nitobe's statements parroted the official army interpretation for the invasion of China, to the despair of his American admirers. In sum, Ota compares the evaluations of Iinuma and Satô, concluding that each author read in isolation persuades him to his point of view, though on balance he leans toward the interpretation of Iinuma. Then Ota concludes that numerous "gray zones" make it impossible to decide whether Nitobe acted in good conscience.

Students of Nitobe stand in debt to Ota for his clear and eloquent definition of the problems. He shows that there is a basis in the written record to question both Nitobe's ability as a cultural interpreter and his dedication to humanitarian internationalism. And it is in Ota's final recognition of the remaining numerous shades of gray that he shows how much work remains before historians can place Nitobe in proper perspective.

The fact is that the garden designer Mori seems in his botanical statement to represent the general appreciation of Nitobe both in Japan and the West at the time of his death. How does one explain that the numerous problems historians now discuss went unnoticed at the time and have not attracted attention in the interval since the end of World War II?

It seems that the general problem has to do with postwar Japanese historians, their understanding of Japan's role in the approach to Pearl Harbor and the events of the subsequent hostilities. This text was originally written on the fiftieth anniversary of the beginning of Hitler's actions against the Jews. In the previous few days wire services had referred to acts of official repentance at the highest levels of the German government, culminating with the retirement of the president of the Bundestag, over what critics called inappropriate statements on this issue which so deeply affects all Germans. Until 1994 there has been no similar reaction in Japan to Japanese brutalities in World War II. On the contrary, one heard only increasing evidence that the Japanese had not come to grips with the consequences of their actions five decades earlier. Only in 1994 have they started to approach the question posed by wartime atrocities: how can a people so otherwise civil and peacefully inclined have wreaked such havoc on their neighbors whom they professed to have "liberated?"

Certainly one cannot find the answer to this stark question in Nitobe's life, but one can find partial answers to it, for Nitobe symbolized a number of elements in the puzzle.

One begins with Nitobe's own personality. His reminiscences tell us that from his earliest days he craved affection and sought it through academic effort. His letters to his adoptive father show how hard he tried to achieve academic distinction, and his activities with the Quakers in Baltimore and Philadelphia demonstrate how their attention assuaged the pain his mediocre academic performance at Johns Hopkins caused him. His critics at Ichikô showed that they considered him unduly shaped by the opinions of others when they called him a *"happô bijin,"* a man who tries to be all things to all people. The government positions which he enjoyed for more than half his days provided him with the prerequisites of high position and contact with the most influential Japanese of his time, while his years in the League of Nations conferred on him the psychic satisfaction of contact with the world's leaders. The favored students who regularly visited his spacious home provided him with an affection more unquestioning than that usually afforded fathers of late adolescent sons. And his purchase of the jizô figure in Shimoda became an oblique admission that he had failed to repay his mother for her affection.

An individual who judges his own worth by his perception of others' attitudes toward him risks his own better judgment, if not his sanity, when cut off from displays of continuing affection. Yet that is precisely what happened to Nitobe after Japan's invasion of Manchuria, for the inner world which Nitobe had constructed required that he remain the center of attention. Numerous individuals close to Nitobe continued to provide such support only as they, with him, found that their ideas, like his, increasingly opposed those of Japan's leaders.

In addition to the dependency reflected in his relations with others, one sees in Nitobe a dedicated personality, one who measures his self-worth in terms of a cause far greater than himself. The cause to which he had dedicated himself was to bring Japan into a position of respect in the Western international community. To do this he had to overcome the disdain of his fellow Japanese for those who evidenced too much their affinity for Western ways. Phrases like *"bata kusai"* which meant the smell of butter in reference to the large amounts of animal fat used in Western cooking or *"seiyô kabure,"* to take on Western ways, indicated in context how little respect those who used the terms held for those whom they described. Nitobe parried their thrusts well, and set a standard of life in the Western manner which earned him respect and admiration. He worked so hard at the attempt because he, like those who shared his training, felt that Japanese must appear sufficiently Western to impress Westerners with their ability at Western skills. Nitobe's admonitions to his newly adopted daughter that she would have to learn to eat Western style lest she embarrass the Nitobes reflected his concern.

But the unconcern for what other Japanese thought of his different ways and his concern for whether Westerners would sanction them reflected his dedication to a greater cause—the acceptance of Japan and its peoples as the equals of Westerners in all respects. This constituted a great ambition at a time when Westerners tended to equate their ways, ideas and values as the only ones worth consideration. Nitobe had to be able to write a persuasive English letter, quote an appropriate Biblical verse or Shakespearean couplet because he knew that these skills would gain him admittance into the company of English gentlemen. By the end of his career he casually used words in his writing which sent educated and sophisticated native speakers of English scrambling to their Oxford dictionaries.

Nitobe's painstaking care enabled him to sponsor those flawless tea parties on the lakeside in front of his Geneva home mentioned by Burkman and there engage Madame Curie and Albert Einstein in polite conversation. Because of this ability he rightfully gained great respect both from Westerners and Japanese.

His success masked another development within himself which Ota notes. The whole purpose which lay behind his drive to perfect himself as a Western gentleman was to advance the cause of Japan. Like other Japanese of his generation, he felt great pride as his nation progressed toward a position of international respect. The increasing nationalism of his introductions to *Bushido* reflected this pride of place he shared with other Japanese. His nomination by them for the post in Geneva, which made him the international symbol of this progress, also demonstrated the trust he had earned at home. As he talked to the young Shôwa Emperor about Japan's position in the world, he found himself in a role like that of his relatives half a century earlier who had received accolades from this young emperor's grandfather. Within Nitobe's own heart, the two sets of honors from his own society and Western leaders reinforced each other. At this time, he personally, more than ever, needed to feel that the actions of his government represented the kind of benign intent that tradition assigned to Imperial rule so that he could represent the Emperor abroad in good conscience.

In his attitude toward fellow East Asians, Nitobe also reflected traditional Japanese thought patterns. Miwa has shown how Japanese had for centuries considered the proper relations with their nearest neighbors in East Asia to be the bestowal of civilization on these lesser barbarians, with the attendant implications of Japanese superiority. The British attitude toward most Asians resembled this traditional Japanese conviction in a number of ways. Always careful to assure that British treated Japanese with respect, Nitobe could with no difficulty accept their attitude toward other "lesser breeds without the law," to use his contemporary Rudyard Kipling's famous enunciation of the British attitude.[2] The assumptions of Nitobe's special field of expertise, colonial administration, led him to consider Koreans and Chinese more as unfortunates in need of assistance rather than individuals who deserved respect. His ideas appear particularly out of place in a vastly different world six decades later.

Let us now return to Nitobe as a cultural mediator. Ota correctly points out the numerous errors of fact, particularly historical fact, in Nitobe's English-language introductory works on Japanese history. Ota goes on to indicate that Nitobe considered some aspects of Japanese civilization good when he addressed Westerners but unworthy of attention when he spoke to Japanese audiences. He adduces Nitobe's attitude toward haiku by way of example, pointing out that when Nitobe wrote for Westerners he considered haiku a positive Japanese contribution to world civilization while in talks to Japanese he found them narrow and constrained. Finally, Ota stresses that Nitobe went out of his way to absolve himself of responsibility by calling himself a simple interpreter.

Specialists on the interpretation of Japan to the West sixty years after Nitobe's death will recognize the perils Nitobe invited with over-generalization. Any historian would blush to find he had made errors like those in Nitobe's treatment of early Japanese history. The Scot James Murdoch had published the first volume of his monumental history of Japan in 1903, a quarter century before Nitobe wrote, so that Westerners had easy access to much more detailed and correct information. Nitobe could have easily checked; in the absence of such verification, he or his publisher needed a knowledgeable editor.

The other two points require further analysis. Can haiku at the same time be accurate representations of a cultural genius and as Ota quotes Nitobe saying page 240, worth no more than the dirt under "Spinoza's... fingernail?" If forced to consider the matter, Nitobe would say, one suspects, that in his terms they could be. His reasoning would rely on his assumptions as a teacher. Since he considered his overriding concern to lift Japan up to the level of the leading Western powers, he welcomed the well disposed interest of Westerners in things Japanese. They, acquainted with the grand universal themes of their own nineteenth-century literature, appreciated the Japanese preference for miniaturization in haiku. Surfeited with the overblown rhetoric of the Romantics, they welcomed the idea that one could exquisitely grasp universal truths in seventeen syllables. And those who had heard of haiku pressed Nitobe for explanations of the differences between the cultures which produced the two types of literature.

Nitobe reacted to a different heuristic imperative when he faced a Japanese audience. They took for granted the haiku as a means to express deep emotions and enjoyed the ambivalence introduced by the economy of expression which allowed the reader to fill in the gaps, but they did not know the grandeur of Western themes. To them, Nitobe felt he must emphasize the majesty of the more complete and precise expression which characterized Western poetry.

So Nitobe could have considered both statements right, and the question of what to emphasize and to whom remained a question of interpretation and the interpreter's knowledge of his audience. This brings up the question of Nitobe's definition of himself as a mere interpreter. In this characterization, he did the enormity of his task a disservice. The chasms, real and imagined, which separated Western attitudes toward Japan and Japanese attitudes toward the West in Nitobe's lifetime baffled the most able analysis. Accurate interpretation required sophisticated understanding of what both parties meant by what they said and gleaned through what they heard. Perhaps the chief difficulty Nitobe faced was the paucity of foreigners who could do the job. He naturally assumed that he alone could do it, and the adulation of audiences captivated by his personal charm and quick-witted rhetoric did not challenge his assumption. No one, save perhaps Mary, seems to have questioned his statements. Few could have felt up to the task because of Nitobe's formidable mastery of the necessary techniques. Both he himself and others saw him as the single individual who could speak across the void of misunderstanding which otherwise separated them. The few cultural middlemen, among whom Nitobe was paramount, commanded vast audiences and garnered great trust. Nitobe's friend Kagawa Toyohiko enjoyed similar adulation and later suffered similar obloquy.[3] A third member of the small group, Uchimura Kanzô, had long given up cultural interpreting on secular matters when his death in 1930 saved him from the worst of what Nitobe and Kagawa would live to face.

The situation calls to mind a similar set of circumstances between North America and China from the foundation of the People's Republic in 1949 and the reopening of diplomatic relations with the United States in 1972. During this period of almost a quarter century, very little information from

China informed Western audiences of the new government's positive achievements. Most Americans feared the dangers posed by what they considered China's role in the international Communist conspiracy. Under these circumstances a native son of Chinese background returned to Canada in the mid-1960s after fifteen years in Beijing. There he had served the Chinese government as an English voice. More than anything else, he wanted to gain stature in world opinion for China's achievements. Thus he used his ability in languages, his debonair ways and obvious sincerity to sketch for Canadians a picture of China hard at work in the solution of massive practical problems. He also parroted every official Chinese shift in official pronouncements on foreign affairs. Canadian opinion makers who listened to him either accepted his comments about the Chinese occupation of Tibet, for instance, though they belied common sense, or politely swallowed their doubts. Other specialists whose experience equipped them to provide another perspective were not asked for their opinions, so "Mr. China" went on unchallenged with his blithe assurances. Since in general he analyzed events more correctly than other North Americans, Canada profited, but it gained less than it might have from its over reliance on one individual and his opinions based in part on his personal magnetism.

Nitobe served a similar function in both Japan and the United States as they blundered toward hostilities through the twenties. Though he continued to command respect, his acceptance of the military's explanations for China policy, necessary for his personal safety at home, and his stubborn reassurance that continuing promotion of mutual understanding would eventually solve all problems eroded his credibility. He died an apparent failure when his self-appointed task became too daunting.

One concludes with reference to his metaphor of the bridge. Historians argue whether as a student he ever in fact said that he wanted to become a bridge between Japan and the West. Whether he did mouth this goal in his university days is not nearly as important as what he went on to do. His career after he started to explain Japan to the good Philadelphia Quaker ladies emphasized cultural mediation just as much as if it had been a conscious professional decision, and his later continued use of the bridge metaphor and acceptance of others' use of it with regard to him tells us that he did not disagree with it.

His acceptance of the metaphor leads us to examine it. In a suspension bridge of the type Nitobe specified *(kakehashi)*, supporting cables anchor its deck to piers at either side of the chasm. The piers must be firmly grounded to support the great stress. One may apply the metaphor to Nitobe by the equation of his tremendous experience in both Japan and the West to the two strong pillars. At the same time, one cannot avoid the melancholy observation that to serve its ultimate purpose the surface of a bridge is routinely trampled upon, a fate which Nitobe appears not to have anticipated. To bridge two cultures on either side of the Pacific turned out to have been far beyond the abilities of any one individual.

Shortly after the end of World War II, two of Nitobe's most dedicated students continued his tradition by the formation of new institutions. They have continued aspects of his legacy since the 1950s while events have brought all Japanese into the mainstream of world affairs.

Resolution

When the peace treaty of 1951 ended the Pacific War, a new Constitution had abolished the institutions which had enabled the military to control Japanese foreign policy and had developed mechanisms to deal with the terrible destruction wrought by that policy. New legislation had given those who wanted a Japan devoted to peace and international cooperation the opportunity to renew efforts in that direction. Most of Nitobe's disciples remained active at the height of their careers. They could themselves attempt to implement Nitobe's ideals to reshape postwar Japan. Two of them who developed institutions consonant with his aims were Takagi Yasaka(1889–1984) and Yanaihara Tadao(1893–1961).

Yanaihara succeeded Nitobe as the professor of colonial policy at Tokyo University. Here his forthright criticism of army atrocities in Manchuria and China elicited the support of other Japanese who considered their national policies unjust. Yanaihara's opposition to the Rape of Nanking in 1937 led to his dismissal from Tokyo University. For the remainder of the war, he supported himself by the publication of a monthly magazine devoted to Bible study. Its social criticism grounded in the transcendence of Biblical injunctions persuaded the government to deny Yanaihara newsprint for the magazine; he then published the essence of his message each month on a postcard. Each subscriber to the magazine received one such postcard.

At the end of the war, Yanaihara's colleagues expressed their respect for his actions by electing him president of Tokyo University. There he initiated widespread reforms to encourage freedom of thought. They included a new two-year Faculty of General Education, which replaced the prewar Ichikô. The Faculty's Department of Comparative Culture became the first Japanese attempt to provide an education similar to that of the new area studies programs in North American universities. Yanaihara's innovative department formed an important part of his program to encourage more comprehensive knowledge of other societies that went beyond the isolated study of a single language and literature. Students were encouraged to compare elements of Japanese experience with those of other countries.

The department and numerous area-studies programs in other universities continue to provide for Japanese students a much more cosmopolitan understanding of the rest of the world. One senses that Nitobe would have been pleased.

The other outstanding disciple to distinguish himself in the Nitobe tradition was Takagi Yasaka. Takagi had been named in the 1920s to a new professorship of American constitutional law at Tokyo University. It had been founded by the descendants of an early American missionary to Japan. Long active in the Japan branch of the Institute of Pacific Relations, Takagi had in 1935 published under its auspices the first report on Japan Studies in the United States. In response to a request from the University of California, he had also recommended one of his best students, Matsumoto Shigeharu, to become an exchange professor at Berkeley. Matsumoto never went to California because University faculty refused to accept a Japanese into their ranks. Matsumoto instead joined the Japanese newspaper service Dōmei in 1933 and served until 1939 in its Shanghai Bureau. Because Dōmei had cooperated so closely with government propaganda efforts, Occupation officials purged Matsumoto after the War. This eliminated all possibility of responsible positions in government or business. Out of conversations between Takagi and Matsumoto and others during his enforced retirement came the idea of a foundation to introduce professionals from outside Japan interested in Japanese problems to Japanese with similar interests. This resulted in the International House of Japan, for which a preparatory committee started plans in 1951.

Matsumoto and Takagi dreamed of a facility that would enable professionals from Japan and other nations to collaborate in congenial circumstances. They felt that such an organization would require housing and dining facilities, a library, introduction to appropriate professional colleagues and an atmosphere conducive to reflection. It should also be moderately priced. In informal surroundings such as these, scholars and researchers could meet to discuss their findings in a way that would benefit the broader general interest of humankind rather than narrow personal or national ends. Given the contemporary devastation of Tokyo, half of which had been leveled by firebombs, the proposal reflected bold imagination.

The Tokyo preparatory committee found a piece of land in a residential district close to the center of the city. It contained a beautiful traditional Japanese garden. Matsumoto and Takagi then approached John D. Rockefeller III, whom they had first met in the 1929 Kyoto Conference of the Institute of Pacific Relations. He provided funds for a new building; Matsumoto and Takagi persuaded three eminent Japanese architects to design it as a team, with the result that its design won an award upon completion in 1955. Enlarged twice subsequently, it continues to serve a vital need in the promotion of better understanding between the peoples of Japan and other nations.

While the building was still being planned, Rockefeller, Matsumoto and Takagi started a program to enable Japanese and American cultural leaders to meet counterparts and address audiences in each other's countries. Under this program, world leaders like Eleanor Roosevelt spoke on numerous occasions in Japan and talked with hundreds of Japanese. Careful preparation enabled her and the others from the United States to learn a great deal about postwar Japan. Japanese leaders benefited even more. Almost one decade before foreign-exchange funds would be made available for Japanese individuals to travel abroad at will, passports were issued only to those who met one of two conditions. Would-be travelers had to demonstrate to the Bank of Japan the national importance of their proposed trip or receive travel money from abroad. Since the funds for the International House program came from the United States, authors, critics and researchers got a very rare opportunity to observe Japan from the outside. Other than a few businessmen and diplomats they became some of the first Japanese to view the great changes that had altered the face of North America during World War II. The program of the International House in ways like these helped reintroduce Japan into the comity of nations after fifteen years' isolation.

Observation of the day-to-day operations of the House four decades later recalls the comfortable ambiance which Inazô and Mary Nitobe provided in Geneva. Corporate memberships in the International House subsidize academic operations and gain corporate representatives admittance to regular lectures by diplomats involved in the practical details of international relations. Simply furnished study bedrooms provide the necessities for itinerant scholars to do their work. The library's impressive collection of Western-language books about Japan provides handy reference for insistent deadlines or substantial works for relaxed study. Breakfast in the coffee shop transforms the unavoidable sharing of a table into a knowledgeable exchange of information about Japanese matters between specialists from throughout the world. And a more formal dining room extends out over the tiny lake nestled in a corner of the garden; there those who know about Nitobe's lakeside tea parties sense a similar dynamic at work.

In International House, one finds the bridge that the elderly Nitobe had in mind. Dedicated professionals from all nations can meet together in quiet and dignified surroundings to discuss common problems. In the midst of one of the world's busiest cities they return from frenzied conferences to find time for the thought and quiet creative individuals require. Regular publications link those temporarily resident in the House with thousands of other members throughout the world. Nitobe felt that the regular contact of individuals from different national backgrounds in circumstances like this constituted one of the best guarantees for the continuation of world peace. Once again, he would have been pleased.

A historian looking back at the group who with Matsumoto and Takagi planned this institution discovers a link in personnel which goes beyond the two of them. A 1962 list of officers and members of the Board of Directors of the House includes the names of at least a dozen individuals who can easily be identified as disciples of Nitobe.[4] The name of Takagi appears on the list. Until the year before when Yanaihara died, his name had also appeared. A number of the same individuals had helped plan the 1929 Kyoto Conference of the IPR a third of a century earlier. In the light of the continuity such statistics imply, the International House resembles a phoenix. It rises out of the ashes of the gutted dreams shared by the tiny group whose members before World War II championed intelligent intercourse with the rest of the world.

Though the International House incorporates so many of the elements which Nitobe considered essential to the promotion of better international understanding, it is not alone. The public awareness of the need for greater knowledge of other nations in the latter years of the twentieth century makes the House one of numerous institutions which offer similar programs. A number of developments stand out as symbols of the changes that have led up to this situation.

The Tokyo Olympics of 1964 started the development with the reintegration of Japan into the world of international sports. They replaced the games of 1936 which had been scheduled for Tokyo but canceled because of the international tension caused by Japan's China policy.

The easing of passport and currency-exchange restrictions in 1969 opened the way for Japanese foreign travel. Travel outside Japan, formerly restricted to the very few, became available to many. The Japanese tourist, filled with a curiosity about the rest of the world and intent upon recording his or her observations, has since then become a familiar feature of the world landscape.

These travels promise to correct the attitudes which so diminished the accomplishments of Nitobe in the minds of his critics after World War II. One of these is Nitobe's attitude toward Koreans. Japanese leaders who had grown up in early Meiji felt so concerned that Japan receive equal treatment from Westerners that they could not understand the needs of others for the same respect they craved. As a result, their ringing declarations of the need for racial equality in fact meant that they themselves desired equal treatment from those who seemed their superiors. Japanese increased wealth and world stature have lessened feelings of inferiority. Widespread travel engenders feelings of normal human warmth toward all individuals the traveler meets. Racial intolerance, particularly against Koreans, continues strong, but increasingly the experiences of individuals with those from other societies who do not fit narrow stereotypes challenge blind prejudice at home.

In no respect have the ideals of Nitobe become more a part of contemporary reality than in the increasingly sophisticated study and use of the English language. Japan has for many years probably spent a higher proportion of its resources to learn English than any other nation has ever invested in the mastery of a foreign tongue. At first, critics felt that the meager results called into question the wisdom of the expense. The concurrent travel abroad of young Japanese and travel to Japan of young people who speak English as a native language have lessened this criticism. At least some among the young students who now arrive in English-speaking countries for their first training outside Japan enjoy a level of English similar to that Nitobe enjoyed when he first went to the United States. In a few years these students will be able to give Japan a voice in international relations which until now only those from Asian nations with colonial pasts have enjoyed. These new Japanese speakers of English will bring Japanese expertise in every field to bear on the common problems of mankind.

One returns to Nitobe's metaphor of the bridge. The cable supports of his bridge were embedded in the rugged mountains of northern Japan and through Mary in the sturdy piety of Philadelphia Quakerism. Even the formidable strength they provided could not withstand the violent winds of international politics in the thirties. Sixty years after Nitobe's death, many crossings have supplanted his lonely span. Their very numbers insure, as nothing else can, that those who in the future share Nitobe's vision of a Japan fully integrated into the mainstream world culture will not themselves experience a tragic end like his.

Notes

1. (Tokyo, Misuzushobô), 1986.

2. "Recessional," 1899.

3. See Yuzo Ota, "Kagawa Toyohiko: a Pacifist?" in Nobuya Bamba and John F. Howes, eds., *Pacifism in Japan: The Christian and Socialist Tradition* (Vancouver: UBC Press, 1979), pp. 169–97.

4. I express my appreciation to Tatsurô Tanabe and Tamiyo Tôgasaki of the International House staff for giving me this information on November 22, 1988.

About the Book and Editor

This collection of essays chronicles for the first time in any language the career and works of pre–World War II Japan's premier internationalist. A self-proclaimed "bridge across the Pacific," Nitobe used his superb command of English to interpret the Japanese people to the English-speaking world and to explain the West to his fellow Japanese. His success led to his appointment as Under Secretary of the League of Nations, before the Japanese invasion of Manchuria in 1931 led to his tragic downfall. Japan had forsaken his cosmopolitan vision, and not even his Quaker charm and eloquence could stand against the raw evidence of the Japanese army's aggression.

At the time of his death in 1933, Nitobe was the best-known Japanese outside his country, yet he has been ignored for six decades, perhaps because his fellow citizens have been unable to face the sober realities of their complicity in their army's excesses. In this groundbreaking volume, historians from North America and Japan revisit the signal contributions of this remarkable man and provide thoughtful new insights into the origins of Japan's road to Pearl Harbor.

John F. Howes is professor of Japan Studies at Obirin University, Tokyo.

Index

Abe Isoo, 108
Adams, Herbert Baxter, 60–64, 66, 68, 69, 74(n51), 179–180
Advice to Women. See *Fujin ni susumete*
Agriculture, 6–7, 11, 70, 161–162, 166, 169, 217
Ainu, 162–165, 169
Akagi, Roy, 265
Akanuma Heitarô, 48
Allegheny College, 10–11, 57–58, 60
Amaterasu, 109
American Legion, 230
Amur Society, 170
Androgyny, 142, 148–149, 151, 154
Anesaki Masaharu, 82, 113, 184, 186–187
Anglo-Japanese Alliance, 17–19, 84–86, 91–94, 97, 185, 202
Angus, Henry F., 197
Aoki Setsuichi, 195, 212(n51)
Araki Sadao, 204
Armstrong, R. C., 98
Arnold, Thomas, 144
Art of War (Sun Tzu), 88
ASEAN. See Association of Southeast Asian Nations
Asiatic Society of Japan, 100
Association of Southeast Asian Nations (ASEAN), 208
Aston, William, 83
Astrology, 281, 290, 291(map), 292, 296–297
Astronomy, 281, 282, 294–300
Athenaeum, 114–115, 247–249
Attolico, Bernardo, 199
Avenol, Joseph A., 199
Awdry, William (bishop of South Tokyo), 83–84, 100
Ayusawa Iwao, 177, 196, 197

Bacon, Francis, 160
Baelz, Erwin, 248
Baltimore, 11, 72(n15)
   See also Johns Hopkins University
Bannen no Inazô (Uchikawa), 53(n41)
Bannerman, Sir Alexander, 89–90, 101
Baradi, Mauro, 125
Batchelor, John, 99, 163–164
Bates, C.J.L., 92, 95, 97, 234–235
Bautista, Marcelino, 125
Benedict, Ruth, 110
Benevolence, 160–162, 166, 172
Bergson, Henri, 190
Bishop, Isabella Bird, 99
Blakeslee, George, 265
Blunden, Edmund, 98
Bocobo, Jorge, 121–123
"Bôkoku," 167
Bokutaku, 235
Bourgeois, Léon, 190
Boutflower, Cecil (bishop of South Tokyo), 84, 91, 93
Bowles, Gilbert, 179
Briffault, Robert, 138, 152
Brinkley, Frank, 83
Brumbaugh, T. T., 113
Bryce, James, 60, 179, 180
Buddha, 217
Buddhism, 67, 98–99, 121, 122, 244, 247, 283
Buell, Raymond, 263, 264
Burkman, Thomas W., 19, 21, 253, 254, 256, 266, 268
Bushido, 121–122, 125, 129, 153–154, 243
   and Christianity, 103(n25), 115, 116
   and militarism, 87–89, 101, 243, 250
   of Nitobe, 7, 89, 100–101, 110–112, 229, 245–247, 249–250

319

origins of, 88, 101, 114–115, 242–243
in the Philippines, 16, 120–122, 124–130, 131(nn 20, 25)
suicide in, 142
in the West, 81, 85–87, 89, 101
Bushidô (Inoue), 243
Bushido (magazine), 242–243
Bushido: The Soul of Japan, 3, 13, 107–113, 117(n1)
and character, 16, 108, 116, 134
criticism of, 12–14, 113–116, 242–243, 245–250
and the Philippines, 119, 129–130
publication of, 13–14, 107, 112
reactions to, 16, 101, 129
sources in, 109, 112, 115, 129
Butler, Nicholas, 261
Byas, Hugh, 83

Calthrop, Everard F., 88–89, 101
Canada, 92–93, 95–97, 266, 267, 310
Carey, James, 65
Carlyle, Thomas, 136, 140, 142, 277
Cartography, 284
Castle, William, 261
Catherine II (empress of Russia), 160
Catholicism, 225
Chace, Anna H., 187
Chamberlain, Basil Hall, 16, 82–83, 85, 100, 109, 113–115
Character, 7, 15
ethic for, 139–140, 142–143, 147–150, 152, 195–196
male development of, 143–150
national, 152–154, 182, 196, 222, 225, 232
Chiang Kai-shek, 256, 258
China, 17–18, 81, 202, 255, 301
and Bushido, 88, 101
as civilization, 169–170
and Japan, 81, 92, 161, 166, 169, 184–185, 272
See also Manchuria; Sino-Japanese War
and League of Nations, 185, 188, 202–204
nationalism of, 171, 203

Nitobe on, 71(n13), 181, 205, 229–230, 233, 257, 266, 308
Nitobe's knowledge of, 239–240, 244
and United States, 228, 309–310
Chinda Sutemi, 187
Cholmondeley, Lionel, 85, 91, 99, 100
Christian Century, 263–264
Christianity, 161, 198, 217, 230
and Bushido, 103(n25), 110–111, 115–116, 129
conversion to, 9–10, 13, 57, 65, 137
in Japan, 9–10, 65, 67, 111, 116
See also Quakerism
Chu Hsiao, 255
Chûô Kôron, 183, 184
Clark, William S., 9–10, 163–164
Coates, H. H., 80, 98
Colonial policy, 3, 17–19, 22, 160–169, 170–173
civilizing goal of, 159, 161, 163, 181, 308
in Korea, 160, 162, 166–170
national defense in, 159–161, 173
of Nitobe, 17–19, 140–141, 159, 161, 173
race in, 164, 168, 172–173
in Taiwan, 165–166, 181
Colonial Policy: Lectures and Essays. See *Shokumin seisakukôgi oyobi rombun shû*
Colonial Studies Association, 165
Committee for Intellectual Cooperation, 271
Commonwealth, 124
Commonwealth Advocate, 124
Communism, 213(n79), 258
Conder, Sir Josiah, 99
Confucianism, 121, 122
Confucius, 9, 109, 227
Congressional Government (Wilson), 179
Copley, Richard Eldridge, 23
Cosmography, 284–285
Curie, Marie, 190

Dai Ajia Kyôkai, 169
Dan, Baron Takuma, 260–261, 275(n63)

Danchôtei nichijô (Kafû), 227
Dazai Shundai, 246
Decline of the West, The (Spengler), 169
Defoe, Daniel, 139
Democracy, 91–92, 94–96, 182–183
Dewey, Davis R., 60
Dewey, John, 179–180
Diagram of Grand Culmination, 285, 286(map), 287
Diplomacy, 4, 17, 21, 178, 182
Diplomat in Japan, A (Satow), 83
Dokusho to jinsei, 239
Dômei, 312
Drummond, Sir Eric, 19, 177, 186–187, 189, 191, 195, 199, 212(n51)
Duguid, Mary, 47–48, 272

East Asia, 92, 161, 171, 173, 308
Eastern Siberia, 171
Ebina Danjô, 186
Economics, 11, 70, 222–224, 227
"Editorial Jottings" column, 201, 221–222, 226–231, 278(n12)
Educational system, 3, 9, 14–15, 82, 90, 101
  Bushido in, 121, 125
  contributions to, 7, 12–15, 222, 225, 227
  English language in, 238–239, 251(n5)
  Nitobe in, 8–9, 238–240
  in the Philippines, 125, 126, 128
  reform in, 3, 139–140
Edward, Prince of Wales, 94
Einstein, Albert, 190
Eliot, Sir Charles, 83, 95, 98
Elkinton, David, 265
Elkinton, Howard, 265
Elkinton, J. Passmore, 205
Elkinton, Mary Passmore. *See* Nitobe, Mary Elkinton
Ely, Richard, 61, 69, 180
Emperor system, 32–33, 85, 101, 107–108, 113, 225
English language, 57, 238–239, 251(n5), 315
  command of, 3, 210(n29), 237, 238, 250(n1)
  writings in, 7, 240–241, 243–246, 249, 305, 308
English literature, 6, 10
English Osaka Mainichi, 201, 217–221, 234–235
  writings for, 20, 43, 220–221, 226, 231, 234, 262, 264, 278(n21)
Essays. *See* Zuisôroku
Ethics, 9, 13, 139, 197
Everyday Japan (Lloyd), 114
Expansionism, 154, 167–168, 171, 181, 185, 304

Far Eastern Crisis, The (Stimson), 213(n79)
Faunce, William, 20
Faust (Goethe), 148
Femininity, 133–134, 138–139, 143, 146–155
First Higher School. *See* Ichikô
Folkways, 168–169
France, 40, 90, 96, 101, 133, 196
France, W. F., 94
Franklin, Benjamin, 145
Freud, Sigmund, 136, 138–139, 143
Friends' Review, 67
Fujin gahô, 150
Fujin ni susumete, 249
Fujin sekai, 150
Fujisawa Rikitarô, 82
Furuya Jun, 11, 138

Gale, J. S., 98
Geneva, 188, 196
Geopolitics, 171
Germany, 17, 91, 96, 171, 192, 199, 306
  Nitobe in, 11–12, 55, 64, 69–70
Gibbons, H. A., 169–170
Giddings, Franklin, 152
Gilman, Daniel, 59, 63, 75(n61)
Goethe, Johann Wolfgang von, 148
Goodman, Grant K., 15
Gotô Ryûnosuke, 171
Gotô Shimpei, 166, 183, 187, 210(n30), 221
Great Britain, 18, 19, 81, 165, 224
  and Bushido, 85, 86, 89, 101, 115–116

and Japan, 17–19, 40, 80–82, 84–97, 101, 185, 202, 308
and Nitobe, 100, 101
Greater Asia Association. *See* Dai Ajia Kyôkai
Greater East Asia Co-prosperity Sphere, 173
Greater East Asia Joint Communique, 173
Great Men I Have Met, 221
Greece, 200
Greene, Jerome, 255
Grierson, Robert, 97
Griffis, William E., 13, 112–113
Gubbins, J. H., 83

Haiku, 240–241, 308–309
Halle University, 11
Hamaguchi Osachi, 222–224, 232
Hamilton, Sir Ian, 87, 90
Hara Kei, 185
Hara Takashi Kei, 165
Harris, J. Rendel, 66, 75(n61)
Harris, Merriman C., 10, 57
Harris, Mrs. Merriman C., 57, 75(n64)
Harris, Townsend, 46, 69
Hashimoto Sanai, 150
Haverford College, 264
Hayashi Gonsuke, 189
Hayashi Shihei, 160, 167, 171
Hearn, Lafcadio, 122
Heaslett, Samuel, 99
Heroes, 140–142, 145, 147, 217
Hibi no shôgai (Uchimura), 227
Hirai Shirô, 288
Hirohita (emperor of Japan), 193, 268, 277(n111), 307–308
History, 4, 152–155, 243–246, 255, 303–304, 308
History of Japanese Religion (Anesaki), 113
History of the Korean People (Gale), 98
Hitler, Adolf, 227, 306
Hobbes, Thomas, 160
Hokkaido, 9, 162–165, 167, 168
Holland, William, 254–255
Holmes, C. P., 91

Home Country Association. *See Kyôdô kai*
Hônen, 98
Hoover, Herbert, 205, 214(n79), 233, 261, 264
Hopkins, Johns, 59, 65
See also Johns Hopkins University
House of Peers, 20, 201
Howes, John F., 22
Hsu Shuhsi, 255, 256
Hughes, Thomas, 141, 144
Hu Shih, 256, 270

Ichikô, 12, 14–15, 147–150, 180, 197, 306
ICIC. *See* International Committee for Intellectual Cooperation
Ienaga Saburô, 246
Iinuma Jirô, 18, 304, 305
Ijin gunzô, 140, 242, 250
Ikeda Satoru, 221
Imai, John, 85
Imai Toshimichi, 113, 115
Imperial Academy, 20, 201
Imperial Rescript on Education, 108
Imperial Reserve Association, 260
India, 188
Industrialism, 133, 153–154
Inge, Dean W. R., 227
Inoue Junnosuke, 223, 260, 275(n63)
Inoue Tetsujirô, 243
In Peace and War (Moore), 80
Institute of International Affairs (Pasadena), 267
Institute of Pacific Relations (IPR), 3, 20–21, 201, 253–256, 272(n1)
  Banff conference of, 43, 208, 267, 269–271
  chairmanship in, 20–21, 43, 201, 218, 254–255
  China in, 202, 255
  Honolulu conferences of, 201, 254
  Kyoto Conference of, 100, 121, 177–178, 201–202, 254–255
  and League of Nations, 201–202, 254
  Shanghai conference of, 21–22, 43, 203–204, 255–256, 258, 274(n30)

writings on, 223, 256
Institute of Politics (Williams College), 206, 232, 265
Institute of World Affairs, 266–267
Intellectual History of Wartime Japan 1931–1945 (Tsurumi), 238
Intercourse Between the United States and Japan, The, 11, 241–242, 248
International Committee for Intellectual Cooperation (ICIC), 189–191, 201
International House of Japan, 312–314
International Institute of Intellectual Cooperation, 191
International Labor Congress, 201
Internationalism, 198–199, 207, 209, 305
writings on, 219, 223, 226, 227
Inukai Tsuyoshi, 185, 233
Invention of a New Religion, The (Chamberlain), 85
Ion, Hamish, 16, 112
IPR. *See* Institute of Pacific Relations
Ishii Akira, 254, 256
Ishii Kikujirô, 189, 191, 198, 200
Ishii Mitsuru, 217
Italy, 200
Itô Hirobumi, 94, 165
Itô Miyoji, 185
Itô Take, 128
Iwate Agricultural Cooperative, 42–43

Jackson, Helen, 164
Jameson, J. Franklin, 59–63, 69, 72(n18)
Japan, 108–109, 153, 171, 222–223, 311
army of, 21–23, 43–44, 86–90, 95–96, 101
and Canada, 80, 92–93, 95–97
"Charter Oath of Five Articles" of, 223, 232
and China, 81, 92, 161, 166, 169, 184–185.
See also Manchuria; Sino-Japanese War
colonial policies of. *See* Colonial policy
Constitution of, 22, 95–96, 108
and East Asia, 92, 161, 173

Foreign Ministry of, 263–264, 275 (n72), 276(nn 78, 80)
foreign policy of, 8, 16, 81, 85–86, 92, 129, 171–173, 207–209, 314
and Germany, 17, 91, 171
and Great Britain, 17–19, 80–82, 84–97, 101, 308
Hamaguchi cabinet of, 223, 232
and Korea, 17, 94, 96–97
and League of Nations, 177–178, 182–189, 193–195, 199–201, 205–208, 266, 268
League of Nations withdrawal by, 20, 44, 203, 205, 207–208, 234, 268, 270
in Manchuria. *See* Manchuria
and Meiji Restoration, 8, 30, 40–41, 108, 121, 153
Nitobe on, 222, 228, 233–234, 258–259
Nitobe's knowledge of, 239–240, 242–246, 250
and the Philippines, 119–120, 122, 124, 129–130
political development of, 91, 93–94, 152–154, 182, 184
and Russia, 160–162, 165, 169, 171
See also Russo-Japanese War
Tanaka government of, 222–224, 232
treaty revisions of, 68, 70
U.S. relations with, 55, 68, 100, 167–168, 182–183, 208, 228, 310
Western ideas in, 56, 68, 85, 86, 248
Western images of, 8–9, 16, 19, 79–85, 97–100, 308–309
Westerners in, 80–94, 97, 99–102
and World War I, 6, 17–18, 91, 93, 161, 305–306
Japan Colonial Association. *See* Nihon Takushoku Gakkai
Japanese language, 238–239
Japanese Nation: Its Land, Its People, and Its Life, 168
Japanese Traits and Foreign Influences, 198, 240, 241, 244
Japan Geopolitical Association. *See* Nihon Chisei Gakkai

Japan League of Nations Association, 193–195, 211(n51)
Japan: Some Phases of Her Problems and Development, 80, 202, 218, 221, 233, 240
Jellicoe, Lord John, 81
Jikei, 142, 143, 149
Jinsei dokuhon, 237
Jitsugyô no Nihon, 15, 149, 182–183, 253
Jitsugyô no sekai, 149
Joan of Arc, 138, 148, 217–218
Jôdai Tani, 270, 276(n78)
Johns Hopkins University, 72(n22), 74(nn 39, 53), 179–180
 arrival at, 55, 59–60
 difficulties at, 11, 56, 64, 69, 74(n51), 306
 participation in, 62–63, 65, 67–69, 72(n23), 74(n42)
 Quakerism at, 65–66, 75(nn 58, 59)
 Satô Shôsuke at, 55, 58–60, 63–64
 Seminary of, 60–63, 73(nn 30, 38)
Journalism, 4, 20, 22, 201, 217–236, 253, 262
 editorial jottings in, 221–222, 226–231, 278(n12)
 editorials in, 220–226
 reprinting of, 228–233, 276(nn 84, 85)

Kafû, Nagai, 227
Kagawa Toyohiko, 43, 309
Kainan Newspaper, 258–260, 275(n45)
Kammu (emperor of Japan), 37
Kasô siting, 288, 289(map), 290
Katô Hiroyuki, 239
Katô Kiyomasa, 242
Katô Takaaki, 94
Katô Takeko, 48, 50
Katô Tomosaburô, 95
Katsura Detached Palace, 287–288
Katsura Tarô, 165–166
Kawaguchi Shûji, 243
Kawai Eijirô, 148, 149
Kawai Michiko, 151
Keenleyside, Hugh, 256, 274(n36), 304, 305

Kellogg-Briand Pact, 201, 205, 265–266
Kelly, Herbert, 100
Kennedy, M. D., 80, 83, 95, 96, 101
Ketsumeidan, 260, 275(n63)
"Ki," 143
Kihara Jitarô, 124
Kikuchi Dairoku, 82, 84
Kimura Shigenari, 142
Kindaichi Kyôsuke, 169
King, Francis T., 65, 75(n59)
Kingsley, Charles, 141
Kinoshita Naoe, 108
Kirkwood, Montague, 166
Kita Ikki, 168, 170
Knox, G. W., 80
Kobayashi Masatsune, 50
Kôdô, 126
Kojiki, 198
Konoe Fumimaro, 171, 183, 187
Koo, V. Wellington, 265
Korea, 17, 18, 94, 96–97, 160, 162, 166–170, 314–315
 Nitobe on, 167, 168, 170, 172, 230–231, 304, 308, 314
"Koshi koku Chôsen," 167
Kôtoku Shùsui, 108
Kunimatsu Toshio, 258, 262
Kyôdô kai, 169
Kyoto University, 12, 14

Landor, A. H. Savage, 99
Landscapes, invisible, 288
Lao-Tsu, 171
Lao-Tzu, 198
Latourette, K. S., 240
Leach, Bernard, 99
League of Nations, 192, 199, 200–202, 211(n51), 254, 266
 and China, 181, 185, 188, 202–204
 and Japan, 177–178, 182–189, 193–195, 199–201, 205–208, 266, 268
 Japanese withdrawal from, 20, 44, 203, 205, 207, 208, 234, 268, 270
 and Manchuria, 178, 181, 182, 202–204, 206, 208, 261, 267–268
 Nitobe at, 19–20, 29, 177–178, 191–199, 204–205, 207–208, 229, 234

Nitobe's appointment to, 3, 12, 180, 186–188
Nitobe's resignation from, 199, 217
Nitobe's support for, 185, 200, 206, 208
organization of, 179–180, 184, 186, 188–189
peace mandate of, 191, 192, 200
Soviet absence from, 192, 205, 206
Tokyo Office of, 211(n51)
U.S. absence from, 192, 193, 199, 205, 206
League to Enforce Peace, 180
Lectures on Japan, 228, 232, 240, 244, 247
Lenin, 227
Liaotung Peninsula, 167
Life of William Penn, The. See *Uiriamu Pen Den*
Lincoln, Abraham, 141, 142
Lippman, Walter, 265
Lloyd, Arthur, 98, 105(n87), 113–115
Locarno Pacts, 200
London Naval Disarmament Conference, 20
London Naval Treaty, 229
Looking Inward and Outward. See *Naikan gaibō*
Lopez, Salvador P., 125
Lorentz, Hendrik, 190
Ludwig, Albert P., 240

Mabini, Apolinario, 124
McLaren, Walter, 265
MacRae, D. M., 97
Madariaga, Salvador de, 199
Maeda Tamon, 213(n71), 254, 256, 274(n28)
Mahan, Alfred T., 181
Makino Nobuaki, 179, 180, 184–185, 187
Manchukuo, 169, 171, 172, 182, 185, 206
Manchuria, 20, 152, 167, 170, 255
atrocities in, 311
and Institute of Pacific Relations, 203, 204, 255, 256
invasion of, 5, 43, 79, 97, 168–169, 171–172

and League of Nations, 178, 181, 182, 202–204, 206, 208, 261, 267
Nitobe's response to, 171–172, 180–182, 203–208, 214(n85), 241, 255–258, 263–267, 306
Nitobe's visit to, 269, 277(n119)
occupation of, 17–18, 21–22, 171–172
and United States, 228, 261–262
Manliness, 133–139, 142–154
Marburg, Theodore, 180, 210(n16)
Masturbation, 145–146
Masuda Meiroku, 254
Matoba Kiyoshi, 46
Matsuda Michikazu, 189
Matsumoto Shigeharu, 213(n71), 256, 312–314
Matsuoka Yōsuke, 128, 170, 188, 206, 213(n68), 255
Matsuura Takeshiro, 163
Matsuyama Incident, 213(n79), 253, 258–262
Meadville, 72(n15)
See also Allegheny College
Medley, A. W., 94
Meiji Restoration, 8, 30, 40–41, 108, 121, 153
Mikami Reiji, 243
Militarism, 43, 95–96, 153–154, 182
and Bushido, 243, 250
in colonial policy, 159–161, 173
and Communism, 213(n79), 258
Mill, John Stuart, 139
Missionaries, 83–85, 91–92, 95–97, 101, 112–113
to China, 206, 230, 266
Miwa Kimitada, 19, 181, 183, 199, 308
Miyabe Kingo, 29, 238, 239
Miyake Setsurei, 109
Modern World Series, 218
Mohammed, 217
Momotarō, 145, 168
Momotarō Doctrine, 180, 181
Monnet, Jean, 199
Moore, Herbert, 80
Morality, 3, 15, 107, 110–111, 115, 139–140

Mori Kannosuke, 279, 281–283, 300–301, 303–305
　See also Nitobe Memorial Garden
Mori Nobu, 45
Morioka, 7–8, 28, 30, 34–44
Morioka Product Corporation, 269
Morris, Roland S., 210(n30)
Morris, Wistar, 66, 75(n64)
Morse, Edward S., 249
Motherhood, 138, 148
Motora Yûjirô, 74(n53)
Motoyama Hikoichi, 217
Munro, Neil, 99
Murdoch, James, 308
Muro Kyûsô, 246
Murray, Gilbert, 190
Mussolini, Benito, 227
Mutô Nobuyoshi, 269
Mysticism, 198, 217
Mythology, 284

Nagai Ryûtarô, 162
Nagata Tetsuzan, 259, 261
Naikan gaibô, 238, 242
Naitô Konan, 170
Nakae Chômin, 109, 163, 243
Nakajima Kenzô, 173
Nakano Seigo, 187
Nambu. See Morioka
Nanking, Rape of, 6, 311
Nasu Hiroshi, 274(n28)
Nasu Shiroshi, 254
Nationalism, 5, 115, 116, 169–171, 194, 203
　of Nitobe, 178, 227, 305, 307
Negishi Yoshitarô, 126
Neill, John, 281
New Map of Asia, A (Gibbons), 169
Newman, Harriet, 196
New Republic, 263
New Tokyo Women's Christian College, 12
Newton, Michael, 53(n41)
New York Times, 263, 264
Nihon bushidô (Mikami), 243
Nihon bushidô ron (Kawaguchi), 243
Nihon bushidô shi (Ninagawa), 243

Nihon Chisei Gakkai, 169
Nihon kaizô hôan taikô (Kita), 168, 170
Nihon Takushoku Gakkai, 169
Ninagawa Tatsuo, 243
Nine Power Treaty, 266
Nitobe family, 30, 32–41, 48, 50–51
　in Sambongi, 34–35, 38–41, 44–46, 50
Nitobe Inazô
　ancestors of, 25–28, 36–41, 50–51
　biographies by, 140–141
　birth of, 28
　and bridge metaphor, 310–311, 315
　Bushido: The Soul of Japan. See *Bushido: The Soul of Japan*
　childhood of, 7–8, 28–32, 134–135, 137
　complete works of, 6–7, 20, 221, 276(nn 84, 85), 304
　controversy over, 4, 16, 239, 303–305, 310, 314
　conversion of, 10, 57, 137
　death of, 3, 4, 21–22, 47, 208, 235–236, 271–272
　depression of, 64, 135–136, 138
　disciples of, 13, 311–312, 314
　Dokusho to jinsei, 239
　education of, 8–9, 238–240
　　See also Johns Hopkins University; Sapporo Agricultural College
　English-language writings of, 7, 240–241, 243–246, 249, 305, 308
　eulogy for, 234–235
　on 5000-yen note, 18, 279
　and Foreign Ministry, 262–264, 275(n72), 276(nn 78, 80)
　Fujin ni susumete, 249
　funeral of, 28, 42, 47–51, 235, 272
　Great Men I Have Met, 221
　honorary degrees of, 264, 267
　Ijin gunzô, 140, 242, 250
　The Intercourse Between the United States and Japan, 11, 241–242, 248
　as interpreter of Japan, 16, 198, 237, 250(n1), 308–310
　Japanese Nation: Its Land, Its People, and Its Life, 168

Index

Japanese Traits and Foreign Influences, 198, 240, 241, 244
Japan: Some Phases of Her Problems and Development, 80, 202, 218, 221, 233, 240
Jikei, 142, 143, 149
Jinsei dokuhon, 237
journalism of. *See* Journalism
Kojiki, 198
Lao-Tzu, 198
Lectures on Japan, 228, 232, 240, 244, 247
legacy of, 79–80, 303, 311, 315
marriage of, 11, 48–49
Matsuyama remarks of, 213(n79), 253, 258–262
as mediator, 237–238, 248, 305, 307–308
Naikan gaibô, 238, 242
nationalism of, 178, 227, 305, 307
neuralgia of, 43, 260
obituaries of, 278(n147)
as Ôta Inazô, 29, 35, 45, 71(n1)
personality of, 56, 134–139, 142, 148–149, 151, 304, 306–307
posthumous attention to, 4–6, 23, 272
racism of, 164
Reminiscences of Childhood, 7–9, 28–30, 32–35, 50–51
Shokumin seisakukôgi oyobi rombun shû, 159
Shûyô, 142, 143, 149, 196
and son's death, 12
Thoughts and Essays, 221, 226
Uiriamu Pen Den, 140–141
unpublished writings of, 27
The Use and Study of Foreign Languages in Japan, 231
Western acceptance of, 82, 100–102, 195, 307
Zuisôroku, 167
Nitobe Inazô, The Twilight Years (Newton), 53(n41)
Nitobe Inazô Zenshû, 6–7, 20, 221, 276(nn 84, 85), 304
Nitobe Jûjirô (father), 28–30, 32–33, 38–41, 46, 50, 134–135

Nitobe Koretami, 36–37
Nitobe Kotoko, 48–49
Nitobe Kun, 45
Nitobe, Mary Elkinton, 46–48, 182, 228, 235, 264–265, 277(n116), 309
  heart trouble of, 44, 267, 271
  on Manchuria, 204, 257
  marriage of, 11–13, 48–49, 112, 138
  on Nitobe family, 27–28, 32–33, 36, 39–40, 48, 50, 135
Nitobe Memorial Garden, 23, 279, 280(map), 281, 288, 299
  astrology in, 281, 290, 291(map), 292, 296–297
  astronomy in, 281, 294–300
  cosmography in, 284–285
  design of, 282–283, 300–301, 301(n15)
  and Diagram of Grand Culmination, 285, 286(map), 287
  Dragon's Horn Tree in, 280(map), 281, 287, 297–299
  kasô siting in, 288, 289(map), 290
  lanterns in, 279, 280(map), 290, 296–297, 299–300
  shadows in, 292–294, 299
Nitobe Memorial Museum, 39, 45
Nitobe Michirô (brother), 29, 32, 34, 45, 135
Nitobe Ryôsuke, 34, 35, 45
Nitobe Seki (mother), 28, 31–36, 46–47, 50, 134–138, 148
  death of, 10, 33, 135–136, 138, 269–270
Nitobe Shichirô (brother), 29, 33–35, 40, 45
Nitobe, Thomas, 12
Nitobe Tsutô (grandfather), 29–30, 33, 34, 37–41, 45–46, 50
Nitobe Waka, 34–35, 45
Nitobe, Yoshio, 47–48
Nogi Maresuke, 96, 101, 122, 141–142
Nôgyô takushoku gaku (Sugino), 162
Non-Recognition Doctrine, 265–266
Norman, Dan, 92
Noyori Hideichi, 149
Number One Higher School. *See* Ichikô

O'Conroy, Taid, 80
Oda Man, 170
Ôi Kentarô, 243, 250
Okakura Tenshin, 112, 238
Okichi, Tôjin no, 138
Ôkubo Toshimichi, 180
Order of the Sacred Treasure, First-Class, 272
Oribe Furuta, 296
Osaka Mainichi. See *English Osaka Mainichi*
Oshikawa Shunrô
Oshiro, George, 21, 22, 304
Osias, Camilo, 125–126
Ôta Inazô. *See* Nitobe Inazô
Ôta Tokitoshi, 29, 31, 45
Ôta Tsunetoshi, 45, 46, 48, 260, 261
Ota, Yuzo, 4, 22, 100, 112, 114, 305, 307–308

Pacific War, 20, 22, 97, 311
Pacifism, 70–71, 145, 178, 182
Parlett, Sir Harold, 83, 255
Patriarchy, 151
Peace Pact, 266
Pearl Harbor, 305
Penn, William, 140–142, 211(n46)
Perry, Matthew, 8, 68, 69
Persia, 188
Philadelphia, 264–265
Philippine Magazine, 124
Philippines, 16, 119–122, 124–130, 131(nn 20, 25)
Piggott, F.S.G., 88, 94
Plato, 227
Plumer, H.C.O., 90
Pluralized Universe or the Filipino Way of Life, The (Osias), 125–126
Portraits of great men. See Ijin gunzô
Powles, Cyril H., 16, 247
Protestantism, 10
P'u yi, Henry, 269

Quakerism, 10–11, 65–71, 112, 140–141, 182, 198, 306
Quezon, Manuel L., 119–126, 128–130, 131(n26)

Race, 92, 164, 168, 314–315
Rappard, William, 177, 189, 199
Reader on life. See Jinsei dokuhon
Reading and life. See Dokusho to jinsei
Religion, 31, 32, 108–109, 138
Religious Values in Japanese Culture (Brumbaugh), 113
Reminscences of Childhood, 7–9, 28–30, 32–35, 50–51
Repington, Charles A'Court, 87
Reservists Association, 213(n79), 259–260
Rizal, José, 124
Robinson, J. C., 113, 115
Rockefeller, John D., III, 312–313
Roden, Donald, 15, 16, 19
Rokumeikan, 248
Roosevelt, Theodore, 144
Rôyama Masamichi, 171–172, 213(n68), 255
Russell, Bertrand, 80, 227
Russia, 17, 160–162, 165, 169, 171
  See also Russo-Japanese War
Russian Revolution, 17–18, 171
Russo-Japanese War, 17, 79, 83, 165, 182, 196
  and Bushido, 13, 86–87, 89–90, 101, 243
Ryûkyû archipelago, 162, 165, 167, 169
Saeki Riichirô, 270
Saeki Yoshi, 85
Saigô Takamori, 141, 142, 167
Saionji, Prince Kimmochi, 187, 188
Saitô Makoto, 95
Saitô Sôichi, 254, 274(n28)
Sakatani Yoshirô, 254
Sakhalin, 17, 167
Sakoji Seizô, 259, 261
Sambongi, 34–35, 38–42, 44–46, 48–51
Sangoku tsûran zusetsu (Hayashi), 160
Sapporo Agricultural College, 9–10, 12, 29, 32–34, 70, 136–138, 161, 164
Sartor Resartus (Carlyle), 136, 140
Sasaki Kô, 275(n72)
Satô Hôryô, 262
Satô Kennosuke, 228, 235
Satô Masahiro, 4, 20, 22, 35, 137, 253, 304–305

Index

Satô Naotake, 189, 195
Satô Nobuhiro, 160, 171
Satô Shôsuke, 29, 69, 70, 161
  at Johns Hopkins, 55, 58–60, 63–64, 72(n18)
Satow, Sir Ernest, 82–83, 85
Satsuma Rebellion, 33
Saunby, J. W., 92
Sawada Setsuzô, 189
Sawayanagi Masatarô, 201
Schaffer, Blanche Weber, 197
Schofield, Frank, 97
Schumpeter, Joseph, 154
Scott, James Brown, 265
Seisho no kenkyû (Uchimura), 227
Self-cultivation. *See Shûyô*
Self-discipline. See *Jikei*
Sexuality, 143, 146
Shakespeare, William, 227
Shaw, Loretta L., 95
Shibusawa Eiichi, 254
Shidehara Kijûrô, 193, 200, 255, 263
Shidô (Yamaga), 115
Shiga Shigetaka, 170
Shimoda, 269
Shinto, 109, 121, 122, 247
Shiratori Kurakichi, 168
Shokumin seisaku kenkyû (Yamamoto), 162
Shokumin seisakukôgi oyobi rombun shû, 159
Shotwell, James T., 20, 197, 198, 255
Shôwa Kenkyû Kai, 169, 171
Shôwa study group. *See* Shôwa Kenkyû Kai
Shûyô, 142, 143, 149, 196
Siam, 188
Siberia, 171, 183
Sino-Japanese War, 14, 17–18, 71(n13), 81, 165, 243, 249
Smiles, Samuel, 139
Society of Friends. *See* Quakerism
Soga no Iruka, 244
Soganoya-Gorô-Geki, 220
Sohô, Tokutomi, 167–168
Somerville, J.A.C., 89
Soviet Union, 192, 199, 205, 206

Spencer, Herbert, 152, 153
Spengler, Oswald, 169
Stead, Alfred, 87
Stimson, Henry L., 205, 206, 213(n79), 261, 264
Stimson Doctrine, 205, 265
Suematsu, Baron Kenchô, 82, 84, 114
Sugimori Kôjirô, 123
Sugimura Yôtarô, 177, 189, 199, 207
Sugino Tadao, 162
Sumi, Roy, 281
Sun Tzu, 88, 95, 101
Suzuki Bunji, 184, 186, 213(n71)

Tachibana Kozaburô, 169
Taft, William Howard, 180
Tagawa Daikichirô, 186
Taishô Nichi Nichi Shimbun (Osaka newspaper), 170
Taiwan, 14, 17–19, 161, 165–166, 180–181
Takagi Yasaka, 49, 135, 179, 197, 254, 272, 311–314
Takaoka Kumao, 169
Takayanagi Kenzô, 203, 254, 256, 274 (n28)
Takeda Kiyoko, 116
Takekoshi Yôsaburô, 165
Tale of Genji (Waley), 98
Tamura Kanzaemon, 41
Tanaka Giichi, 185, 201, 222–224, 232
Terauchi Masatake, 94
Things Japanese (Chamberlain), 16, 113
Thoughts and Essays, 221, 226
Tôgo, Heihachirô, 94
Tokugawa Iesato, 266
Tokugawa Iyeyasu, 245
Tokutomi Roka, 148
Tokutomi Sohô, 109
Tokyo Geographic Society, 169
Tokyo Nichi Nichi, 201, 217–221
Tokyo Pan-Pacific Club, address to, 221
Tokyo University, 10, 12, 14, 159, 161, 181, 311–312
Tokyo Women's Christian College, 15, 150, 186

Tom Brown's Schooldays (Hughes), 144
Towada-shi, 35
Toynbee, Arnold, 100
Treaty of Portsmouth, 17, 79, 83, 87
Treaty of St. Petersburg, 162
Treaty of Shimoda, 162
Treaty of Shimonoseki, 165
Tristam, Canon, 99
Trolope, Mark Napier, 98
Tsurumi Shunsuke, 100, 238, 250, 305
Tsurumi Yûsuke, 49, 179, 213(n71), 254, 256, 274(n28)
Tsushima, 162
Turner, Frederick Jackson, 179, 180

Uchida Ryôhei, 170
Uchikawa Eiichirô, 260, 275(n72), 277 (n119)
Uchikawa Eijirô, 42, 43, 47, 48, 53(n41)
Uchimura Kanzô, 51, 99, 100, 135–137, 184, 309
  on Bushido, 103(n25), 246
  and Christianity, 10, 15, 111, 108
  friendship with, 5, 29, 235
  pacifism of, 5, 6, 182
  and Quakers, 66–67, 75(n64)
  as student, 8–10, 163
  works by, 32, 227, 238
Udai kondô hisaku (Satô), 160
Uemura Masahisa, 242, 243, 249, 250
Uiriamu Pen Den, 140–141
Undertones of War (Blunden), 98
UNESCO. See United Nations Educational, Scientific, and Cultural Organization
United Nations, 208
United Nations Educational, Scientific and Cultural Organization (UNESCO), 3, 189, 208
United States, 9, 115, 228, 261, 309–310
  Immigration Act of 1924, 44, 188, 199, 261
  and Japan, 55, 68, 100, 167–168, 182–183, 208, 310
  Japanese immigrants in, 57, 71(n12), 199
  and League of Nations, 192, 193, 199, 205, 206

Nitobe on, 56–58, 212(n64), 230, 233
  and the Philippines, 119, 120, 128–130
  visit of 1932 to, 44, 204–208, 228, 230, 233, 241, 261–268
University of California at Berkeley, 266, 277(n100), 312
University of Halle, 55
University of Southern Califorrna, 267
University of Tokyo. See Tokyo University
Uno Shûhei, 45
Use and Study of Foreign Languages in Japan, The, 231

Vargas, Jorge B., 131(n20)
Veblen, Thorstein, 152, 154
Verzosa, Paul Rodriquez, 131(n25)
Vespa, Amleto, 80
von Raichffeisen, Friedrich Wilhelm, 42

Waley, Arthur, 98, 283–284
Walters, F. P., 190, 199
Wan Yang Ming, 109
Washio Shôgorô, 183
Watase Shôzaburô, 74(n53)
West, 81, 85–87, 160–162
  Japanese image in, 8–9, 16, 19, 79–85, 97–100, 308–309
  Japanese views of, 8–9, 56, 68, 85, 86, 248
  Nitobe's acceptance in, 82, 100–102, 307
Western Influences in Modern Japan, 255
Weston, Walter, 99
Wheeler, Rev. David H., 57, 58
Whelen, F. L., 19
"White peril," 162
Why I am not a Christian (Russell), 227
Wilson, Woodrow, 59, 60, 73(nn 24, 30, 32), 108, 170, 172, 182–184, 202
  and Nitobe, 179, 183, 186
Women, 108, 111-112, 146, 148, 230, 232–233
  as advocate for, 150–151, 192, 217
  See also Femininity

Women's Foreign Mission Association of Friends of Philadelphia, 66–67, 70, 138
Women's magazines, 150–151
World War I, 17–18, 90, 91
World War II, 6, 304–306

Yamaga Sokô, 109, 115, 133
Yamagata Aritomo, 94, 95
Yamamoto Mitono, 162
Yanagita Kunio, 169, 284
Yanaihara Tadao, 159, 161–162, 167, 173, 230, 311, 314
Yano Jun'ichi, 170
Yap island, 17
Yate, C.A.L., 89

"Yellow Peril," 81, 92, 162
Yin-yang diagram. *See* Diagram of Grand Culmination
Yoda Shokei, 88–89
Yokota Kisaburô, 213(n71)
Yo no sonkei suru jimbutsu (Yanaihara), 167
Yoshida Shigeru, 255
Yoshida Shôin, 114
Yoshino Sakuzô, 184, 185, 230
Young, A. Morgan, 80, 82, 83
Young, Robert, 99, 104(n66)
Young, Walter, 255
Yûgen, 283–284

Zuisôroku, 167